D0953769

IT
Portfolio
Management
Step-by-Step

IT
Portfolio
Management
Step-by-Step

*Unlocking the Business Value
of Technology*

BRYAN MAIZLISH
AND
ROBERT HANDLER

(For Gartner, Inc.)

WILEY

John Wiley & Sons, Inc.

This book is printed on acid-free paper.

Copyright © 2005 by Bryan Maizlish and META Group, LLC, a subsidiary of Gartner, Inc. All rights reserved.

Published by John Wiley & Sons, Inc., Hoboken, New Jersey.
Published simultaneously in Canada.

No part of this publication may be reproduced, stored in a retrieval system, or transmitted in any form or by any means, electronic, mechanical, photocopying, recording, scanning, or otherwise, except as permitted under Section 107 or 108 of the 1976 United States Copyright Act, without either the prior written permission of the Publisher, or authorization through payment of the appropriate per-copy fee to the Copyright Clearance Center, Inc., 222 Rosewood Drive, Danvers, MA 01923, 978-750-8400, fax 978-646-8600, or on the web at www.copyright.com. Requests to the Publisher for permission should be addressed to the Permissions Department, John Wiley & Sons, Inc., 111 River Street, Hoboken, NJ 07030, 201-748-6011, fax 201-748-6008.

Limit of Liability/Disclaimer of Warranty: While the publisher and author have used their best efforts in preparing this book, they make no representations or warranties with respect to the accuracy or completeness of the contents of this book and specifically disclaim any implied warranties of merchantability or fitness for a particular purpose. No warranty may be created or extended by sales representatives or written sales materials. The advice and strategies contained herein may not be suitable for your situation. You should consult with a professional where appropriate. Neither the publisher nor author shall be liable for any loss of profit or any other commercial damages, including but not limited to special, incidental, consequential, or other damages.

NOTE TO THE READER: Unless otherwise noted, all of the studies (including percentages shown), and exhibits that appear in the book were either adapted from or are the original material copyrighted to META Group, LLC, a subsidiary of Gartner, Inc.

For general information on our other products and services, or technical support, please contact our Customer Care Department within the United States at 800-762-2974, outside the United States at 317-572-3993 or fax 317-572-4002.

Wiley also publishes its books in a variety of electronic formats. Some content that appears in print may not be available in electronic books.

For more information about Wiley products, visit our web site at www.wiley.com.

Library of Congress Cataloging-in-Publication Data:
Maizlish, Bryan.
    IT portfolio management step-by-step: unlocking the business value of technology / Bryan Maizlish and Robert Handler.
        p.   cm.
    ISBN-13   978-0-471-64984-8 (cloth)
    ISBN-10   0-471-64984-8 (cloth)
        1. Information technology—Management.   2. Information technology—Cost effectiveness.   I. Handler, Robert.   II. Title.
    HD30.2.M346 2005
    004'.068'1—dc22

2004024583

Printed in the United States of America

10 9 8 7 6 5 4

To my wife Robin, the love of my life, my best friend, and the voice of sanity and reason in our household—thank you for your unconditional support and providing the unwavering encouragement, confidence, and inspiration to write this book and achieve my dreams. Thank you to my children Jennifer, Evan, and Emily for bringing joy and happiness into my life, for your incredible patience in this journey, and for your wisdom and counsel in helping me keep things in perspective. And, thank you to my mother, Sondra, for your wonderful advice throughout the journey.

Bryan Maizlish

Words cannot express the appreciation I have for my wife, Jennifer, my son, Charles, my daughter, Alexis, my two golden retrievers, and many others. The effort required to create this book took me away from them more than I had anticipated, yet they stood by me. Thank you also to my parents, David and Claire, who, via nature or nurture, gave me the fortitude to complete this project. It is to all my loved ones who supported me in life that I dedicate this book.

Robert Handler

Acknowledgments

IT Portfolio Management Step-by-Step: Unlocking the Business Value of Technology is the result of 15 years of effort, beginning with our research on financial portfolio management and branching out to information technology (IT) portfolio management. The content in this book was shaped and sculpted based on the stellar research from META Group, Inc. (now owned by Gartner, Inc.), studies from academia, collaboration with IT portfolio management software providers and consultants, and input and feedback from leading practitioners. Thank you for your support, encouragement, and counseling.

There are a few key individuals who deserve special mention. Without the steadfast support of Richard Buchanan, CD Hobbs, Val Sribar, Dale Kutnick, Gene Hall, Peter Sondergaard, Joe Baylock, and Tom Hayes, and their willingness to allow us utilize resources and key personnel, this book would have not succeeded. Also, a profound thank you to Mike Thomas, Roland Wiltz, and Roger Mann, for providing a foundation that supported our inspiration and creativity. We are deeply grateful to these individuals for allowing us to follow our passion.

We are very appreciative and truly humbled by the generous contributions made by the analysts at META Group, LLC, a subsidiary of Gartner, Inc. and Gartner, Inc. Their tremendous talent, intellect, professionalism, and in-depth research and knowledge provided both content and spirit to our book. Many of these individuals supported our efforts on their own time. Thank you very much for your time, research, and perspectives. Their names, listed below as contributing authors to this book, are as follows (in alphabetical order):

Phil Allega
Willie Appel
Melinda Carol-Ballou
John Brand
Andreas Bitterer
Scott Bittler
Linda Bastoni
Louis Boyle
Richard Buchanan
Michael Buchheim
Brian Burke
Enrico Camerinelli
David Cearley
Phil Dawson
Michael Doane
Jim Duggan
Mike Egan
Hams El-Gabri
Rich Evans
Corey Ferengul
Morgan Gerhart
Nick Gall
Phil Goodwin
Mike Gotta
Marc Halpren
Simon Hayward
CD Hobbs
Matt Hotle
Ted Kempf
Rakesh Kumar

Dale Kutnick
Carl Lehmann
Nicole Latimer
Matt Light
Carole McPherson
Thomas Murphy
David Newman
Glenn O'Donnell
George Paras
Al Passori
Jean-Louis Previdi
Jonathan Poe
Wissam Raffoul
Bruce Robertson
Elizabeth Roche
Bill Rosser
Dr. Howard Rubin
Rob Schafer
Kurt Schlegel
William Snyder
Val Sribar
Dan Stang
Christophe Toulemonde
Mark Vanston
Dan Vogel
Graham Waller
Tim Westbrock
Barry Wilderman
David Yockelson

A special thank you to Michel Delifer, Dr. Peter A. Koen, and Jane Seago. Michel Delifer from Stage-Gate, Inc., along with the stellar research from the highly acclaimed members of the leadership team at Stage-Gate, Inc., including Robert G. Cooper, Scott J. Edgett, and Elko Kleinschmidt, provided invaluable insight and support for the Stage-Gate® processes and other areas discussed in our book. Dr. Peter A. Koen, Associate Professor at The Wesley J. Howe School of Technology Management, Stevens Institute of Technology, and one of the world's leading experts in the front end of innovation, provided very relevant input to the discovery phase sections of our book. And, Jane Seago from the IT Governance

Institute (ITGI) contributed incredible insight and research in the areas of governance and regulatory compliance.

There were also many important contributions made by other individuals that we would like to thank (in alphabetical order): Shawn Bohner, Michael Bogin (Sive, Paget & Riesel), Michael Booker, Brad Boston (Cisco Systems Inc.), Michael Carlson (Xcel Energy), Casey Chaloux, Kim Cook (In-Q-Tel), Dennis Crowley (Cutter Consortium), Martin Curley (Intel Corporation), Basel Dalloul, Matt Dezee (Cisco Systems Inc.), Vince DiGennaro, Don DiNunno, Sabina Gargiulo (Institute for International Research), Ray Gogel (Xcel Energy), Mike Gruia (United Management Technologies), Dr. Thomas Handler, Ian S. Hayes (Clarity Consulting), Brian James (Mercury Interactive), Carrie Kalish, Kenneth J. Kraemer (CRITO, U.C. Irvine), Doug Laney, Rick Laubscher, Kevin Laughlin (Cisco Systems, Inc.), Harry Lee (The Department of Treasury), Heather Pemberton Levy (Gartner, Inc.), David Lindheimer, Gilman Louie (In-Q-Tel), Doug Lynn, Bruce Miller (Project Management Solutions, Inc.), Matt Odel, David Perko (Teradyne Inc.), Dave Peterson (Mercury Interactive), Rachel Quercia (Pacific Edge Software), Sue Reber (ProSight, Inc.), John Reece (John C. Reece & Associates), Marnie Ross, Terry Ross (Pacific Edge Software), Karen Rubenstrunk, Shvetank Shah (Corporate Executive Board/CIO Executive Board), Gary Silverman (Silverman & Associates), Dr. Malcolm Slovin, Mitch Taylor (Cisco Systems, Inc.), Rick Turoczy (ProSight Inc.), Herb VanHook, Kris van Riper (Corporate Executive Board/CIO Executive Board), Katherine Vogt, Gayle von Eckartsberg (In-Q-Tel), Dr. Sami Zahran (IBM), and Aaron Zornes.

We would like to thank Suzanne (Meier) Dvorchak for balancing her family life and the editing needs of this book. Her insight, suggestions, and pragmatic approach helped bring many concepts together. A special thanks to Barbara Koning, who went into overdrive in providing many of the graphics. Thank you for your personal attention and collaborative support. And, our incredible gratitude to Rose Lambert for her unwavering support and commitment to this book.

We are also thankful for the contributions and foresight from Gary Calabrese (Chief Technology Officer, Rohm & Haas), Clint Brooks (Senior Vice President of Research & Development, International Flavors & Fragrances), and Todd Abraham (Vice President of Global Research, Kraft Foods, Inc.).

We are very appreciative toward Ron Nelson for taking time out of his busy schedule to write the outstanding Foreword to our book.

Our editor, Tim Burgard, and editorial support from Helen Cho and Kim Nir deserve special praise for supporting this book, teaching us the art and science of the English language, and tolerating our often strong opinions. Thank you for seeing the value of IT portfolio management, and for guiding us through the publishing process.

We are also deeply grateful to our families who endured the long hours and collaboration that went into this book and supported us all along the way. To Robin Maizlish and Jennifer Handler, our heartfelt love and gratitude cannot be expressed with words. Through it all, we built a strong and enduring friendship.

Also great thanks to our children who were remarkably understanding of the time and commitment it took to write this book. Thank you Alexis Handler, Charles Handler, Jennifer Maizlish, Evan Maizlish, and Emily Maizlish. You kids rock!

Most of all we'd like to thank you, the reader, for supporting this effort. We have deep respect for you, the change agents, who must do one of the most difficult things there is to do—exercise positive change in the face of often extreme resistance. We did our best to put together something that was useful to the change agents, providing context, a usable approach, and lessons learned, but we know that effecting positive change in any organization is usually no small task. Thank you.

Foreword

In the information age, knowledge provides a competitive edge that no business can ignore. The challenge, however, is that with all of the hype, complexity, and confusion around information technology (not to mention a healthy dose of jargon) it is often difficult to distinguish between good and bad technology investments. That's problematic, or at least it should be, because information technology is the central nervous system of most organizations, providing the tools to act rapidly to changes in the business environment. If the information technology is optimized, the organization can thrive, even in the most chaotic times. Optimizing information technology investments is not an option—it is a business mandate.

Information technology investments currently account for the majority of capital expenditures within many companies; therefore it must be treated with at least the same due diligence rigor as any other capital investments. A sound business case must exist; it must support the strategy of the organization; and it must support, and in many ways adhere to, new legislation.

We are increasingly expected to provide accurate information to multiple shareholder and stakeholder groups at light speed. But that should not be a justification for throwing caution to the wind and spending whatever it takes to accomplish that goal. Like any other investment, information technology must be actively managed throughout its entire life cycle, ensuring that both its initial and ongoing costs do not exceed the benefits it provides. We cannot afford to treat investments in information technology as unmanaged operating expenses, as they provide far too many opportunities for value creation, cost savings, and relevant, timely, and accurate information that serve as seminal elements of competitive advantage.

IT portfolio management provides a sound and proven business approach to optimizing investments in information technology. The investment portfolio metaphor provides a mechanism to govern investments in information technology that accounts for their value, risks, costs, useful life, and interrelationships. Much the way an investment manager dynamically manages a portfolio of financial investments, business leaders must make intelligent buy, sell, and hold decisions around their investments in information technology to optimize revenue and growth opportunities, improve customer experience, and streamline operations; when done properly, the productivity improvements and cost savings that result will positively impact the bottom line and allow us to fulfill our primary obligation: driving shareholder value. For example, automated transaction processing through online order making and order taking has created opportunities to offer complex services through dynamically packaging new customized offerings, generating additional fees, and better meeting the customer needs of a global audience. The online travel business is a good example of how information technology has served as a powerful enabler, facilitating streamlined fee-for-service and inventory management models, and providing greater access to published air, car, cruise, and hotel fares, and travel packages worldwide for both leisure and business travelers.

With the growing investment in information technology and the profound contribution of information technology within many companies, it is imperative that the interactions between risk, reward, and value for information technology investments are proactively identified, evaluated, prioritized, and managed. *IT Portfolio Management* makes this case strongly and logically, providing evidence and case studies to support this argument. *IT Portfolio Management* highlights the impact of adopting this technique, from organizational change to governance impacts down to the bottom line. Many books present approaches to effecting positive business change, but *IT Portfolio Management* presents the approach and provides the steps required to transform an organization from ad hoc information technology management to information technology optimization, replete with lessons learned. *IT Portfolio Management* is not a revolutionary approach. It is an evolutionary approach that works. The authors thoughtfully provide tools to measure your organization's abilities and to help it evolve over time to information technology excellence.

Following the guidance of this book, organizations can evolve into adaptive real-time enterprises that thrive in a world of change. *IT Portfolio Management* provides an answer to every senior business leader's questions around the black hole of the IT budget. *IT Portfolio Management* also provides answers to how IT professionals should breakdown the barriers and effectively communicate with business leaders in their language. Maintaining a strong balance sheet, alignment of assets, occupying and sustaining a leadership position, and achieving profitable and relevant return on investments cannot be separated from sound practices of IT portfolio management, and are the fiduciary responsibilities of leaders in an information technology era.

Ronald L. Nelson
President and Chief Financial Officer
Cendant Corporation

Overview of the Book

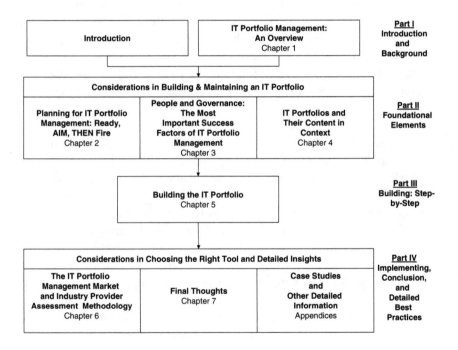

Part I: Introduction and Background

The Introduction provides the readers with a brief overview of IT portfolio management and a description of what lies ahead. It sets the stage for readers who are new to IT portfolio management. Experienced readers should skim this section.

Chapter 1, IT Portfolio Management: An Overview, provides the foundation building for the remainder of the book. For readers who are new to IT portfolio management, Chapter 1 provides a good overview with a description of the definitions and characteristics, and a discussion on the value and risk associated with IT investments. For readers who are experienced at IT portfolio management, we recommend skimming through this chapter.

Part II: Foundational Elements

Chapter 2, Planning for IT Portfolio Management: Ready, Aim, THEN Fire, provides a description of some of the assessments and readiness dimensions related to IT portfolio management. Readers who are new to IT portfolio management should carefully read this section. For experienced readers, we suggest, at a minimum, skimming this section. This chapter touches upon many of the organizational relationships that are often missed by even experienced practitioners, so it is definitely worth the time to read this chapter. Chapter 2 also provides important insight with respect to the IT portfolio management maturity model. We recommend that all readers focus on this section of the chapter. Balance and alignment across the elements of the maturity model is critical to optimize one's performance.

Chapter 3, People and Governance: The Most Important Success Factors of IT Portfolio Management, describes how regulatory changes are affecting management's approach to monitoring, controlling, and responsible risk-taking. The Sarbanes-Oxley Act and other compliance requirements are driving a focus on governance, and the associated policies and principles. For readers who are new to governance, we suggest reading this chapter. For readers who have efficient and effective governance structures in place, we advise skimming this chapter.

Chapter 4, IT Portfolios and Their Content in Context, describes the linkage between the IT life cycle phases and the three IT portfolios. In addition, detailed information is provided regarding the structure and content of each portfolio. For readers who are new to IT portfolio management, we suggest skimming this chapter and referring back to it on a frequent basis. There are many areas within Chapter 4 that cross over to Chapter 5. For readers who are experienced at IT portfolio management, Chapter 4 provides examples of how other companies approach this subject, and therefore should be read in depth.

Part III: Building: Step-by-Step

Chapter 5, Building the IT Portfolio, discusses in detail the eight key stages in building the IT portfolio. This is the longest chapter, and, for most readers, will represent the most important material in this book. Each stage, and its sub-elements (e.g., tasks, outputs, and skill requirements), are shown along with images to illustrate the steps and processes. While Part I and Part II provide important foundational elements, readers, both novice and experts, are encouraged to focus on the valuable and extensive information provided in this chapter.

Part IV: Implementing, Conclusion, and Detailed Best Practices

Chapter 6, The IT Portfolio Management Market and Industry Provider Assessment Methodology, discusses the current and future state of the IT portfolio management software marketplace, and provides a comprehensive industry provider assessment methodology. Functional capabilities, presence, and performance criteria form many of the critical decision factors companies should consider in evaluating and selecting an IT portfolio management tool. This chapter targets information for readers at all levels.

Chapter 7, Final Thoughts, summarizes many of the important points raised in this book. The future vision of adaptive technologies, the impact of legislation, and other factors are brought forward for consideration. This chapter, although optional, helps to put it all in perspective.

The Appendixes provide detailed case studies from three exemplar companies—Cisco Systems, Inc., In-Q-Tel, and Xcel Energy. Many of the core principles and process are illustrated in these case studies. Readers will find these case studies very illuminating.

Contents

Introduction

Information technology (IT) is at a critical juncture in today's business climate. The pressure of managing and optimizing IT investments across multiple business units/divisions in alignment with key business drivers and their associated risks, cost, value, performance in light of limited resources (people, funding, facilities, etc.) and a demanding legal and regulatory environment is a challenge for all companies. The measurement for return on IT investments has shrunken from yearly to quarterly to monthly. The increasing velocity in the pace of change and innovation is requiring a corresponding increase in the ability to adopt structure, discipline, and rigor in delivering value and meeting customer needs; a Darwinian shakeout is happening in front of our very eyes. Information technology can be either a strategic enabler that adds value, drives growth and transforms a business or a source of distracting noise that results in increased costs just to maintain the status quo. It is up to companies to decide how to manage IT. Unfortunately, most business executives have little regard for IT and minimal visibility into their IT investments. With IT investments ranging from 1.5% to almost 7% of revenues (a few companies spend as high as 20%), it is clear that an approach is needed to ensure these investments meet or exceed expectations. This book prescribes a logical, consistent, common-sense approach to aligning, rationalizing, prioritizing, selecting, optimizing, managing, and monitoring the portfolio of information technology investments for optimal benefit and balance, identifying and eliminating low value-add and redundant investments while maximizing the allocation of resources at acceptable levels of risk. Constraints based on available funding, core capabilities, risk thresholds, labor and material resources, complexity and maturity, time, organizational priorities and requirements, compliance and standards, and value and benefits serve as important factors that must be assessed, prioritized, and balanced in a portfolio of IT investments. While it is not a silver bullet, IT portfolio management is the next best thing—a proven, rational, and practical value-revenue generation and cost reduction approach that works, enabling companies to create and maintain a sharp focus while having visibility and control of their investments across their organizations.

Beginning in the late 1940s through the next few decades, management of IT was simple and straightforward. IT hardware was prohibitively expensive, and applications were costly and custom built to fit a company's needs. Rogue buying patterns were nonexistent. As the IT market began to mature and as standards and commercial off-the-shelf technologies gained acceptance, the cost of hardware and software dramatically declined, allowing divisions and business units to bypass corporate IT to procure technology independently. Y2K, the birth of the Internet, and the dot.com era helped propel a period of double-digit IT spending, further compounding an off-cycle, often hidden IT spending frenzy. As IT spending took on an increasing percentage of a company's expenses, many companies began to take inventory of their IT assets and uncovered a large number of duplicative systems and solutions.

When the dot.com implosion occurred and revenue growth slowed, the pipeline of new innovations and product development exposed a large number of issues regarding the poor quality and abundant (and redundant) quantity of IT investments, misalignment with strategy/objectives, and imbalance of aggregated risks. Companies could no longer afford to be kept in the dark with respect to the number of ongoing projects, the resources allocated to these projects, and the inventory and lack of integration and interoperability between existing IT assets. All of these factors were draining valuable resources, resulting in a high degree of company-wide risk. Companies could no longer afford to ignore the interdependencies, intradependencies, support, and constraints that these IT assets individually and collectively had on other assets, thus affecting cost, risk, and value.

The complexity, rapid changes, and volatility in the technology sector have continued to proliferate, making technology investments increasingly risky and uncertain. For example, changes can occur as a result of:

- Adjustments to the mix of business/mission needs and product versus service offerings
- Industry trends
- Economic shifts
- Customer and constituent demands
- Supplier offerings
- New disruptive technologies

- Regulatory requirements
- Competition and/or business intelligence

A key discriminator for adaptive organizations is moving the bar to the left, sensing these trends and changes earlier in the cycle and responding with near real-time precision. Web services, model and service-oriented architectures, composite applications, offshore IT outsourcing, thin client architectures, on-demand computing, ubiquitous computing with nodes virtually everywhere, and other innovations will continue to fundamentally change the paradigm of IT spending and management, creating unprecedented opportunities for flexibility and agility. In addition, IT management's role has changed and transformed from code development, primarily for internal purposes, to integration of standards-based, open-source/commercial off-the-shelf technologies targeted to both internal and external users—and many pundits think this is just the tip of the iceberg.

IT management's role has expanded into the formulation and development of the corporate strategic plan. The chief information officer (CIO) in many companies reports directly to the chief executive officer (CEO), working closely with corporate leadership to establish the governance and charter for IT portfolio management as well as the criteria and target performance associated with measurements and metrics. The job description for IT management now encompasses a combination of leadership, technological know-how, and expertise in business financial processes and strategy. IT management is under tremendous pressure to reduce cycle times, decrease the amount of time to change business processes, and handle a growing multitude of information sources that are generating more information in shorter periods of time. Organizing, managing, and responding in near real time to changing conditions is a core competency required to compete in today's market.

For decades, researchers have studied the possible correlation between information technology investments and productivity. Although study findings are not always consistent, IT's growing contribution to a company's core competencies cannot be debated; nor can the growing reliance of IT on delivering value and quality of service to customers, suppliers, employees, distributors, and partners. Failure to deliver value and quality of service from IT investments or assets can be costly and catastrophic.

IT portfolio management is not an alien term within most companies. But the definitions and practical aspects of IT portfolio management are not obvious or widely accepted. According to a recent study, less than 20% of companies maintain an active IT portfolio management framework.

The goal of an IT portfolio is to deliver measurable business value—tangible and intangible—while aligning and improving the business and IT strategy. Similar to the portfolio management framework utilized in the financial services sector, IT portfolio management is a combination of people, processes, and corresponding information and technology that senses and responds to change by:

- Communicating effectively, with appropriate agility to rapidly reprioritize and rebalance investments and assets
- Creating and cataloging a detailed, value-based, risk assessment of the inventory of existing assets
- Eliminating redundancies while maximizing reuse
- Scheduling personnel and other resources optimally
- Monitoring and measuring project plans (costs, schedule, scope, timing, yield, risk, benefits, etc.) from development through post-implementation, including disposal

IT portfolio management provides the tools, processes, and disciplines needed to translate information technology into a common taxonomy that both business and IT executives understand. Using business-oriented values of measures, establishing views of interest to specific stakeholders, and measuring and monitoring the health and status of all IT investments through the use of key performance indicators, metrics, balanced scorecards, and service-level agreements reinforces the importance of the communication and collaboration between IT and business. IT portfolio management is conveyed in business terms, and business management is responsible for making IT investment decisions. The critical importance of alignment to corporate strategy and planning, and the sequencing of priorities to migrate from the current as-is state to the future to-be state, is driven primarily by business needs and supported by IT.

IT portfolio management provides the day-to-day management and operations of IT investments, assuring IT investments are performing according to plan, scope creep, redundancies, and risks are identified early, limited resources are providing maximum benefit, and any changes to the IT portfolio as a result of business redirection are efficiently and effectively executed. In addition, IT portfolio management tracks and reports on IT forecasts, road maps, and trends, providing business, technology, integration, and solution views in support of the guidance and direction of the future to-be business strategy.

The communication and collaboration between IT and business are the most critical aspects of IT portfolio management. Trying to create an active IT portfolio management framework will not work without clearly defined and measurable business and strategic objectives and accountability that are embraced by employees, partners, suppliers, customers, and distributors. Culture, organizational barriers, isolated (stovepipe) processes and rogue systems, undocumented and convoluted (spaghetti) architectures, lack of governance and control points, and metrics-based decision making based on yesterday's behaviors and parameters must be resolved to assure the success of IT portfolio management.

This book provides a pragmatic, step-by-step road map, describing IT portfolio management and its major elements. Chapter 1 provides an overview of IT portfolio management. Chapter 2 describes the planning aspects of IT portfolio management. It explains the IT portfolio management maturity model and the key people, process, and technology aspects at each of five levels within the model. Chapter 3 describes the IT governance aspects of the IT portfolio. It discusses the relationship between IT and corporate governance, and the impact of legislation and compliance rules, such as the Sarbanes-Oxley Act, on the IT portfolio. Chapter 4 covers the IT life cycle and IT subportfolios. Chapter 5 provides step-by-step aspects of building the IT portfolio. Chapter 6 describes the request for information and the request for proposal parameters that companies should consider when evaluating and assessing IT portfolio management software providers. Chapter 7 covers the way forward, discussing the impact that adaptability and new technologies have on IT portfolio management. The book concludes with detailed case studies of Cisco Systems, In-Q-Tel, and Xcel Energy, which are exemplar companies that actively practice IT portfolio management.

For leading companies, the IT portfolio is measurable, manageable, traceable, and constantly being monitored and improved, enabling IT investment decisions of buy, hold, sell, migrate, reengineer, or replace projects and/or assets with near real-time quantitative and qualitative impact assessment. Reliable information and data regarding the current architecture enhances a company's ability to monitor and measure the existing portfolio of assets, identifying gaps and shortfalls, leading to the possibility of retiring investments, creating new projects, or generating the need for discovery and innovations to solve complex problems not addressable by current solutions. Duplicative, superfluous investments that are not in line with business objectives are identified early in the process and terminated. Pioneering companies that actively practice IT portfolio management realize its value is more than simply maximizing tangible financial payback, achieving the largest net present value, or attaining the highest rate of return. They understand that value is also derived from investments that optimize and provide soft benefits such as legal and/or regulatory compliance and intangible, nonfinancial benefits such as higher customer satisfaction.

One size or one road map does not fit all companies for IT portfolio management, but the essential ingredients to move forward for new adopters, novices, and experts are encapsulated in this book. If you are new to IT portfolio management, we provide a starting point, defining the scope, objectives, governance, key decision criteria, and associated processes. You are encouraged to identify IT investment opportunities that offer high impact and low levels of complexity (e.g., IT project portfolio and discretionary investments), analyze these potential investments against business alignment, risks, benefits, and costs, and make a selection. Taking small, balanced, and aligned steps and incorporating lessons learned are important elements for early success. For those who are experienced in IT portfolio management, this book offers insight into leading practices of optimizing the entire portfolio, case studies, important legislation and compliance requirements, and the suggested parameters for evaluating IT portfolio management software companies.

Companies will continue to harness IT to automate new forms of collaboration, innovation, analytics, operational excellence, resource sharing, and sourcing. As IT becomes more commoditized, or as Nicholas Carr's *Harvard Business Review* article "IT Doesn't Matter" states, "What makes a resource truly strategic . . . is not ubiquity but scarcity,"[1] competitive advantage will increasingly be defined by companies that leverage IT in the areas of adaptability, productivity and response times, inventory and cost per transaction, visibility and transparency across processes, and metrics to monitor and control risks and uncertainty. IT portfolio management is the nucleus to assure that IT is aligned with business, avoiding the costly problem of overspending/unnecessary spending, and bucketing investments according to categories that help run the business, grow the business, and transform the business. IT portfolio management provides the discipline of balancing risk against expected returns, evaluating the performance and utilization of existing systems, analyzing and assessing alternatives and trade-offs, and removing waste resulting in significant efficiencies and cost savings. The analysis and results of IT portfolio management will increasingly play an important role in shaping, molding, and defining the corporate and strategic plan. IT and business, once thought of as separate and distinct, are morphing together. IT portfolio management is the change agent that makes this happen with the most efficiency and best results.

NOTE

1. Nicholas G. Carr, "It Doesn't Matter," *Harvard Business Review* Vol. 81, No. 5, May 2003.

CHAPTER 1

IT Portfolio Management: An Overview

CHA CHA CHANGES IN THE CURRENT ENVIRONMENT

The unabated growth in information technology (IT) spending, a primary means of economic expansion before 2000 due to large-scale enterprise resource planning (ERP) implementations, Y2K, and the hypergrowth attributed to dot.com and e-business, is, for the time being, over. In today's turbulent environment, companies face new hurdles from:

- Greater uncertainty
- Increased commoditization
- Nontraditional entrants with competitive offerings
- Shorter half-life of information (moving strategic enablers to commodity)
- Tighter spending
- New technologies
- Changing customer demands and higher levels of personalized preferences
- Multiple pricing, service, and utility models
- Government regulations, legal compliance, and safety standards
- Increased transparency of information due to the blurring between customers, competitors, and suppliers

While many of these challenges are externally driven, the internal challenges faced by many companies include:

- Clearly defined and clearly communicated business and strategic objectives, and consensus building around these objectives
- Complexity associated with introducing and infusing change and innovation
- Identifying and managing investments across multiple divisions and business units
- Product versus service focus
- Value chain partners
- Sourcing relationships
- Cost reductions
- Responsiveness improvements
- Efficiency enhancements

Although change will continue to accelerate and have more impact, many companies continue to either reduce or maintain current levels of IT spending. CIOs and other IT management leaders are now being called upon to justify the business value of IT. Critical capabilities to supporting the business value of IT include:

- Prioritization and alignment with the corporate vision
- Balanced investments across business units
- Pragmatic cost and risk-control mechanisms
- Rational decision-making processes
- Flexibility to reassess and rebalance priorities in the face of a fluid environment
- Adherence to mandated compliance and regulatory requirements

Achieving growth and business value in today's challenging economy has driven many companies to focus on their core competencies: the unique and differentiated knowledge contained within their processes, technologies, relationships and extended enterprises, skills, and culture that provide a leveragable competitive advantage. Focusing on core competencies also means developing a closer alignment between business and IT, as IT represents a sizable percentage of the budget spending for companies and is quickly developing into a valuable strategic asset. In fact, according to recent research, IT spending as a percentage of gross revenues is currently 1.5% to 7.0% and represents greater than 70% of capital spending for most companies.

FOCUS ON IT INVESTMENTS

IT can have a significant impact on the quality of services and solutions and the performance of a company. Efficiently and effectively managed IT investments that meet business and mission needs can create new value-revenue generation, build important competitive advantages and barriers to entry, improve productivity and performance, and decrease costs. Similarly, poorly aligned and unmanaged IT investments can sink a company.

IT investments represent a profound hole within companies. There are no other investments within a company that occupy such a large and growing expenditure yet lack disciplined management, processes, and performance measurements. However, a majority of companies are aggressively scrutinizing the amount of investment allocated to IT in an effort to cut costs, achieve economies of scale, and drive shareholder value to get more and do more for less. The primary focus on IT investments is on short-term projects and priorities with near-term benefits, delaying and in many cases eliminating long-term strategic investments.

Concurrent to cutbacks in IT spending and a short-term focus, management within companies is demanding an increase in IT productivity, expanding IT's role from internally focused to customer facing and making IT more relevant to the business strategy as resources are scaled back. Customers are demanding more rapid, real-time, customized, total solutions, while competitors are forcing companies to frequently innovate to maintain their market position. Additionally, regulators are requiring new levels of accountability and traceability of corporate behavior (e.g., the Sarbanes-Oxley Act), prompting increasing levels of compliance. The information systems department is not immune to compliance requirements mandating microscopic examinations of areas such as careless project overruns.

Besides deploying Six Sigma practices and cutting costs by freezing projects, laying off employees and contractors, or renegotiating supplier contracts, many companies are utilizing supply-side self-funding IT activities to get through turbulent times, including:

- Simplifying, migrating, retiring, and/or consolidating legacy systems to decrease operations and maintenance costs and increase flexibility and agility
- Standardizing, reengineering, and utilizing commercial off-the-shelf technologies and open standards for new product development to speed time to market and avoid the expensive use of proprietary technologies
- Externalizing processes through outsourcing and establishing value-network partner ecosystems and shared services, resulting in lower costs and focus on core competencies

IT portfolio management is a tool that supports companies during times of both robust growth and economic downturn. IT portfolio management supports disciplined improvement and thrives on consistency, repeatability, and accountability. However, a key challenge for companies during periods of boom or bust is aligning to the corporate strategic intent and developing a framework for measuring, balancing, prioritizing, selecting, and flexibly changing the composition of IT investments and assets. Many companies are hemorrhaging in IT spending due to:

- A prevalence of pet projects
- A reluctance to kill projects and/or retire assets
- Too many active projects and a huge backlog of projects
- A myopic focus on exotic and cool technologies
- A lack of a detailed cataloged, organized, and aggregated view of critical versus immaterial assets
- Inconsistent and incomplete criteria to assess IT investments
- Underestimation of the total cost of ownership
- Inadequate governance
- Ad hoc program management processes

This situation is reflected in the following survey results that highlight the shortfalls of the majority of companies in attaining optimal value at acceptable risk levels for their IT investments:

- 84% of companies either do not do business cases for their IT projects or do them on a select few key projects.
- 83% of companies are unable to adjust and align their budgets with business needs more than once or twice a year.
- 67% of IT organizations are not market ready. Benchmarking is done less frequently than once a year.
- 89% of companies are flying blind, with virtually no metrics in place except for finance.
- 57% of companies perceive they are balancing the pressures of cost cutting and IT effectiveness.

Most companies maintain a list of more IT projects than their budgets can support. Ironically, many business and IT managers are unaware of:

- The types of ideas and concepts being worked on within research and development
- How many IT projects are in the development cycle and their alignment with the future strategic direction
- The amount of resources allocated to, or the risks associated with, each IT investment

- The reason why IT investments were initiated or the criteria used to approve IT investments

In addition, information regarding the size and magnitude of the operations and maintenance budget as a percentage of IT spending, and how this funding is allocated among new systems versus legacy systems, is typically not readily available. Hiding IT costs associated with pet projects, political power plays that override strategic objectives, and implementation and execution of rogue systems is easy and commonplace. Unfortunately, most companies lack the discipline to continuously measure performance. To complicate matters, it is not unusual that accountability to initial assumptions made in IT investments is nearly impossible to trace, since roles, responsibilities, and ownership are vaguely defined. Welcome to the world of configuration management, change management, transition management, and governance processes at the lowest levels of maturity. It is impossible to effectively and efficiently manage IT resources without awareness and a detailed catalog of all IT investments, identifying who is accountable, and relevant metrics.

The flaws and disconnects as discussed are manifested in the figures from PMI:

- 72% of IT projects are late, overbudget, lacking in functionality, or never delivered.
- Of the 28% "successful" projects, 45% were overbudget and 68% took longer than planned.
- 50% of managers said they could have realized value with 50% of the cost.
- Only 52% of the projects realized strategic value.

According to the Project Management Institute, North American firms spent more than $1 trillion on IT deployments and surrendered nearly $300 billion on late, overbudget, or failed implementations during 1999–2001.[1] Focus, direction, and control mechanisms are not core competencies within many companies. These figures are particularly alarming considering that projects and initiatives in the pipeline should represent the engines for growth, modernization, and transformation. Projects and initiatives typically average approximately 25% of the total IT budget (the remainder allocated to assets within operations in such areas as existing applications, infrastructure, people, processes, etc.). Assuming a 30% success rate, only $1 out of $14 spent by the average company's IT budget can be correlated with new benefits. This is a relatively accurate assertion.

IT continues to subsume a larger percentage of the enterprise budget. The criticality of IT to business operations and the rising cost of downtime will increasingly impact the bottom line. As customer demands continue to increase and as companies expand their operations beyond their own facilities, it is imperative that they focus on demand-side efficiencies and provide impeccable quality, service, integrity, and continuous innovation. As a result, converting fixed IT costs into variable costs through such mechanisms as utility-based on-demand offerings and outsourcing (e.g., infrastructure, application development, application maintenance, business processes) allows companies to focus on their core value propositions. This practice has recently gained traction.

Many companies maintain a sequential series of tightly coupled, hardwired systems that dictate business logic and processes. The resulting infrastructure is inflexible and ineffective in data aggregation and synchronization. Costly overruns are commonplace in extending or adding new processes across divergent and distributed environments. The ability to extend, migrate, refurbish, or retire systems or applications is very difficult as key dependencies, support, and constraints with other applications and systems are often unknown. Thus, it is not surprising to find multiple and redundant enterprise resource planning, supply chain management, portals, customer relationship management, middleware, and operating systems consisting of undocumented ad hoc upgrades and patches analogous to a "spaghetti" architecture.

Technical, business, operating, system, logical, and physical views of the architecture are typically outdated or nonexistent. Misalignment between IT and the strategic intent, inability to establish a common IT architecture, and a highly redundant and undocumented as-is architecture will result in high operations and maintenance costs. Furthermore, this will limit a company's ability to rapidly respond to unforeseen events and prioritize and reprioritize investments. In today's unforgiving economy, the result of not conforming to a disciplined IT portfolio management framework is undisciplined growth and drift of business processes that are typically expressed through lack of innovation, slow market responsiveness, and dissatisfied customers. These shortfalls are exposed swiftly, causing debilitating and adverse effects on valuation and the sustainability of a company as an ongoing entity.

To further complicate matters, the emergence of web services, business process management systems, and services-oriented development of applications (SODA), which enable more specialized, plug-in applications, are seminal elements in realizing the vision of an agile enterprise. These flexible new technologies are creating an unprecedented demand for systems to interoperate. Web services and SODA will continue to make the business and IT relationship more critical as IT continues to become increasingly more integral to business processes. The layers of abstraction added to technologies are becoming more visual and model driven. In addition, the introduction of emerging technologies or often just the hype around them (e.g., nanocomputing, grid computing, and peer-to-peer computing) will continue to add to the complexity of IT, making IT portfolio management an increasingly critical capability.

FORMING, NORMING, STORMING: THE IT LIFE CYCLE

Unfortunately, there is no single point of failure that is causing breakage. In fact, there are failure points across the entire IT life cycle that contribute to poor planning, execution, and alignment of projects and initiatives. According to research, fewer than 25% of Global 2000 IT staff have been formally and effectively schooled in project management. The IT life cycle is comprised of three primary phases: the IT discovery phase, the IT project phase, and the IT asset phase.

IT Discovery Phase

Sometimes called the fuzzy front end, the IT discovery phase occurs during the concept and idea stages of basic research. This phase matures IT investments that are typically longer term, riskier, and more uncertain than the other two phases discussed below. The IT discovery phase provides the locomotive that companies utilize to grow and transform the business. Investments in this phase are inventoried, assessed, balanced, optimized, and selected in the IT discovery portfolio.

IT Project Phase

Sometimes called new product development, this phase is governed by a series of stages and gates for managing the life cycle of projects. Investments made in the IT project phase typically are medium- to short-term investments that companies use to help transform and grow the business. Investments in this phase also include mandatory requirements (e.g., legal, compliance, and safety regulations). Investments in the IT project phase are inventoried, assessed, balanced, optimized, and selected in the IT project portfolio.

IT Asset Phase

The IT asset phase describes the portion of the IT life cycle that are currently in operations and maintenance. This phase monitors and evaluates the existing infrastructure, software, human capital management, processes, data, and information. Investments in the IT asset phase are used to help run the business and are inventoried, assessed, balanced, optimized, and selected in the IT asset portfolio.

Shortfalls in the IT Life Cycle

Exhibit 1.1 describes the three primary phases of the IT life cycle, the shortfalls within each of these phases, and the impact as a result of these shortfalls. The bullet points shown in the shortfall areas under the specific phases in Exhibit 1.1 do not necessarily correspond to the phases under which they reside. The majority of companies have formal return on investment, payback period, internal rate of return, and/or economic value-add metrics. However, most do not consistently apply both financial and nonfinancial measurements and processes for evaluating projects and initiatives, and most do not track metrics after implementation.

Decentralization and lack of visibility of IT spending create misalignment, leading to redundancy and lack of reuse. Many groups within companies do not see the IT department as an entity that can quickly and effectively resolve their issues; therefore, business units typically will design and build their own "sandbox" of systems and solutions completely under the radar screen of corporate IT governance. Unfortunately, maintenance, product, and service enhancements form the majority of IT spending, many utilizing nonstandard processes, leading to high total cost of ownership. Companies frequently underestimate the total cost of ownership for investments: ongoing maintenance and enhancement costs, licensing, upgrades, training, and other ongoing costs associated with the "tail" of an investment.

DOES IT *REALLY* MATTER? THE IT PRODUCTIVITY PARADOX

Many executives question whether they are receiving full value from their IT spending and whether this spending is being properly directed. In the 1980s, a series of studies found that despite the improvements made by technology, the correlation between how much a company spends on IT and the accompanying productivity generated as a result of IT investments is minimal. This is referred to as the IT productivity paradox. The IT productivity paradox has recently been examined in numerous studies including one by Dedrick, Gurbaxani, and Kraemer, who concluded that "the productivity paradox as first formulated has been effectively refuted . . . greater investment in IT is associated with greater productivity growth."[2] Appendix 1A provides a summary of selected studies on the IT productivity paradox.

One of the more interesting research studies conducted recently is from Mainstay Partners. In 2002, Mainstay surveyed 450 companies across the energy, financial services, health care, manufacturing, retail and consumer products, and telecommunications industries. The survey showed that IT-smart organizations—defined by companies that actively and effectively manage their IT investments through the use of IT portfolio management—derive measurable value from IT investments. Although the number of these companies is small, the research concluded that for IT-smart organizations:

EXHIBIT 1.1   THREE PHASES OF IT LIFE CYCLE

IT Discovery Phase	IT Project Phase	IT Asset Phase

Shortfalls

IT Discovery Phase

- Requirements, future capabilities and as-is versus to-be architecture not adequately considered when assessing concepts.
- IT concepts are not linked to business, functional, or divisional strategy.
- Poorly defined, nonstandardized business cases; assumptions that are not complete or accurate and do not consider risk outliers, feasibility, correlation with other investments, and other dependencies and constraints; lack of decision criteria.
- Lack of weighting of attributes.
- Distributed, siloed repository of concepts.
- Too many concepts in the pipeline, with too few support resources; best resources are not allocated to concepts and ideas.
- Few concepts considered that will transform the company; many initiatives are disassociated with the long-term strategic objectives; moving fast can be difficult.
- Deficient communications result in fragmented efforts, as resources are not optimally aligned and deployed.

IT Project Phase

- No centralized project management office; no single and consistent project manager throughout the cycle.
- No central and visible repository of all projects.
- Lack of governance and cross-participation from key executives.
- Inadequate gating and filtering mechanisms; ad hoc entry and exit criteria at each major phase.
- Inability to optimally scope, cost, schedule, and allocate resources to projects.
- Gaming the system with pet projects.
- Unwillingness to "kill" projects.
- Development methodologies such as spiral, rapid application, and time-box approaches are not utilized; customer/end user feedback is inadequate.
- Assumptions are never revisited.
- Lack of headroom for resources/funding for unexpected events prohibits ability to rapidly reprioritize and switch directions.
- Never turning down a customer, senior management, or marketing request.

IT Asset Phase

- Employee skill sets and processes needed to support new solutions are not adequately considered.
- Integration and interoperability with existing systems and business processes are not fully assessed.
- Refusal or inability to continuously assess as-is versus to-be architecture and optimally decide whether to retire, migrate, or keep existing systems and solutions.
- Ineffective feedback loop to IT or corporate strategy.
- Distributed and siloed repository of assets.
- Lack of metrics prevents objective evaluation of performance and development of sustainable service levels.
- Applications and systems define business logic.
- Opportunity to outsource maintenance and support of applications and systems is not given adequate consideration.
- Benchmarking performance against similar entities does not occur on a regular basis.
- Above-average IT spending occurs in maintenance and support, with little left to grow or transform opportunities.

Results

IT Discovery Phase

- Inaccurate prioritization of IT investments; investment imbalance, as important and strategic projects are underfunded.
- Duplicative spending and redundant R&D investments.
- IT portfolio risk profile reaches an unacceptable level.
- Nonstandardized initial business cases create difficulty comparing and contrasting various types of IT investments.
- Sustaining innovations that do not create long-term competitive advantage.
- Resources not optimally aligned.

IT Project Phase

- Majority of projects do not meet expectations.
- Costs exceed budgeted levels; scope creep and project drift are commonplace.
- Projects are late or projects go on for years and are never "killed."
- No flexibility to rapidly reprioritize.
- Committees are powerless and lose the trust of senior management as well as employees.
- Too many projects in the pipeline prove costly and divert resources.

IT Asset Phase

- Projects meet objectives but do not meet customer needs (suboptimal performance).
- Misalignment and lack of interoperability with enterprise architecture; scaling of solutions is virtually impossible.
- Elements of cost such as upgrades, maintenance, user support, etc., are improperly calculated, resulting in exorbitant life cycle costs; many costs buried in line item areas and true costs are difficult to uncover.
- Rogue systems and redundant solutions increase error rates, support costs, and stifle flexibility and agility.

The correlations, constraints, and dependencies of IT investments are not typically combined and aggregated under one view to enable the representation of the holistic and complete alignment with strategy, balance across the company, and assessment of overall risks, costs, benefits, timing, and value.

- Optimizing existing processes for incremental productivity improvements resulted in 10% to 15% general and accounting savings
- Reconstructing core processes for changes in productivity and efficiency resulted in 2% to 3% operating margin improvements
- Inventing new processes and organizational capabilities for growth typically resulted in a ten-fold return on invested capital (ROIC)

The research also showed many areas of breakdown for the non–IT-smart organizations, including:

- Companies spent a lot more on IT than their budgets indicated, since IT budgetary control leaked from the CIOs/CFOs into the lines of business.
- Ad hoc decision processes were used for prioritizing and managing technology investments.
- Poor visibility to accurately measure the business impact of technology investments with unclear business metrics. Very few companies measured the actual results of execution.
- Ineffective ability to tie IT investments with business strategy and goals.
- Lack of business management involvement, poor communication of IT strategies across the company, and an absence of effective governance.[3]

Another research study conducted by Bruque and Medina in 2002 identified areas that probably contribute to the IT productivity paradox:

- Not properly focusing on and managing critical areas within the life cycle
- Reactive moves that defy standardized evaluations, such as defensive postures as a result of a competitor announcement triggering an IT investment
- Value generated by IT investments not being the same for all companies and to a large extent being dependent on the nature of their business
- The effect and importance of complementary resources such as certain human and management elements
- Unrealistic business models bound to fail irrespective of the investments made[4]

Companies witness a positive correlation between IT spending and increased productivity when:

- Senior leadership is strongly supportive and commited
- Governance boards adhere to policies and guidelines yet maintain agility
- Organizational structures and cultures are incentivized and motivated to integrate and align IT and business management

It has been said that "we have a lot of common sense . . . because we don't use it much." Deferring to common sense, if automation is applied poorly to suboptimal processes and bad data, processing, analysis, portfolio management, or just about anything will show that bad results occur with greater frequency. IT portfolio management is reliant on a solid foundation of supporting processes and grounded data. Assuming these are in order, IT portfolio management is an integral framework, language, and tool in realizing the positive correlation between the amount spent on IT and the corresponding increase in productivity.

IT PORTFOLIO MANAGEMENT IOI

Overview

There are elements of IT portfolio management that exist in all companies. They have very similar goals and objectives: maximizing value (tangible and intangible) while managing risks and costs. Most companies utilize simple and straightforward financial models to make investment decisions. For these companies, the IT portfolio management framework is incomplete; it is missing key criteria, is not conducted uniformly, and is not applied across the entire organization nor over the entire life cycle of an IT investment. The framework contains information about each portfolio and the investments that comprise each portfolio, highlighting both the positive and negative aspects of these investments. Analysis of the IT portfolio identifies specific areas in need of improvement, holes in the requirements and architecture, misalignment to the strategic intent, areas that are being overserved and underserved, and so on. There are three primary areas of IT portfolio management:

1. Processes and a framework to plan, create, assess, balance, and communicate the execution of the IT portfolio. For best-practice companies, these processes are standardized, consistent, and visible across the enterprise.

2. Tools that analyze information and data, such as value, costs, risks, benefits, requirements, architecture, and alignment to business and strategic objectives. Information and data are derived from the strategic intent, strategic plan, and business and strategic objectives. Information and data are fluid. Weighting and scoring are applied against information and data in order to prioritize and rank investments. What-if analysis can be performed, which will impact and alter the ranking and prioritization of IT investments.

3. A common business taxonomy and governance that communicates and defines the principles, policies, guidelines, criteria, accountability, range of decision-making authority, and control mechanisms.[5]

The IT portfolio management step-by-step methodology presented in detail in Chapter 5 is a proven process for applying IT portfolio management and has eight stages. These stages are not intended to be applied in a waterfall manner (i.e., serially). They serve as a framework that should be adjusted based on the reader's objectives. In today's fast-paced world, waterfall approaches to delivering anything are proving less and less effective. Nonetheless, the eight basic stages are:

1. Developing an IT portfolio management game plan
2. Planning the IT portfolio
3. Creating the IT portfolio
4. Assessing the IT portfolio
5. Balancing the IT portfolio
6. Communicating the IT portfolio
7. Developing and evolving IT portfolio governance and organization
8. Assessing IT portfolio management process execution

The first stage, the game plan, determines the objectives for IT portfolio management and assesses the main points to establish the most practical areas to address. It encourages users of IT portfolio management to avoid analysis paralysis and begin to make decisions.

The second step, planning, involves building upon the efforts of phase 1 and providing the foundation to plan the investment strategy and portfolio/subportfolio structures.

The third step, creating, inventories all significant IT investments, both current and planned. Each potential IT investment is captured in a standardized business case and located in a centralized database. Assumptions are cataloged, screening decisions are memorialized, and alternatives are identified in each business case. Metrics are defined and portfolio views are built. In the creating stage, weighting information and data form the criteria for screening new or existing investments. Companies should develop a consistent and standardized set of criteria with threshold levels (e.g., risk tolerance, funding and resource capacity and constraints, cost limitations, must-have versus nice-to-have requirements, investment categories). The level of detail associated with the screening process can vary based on the size, risk, complexity, technology, and business/mission maturity of the investment, and if the investment is based on a mandatory requirement. For the IT asset portfolio, analysis of IT investments includes assessment of technical condition, business value, and risk as shown in Exhibit 1.2.

The screening mechanism serves as a check and balance that ensures multiple, relevant, and timely criteria are assessed against each IT investment to assure IT's success in enhancing business and mission performance. The screening

EXHIBIT 1.2   ANALYSIS OF IT INVESTMENTS

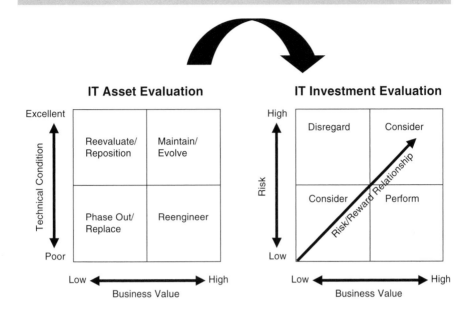

process helps to identify related investments that might be candidates for consolidation. The process also helps to identify potential candidates for acceleration or decommissioning before a large dollar exposure is incurred. As part of this screening process, detailed gaps in requirements, standards, stakeholder analysis, architectural views, and a detailed catalog of the description of IT assets should be published and made available to key employees so that IT investments can easily be mapped to these areas. The criteria used for the screening process should also be made available so that answers to many questions can be anticipated in advance and addressed in the business case.

The fourth stage, assessing, measures the portfolio against targets and monitors internal and external conditions for possible trigger events. IT investments are tracked and monitored both individually and within the IT portfolio. Status reviews evaluating actual versus forecasts made in costs, schedule, value, benefits, scope, and so on, are conducted at least on a quarterly basis (more often depending on the costs, complexity, risks, and value of the IT investment). As mentioned, data and information can change, which could alter the path of IT investments. Balanced scorecards, key performance indicators, critical success factors, service-level agreements, and other metrics provide valuable warning signs relevant to the health and well-being of IT investments. Large deficiencies and imbalance, such as poor project management or risks surpassing threshold levels, can trigger changes to the IT portfolio. As investments are evaluated, the business case for each IT investment should be frequently evaluated and updated. This serves as important feedback for other IT portfolio management processes.

The fifth stage, balancing, identifies tuning options and determines trade-offs within the portfolio. A committee of senior management personnel performs a what-if analysis, adjusting key constraints, variables, and other parameters of the portfolio; assesses the impact of alternative investment options; and determines the optimal allocation of investments into pools (categories). Research indicates that high value is obtained by dividing the overall IT investment pool in a manner that mirrors the enterprise strategy and its time horizon. The same committee serves as the decision authority and selects which investments get funded. The selected investments are mapped into an IT portfolio.

The sixth stage, communicating, creates a consistent approach for driving awareness around the portfolio, goals, status, and what needs to change. This awareness needs to be driven by a communication plan that tailors messages to specific audiences and makes sure these messages are received and acted upon. Communications must occur throughout all phases. Communication is of such critical importance to IT portfolio management that it must be considered at the onset. People, communication, and collaboration form the most seminal aspects of IT portfolio management.

The seventh stage, governance and organization, identifies the roles, responsibilities, and processes for governing the portfolio management process.

The final stage, assessing execution, evaluates program execution and the actual portfolio performance against objectives defined in the game plan. It's the capstone phase where value is demonstrated. If initial objectives were met or exceeded and metrics validate this fact, license exists to evolve the IT portfolio management process, ultimately weaving it into the fabric across all divisions/business units of the organization.

Lessons learned from the performance of investments and the IT portfolio form the golden nuggets (*keisen*) to improve the processes, data, and information as well as the communication and collaboration aspects of IT portfolio management. An example of some areas of input that serve as feedback into IT portfolio management for continuous improvement include:

- Evaluation of the quality and accuracy of assumptions used as the basis of the investment (e.g., actual versus planned schedule, deliverables, costs, and risks)

- Level of support to the customer's business processes, and customer satisfaction with the IT investment

- Achievement of target objectives and benefits (e.g., reduction in cycle time, compliance with regulatory requirements, increase in productivity, and cost savings)

- Utilization of the IT investment (e.g., adequate training, features and functionality, and forecast versus actual users)

Taking corrective actions to enhance the IT portfolio management process, the quality and accuracy of the data and information, and communication and collaboration is a never-ending, fluid aspect of IT portfolio management.

An IT portfolio planning and management approach forces companies to think through the enterprise implications of their IT spending. Research consistently finds that when companies initially institute a portfolio approach, IT expenditures decline by 15% to 20% with no significant negative impact. Given the potential savings and the fact that IT expenditures tend to run between 1.5% and 7% of a company's revenue, using a portfolio approach is a no-brainer. Studies indicate organizations that are mature in IT portfolio planning and management tend to be industry leaders. These organizations consistently maintain sharp focus, balance the needs of current market areas and new growth segments, and exhibit higher performance levels than their competitors, rapidly eliminating underperforming IT investments and reallocating funds to new value-revenue generation opportunities.

IT Portfolio Approaches and IT Subportfolios

IT portfolios are defined using two approaches. The tactical, bottom-up approach leverages existing IT assets and IT projects in the pipeline to define the composition of the portfolio. The strategic, top-down approach decomposes the corporate strategic intent to business and strategic objectives and the IT plan, which records the priorities, timing, and metrics required to achieve the defined goals of the company.

Funding and resource allocation decisions made to specific pools (investment categories) of the IT portfolio are formed based on the top-down approach. We believe that incorporating both the top-down and bottom-up approaches are representative of best practices. Irrespective of the approach, IT portfolio management is a major element of the IT plan and is usually managed by the CIO. IT portfolio management, as shown in Exhibit 1.3, provides an analysis and decision-making framework between employees, customers, partners, suppliers, and distributors. It is supported by many key skills and areas, and it is an aggregation of three subportfolios that provide the entire, holistic, risk-versus-value cost perspective:

1. *IT discovery portfolio:* comprised of longer-term investments in the IT discovery phase
2. *IT project portfolio:* comprised of medium- to short-term investments in the IT project phase
3. *IT asset portfolio:* comprised of existing investments in the IT asset phase

EXHIBIT I.3 IT PORTFOLIO MANAGEMENT

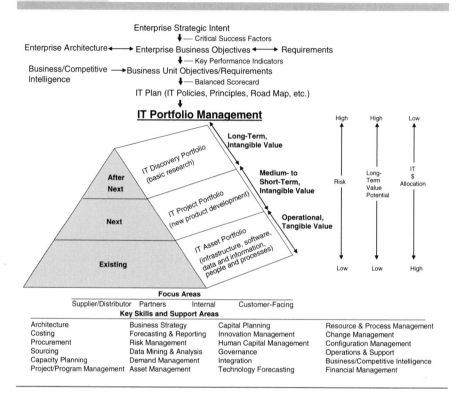

Exhibit 1.3 is for illustrative purposes only; for ease of use, there are some feedback loops purposefully not reflected. Business objectives, requirements, critical success factors, key performance indicators, balanced scorecard, IT subportfolios, and key skills and support areas are discussed in detail throughout this book.

"To Boldly Go Where No Man Has Gone Before": The IT Discovery Portfolio

The IT discovery portfolio is a framework used in the front end of the IT life cycle. In the discovery phase, investments are classified as concepts or ideas; thus, value, costs, benefits, and risk are somewhat difficult to quantify. The IT discovery portfolio aligns, prioritizes, and balances new technologies, which form the basis of strategic enablers and transformation. It has been susceptible to cost cutting, as many organizations focus on short-term, sustaining, low-risk initiatives and bypass the experimental, higher-risk, longer-term innovation and incubation initiatives. The IT discovery portfolio only functions optimally when IT and business have a highly functional relationship, which according to research occurs in only 2% of companies.

Many companies now recognize that mergers and acquisitions, geographic expansion, increase in business development, or cost-cutting efforts will not drive consistent and sustainable growth. As resources have become tighter over recent years, discovery and research have become accountable and performance oriented. They are inextricably linked to delivering elements of the business and strategic objectives, producing targeted and measurable results that increase value and growth consistent with the strategic intent.

Unlike the mid to late 20th century, when discovery and research could take a decade or more from initial idea through commercialization, the majority of companies today cannot afford to spend a sizable amount of resources over such a long period of time. The IT discovery portfolio provides the framework to assure investments are in line with expectations.

Ready, Aim, Fire: The IT Project Portfolio

The IT project portfolio takes input and direction from the corporate strategic plan, external and internal requests, the discovery portfolio, and the IT asset portfolio. IT projects are evaluated based on the input and assumptions made in the business case. The business case details the alignment to the business and strategic objectives, assessment of key stakeholder needs, critical dependencies and constraints, risks, value, costs, benefits, and adherence to compliance/regulations. IT projects are intangible assets in that they have not proven their mission or business value. However, investments in the IT project portfolio are the seminal building blocks in the execution of strategies—vehicles to execute change that are critical to a company's survival. Failure to efficiently manage projects in a repeatable way will destroy a company.

The IT project portfolio focuses on all the projects in development across a company and consolidates one view of the overall value and risks. It serves as a gating mechanism for assuring projects are in alignment with the strategic intent, assumptions in the business case are adhered to, and decisions are based on accurate and timely data.

IT portfolio management is dependent on expertise in project, program, and enterprise program management:

- Project management is focused on single project execution usually in support of a business objective (e.g., upgrade network servers, install desktop operating system). Project management is concerned with project timelines, budget, tasks, and deliverables. Close coordination with people (employees, customers, suppliers, regulators, etc.) is important in managing this aspect of the portfolio.

- Program management is focused on coordination of multiple related projects usually in support of one particular mission or business theme (e.g., customer relationship management, supply chain management). Program management is concerned with synchronized delivery of project results, inter-project dependency management, resource sharing (e.g., people, time, and money), issue and risk management, and budget control to achieve program success.

- Enterprise program management is a holistic view of the coordination and oversight management of all programs/projects within the enterprise. Enterprise program management is concerned with the integration of planning, strategy, resource allocation, and architecture management to achieve best value to the company. This includes value management, process management, and human capital management. The enterprise program management office plays a critical role in IT portfolio management, ensuring that projects and programs are aligned with the business direction. This office provides the management framework for improving project performance through consistency of management approach and process knowledge.

An efficiently run IT project portfolio results in driving higher project success rates. The IT project portfolio does not help companies attain 100% project success, but it improves the successful track record of project investments and helps companies learn how to "fail" properly and faster.

If It Ain't Broke, It Probably Will: The IT Asset Portfolio

An IT asset is defined as anything in the operational baseline under the domain of IT (e.g., hardware, software, data and information, people, and processes). The IT asset portfolio provides a framework to catalog and continuously monitor the business alignment, value, risks, costs, benefits, and balance associated with infrastructure, software, human capital management, processes, data, and information. It represents the largest expenditure for the IT organization.

Applications, typically one of the largest subportfolios in the IT asset portfolio, are categorized according to technical condition (e.g., architecture, adaptability, stability, etc.) and functional/business value (e.g., scope of use, reusability, criticality, completeness, ease of use, stability, cost, dependencies). Assessment and analysis of the IT asset portfolio is partially based on the weightings of these criteria. Weighting can be defined according to different users, industries, and the maturity stages of an application's life cycle. Depending on the technical condition (high versus low) and the derived business value (high versus low), Exhibit 1.2 will facilitate the decision to maintain the existing application, reengineer, retire, or migrate an application.

Of the three portfolios, the IT asset portfolio typically represents the largest expense. Companies have a long way to go to fully map their IT assets and develop a holistic view of the business processes, constraints, dependencies, value, total cost of ownership, metrics, and risks associated with these assets. This analysis provides important feedback to the project portfolio and is used as a basis to consolidate and streamline, retire, wrap, outsource, upgrade, or replace assets. Chapter 6 discusses the maturity of the IT portfolio marketplace and provides insight into the maturity and direction of the IT asset portfolio.

IT portfolio management, encompassing the IT discovery portfolio, the IT project portfolio, and the IT asset portfolio, is shown in Exhibit 1.4. For illustrative purposes only, the processes shown in Exhibit 1.4 in each IT subportfolio are shown in a sequential manner. In reality, many of these processes can occur concurrently, nonsequentially, and nonlinearly. In addition, for ease of representation, many feedback loops were purposefully not shown in this exhibit.

The IT Portfolio Focus on People

Critical and often underestimated elements of the success of IT portfolio management are the people and cultural aspects. Research shows that while financial and operational metrics are important, the attitude, perceptions, and measures of customers, employees, suppliers, regulators, and shareholders are the largest differentiators between high- and low-performance companies. At least on a quarterly basis, measuring, analyzing, and creating course-correction action plans based on asking questions and gathering input from end users and managers of the IT portfolio management process are viewed as best practices. Although understanding individual behaviors and outliers is important, group trends and patterns are critical leading indicators.

IT portfolio management engages cross-functional management and end-users, providing information and data to multiple stakeholders to obtain buy-in regarding prioritization of limited investment dollars, allocation of resources, and a plan to proceed forward. According to research, individual productivity is significantly higher when work is proactively structured around goals. Training to improve learning effectiveness, early and prudent risk taking, and employee empowerment also improve productivity and serve as important behaviors for IT portfolio management. However, resistance to adopt IT portfolio management within business units and divisions that have become accustomed to operating

EXHIBIT 1.4   IT PORTFOLIO MANAGEMENT PROCESSES

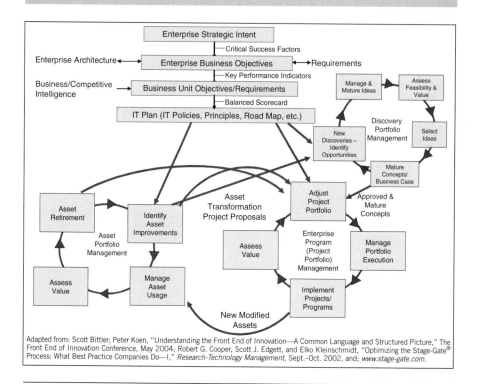

Adapted from: Scott Bittler; Peter Koen, "Understanding the Front End of Innovation—A Common Language and Structured Picture," The Front End of Innovation Conference, May 2004; Robert G. Cooper, Scott J. Edgett, and Elko Kleinschmidt, "Optimizing the Stage-Gate® Process: What Best Practice Companies Do—I," *Research-Technology Management*, Sept.–Oct. 2002, and; *www.stage-gate.com*.

within their siloed environments is not unusual. Many people simply despise change, and IT portfolio management for many companies and their employees involves making numerous changes to the status quo.

Currently, many business units are meeting the near-term needs of their customers without having to justify, or perhaps prolong, the decision-making process by adopting a holistic IT portfolio management framework. While operational decisions and measures should be kept locally within business units, strategic decisions and linkages to key performance measures must be centralized in order to create the ideal enterprise architecture. One of the most effective ways to change behavior is to create clear metrics, linking individual performance strategic objectives with incentives based on desired behavior and positive adjustments to meet performance and objectives.

Key performance measures must be clearly defined, well communicated, and reinforced. Measurements must be linked to performance standards, reviewed frequently, and closely tied to reward and recognition systems. Without a clear understanding of how key measures relate to both individual and group performance and accountabilities, resistance to change will be pervasive.

COMPARISON OF IT PORTFOLIO MANAGEMENT AND FINANCIAL PORTFOLIO MANAGEMENT

Stock traders and money managers of mutual funds tailor a portfolio of investments based on their customers' risk and reward profile, with a keen understanding of the fundamentals associated with investments in the portfolio. Regardless of whether money managers oversee a risk-averse or a highly risky portfolio, the objective is to maximize investment return at an acceptable risk level. As conditions change, money managers must make buy, sell, and hold decisions concerning individual projects and initiatives within portfolios. Money managers are able to communicate in real time the overall performance and value of the portfolio they manage. The liquidity of the majority of their investments means that investments can be bought, sold, or traded with minimal effort.

In addition, money managers have many metrics to compare their performance with other fund performance and investment alternatives. It is important to note that money managers have an immense amount of relatively reliable and standardized information regarding individual assets within their portfolio such as annual reports, financial statements, industry and analyst reports, competitor information, and so on. The tools used for analysis of financial portfolios are generally well established. However, Enron and Worldcom remind us that surprises can occur from time to time.

IT portfolio management leverages many of the rigorous constructs and best practices from the financial marketplace. But there are numerous differences due to the complexities, high exit costs, low salvage value, and lack of securitization associated with some elements of IT. As opposed to a portfolio of investment that might consist of treasury bills, bonds, precious metals, money market, fund shares and private and public equity, IT portfolio management is applied within companies and government agencies to assess and arbitrate alternative investments that compete for limited resources. Unraveling IT investments is usually more complex and takes more time than a publicly traded instrument.

A failed IT investment could have a sizable impact on business continuity and mission critical operations. Some IT investments may not produce the optimal level of financial return due to mandatory, legal, safety, and regulatory constraints, which can trump ROI calculations. The decision support tools and information regarding an IT portfolio are not as well established or as robust as the resources available to money managers. IT portfolio management involves more factors than financial portfolios. Similar to how money managers operate their financial portfolio, IT portfolio management provides reporting and performance metrics that constantly assess, reprioritize, and rebalance a series of buy, hold, and sell decisions related to a suite of technology, process, and tradecraft investments as market conditions and corporate needs change.

An important similarity between a money manager's financial portfolio and an IT portfolio has to do with correlation, or the interdependency between investments in the portfolio. With constrained and limited resources and constant change, it is important to understand not only the risks associated with each individual investment but also the impact, dependencies, and uncertainty across investments. Understanding these relationships and effectively diversifying high-, medium-, and low-risk investments in short-term, medium-term, and long-term initiatives across business and functional areas will minimize the level of risk associated with a portfolio at any given time. The Efficient Frontier, a tool that was originally established for the financial market, is being used to calculate risk versus value of the entire IT portfolio and the effect of individual investments on the IT portfolio (see Chapter 5 for more information regarding the Efficient Frontier).

VALUE AND RISKS

Investors must have some willingness to commit to a level of uncertainty. For investments that have a low probability of an expected result and a high number of possible outcomes, investors expect to receive a higher rate of return due to the potential volatility (investment A in Exhibit 1.5). In contrast, for investments that have a high probability of an expected result and a low number of possible outcomes, investors expect to receive a lower rate of return due to the increased certainty (investment B in Exhibit 1.5). Triangular or normalized probability distribution curves are used to visually show the range of possible outcomes for investments.

For many investments, there is typically a positive correlation between risk and the variability potential for reward—the higher the risk, the higher the variability in the return (or, conversely, the higher the risk, the lower the probability of obtaining a desired outcome). In 1952, Dr. Harry Markowitz, Nobel Laureate and pioneer of portfolio management, published "Portfolio Selection" in the *Journal of Finance*,[6] which showed that a diversified portfolio of high- and low-risk investments yields a higher return than a portfolio comprised of solely high-risk investments or a portfolio of only low-risk investments. Dr. Markowitz described a concept called modern portfolio theory—an efficient suite of investments at a defined level of risk that will maximize return. Modern portfolio theory states there is no single optimal portfolio, but at a given level of value and risk that an investor is willing to incur, an efficient portfolio can be created to maximize returns. Dr. Markowitz made the assumption that investors know and can

EXHIBIT 1.5   SAMPLE PROBABILITY DISTRIBUTION
OF INVESTMENTS

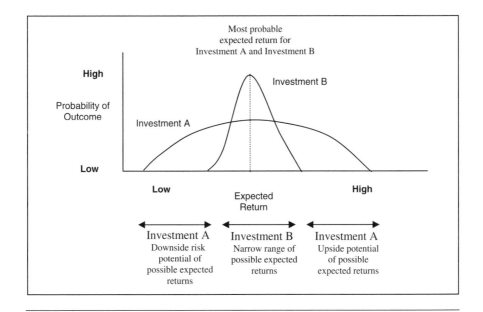

accurately define their objectives. For some companies, the strategic intent and strategic objectives are not clearly defined and clearly articulated, making the IT portfolio difficult to manage in these instances.

Through the capital asset pricing model, Nobel Laureate William Sharpe showed the interrelationships between investments in a portfolio, which we defined earlier as correlation, and how these interrelationships can be risk elements that are just as vital as the individual risks associated with each investment.[7] In 1984, Elton and Gruber mathematically defined an efficient frontier curve, which displays the set of efficient portfolios, demonstrating optimal portfolio combinations for various levels of expected returns versus covariance of return.[8]

Currently, IT portfolio management has become the framework used by leading private- and public-sector entities. Within the public sector, both the U.S. General Accounting Office (GAO) and the Office of Management and Budgeting (OMB) advocate IT portfolio management as a central tenet to sound IT investment management. In Circular A-130 in 2000, the OMB found, "The portfolio will provide information demonstrating the impact of alternative IT investment strategies and funding levels, identify opportunities for sharing resources, and consider the Agency's inventory of information resources."[9] The GAO considers portfolio management as a nucleus for IT investment decision-making. The GAO provides a sound approach to IT portfolio management, and Exhibit 1.6 illustrates how the process works. The three seminal phases shown in Exhibit 1.6 are:

1. *Selection phase:* identifies and chooses IT projects that maximize mission needs using standardized, up-to-date data (risks, proposed benefits, etc.).

2. *Control phase:* progress reviews that measure and monitor actual versus forecast costs, schedule, and benefits. Areas of concern are quickly identified and actions to continue, modify, or cancel are assessed.

3. *Evaluation phase:* determination of the impact on performance. Lessons learned are fed back into the IT portfolio management process for future improvements.[10]

Companies use portfolio management as a strategic and tactical tool to deliver

EXHIBIT I.6   GAO IT INVESTMENT MANAGEMENT PROCESS

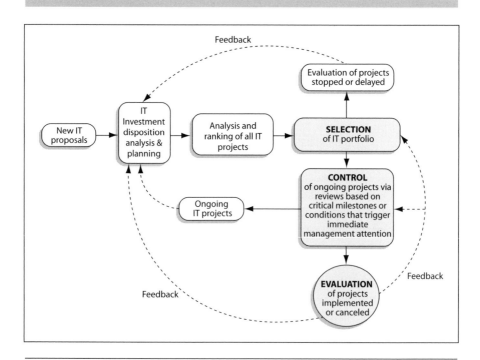

Source: "Assessing Risks and Returns: A Guide for Evaluating Federal Agencies' IT Investment Decision-making," United States General Accounting Office, February 1997.

business value and gain maximum benefit from investments (e.g., productivity increases, decreasing time to market, cost savings resulting from retiring legacy systems and solutions). Value from IT portfolio management is also gained from the ability to anticipate change, maintaining a readiness state for future needs and adjustments while demonstrating the traceability to strategy and planning, architecture, and program management. Some best practices to raise awareness and management control of critical performance and value drivers include:

- Scorecards that track IT's contribution to operational excellence, product leadership, customer intimacy, and financial metrics visually represented via a dashboard interface
- Benchmarks to compare resources and performance by unit
- Benchmarking to compare practices within the same or different industries

Understanding the balance of forces enables IT to take control of value creation.

Attention to risk management and business continuity has increased substantially since September 11, 2001. By incorporating risk-scenario planning within IT portfolio management, IT investments can be aligned with organization risk tolerance. Failure to incorporate risk-scenario planning up front forces organizations to rely on reactive risk management, luck, and firefighting.

A main goal of portfolio management is to spread risk among multiple decisions. By determining what percentage of investment dollars should go into run-the-business versus grow-the-business versus transform-the-business categories, an organization is asserting its risk tolerance on its IT portfolio. Organizations that are risk adverse will spend less resources in transformation-based investments. However, portfolio risk management and tolerance should also evolve to embrace change as the organization's portfolio management skills evolve. The enterprise program management function must instantiate an actionable risk management approach based on culture and risk tolerance. This must incorporate regularly updated standardized risk assessments for initiatives that include traditional risks (e.g., critical skills shortage, technology failure) and dynamic risks arising from less predictable environmental changes (e.g., regulatory changes, market risk, political instability).

Similar to other assessments made to secure an investment, the majority of companies never revisit risk assessments during development or post-implementation. According to research, less than 20% of global organizations have adopted an IT risk management framework such as CobiT (control objectives for information and related technology). CobiT, developed by the Information Systems Audit and Control Association, is a generally accepted standard for IT security and control practices and provides a framework for management, users, and IT audit professionals. Further discussion on CobiT can be found in Chapter 3.

A major challenge with risk management is determining the probability and potential impact of a major problem when an initiative is a complex one-time event. No historical information exists to apply in a probabilistic manner. To manage risks for complex one-time initiatives, scenario planning is used to identify possible issues.

Risk-scenario planning involves several steps that must be performed regularly, providing a means to minimize the IT portfolio's variance of return. The first step in scenario planning involves determining a suitable time horizon. The duration must be reasonable to accommodate risks that emerge in the current fast-paced environment and span no further than the life expectancy of initiatives in the IT portfolio. Next, a wide range of scenarios must be developed to describe possible future events. In Exhibit 1.7 scenario planning determines the potential risks as a result of the cultural, conditional, complexity, and cooperation aspects.

The probability of each risk scenario transpiring is determined, as well as the impact of each risk scenario on initiatives in the IT portfolio (Exhibit 1.8). This information is used to:

- Fine-tune the portfolio to add or remove initiatives that have other-than-expected risk-adjusted value

EXHIBIT 1.7   SCENARIO PLANNING EXAMPLE

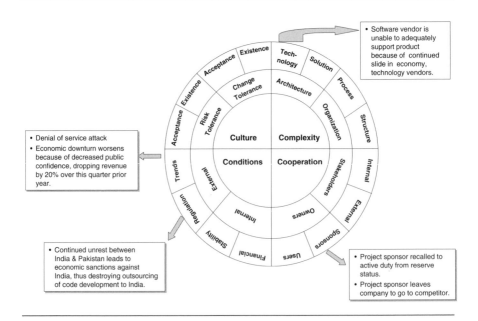

EXHIBIT 1.8 SCENARIO PLANNING PROBABILITIES

Scenario	Magnitude	Probability	Impact	Mitigation Strategy
Denial-of-service attacks	$2,500,000	20%	$500,000	Put appropriate technology in place and ensure for cost containment of $100,000
Economic downturn worsens because of decreased public confidence, dropping revenues by 20% over this quarter prior year	$42,857,143	70%	$30,000,000 (IT budget reduction)	Institute IT portfolio program and proactively attach attributes to projects to determine which are discretionary
Continued unrest between India and Pakistan leads to economic sanctions against India, thus destroying outsourcing of code development to India	$50,000,000	40%	$20,000,000	Require source to be archived to local servers nightly; create alliance with offshore developers in other nations
Software vendor is unable to adequately support product because of continued slide in economy, technology vendors	$16,666,667	30%	$5,000,000	Require source to be held in escrow; check media quarterly
Project sponsor recalled to active duty from reserve status	$14,285,714	70%	$10,000,000	Develop relationship with heir apparent to existing project sponsor
Project sponsor leaves company to go to competitor	$500,000,000	2%	$10,000,000	Nothing

- Determine risk-adjusted portfolio value
- Develop enterprise risk-mitigation strategies including cost-containment insurance

Risk-scenario planning is an effective tool to maximize IT investment returns by minimizing transformation risk.

CONCLUSION

Mercy Health Partners implemented IT project portfolio management. According to James J. Albin, vice president and CIO of Mercy Health Partners, and

Pacific Edge Software, Mercy's enterprise portfolio management solution provider, Mercy has achieved results within 18 months:

- Reduced IT costs by $4 million.

- Gained a highly satisfied customer base by involving customers in the project approval process. Customers set priorities based on the current number of projects in the queue and resource availability.

- Strategically aligned how resources are allocated to projects. Resource tracking helps the information systems (IS) department prioritize projects based on availability.

- Communicated and improved the understanding of IT's direction. With clear visibility into project portfolios and easily accessible reports, executives and senior management make better business decisions based on strategic goals. They can analyze budget and time information, easily obtain project completion reports, prioritize projects based on criteria, and explain impacts of resource management.

- Enhanced project approval and prioritization process.[11]

As you can see from the benefits for Mercy Health Partners, the results of IT portfolio management are tangible and measurable:

- Duplicative efforts are eliminated, resulting in dollar savings.

- Pet project and uncoordinated funding are minimized.

- Low value-added investments are identified early in the process, and action is taken to revector resources to more critical priorities. Alignment and balance is quickly achieved.

Diversification of risks is an important aspect of IT portfolio management. Risks are minimized by spreading and diversifying resources across short-term and long-term investments, high- and low-risk projects, existing infrastructure and new innovations, and by project types, product lines, strategic versus nonstrategic, regions, and market segments. Most companies passively manage their IT portfolios. Migrating to active IT portfolio management takes many years. The next chapter discusses the planning aspects of IT portfolio management and the IT portfolio maturity model.

NOTES

1. Project Management Institute, www.pmi.org.
2. Jason Dedrick, Vijay Gurbaxani, and Kenneth L. Kraemer, "Information Technology and Economic Performance: A Critical Review of the Empirical Evidence," Center for

Research on Information Technology and Organizations, University of California, Irvine, March 2003, www.crito.uci.edu; http://portal.acm.org/citation.cfm?doid=641865.641866 pp. 1 and 24 for appendix.

3. Amir Hartman, "Why Tech Falls Short of Expectations," Optimizemag.com, July 2002, http://www.optimizemag.com/article/showArticle.jhtml?articleId=17700745; pp.22–27.

4. Sebastian Bruque and Jose Medina, "The Technology Paradox: Characteristics, Causes and Implications for IT Management," *International Journal of Information Technology,* Vol. 8, No. 1, August 1, 2002, http://www.icis.ntu.edu.sg/scs-ijit/81/81-5.pdf; pp. 79–88.

5. Adapted from "Assessing Risks and Returns: A Guide for Evaluating Federal Agencies' IT Investment Decision-making," United States General Accounting Office, February 1997, http://www.gao.gov/special.pubs/ai10113.pdf.

6. Harry M. Markowitz (1952), "Portfolio Selection," *Journal of Finance,* 7:1, pp. 77–91.

7. William F. Sharpe 1964, "Capital Asset Prices: A Theory of Market Equilibrium under Conditions of Risk." *Journal of Finance,* 19:3 pp. 425–442.

8. Edwin J. Elton and Martin Gruber, *Modern Portfolio Theory and Investment Analysis,* 2nd edition, New York: John Wiley & Sons, 1984.

9. Office of Management and Budget, Circular No. A-130, Section 8 (b) 1b VII, November 30, 2000, http://www.whitehouse.gov/omb/circulars/a130/a130trans4.html#8.

10. United States General Accounting Office, *Assessing Risks and Returns: A Guide for Evaluating Federal Agencies' IT Investment Decision-Making,* February 1997, http://www.gao.gov/special.pubs/ai10113.pdf; diagram is on page 9.

11. Pacific Edge, Mercy Health Care Partners Case Study, www.pacificedge.com/solutions/case_studies/case_mercyhealth.asp; and James J. Albin, "Project Portfolio Management: The Future of IT," *Portfolio Knowledge,* Issue 1, p. 11, 2002, www.portfolioknowledge.com.

Selected Firm-Level Studies of IT Returns

Study	Data Sample	Findings
		IT and Firm Performance
Strassmann [1990]	38 U.S. companies	No correlation between IT spending and firm performance.
Loveman [1994]	60 Business units in 20 U.S. companies	IT investments add nothing to output.
Barua et al. [1995]	Same as Loveman [1994]	IT improves intermediate output if not final output.
Brynjolfsson and Hitt [1993]	Large U.S. manufacturers	Gross-marginal product of IT is over 50% per year in manufacturing.
Brynjolfsson and Hitt [1995]	Large U.S. manufacturers	Firm effects account for half of productivity benefits of earlier study.
Lichtenberg [1995]	U.S. firms, 1989–1991	IT has excess return; one IS employee can be substituted for six non-IS employees without affecting output.
Brynjolfsson and Hitt [1996]	367 Large U.S. firms	Gross return on IT investments of 81%. Net return ranges from 48% to 67%, depending on depreciation rate.
Hitt and Brynjolfsson [1996]	370 U.S. firms	IT investments increase firm productivity and consumer welfare, but not profitability.
Dewan and Min [1997]	300 Large U.S. firms	IT is a net substitute for both capital and labor, and shows excess returns relative to labor input.
Black and Lynch [1997]	1621 U.S. manufacturing establishments	Productivity not affected by presence of a particular management practice but by implementation, especially degree of employee involvement.

Study	Sample	Finding
		Nonmanagerial use of computers related to productivity.
Brynjolfsson et al. [1998]	Sample of *Fortune* 1000 U.S. firms, 1987–1994	The stock market value of $1 of IT capital is the same as $5–$20 of other capital stock.
Gilchrist et al. [2001]	Sample of *Fortune* 1000 U.S. firms	IT productivity is greater in IT producer firms than in user firms and in durable manufacturing.
Greenan et al. [2001]	French firms	Gross returns to IT investment are positive and greater than returns to non-IT investment.

Organizational Complements and IT Returns

Study	Sample	Finding
Bresnahan et al. [2002]	400 Large U.S. firms, 1987–1994	The effects of IT on labor demand are greater when IT is combined with particular organizational investments.
Brynjolfsson et al. [1998]	Sample of U.S. firms, 1996	Decentralized organizational practices, in combination with IT investments, have a disproportionate positive effect on firm market value.
Ramirez et al. [2001]	200+ U.S. firms, 1998	Firm use of employee involvement and total quality management enhances IT returns.
Francalanci and Galal [1998]	52 U.S. life insurance companies, 1986–1995	Productivity gains result from worker composition (more information workers) and IT investments.
Devaraj and Kohli [2002]	8 Hospitals, over 3 years	IT investment combined with business process reengineering positively and significantly influences performance.
Tallon et al. [2000]	300+ U.S. firms, 1998	Perceived business value of IT is greater when IT is more highly aligned with business strategy.

Source: Jason Dedrick, Vijay Gurbaxani, and Kenneth J. Kraemer, "Information Technology and Economic Performance: A Critical Review of the Empirical Evidence," Center for Research on Information Technology and Organizations, University of California, Irvine, March 2003, www.crito.uci.edu; http://portal.acm.org/citation.cfm?doid=641865.64866, p.24 for appendix.

CHAPTER 2

Planning for IT Portfolio Management: Ready, Aim, THEN Fire

INTRODUCTION

Unfortunately, it is all too common for organizations to latch on to a technology or technique, assuming it is the ever-elusive silver bullet, and dive into execution without being grounded in reality. The technique of IT portfolio management is no exception. Many IT portfolio management efforts have failed or been derailed because of improper planning prior to embarking on the journey. Recently, the focus of IT portfolio management has been on eliminating and consolidating IT assets (e.g., servers, applications). Given the volatility in the marketplace, this is a logical use of IT portfolio management. However, it is not leading practice—it is common practice. Best practice companies look at the big picture within the context of their objectives, risk tolerance, and the interrelationships between IT investments.

This chapter explains the importance of planning for IT portfolio management. Of key importance is aligning the IT portfolio management efforts with business objectives, the capabilities of the team responsible for the effort, the degree of engagement of key stakeholders, and the culture of the organization. Just as a pilot creates a flight plan before getting into the cockpit, the IT portfolio management effort must create an achievable game plan prior to execution.

This chapter also describes the steps needed to generate a plan for establishing and maintaining the IT portfolio. Careful attention is placed on establishing the value proposition and identifying the objectives, scope, and associated work effort of the next phase of the portfolio management process. The goal is to create an achievable game plan that positions IT portfolio management for success on the initial iteration and subsequent iterations. To achieve this goal, the processes that must occur include:

- Assessment of the readiness of the company for IT portfolio management
- Assessment of the maturity of the IT portfolio management process within the company
- Assessment of the capabilities of the team responsible for IT portfolio management
- Bounding of the scope of the IT portfolio management effort
- Establishment of reasonable, attainable, and measurable objectives
- Creation of a charter for the effort—a contract to establish what will be done by whom (and by when)
- Creation of an actual task plan replete with milestones and assignments of responsibilities
- Creation of a communication plan to set and manage expectations
- Selection of the tools to be used in the current iteration of the IT portfolio management process
- Validation of the game plan with appropriate stakeholders

It is assumed that initial objectives for IT portfolio management exist. As a rule of thumb, objectives of any initiative should drive the tasks performed and the appropriate deliverables created by said tasks. Using this rule of thumb will minimize time expended on tasks that provide little, if any, value to the organization. If initial objectives for IT portfolio management do not exist, the benefits that will help in their creation include:

- Has historically reduced project spend by 15% to 20% with no significant downside to the business
- Identifies opportunities for reuse of existing assets on proposed projects
- Provides an approach to minimize spending and maximize return on information when applied to assets
- Provides a top-down approach to optimizing IT performance when applied holistically
- Balances IT investments with organizational objectives and tolerance for risk
- Provides a mechanism to prevent overinvesting in business areas or product lines that are nearing the end of their life cycle

- Surfaces interdependencies between projects and/or assets that were previously hidden, possibly averting the domino effect
- Identifies mismatches between desired and actual spending on operational, growth, and transformational investments

With all these potential benefits in mind, it is no wonder that many jump into IT portfolio management with ungrounded enthusiasm. The subsequent sections show the steps needed to temper unbridled enthusiasm and embark on IT portfolio management with the most salient and attainable objectives driving the effort.

BASELINE ASSESSMENTS

Baselines are critical to demonstrating success with change initiatives. In the absence of baselines, ex post facto improvement of change initiatives is subjective. Research found that 70% of IT projects are deemed unsuccessful. The root cause is failure to define success criteria at the start of the projects. This lesson must be applied to IT portfolio management initiatives. Of note in the aforementioned statistic is that of the 30% of IT projects deemed successful, 50% changed their objectives during the project. This is an acceptable practice called expectations management. Expectations management requires communication with key stakeholders, which is why communication planning and stakeholder analysis are also covered in this chapter.

Nonetheless, baselines must be obtained to measure improvement after the application of IT portfolio management and to temper objectives prior to beginning. The areas that are the most commonly baselined are:

- Organizational readiness to embrace the IT portfolio management process
- IT portfolio management process maturity
- Capabilities of the enterprise based on current abilities and organization readiness
- Credibility of the IT organization in the eyes of the business

If this is the initial foray into IT portfolio management, the catch-22 is that objectives and associated tasks at this stage have not been firmed up, so staffing requirements are unknown. Generally, the initial phase of IT portfolio management is sponsored by the CIO, and early tasks are performed by a direct report to the CIO responsible for special projects. While this is by no means an absolute, someone must perform the initial assessments, identify the target objectives for IT portfolio management, build a plan to perform IT portfolio management, and find adequate resources to successfully execute the plan. In organizations that are evolving their existing IT portfolio management function, the team responsible for IT portfolio management carries out the tasks outlined in the following section.

ORGANIZATION READINESS

Organization readiness involves looking at critical dimensions within a company to determine how much IT portfolio management it can absorb. Assessing the readiness of the organization for IT portfolio management enables pinpointing where IT portfolio management can provide the most value within the enterprise. As it is embraced by the enterprise, reassessment of organization readiness helps target future objectives for expanding the scope of IT portfolio management. Whereas some organizations have clearly defined IT investment processes, others lack structure for IT investments. Some organizations view IT as a necessary evil; other organizations view IT as a valuable strategic enabler.

Various factors must be considered to determine the organization's readiness for IT portfolio management. Exhibit 2.1 lists factors to consider when assessing readiness for institutionalizing IT portfolio management. While the dimensions in Exhibit 2.1 do not provide a scientific method for quantifying IT portfolio management readiness, analyzing each dimension will provide adequate information to temper often overly optimistic objectives or scope.

IT PORTFOLIO MANAGEMENT MATURITY

The overall goal of IT portfolio management is to optimize the risk reward trade-off when allocating resources in support of organizational objectives. When reviewing individual financial portfolios, the individual portfolio manager must analyze financial objectives, tolerance for risk, and available resources, then make appropriate decisions. In the case of individual financial portfolios, adequate metrics exist to make rational decisions with relative precision and appropriate accuracy. Most IT organizations, however, lack infrastructure for real-time reporting, performance measurement, and business analytics. Additionally, several key obstacles to IT performance exist, many of which tie back to a lack of metrics (see Exhibit 2.2).

Unlike the portfolios used by money managers in the financial marketplace where the underlying data come from mature processes governed under generally accepted accounting principles (GAAP) and generally accepted auditing standards (GAAS), IT does not have generally accepted governing principles and standardized rules and processes. Therefore, this chapter identifies a maturity model that helps meter the progress made by companies in the IT portfolio management

EXHIBIT 2.1   ORGANIZATION READINESS DIMENSIONS

Value	What is the business's perception of IT's value?
IT Plan and IT Principles	Does an IT plan and/or IT principle document exist? Are they frequently evaluated and updated? Do these documents explain how IT delivers value within the organization?
IT Governance Committee	Does the company have an existing IT governance committee that can be leveraged?
IT Discovery	Is there a tie between IT discovery and the strategic plan?
Project Prioritization Process	Is there a project prioritization process in place? If so, is it resistant to change?
Project/Program Management Competency	Do project/program competencies exist? If so, at what level of maturity?
Enterprise Architecture	Has a clear vision of the enterprise's future been articulated through an enterprise architecture or similar mechanism?
Measurement Program	Do metrics exist within the IT organization? Are they reliable? Are they accurate? Are they precise?
Products/Service Catalog	Is there an accurate listing of IT assets? Are they portrayed as products and services to be offered to the customers of IT, or are they portrayed as depreciable assets?
Leadership/Sponsorship	Is there strong leadership within the business and IT to support decisions made with a portfolio approach?
Organization Culture	Does the organization's culture promote consensus decision making? What is the organization's tolerance for risk?
Operational Processes	Are operational processes stable enough to provide reliable data and information for portfolio decisions?
Resources	Do adequate resources exist to institute portfolio management (e.g., people, funding, time)?
Technology and Support	Is there an adequate infrastructure and support mechanism in place (help desk, networked services, integrated systems and solutions, etc.)?

process. The IT portfolio management maturity model allows IT organizations to benefit from rudimentary portfolio management initially but requires operational processes to be refined and matured to enable the nirvana of IT portfolio management—an optimized, fluid, dynamic portfolio of projects and assets that provides the most efficient and effective use of a company's IT resources and is capable of being reprioritized and rebalanced based on changing conditions.

The Software Engineering Institute (SEI), a federally funded research and development center operating at Carnegie Mellon University, developed the capability maturity model (CMM) as a framework to guide software process improvement efforts. It is comprised of five levels that provide a framework for

EXHIBIT 2.2 OBSTACLES TO IT PERFORMANCE

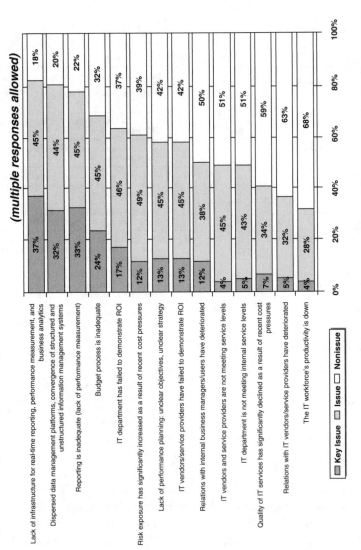

(multiple responses allowed)

	Key Issue	Issue	Nonissue
Lack of infrastructure for real-time reporting, performance measurement, and business analytics	37%	45%	18%
Dispersed data management platforms, convergence of structured and unstructured information management systems	32%	44%	20%
Reporting is inadequate (lack of performance measurement)	33%	45%	22%
Budget process is inadequate	24%	45%	32%
IT department has failed to demonstrate ROI	17%	46%	37%
Risk exposure has significantly increased as a result of recent cost pressures	12%	49%	39%
Lack of performance planning: unclear objectives, unclear strategy	13%	45%	42%
IT vendors/service providers have failed to demonstrate ROI	13%	45%	42%
Relations with internal business managers/users have deteriorated	12%	38%	50%
IT vendors and service providers are not meeting service levels	4%	45%	51%
IT department is not meeting internal service levels	5%	43%	51%
Quality of IT services has significantly declined as a result of recent cost pressures	7%	34%	59%
Relations with IT vendors/service providers have deteriorated	5%	32%	63%
The IT workforce's productivity is down	4%	28%	68%

IT organizations blame lack of measurement or inadequate measurement as key performance roadblocks maturing application development from ad hoc software development processes that produce unpredictable results to a self-improving environment that produces quality software with predictable results. The CMM is effective in this regard and has spawned maturity models in other knowledge areas (e.g., project management) to bring discipline and corresponding quality to them. It is in this spirit that we put forth an IT portfolio management maturity model to bring quality and self-improvement to the application of portfolio management and enable better IT decision making.

Exhibit 2.3 shows the five basic levels of the model, along with the key objective(s) that would drive an organization to want to progress to the next level. Level 0, admitting, is the starting point. At level 0, recognition of the benefits of applying portfolio management to IT is identified. Moving to level 1, communicating, requires that a portfolio be created to communicate interrelationships of IT assets and/or projects. Level 1 can be thematic or holistic. Relative accuracy is more important than precision at level 1. Whereas level 1 can be a one-time event, level 2, governing, requires that IT portfolio management be officially recognized with governance—prescribed processes, allocated people, and approved policy—to enable it to live within a company.

EXHIBIT 2.3   IT PORTFOLIO MANAGEMENT MATURITY MODEL

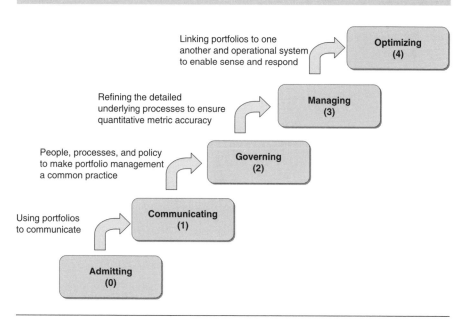

At level 3, managing, the accuracy of information feeding the portfolio becomes pertinent. In fact, level 3 cannot be obtained or exceeded without the underlying operational processes being mature enough to provide reliable quantitative input for the portfolio. Level 3 is the most difficult level to obtain. For asset portfolios, asset management must be operationally effective. For projects, project and program management must be mature enough to provide consistent and reliable project and program estimates and actuals to feed the project portfolio. The IT portfolio in its entirety cannot attain or exceed level 3 until all subportfolios are at level 3 or greater. Level 4, optimizing, is nirvana for IT portfolio management. At level 4, metrics are acted upon to improve the portfolio. Interdependencies between portfolio components, as well as interdependencies between subportfolios, are recognized and measured. Measurements at level 4 are used to guide improvement. A more detailed description of the maturity model can be found in Appendix 2A, enabling readers to determine their current and desired IT portfolio management maturity.

Raising the level of IT portfolio management should not become the primary objective. Many improvement initiatives have maturity models (e.g., Software Engineering Institute's capability maturity model and Program Management Institute's organizational project management maturity model). A maturity model is a diagnostic and nothing more. Frequently, the primary goal of organizations becomes either moving to the next level or advancing to the highest level. While there may be merit in advancing in maturity, failure to address business issues and provide demonstrable value will most certainly derail the most well-intentioned IT portfolio management initiatives. Determining the current level of IT portfolio management maturity, however, will provide an excellent mechanism to ensure that the objectives are neither too lofty nor too unambitious.

IT PORTFOLIO MANAGEMENT CAPABILITY ASSESSMENT

After analyzing the organization's pain points, readiness for IT portfolio management, and maturity of the IT portfolio management discipline within the organization, the capabilities to do IT portfolio management can truly be ascertained—the current state of the enterprise's use of IT portfolio management, coupled with the enterprise's readiness for change, enables a relatively accurate assessment of the extent to which IT portfolio management can be applied successfully. The capability to perform IT portfolio management within your organization should temper the initial objectives. At this juncture, ask yourself if, "based upon what I've learned with the assessments, and given my resource constraints, are my objectives for IT portfolio management doable?" If the answer is "no," which it usually is, adjust the objective for attainability. Set yourself up for success.

STAKEHOLDER ANALYSIS

This step is not optional! Many practitioners assumed it was, leading to derailment of the effort because of a failure to address the issues of a key stakeholder. Stakeholder analysis is designed to identify key players who have a stake in IT portfolio management and their attributes so that they can be addressed appropriately. In rudimentary stakeholder analysis, individuals who have a stake in an effort are identified, then their issues are captured and addressed. We advocate taking stakeholder analysis a bit further. While IT portfolio management has its roots in mathematics, people are the critical element to its success. Key stakeholders must be identified and their support secured. To do this, however, the personal benefits to them must be identified, associated with the IT portfolio management effort, and subsequently communicated to them to secure their involvement and support.

Key stakeholders are generally identified as those with formal or informal power. Formal power can often be associated with funding ability. Informal power relates to the ability to influence others (often those with funding ability). Stakeholder groups can also be identified. For example, the team of project managers might be considered a stakeholder group. If the IT portfolio management exercise involves projects and project metrics are required, project managers must be addressed to fulfill this need.

Once key stakeholders are identified, their attributes must be collected. Often, these attributes are qualitative or even educated guesses. The minimum attributes about each stakeholder (or stakeholder group) are included in Exhibit 2.4.

The perceived level of support is identified to enable portfolio management stakeholder triage. Those with high support for the effort can be enrolled in providing active sponsorship and participation. Those on the fence should be addressed directly to increase their level of support. Those who are naysayers should be addressed to increase their level of support or minimize the damage their negativity could bring to the initiative. Power level and other influences such as lead end users are also major considerations. It is optimal to have those with the most power or who are the most influential lead the IT portfolio management initiative. In fact, this often turns out to be the case.

Who is the most powerful person in a company? Often, it is the chief financial officer (who controls the money). Ironically, CFOs understand and even embrace IT portfolio management. It resonates with their philosophies around risk, return, and control. Often omitted, learning and communication styles are of critical importance. Highly analytical individuals (or groups) will require massive amounts of data to engage them and maintain their support and participation. Those who are behavioral in nature—concerned with the human aspects of IT portfolio management—must be made to understand that IT portfolio management enables more effective communication and minimizes conflict. Directives tend to be those

EXHIBIT 2.4   STAKEHOLDER ANALYSIS ATTRIBUTES

Who	Level of IT Portfolio Management Support	Power Level	Learning/ Communication Style	Perceived Risks with IT PfM	Business Issues/ Opportunities
• Senior Management	• Supporter	• High	• Analytical	• Loss of Power	• Reduce Costs
• Line of Business Management	• Fence Setter • Naysayer	• Medium • Low	• Behavioral • Directive	• Loss of Control	• Increase Revenues
• IT Management			• Conceptual		• Improve
• Line of Business Staff					
• IT Staff					
• Business Partners					

who just want an answer to their problems to be acted upon with immediacy—details be damned! Directives will want the big picture and the bottom line. Give it to them.[1] Conceptuals, however, just want the big picture—the bottom line is irrelevant as long as the big picture makes sense. The risks to the stakeholders of adopting an IT portfolio management approach must also be identified so that they can be mitigated. Most frequently, the risks are loss of power and loss of control. No longer will projects be approved based on who screams the loudest.

The business issues and opportunities to the key stakeholders must be identified and associated with the success of IT portfolio management. The issues and opportunities of key stakeholders are generally apparent based on their role in the organization. For CEOs, the most common issue is improving the stock price; however, compliance with legislation is also rapidly becoming a key issue. For CFOs, legislative compliance, control of expenditures, and return on capital are key issues. For CIOs, the issues include improving the IT landscape and avoiding a major system failure. These are further defined in Chapter 5. Often, stakeholders make their issues and opportunities known. These become the objectives of their subordinates and are included in internal communications. Stakeholder analysis will enable extremely effective communication and can make the difference between success and failure. Stakeholder analysis is generally considered to be a working paper or unpublished document. It almost never should be published or discussed outside the core IT portfolio management team.

REFINING IT PORTFOLIO OBJECTIVES

With IT portfolio management capabilities known, scope and objectives must be documented for the current iteration of the IT portfolio management process. These objectives are generally developed with the IT portfolio manager and CIO. If business sponsors have been identified at this juncture, they most certainly should be included in these tasks. Refining IT portfolio objectives consists of two steps: identifying the scope and applying the scope, along with the capabilities, to the initial objectives.

Scope

When determining the scope, pain points within IT and the business, coupled with IT portfolio management capabilities, should suffice to provide appropriated bounding. In general, the scope of IT portfolio management covers the areas within IT listed in Exhibit 2.5.

Embarking on IT portfolio management is a journey. Those who successfully complete it do so by understanding the terrain. There are some dependencies between the subportfolios that become critical as the use of IT portfolio management within the organization matures. However, when an organization is early in its journey toward embracing IT portfolio management as a common governing discipline, it is advantageous to have early successes to build upon. In Exhibit 2.6, the most common subportfolios are listed, showing their relative degree of value and complexity. For this purpose, complexity includes not just the creation of the portfolio but also the ability to act upon it.

EXHIBIT 2.5   SCOPE OF IT PORTFOLIO MANAGEMENT

Digital Innovations	Assets	Projects
Tactical Digital Innovations	Applications	Initiatives
Strategic Digital Innovations	Infrastructure	Projects
Transformational Digital Innovations (i.e., the Discovery Portfolio)	People, Information, Processes, Services	Programs

EXHIBIT 2.6 VALUE COMPLEXITY TRADE-OFF

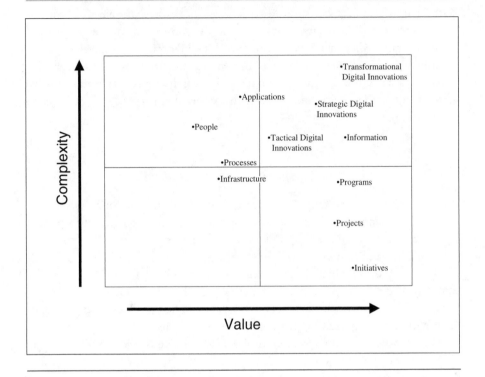

For example, using IT portfolio management to analyze the application portfolio might unearth an enormous financial waste and strategic alignment opportunity. If it were discovered that four versions of SAP with overlapping functionality and data stores existed in the current baseline, there would be a high likelihood that three systems would be decommissioned, improving governance, increasing data quality, and possibly reducing licensing and maintenance fees.

Digital innovations are IT-driven changes to short-, medium-, and long-term business strategy. If the IT organization lacks credibility in the eyes of the business, which it does at least 70% of the time, a discovery portfolio is most probably inappropriate. Most organizations begin with projects, skipping the discovery phase altogether. Specifically, they apply the IT portfolio management process to initiatives being proposed for funding. It is the least complex approach to derive benefits from IT portfolio management. Applying IT portfolio management to initiatives tends to be timed with a funding cycle (i.e., traditional budget planning process).

If IT portfolio management is being instituted after a completed budgeting cycle, projects and programs tend to be the next logical starting point. They are more complex than initiatives because they are generally funded and underway, but they are less complex than decommissioning assets in production. Adjusting the project mix to align it better with organization strategy and tolerance for risk tends to positively impact the business. This is because 80% of project portfolios are out of alignment with business objectives and strategy.

Additionally, in most instances, applying IT portfolio management to an existing project portfolio can identify 15% to 20% in excess spending. IT spending on average is between 1.5% and 7.0% of revenues. Roughly 25% of IT spending can be tied to projects; in research surveys, 22% of IT spending was devoted to transforming the business and 26% was capitalized—two facts supporting the reasonableness of the 25% estimate. Thus, on average, applying IT portfolio management to an organization can save a hard dollar percentage between 0.5% and 1.25% of the firm's revenue. The magic, however, is not in the technique itself but in how and where it is applied—it must be to an area or subportfolio that would benefit.

Defining Portfolio Management Objectives

By now, a thorough understanding of capabilities exists. Pain points that might be alleviated through IT portfolio management have been identified. Ideally, the business vision has been supplied to the IT portfolio management team as an input to assist with prioritization of IT portfolio management. This business vision can come from the enterprise architecture group, the IT strategy group, or the CIO. Ah, but if only the world were perfect. Often, the IT portfolio management team must "explore strange new worlds . . . seek out new life and new civilizations . . . boldly go where no IT professional has gone before"—the IT portfolio management team must extract the business vision from existing documents or facilitate the development of a business vision.

With the business executives, the spirit of a business vision within the IT portfolio management effort is to find agreement between IT and business management on a common and cohesive vision of the business and key business challenges, as well as the opportunities and problem corridors the company expects to encounter in a defined planning horizon. The focus will be on the most important driving strategies influencing significant change in the enterprise. Unlike a traditional set of strategies commonly generalized in corporate communications, the business vision applied to IT portfolio management is a key input for the IT portfolio. If those involved in balancing the IT portfolio can do so in the context of the business vision, a key objective of IT portfolio management has been met—alignment between business and IT.

The business almost invariably exists in the collective consciousness of the company. However, extracting it from the collective consciousness and organizing it into a coherent form that drives consensus among key members of a broad stakeholder group is an art form. Generally, the steps that must be taken are:

1. Collect and analyze business and strategic documents (e.g., internal communications, annual reports, budgets, SEC filings, business plans, strategic plans)

2. Analyze business and strategic documents for trends and patterns (e.g., unmet customer needs, current versus new target markets, operational and service processes and systems, and performance levels), and select the key strategies that are common, coherent, and consistent; will drive change; and will have broad impact across the organization

3. Analyze internal and external trends and value drivers (e.g., technology forecasts) to determine if any strategies are missing, obsolete, or erroneous

4. Pull together a business vision comprised of realistic business and strategic objectives that will drive change across the organization in support of its desired future state.

While seemingly trivial, the creation and subsequent use of the business vision is one of the most important components of effective IT portfolio management. If projects are the building blocks of implementing business and strategy objectives and they fail to map against validated enterprise strategies (and business requirements) in the business vision, why are they being performed? This is one of the key reasons a business vision is required, and it is an indicator of the value and power of IT portfolio management. At this stage, however, the business vision is used as an additional input to determine the appropriateness of the objectives for IT portfolio management. If the goals do not align with the strategy of the business, an alignment issue must be reconciled prior to using IT portfolio management as a decision-making framework.

Once a business vision exists and a scope is defined, the present objectives of IT portfolio management become apparent. Initial objectives either existed or were implicit. These objectives were subjected to a reasonableness test against the organization's capabilities. This generally leads to an adjustment of IT portfolio management objectives, making them more attainable. Then the scope of the initiative is factored into the equation based on tempered objectives and an understanding of the capabilities of the IT portfolio management team. The organization that must adapt to the new process is assessed. Finally, the objectives are reconciled against the strategy and business vision of the organization. The results are objectives for IT portfolio management that are meaningful to IT and the business, valuable in support of strategy, and attainable based on the capabilities and constraints of the business. The IT portfolio management effort is now set to succeed.

PORTFOLIO METRICS

It is ironic that a discipline like IT, evolving out of mathematics, is so resistant to metrics. Business cases are often based on intuition. Metrics evade. Devoid of quantitative measures to demonstrate the value of portfolio management, however, value gained is left to the perception of key stakeholders. Thus, it is critical to plant the seed that measurable value will be derived from incorporating the discipline of IT portfolio management into the fabric of IT and the company. As with all new initiatives, there is a time lapse between inception and value delivery. Depending on the scope and subportfolio(s) selected, this value delivery time lapse can vary. For example, if IT portfolio management is applied during the funding cycle to eliminate superfluous requests from being funded, each instance of a non-approved project could conceivably be attributed to IT portfolio management and counted as part of the return on investment. However, failure to consider metrics before embarking on IT portfolio management will lead to a reverse engineering exercise to demonstrate value after IT portfolio management has been performed. This is often fruitless.

There are two fundamental types of metrics that must be considered before commencing with IT portfolio management: value delivery and process improvement. Value delivery consists of cost reduction, increase in revenue, increase in productivity, reduction of cycle time, and reduction in downside risk. Process improvement refers to improvements in the IT portfolio management process. While the metrics are similar and in many ways interrelated, process metrics focus on the effectiveness of the IT portfolio management process. Is the process improving? Is the process providing perceived value? Is the process expanding in scope? More and more, leaders are looking into the metrics microscope to eliminate non–value-added activity and focus on value-added activity. The IT portfolio management discipline must therefore demonstrate its value with metrics.

Prior to embarking on IT portfolio management, metrics must be identified to demonstrate the effectiveness of the process. The scope and objectives are considered, along with the infrastructure and quality of the source data to identify baselines and targets for improvement. This is true of both value delivery metrics and process effectiveness metrics. These metrics must be built into the process so that at the end effectiveness can be determined and lessons learned can be supported.

For the discovery and project portfolios, reduction in project spending is an excellent metric to monitor. Generally, the historical IT project budget can be used as a baseline and adjusted for overall budget changes that often occur in lockstep with changes in the overall budget. Raw quantity of active projects is often an effective metric as well; it is common to see IT organizations working on more projects than the available resources can support. Thus, a reduction in concurrent projects is a valid metric. Coupled with improvements in metrics around project effectiveness (e.g., budget to actual, customer satisfaction), a reduction in the quantity of active projects can tell a compelling story.

For the various IT asset portfolios, however, the metrics must often come from source systems such as corporate accounting systems, asset management systems, and human resource management systems. The data in these systems are often suspect. While the book data on IT assets are accurate for financial reporting systems, often total cost of ownership of IT assets is lost in the morass of IT operational expenses that are not directly costed back to the individual assets. It is common to see IT assets (e.g., hardware and software) depreciated using an accelerated approach. Once the IT assets are off the books or have a zero book value, costs are not associated with them in the financial system, and linkages from IT operational systems to financial systems have historically been weak. Regardless, improvement metrics must be obtained and compared against a baseline to truly demonstrate success of IT portfolio management when applied to IT assets. In the absence of precise metrics, metrics can be derived from agreement. By developing baseline estimates from key knowledgeable stakeholders and documenting these baseline metrics, the spirit of applying them to demonstrate IT portfolio management is achieved.

Metrics serve a vital gauge for the IT portfolio management process, demonstrating the value of the process and refining it for subsequent iterations. Identify metrics that associate back to realistic objectives so that attainment of these objectives is apparent. Build metrics capture into the IT portfolio management process to avoid an ex post facto scavenger hunt. Demonstrate value by demonstrating value. Chapter 5 contains further discussion regarding metrics and shows examples of metrics used in IT portfolio management.

CHARTERING THE EFFORT

A project charter is an agreement between all interested stakeholders (e.g., perform team, sponsors, subject matter experts, end users) regarding:

- Objectives
- What will be done
- How it will be done
- By whom
- Risks and mitigation strategies
- Assumptions
- Success criteria

Think of the charter as a contract between those sponsoring the initiative and those performing the initiative. It documents understanding to minimize the impact of such conditions endemic in organizations as selective memory. The project charter is a living, breathing document that is subject to change. However, changes must be understood and often signed off by key stakeholders. Second only to performing stakeholder analysis, an IT portfolio management charter is one of the most important items to create and the least frequently created in practice.

TASK PLANNING

While IT portfolio management is a process that should be adopted as a normal business practice, it should be managed as a project. Therefore, a task plan must be created and managed for each iteration of the IT portfolio management process. Previously, objectives were articulated. The tasks to populate the work plan will become apparent as you progress through this book. In general, however, objectives for doing IT portfolio management should drive the tasks performed and the deliverables created. If doing or creating something supports the objectives of IT portfolio management, then do it; if not, don't!

Time is a scarce commodity for you and for those being asked to participate in the IT portfolio management process. Being judicious about what is produced, who is involved in the process, and what is expected of them is a key to success. Objectives drive the deliverables and tasks of the IT portfolio management process. If doing or creating something does not satisfy an objective as outlined previously, simply do not do it. Conversely, a task plan must be reconciled against the objectives to determine if the task(s) and deliverables being created do, in fact, satisfy objectives.

Chapter 5 walks the reader through the stages and associated tasks and deliverables of the IT portfolio management process. Suffice it to say, a simple understanding of these stages will enable a skeleton of the plan to be created. As you read this book, the skeleton should evolve into a workable and effective plan to apply IT portfolio management to your specific situation.

COMMUNICATION PLANNING

Communication is critical to the success of any change initiative. It is not a web site or an onslaught of unplanned e-mails—that is spam! Effective communication involves preparing messages for a specific audience, delivering those messages, and validating they were received. Many organizations have internal communication departments because of the criticality of effective communication to the successful operations of an organization. Leading IT organizations have an internal communication department devoted to communicating IT issues to the appropriate stakeholders. In general, people abhor change much the way nature abhors a vacuum. Stakeholder analysis is the foundation for effective communication. It identifies the audiences, their issues, and how they should be communicated to. From this foundation, a plan must be derived that is lockstep with the execution plan and provides targeted messages to support organization change management.

Exhibit 2.7 shows an effective communication planning process. The activities that must occur are:

1. Building awareness
2. Soliciting support
3. Facilitating collaboration
4. Obtaining approval
5. Communicating results

EXHIBIT 2.7 COMMUNICATION PLANNING

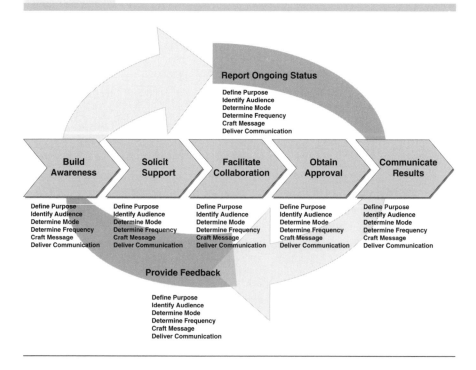

The key point is that key stakeholders and their issues must be identified, purposeful messages must be delivered to the key stakeholders in a manner consistent with their preferences for communication, and validation of receipt and understanding of the messages must transpire. Effective communication is key to the success of IT portfolio management. Without it, IT portfolio management will appear to be an academic exercise devoid of value. It will fail.

IT PORTFOLIO MANAGEMENT SOFTWARE SELECTION

There are excellent IT portfolio management software products. In Chapter 6, we provide a template for readers to consider as they prepare a request for proposal (RFP) or request for information (RFI) from leading IT portfolio management solution providers. During the planning phase, attention must be given to solution providers. IT and business alike have a tendency to jump toward adoption of a solution, hoping it will provide silver bullet functionality. It will not! Many IT portfolio management efforts have been hugely successful with simple office automation tools (e.g., Microsoft Excel). As the process and size of the IT portfolio grow and different views of the portfolio are required to support different stakeholders, simple office automation tools falter.

Software selection is dependent on functional requirements (i.e., what is required to support the objectives and corresponding tasks and deliverables of the process), the resources available including funding and people/skills, and the magnitude of the IT portfolio. In general, the three categories of IT portfolio management solutions are:

1. General IT portfolio management solutions
2. Project/discovery portfolio management solutions
3. Asset portfolio management solutions

The initial focus of IT portfolio management is usually centered on projects. Asset and discovery portfolio management are not typically a primary considerations. Project portfolio management, general IT portfolio management, and office automation solutions should show up on the long list of candidates. Conversely, if the asset portfolio is the initial focus, general IT portfolio management solutions, asset portfolio management solutions, and office automation tools make the short list; project portfolio management tools are not identified as near-term needs. If the entire IT portfolio is the current focus, all tool categories are fair game. The authors predict that all three portfolio management solutions will converge under a single solution offered by many competing entities. Chapter 6 provides more detail on the current and future trends in these markets.

The long lists can be shortened by reviewing the objectives and capabilities of the team/organizations. If the objectives are lofty, the team is strong, and resources permit, a larger investment in portfolio automation solutions is called upon. If, however, resources are constrained or objectives are seemingly simple, begin with office automation tools. The tools must be enablers to the process and must therefore support attainment of objectives in the context of the capabilities and available resources.

CONCLUSION

At this point, you should have an understanding of the objectives of IT portfolio management and the capabilities required to perform IT portfolio management. Key stakeholders should be identified. A charter or contract between key stakeholders and those responsible for facilitating the IT portfolio management process should exist. A skeleton plan should be created that will subsequently be expanded upon. Success criteria and measures of success and value creation should exist. The IT portfolio management process is positioned to successfully provide value to the enterprise. However, the governance aspects still need to be established. Deciding who has authority versus input over decisions, what decisions are made in which forum, how decisions are made, and how these decisions impact both business and strategic objectives as well as specific metrics is very complicated. In the next chapter, the people and governance aspects of IT portfolio management are discussed.

NOTE

1. Rowe, A. J. and R. O. Mason, *Managing with Style: A Guide to Understanding, Assessing, and Improving Decision Making,* San Francisco: Jossey-Bass, 1987.

IT Portfolio Management Maturity Levels

LEVEL 0: ADMITTING

Although the CMM starts at level 1, the IT portfolio management maturity model starts at level 0 because most organizations start from nothing. Level 0 is the recognition that a better way exists. Following are the characteristics of each sub-portfolio and aggregate IT portfolio at level 0:

- *Projects:* The focus is on determining what projects are active and in the pipeline. The focus is on data collection.
- *Applications:* The focus is on determining which applications exist, their purpose, and their owners. The focus, again, is on basic data collection.
- *Infrastructure:* The focus is on determining what infrastructure assets exist within the organization. The focus remains on basic data collection.
- *People:* The focus is on determining what people exist and what their skills are. The focus, again, is still on basic data collection.
- *Process:* The focus is on determining what processes are performed by the enterprise and identifying their owners. The focus remains on basic data collection.
- *Information:* At this level, the key entries (e.g., customer, employee, item) are identified. Associative entities or reports are excluded. Only a baseline of entities critical to the operations of the enterprise is captured. This is the genesis of an enterprise metadata repository.

- *Overall IT portfolio:* The simple recognition of a need for an overall IT portfolio is adequate.

LEVEL 1: COMMUNICATING

The focus of level 1 is structuring things to show relationships and aspects to make less-siloed decisions. At level 1, the benefits of the portfolio management approach become apparent visually; however, accuracy is relative and precision is suspect.

- *Projects:* The focus of the project portfolio is aggregating and interrelating the projects based on available information. A standard for obtaining project information exists, but the project management processes are not standardized. Initiative requests are included as well. A basic yet consistent business case or initiative request form exists to support clear communication.
- *Applications:* For the application portfolio to be at level 1, a listing of all applications, replete with attributes that enable high-level decision making, is required. Candidate attributes include business value, technical condition, process supported, and affected entities.
- *Infrastructure:* Infrastructure portfolio requires a list of all (major) infrastructure assets with sufficient attributes to enable decision making regarding their use. Ideally, at this level infrastructure assets are compared relative to the technical standards outlined in the enterprise technical architecture.
- *People:* People portfolios require a listing of all IT personnel, their skills, and skill levels. To be of optimal value to the enterprise, an understanding of skill demand is required. Thus, the people portfolio will tend to lag behind the projects, applications, and infrastructure to support intelligent future-based staffing decisions.
- *Process:* Process portfolios require all major processes to be documented in sufficient detail to enable similarities and differences to be identified. A process portfolio generally augments other portfolios (e.g., information, application, people) to enable more refined decision making.
- *Information:* Information portfolios require sufficient documentation to identify overlaps, inconsistencies, and opportunities. At level 1, the information portfolio generally consists of a listing of entities critical to the organization's operations.
- *Overall IT portfolio:* To attain level 1 throughout the entire IT portfolio, all subportfolios must be documented, highlighting key interrelationships and interdependencies between portfolios.

LEVEL 2: GOVERNING

At level 2, the focus is on putting the people, processes, and policies in place to support more refined portfolio decisions. It is at level 2 that the link between operational processes (and their supporting metrics) and the decision support process of portfolio management begins to surface.

- *Projects:* Project and program managers provide consistent information to the portfolio manager. Processes with defined frequency exist to provide consistency. Policy exists around providing project information to the project portfolio. Policy also exists to support active portfolio management. An executive steering committee meets regularly to provide strategic information and decision support.

- *Applications:* Applications are assigned owners. Processes exist to manage application life cycles, and policies exist to provide business rules over application life cycles. A defined process with named individuals and business rules periodically reviews the application portfolio. An executive steering committee meets regularly to provide strategic information and decision support.

- *Infrastructure:* Basic asset management exists. Processes exist to periodically create and balance the portfolio of infrastructure assets. Policies surrounding asset management support the portfolio balancing. Named individuals participate regularly in the infrastructure portfolio management process. An executive steering committee meets regularly to provide strategic information and decision support.

- *People:* Basic human capital management practices exist to proactively update skills in a skills (management) database and assist with updating information on people. IT HR policies support the creation and maintenance of the people portfolio. An executive steering committee meets regularly to provide strategic information and decision support.

- *Process:* Process portfolios are generally enabled with a business improvement methodology and team (e.g., Six Sigma). Processes are documented consistently and stored in a common repository. The contents of the process portfolio are reconciled to minimize redundancies. An executive steering committee meets regularly to provide strategic information and decision support.

- *Information:* Information portfolios are enabled through information management. People, process, and policy exist to ensure data are treated as a corporate asset. People, processes, and policies also exist to ensure that the information portfolio is updated and balanced regularly. An executive steering committee meets regularly to provide strategic information and decision support.

- *Overall IT portfolio:* For the entire IT portfolio to be at level 2, all subportfolios must be at level 2 or greater. An IT portfolio manager must be named. A defined IT portfolio management process must exist replete with supporting processes. All governing processes for each subportfolio are synchronized with the overall IT portfolio management process. Interdependencies between subportfolio components are managed and used to balance the portfolio. An executive steering committee meets regularly to provide strategic information and decision support.

LEVEL 3: MANAGING

Level 3 focuses on having mechanisms and metrics in place to measure the effectiveness of the technique and ensuring effectiveness of governance.

- *Projects:* Metrics for governing processes and key supporting processes are identified and captured, preparing for level 4, where these metrics can be used to analyze and optimize both the subportfolio and the portfolio management process.

- *Applications:* Metrics for governing processes and key supporting processes are identified and captured, preparing for level 4, where these metrics can be used to analyze and optimize both the subportfolio and the portfolio management process. Applications are treated as assets, with costs and benefits captured against these assets, much the way plant machinery is managed through a maintenance, repair, operations (MRO) system.

- *Infrastructure:* Metrics for governing processes and key supporting processes are identified and captured, preparing for level 4, where these metrics can be used to analyze and optimize both the subportfolio and the portfolio management process. Infrastructure is treated as assets, with costs and benefits captured against these assets, much the way plant machinery is managed through an MRO system.

- *People:* Metrics for governing processes and key supporting processes are identified and captured, preparing for level 4, where these metrics can be used to analyze and optimize both the subportfolio and the portfolio management process.

- *Processes:* Metrics for governing processes and key supporting processes are identified and captured, preparing for level 4, where these metrics can be used to analyze and optimize both the subportfolio and the portfolio management process.

- *Information:* Metrics for governing processes and key supporting processes are identified and captured, preparing for level 4, where these metrics can be used to analyze and optimize both the subportfolio and the portfolio management process.

- *Overall IT portfolio:* Metrics for governing processes of each subportfolio and key supporting processes are identified and captured, preparing for level 4, where these metrics can be used to analyze and optimize both the subportfolio and the portfolio management process. Metrics are captured on the overall IT portfolio management process as well. The overall IT portfolio management process resembles a financial consolidation of the subportfolios.

LEVEL 4: OPTIMIZING

Level 4 focuses on being able to sense and respond appropriately to optimize allocation of resources across the IT organization.

- *Projects:* Project/program operations are providing reliable information supported by excellence in project management and execution. The project portfolio reflects and is balanced against near-real-time project information. The project portfolio is integrated with other portfolios, most specifically people, infrastructure, and applications.

- *Applications:* Application performance and life cycle information are affecting the application and IT portfolio; information from other portfolios is used to balance the application portfolio as well. It is common to see applications feeding information to the process portfolio (i.e., process metrics).

- *Infrastructure:* Asset management information is used to balance this subportfolio and associated to related portfolios, including the project, people, and process.

- *People:* The people portfolio is balanced against the process, project, and infrastructure portfolio to ensure that the optimum mix of skills exists in sufficient quantities to support current and future needs, and skill and resource shortages are identified proactively and acted on through defined human capital management processes.

- *Process:* All processes exist in the portfolio with supporting metrics and ties to the applications supported by these processes and the information touched by these processes. Processes can be adjusted based on information from other subportfolios. The overall portfolio management process and each subportfolio's management process are captured and optimized.

- *Information:* An optimized information portfolio enables adjustment of information management to balance other portfolios. Data quality flows into the portfolio, enabling rapid corrective action to be taken through information.

CHAPTER 3

People and Governance: The Most Important Success Factors of IT Portfolio Management

"IT Governance is the system by which an organization's IT portfolio is directed and controlled. IT Governance describes (a) the distribution of IT decision-making rights and responsibilities among different shareholders in the organization, and (b) the rules and procedures for making and monitoring decisions on strategic IT concerns"[1]

INTRODUCTION

Conflict and competition drive each business unit to its peak performance. However, unrecognized or poorly managed conflict will lead a company into disarray. Governance is foremost a process designed to resolve ambiguity, manage short- and long-range goals, and mitigate conflict within a company and between divisions, business units, and corporate. IT governance is a systematic relationship between information policy, processes, and people enacted to enable the freedom of thinking (innovation), decision making, and action (initiative) without compromising the overall objectives of the company. It defines and mandates the parameters (e.g., aligning IT activities to business objectives, setting cost and risk thresholds, and providing IT value goals) within which individual employees are given freedom and autonomy to react to their marketplace and customers while maintaining consistency with the business policies that drive the company.

IT governance serves the primary role of focusing IT efforts and resources on high value-added support of the business, application of best practices, and reuse while keeping the company out of low value-added investments. Enterprise governance must establish policy that articulates guidelines within which expected behaviors occur defining the processes and defining and delegating responsibility and accountability for operating the business accordingly. IT governance has two primary functions:

1. *Policy development (structure):* policy must articulate the guidelines within which expected behaviors occur, with the intent of directing the enterprise toward an acceptable level of commonality.

2. *Policy compliance (process):* after policy is established (i.e., reviewed and agreed upon in the level of formality warranted for a particular company), governance is responsible for providing the means (controls and checks) to ensure compliance with established policy. This includes defining, communicating, gaining agreement upon, and applying the consequences of noncompliance.

There is a strong relationship and dependency between IT governance and IT portfolio management. The criteria used to evaluate IT investments in the IT portfolio are derived from many of the policies and principles created and approved by governance bodies. Conversely, IT portfolio management provides the framework, language, and tools to support IT governance. IT portfolio management provides the analysis and common taxonomy between business and IT so that governance bodies can communicate and mutually understand how investments are aligned, balanced, and managed across the company. Quantification of risks, costs, value, and performance shown in views that speak to important issues of concern to members of the governing bodies dissipate many of the political biases in the decision-making process. Because IT portfolio management ensures consistency in the process of making decisions, clearly delineated criteria to proceed forward or halt an investment are rapidly decided. In addition, IT portfolio management provides the framework for governing bodies to save money by scrutinizing IT investments and eliminating nonstrategic and poorly performing investments.

The increasing requirements on corporate governance brought on by Sarbanes-Oxley and other legislation have a direct impact on both the importance and the specificity of IT governance. This chapter articulates the importance of the role of people, policies, and principles in IT governance. It describes the relationship between IT governance and IT portfolio management.

A DEMANDING ENVIRONMENT

Overview

Investors and stakeholders expect a company to:

- Generate higher profits and provide meaningful return on investment
- Maintain risk mitigation strategies such as business continuity plans
- Optimize limited resources
- Hold senior leadership accountable for their actions
- Have control and measurement practices in place, monitoring the right set of leading and lagging indicators

Customers expect extraordinary levels of flexibility and customization, greater functionality, fair pricing and quality, and unprecedented levels of service and support. Regulators expect increased control and accountability from management in both the private and public sectors. Competitors are creating new innovations at a record pace, compressing the time and cost of product life cycles, and redefining and blurring industry and organizational boundaries.

These demands have created an unprecedented need for companies to maintain or improve current levels of performance as they transform their architecture and business model to accommodate many of these changes and uncertainties. Many companies are transforming by exploiting new strategies and executing multiple value drivers while hanging on to their traditional business models and markets through waves of change and generational shifts. It is a bit like the proverbial changing of the tires on a moving car. Successful planning, development, execution, and refinement requires efficient and effective:

- Leadership
- Organizational structures
- Policies and principles
- Decision-making processes
- Collaboration
- Integration
- Management

IT is an enabler of these areas, enhancing the planning, design, manufacturing, and knowledge management aspects of business. IT also facilitates:

- Increasingly automated business processes, be they collaborative, analytical, or transactional

- The creation of new business models (e.g., Dell, eBay, and Amazon)
- Cost efficiency and focus on core competencies (e.g., IT outsourcing)

IT enables the business and is rapidly morphing into the business. As discussed in Chapter 1, current research shows a definitive link between intelligent investments in IT and productivity improvements. For many companies, efficient and effective performance of IT has a direct impact on their profitability.

However, in many companies, the business does not actively engage the IT organization early or often enough in the planning and decision-making processes. Security, scalability, integration issues, and other areas within IT that should be of concern in planning and IT decision-making criteria are not given adequate attention or weight. Unfortunately, planning activities and decisions made within companies are often a result of who carries the most political clout.

Many poor business decisions will result in significant IT change management issues. A fundamental truism is that when bad business processes are automated, things get worse faster. Conversely, when good business processes are automated, they generally lead to productivity improvements and cost reductions. Likewise, poor technology decisions will result in subpar business agility, slow responsiveness, poor integration, and potential loss of goodwill with key partners, suppliers, employees, and customers. There is no longer a distinction between business and e-business—they are one in the same.

Self-Diagnosis: Preventive Measures

The dependency and importance of information technology and IT portfolio management influence and shape effective IT governance. Companies should consider some of these questions as they assess their IT governance maturity level:

- Are the board of directors and executive management engaged in decisions regarding the focus and direction of IT, the prioritization of IT investments, and risk setting and monitoring? Are these communicated in business nomenclature? Is a senior IT representative a member of the executive management team?

- Are the processes to ensure that IT is aligned with business and strategic objectives consistent and repeatable? Are there consistent and standardized weighted criteria and business users in place to assess each IT investment? Have these been socialized and agreed upon by the members of the governance bodies? Are they aligned to the critical success factors, key performance indicators, and balanced scorecards? Are they widely and frequently communicated across the company?

- Is the budget cycle performed only on an annual basis? Does the budget horizon project out for at least two years? Are savings achieved by migrating or retiring IT investments actively factored back into the IT budget? Is spending on IT commensurate with industry averages?

- Are there business, information, and technology policies and principles in place? Are they available throughout the company?

- Do specific projects deliver their intended value within the cost, schedule, and resource allocation as promised?

- How easily can the governance bodies assess alternative investments and perform what-if analyses? Are there sufficient infrastructures, processes, rules, resources, and communication channels and vehicles in place to rapidly redirect resources and absorb the impact of change?

- Has the company's tolerance for risk been clearly defined and communicated?

- Are legal compliance and regulatory issues addressed proactively?

- Are there internal control mechanisms in place to adequately identify and mitigate risks before they become unwieldy? Are there appropriate change management processes in place?

- Is the company focusing on its core competencies and leveraging the fabric of a network and net-centric environment to create a web of partnerships, alliances, and outsourcing relationships?

- Are intangible assets such as information assets, branding, human capital management, and customer relationship management being fully exploited (or even monitored)?

- Do governing bodies have easy access to and visibility of all investments across the IT discovery, IT project, and IT asset portfolios? Are these rolled up into a holistic end-to-end perspective showing risks, value, timing, and costs of all combined IT investments? Are meetings held frequently to assess both new and existing IT investments?

- Are there pools (categories) of investments with defined levels of IT spending defined for each category? What percentage of resources from IT are allocated to running the business versus transforming the business or growing the business? Are these figures actively tracked?

- Are performance measurements, service-level agreements, and postmortem project assessments, actively tracked, captured, communicated, and fed back into the system for continuous improvement? Are these valued in hard dollars?

- Are customers and/or end users satisfied with the service delivered by IT? Do they believe that IT is responsive within an acceptable timeline to meet their needs? Do customers have a voice in IT decisions?

- Are different functional areas, business units, and divisions incentivized to work together and support one another for the common good of the company? Are there incentive compensation triggers in place to reward employees for desired behavior and acceptable risk taking?

- Is the ownership for IT decisions clear to management, employees, stakeholders, and partners—that is, who is responsible, accountable, consulted, and informed (i.e., RACI) for all key IT decisions? Has the culture of the company been taken into consideration as to how decisions are made and who makes them?

- Is there a governance process/framework that has been defined, documented, and is working effectively and efficiently? Does this framework incorporate best practices from CobiT, ISO 900X, SEI CMM, COSO, ITIL, as well as other common frameworks used in both the private and public sectors?

This chapter addresses the answers to these questions and provides insights on how to move ahead.

The Conundrum

For many companies, the answer to most of the questions posed in the previous section is no. However, in many cases, key stakeholders believe the opposite is true. Perceptions are clearly not meeting reality. This situation is typically borne out once it becomes evident that IT investments are overschedule, overbudget, and not in alignment with business and strategic objectives.

Inadequate and in many cases ad hoc IT governance is one of the primary reasons why perceptions do not meet reality. IT governance requires a common understanding and taxonomy between business and IT. Due to the complexities associated with the nascent but rapidly maturing field of IT, IT governance traditionally has been isolated and disjointed from other governance areas, with limited board of director involvement. This must change for companies to realize real value from their IT strategy.

Executives within companies realize that much of the value of their company has migrated from tangible assets (equipment, inventory, land, etc.) to intangible ones (intellectual property, processes, patents, etc.) that are dependent on IT to deliver and fully realize their value. Another conundrum faced by companies is how to analyze and assess the value of intangible assets. Take, for example, some of the challenges CIOs face in gauging intangible assets such as information:

- What information do we (or do we not) have?
- How good is our information's quality, and how can we measure and improve it?

- How well do we manage and leverage information?
- How do our information management maladies affect our ability to achieve regulatory compliance?
- How much can our enterprise processes be improved through better/faster/more accessible information?
- Insurers are now excluding information assets from property policies. . . . What is our exposure/risk?
- Can our information be marketed or bartered?
- How much should we be spending on acquiring, managing, and leveraging information?
- How can we gauge the financial value of our information assets?
- What policies, practices, and technologies should we put in place to improve information's value?

Understanding how to value intangible assets remains a difficult challenge that IT governance and accompanying policies and principles must address.

THE NEW FOCUS FOR IT: BUSINESS

Historical Perspective

It used to be so simple when IT was a staff function—a cost center that served primarily as a support-based entity. In the early days, IT was called data processing. Rudimentary information technologies introduced in the late 1940s were expensive and limited in functionality. In fact, the technology was so expensive that a conscious decision to have two-digit date fields was made to save two bytes of memory even though it was known that it would be problematic at the turn of the century. The core purpose of computing in business was to perform massive amounts of calculations, primarily tabulations. In government, computers were leveraged to enable basic calculations such as census tabulations with greater speed and accuracy. In the private sector, computers were leveraged in accounting departments, primarily to improve the speed and accuracy of bookkeeping. The introduction of computing hardware virtualized and commoditized calculation and tabulation, displacing the clerks in green visors.

As IT evolved with the emergence of second- and third-generation languages, the utility of the hardware expanded. Computers enabled decision support with advances in memory, storage, and processing capabilities as well as software. The distinction between data and information surfaced. Data equated to records; information equated to reports or processed records. Thus, the management information systems (MIS) department was born. The MIS department was a centralized unit, and the Chief Information Officer (CIO) reported to the Chief Financial Officer (CFO). IT was leveraged to generate massive quantities of reports to enable more effective decision making (at least in theory).

The CIO was typically not part of the executive leadership group and did not have input into the formation of, and alignment to, the strategic plan. The CIO served, at best, in an advisory role to executive management and was called upon to support mostly inward-facing systems delivery. As software capabilities expanded, hardware became commoditized, having to support initially standardized languages and subsequently standardized commercial off-the-shelf software applications. Traditional planning and budgeting processes were augmented by formalized IT planning approaches. Annual strategic information system plans (SISPs) were created. The trigger to the SISP was the completion of strategy development. As part of the SISP, the CIO was to:

- Assimilate the organization's strategy
- Perform a current state assessment
- Design a desired future state aligned with corporate strategy
- Develop a plan to migrate from the current state to the desired future state
- Obtain funding approval to execute the plan

This process, while effective for a period of time, soon became too slow to adapt to the rapid technology-enabled pace of business change. As an interesting factoid, many SISP approaches included IT portfolio management as a technique to optimize the creation of a migration plan.

Further commodization of hardware due to the software effect and rapid advances in price-performance ratios caused downward price pressure on hardware to the point where business units, divisions, and smaller businesses could afford to directly buy their own information technology. Notions of distributed computing, coupled with an "empower the end user" collective consciousness, led to the movement of information technology from centralized IT departments to business units.

Business units, requiring IT support to be competitive and unwilling to wait for the centralized IT backlog to clear, took matters in their own hands, ushering in the age of information technology anarchy. While business units were able to develop functional systems to support their needs, these systems most often did not adhere to corporate standards around approved technology, security, scalability, and interoperability, leading to islands of automation. Advances in networking standards and improvements in personal computing further exacerbated the situation by enabling business units to develop mission critical applications on technology not designed for mission critical applications.

In the early 1990s, however, business process reengineering, enabled with client-server technologies, provided the false promise of the optimal and agile process-centered enterprise. In a few select cases, successes spawned a flurry of process rework and enterprise resource planning (ERP) implementations. This wave was followed by the recognition that two-digit date fields would, in fact, be problematic at the turn of the century. Y2K fears ushered in unbridled IT spending. It was not uncommon to see absurd IT projects justified as necessary as part of Y2K remediation. In one instance, a company footed the bill for new personal digital assistants (PDAs) for its IT department because the old PDAs were not certified as Y2K ready; the prior PDAs were called legal pads! Much hard work enabled the universe to transcend the perils of Y2K.

Directly following the success of Y2K, however, the extraordinary madness of crowds led to the irrationally exuberant age of e-business. Whereas today the value of e-business is being discovered, many of the proposed e-business projects (or pure play dot.com start-ups) immediately following Y2K had little merit. The notion of funding a project or business because it was "sticky" or because there was not enough time to think things through was, in retrospect, absurd.

Eventually, the collective consciousness of the business and IT community discovered that not only was the emperor not wearing any clothes, he was corpulent—the Nasdaq crashed, innovation dollars shriveled, and IT budgets had to go on a starvation diet. Corporate accounting scandals also surfaced to add fuel to the fire, with Enron stock plummeting from $84.87 per share in 2000 to less than $1 per share in 2001. Not long afterward, in June 2002, an internal audit of Worldcom discovered that $3.8 billion had been "misaccounted," kicking off a Securities and Exchange Commission (SEC) investigation. The largest accounting firm in the world, Arthur Andersen, closed its doors. An avalanche of additional corporate accounting scandals followed.

Fueled by some of the events and factors in the preceding paragraph, there are three key factors leading to the increased importance of IT governance. First, an overall increase in corporate governance has impacted all areas including IT. In many instances, IT governance is mandated by legislation.

Second, the CIO's role has evolved over recent years as IT has taken on a more prominent role within companies. When IT was the Darwinian equivalent of an amoeba, the CIO's role was easy and of less importance. Now, IT is the evolutionary equivalent of a Portuguese man-of-war—a loosely coordinated colony of cellular interactions—and the CIO's role has dramatically evolved. If the pace of technological innovation continues, within 10 years IT will be the digital Darwinian equivalent of an elephant. Tamed, an elephant can perform amazing feats. Untamed, an elephant is capable of just about anything.

Third, and most importantly, are the increasing demands for return on IT investments. When modern digital computing was first introduced to organizations, high costs demanded good investment management. As the costs of technology declined, investment management fell by the wayside. Technology investments, once previously capitalized and depreciated over a period of years, were taken as operating expenses or accelerated depreciation. They were taken off the books as quickly as possible, and this was justified by a perception of rapid obsolescence. Of course, once removed from the books, it is difficult to track costs and benefits associated with these investments. Now there is an understanding that technology investments left unchecked are costly to maintain regardless of the obsolescence of their underlying architectures. Organizations' IT budgets are being largely consumed by maintenance of legacy systems as these arcane and rigid systems enter into a never-ending "fix a bug, make a bug" cycle.

Regulatory Changes

In 2002, the Sarbanes-Oxley Act was passed in the United States, which fundamentally stipulated that the information being reported on corporate performance within publicly traded companies must be an accurate depiction of corporate performance. Specifically, as directed by Section 404 of the Sarbanes-Oxley Act, the SEC released "Management's Report on Internal Controls over Financial Reporting and Certification of Disclosure in Exchange Act Periodic Reports," which states, "The internal control report must include:

- A statement of management's responsibility for establishing and managing adequate internal controls over financial reporting for the company
- Management's assessment of the effectiveness of the company's internal control over financial reporting as of the end of the company's most recent fiscal year
- A statement identifying the framework used by management to evaluate the effectiveness of the company's internal control over financial reporting
- A statement that the registered public accounting firm that audited the company's financial statements included in the annual report has issued an attestation report on management's assessment of the company's internal control over financial reporting"[2]

Perhaps one of the more intimidating points alluded to in the report is that Chief Executive Officers (CEOs) and CFOs must validate, certify, and sign the results. Intentionally misleading statements could result in severe personal penalties. Although not mandated by Sarbanes-Oxley, some companies are requiring sign-off by the CIO. This legislation alone has dramatically altered the role and function of the CIO and the governance framework within companies. Appendix 3A shows the IT road map for meeting the challenges imposed by Sarbanes-Oxley.

IT portfolio management is integral to supporting Sarbanes-Oxley compliance. IT portfolio management is particularly useful for companies that have:

- Immature processes for gathering information to assess IT investments
- Inconsistent processes and nonstandardized information and data across the company
- Sole reliance on financial measures to assess material changes and impacts[3]

IT portfolio management supports compliance with the Sarbanes-Oxley Act by keeping companies and management focused, aligned, and balanced, serving as a preventive framework and tool to minimize material changes due to IT investments. It enhances interim record and document management policies, provides support for identifying secure and trusted repositories and for safeguarding relevant and important data, and helps guide ready access to essential documents.

A 2004 study on Sarbanes-Oxley compliance efforts within companies demonstrates:

- 54% of Sarbanes-Oxley compliance efforts are not integrated with other compliance efforts.
- 92% expect to change the way systems are rolled out to comply with Sarbanes-Oxley.
- 93% expect to undertake Sarbanes-Oxley security control remediation.
- 82% expect to reevaluate their security strategy to ensure compliance with Sarbanes-Oxley.
- 71% are currently defining their Sarbanes-Oxley compliance blueprints; only 20% claim to have a completed blueprint.
- 43% are currently executing on their Sarbanes-Oxley blueprint; only 20% have a completed blueprint for execution.
- 59% expect to be able to certify outsourced functions or processes.
- 52% view Sarbanes-Oxley as a necessary cost of doing business; 41% believe it will ultimately make them more competitive.

As shown, many firms are recognizing the seriousness and breadth of Sarbanes-Oxley but are failing to address it in an optimal manner. This will change. Sarbanes-Oxley and other legislative and regulatory requirements are requiring better management of information, which is enabled through IT portfolio management. The Xcel Energy case study, as shown in the last section of this book, provides further insight on how a leading company is utilizing IT portfolio management as one important means of complying with Sarbanes-Oxley.

Other legislation has also contributed to the changing role of the CIO, including the Clinger-Cohen Act, the Food and Drug Administration 21 CFR Part 11, the Health Insurance Portability and Accountability Act (HIPAA), Graham-Leach-Bliley, DoD 5015.2, Office of Management and Budgeting's (OMB's) Exhibit 300, and The USA Patriot Act. In Europe, the New Basel Capital Accord (Basel II) and the Higgs Report paralleled many of the relatively new regulations in the United States—an effort to reinforce the criticality of disciplined and accountable (corporate) governance practices.

Increased legislation around accuracy, privacy, and timeliness of information is a trend, not a fad. Organizations must accept this and build for it or face the consequences. An overall compliance program is called for, reminiscent of Y2K remediation efforts, and should be orchestrated in concert with enterprise architecture activities.

Companies are facing ever-increasing legislation with which they must comply, both locally and globally. Failure to accept this trend and address it will lead to excessive fines and possible criminal penalties. By applying lessons learned from Y2K remediation, organizations can formulate a blueprint and execute a plan to maximize return and minimize risk.

Within the federal government, the OMB mandates agencies to submit the Exhibit 300 document, which requires agencies to align their budget proposals with their mission needs and federal enterprise architecture. Detailed business cases are scored against:

- Acquisition strategy
- Project (investment) management
- Enterprise architecture
- Alternative analysis
- Risk management
- Performance goals
- Security and privacy
- Performance-based management systems
- Life cycle cost formulation
- Support to the president's management agenda

The Value Measuring Methodology developed by the Federal CIO Council provides the foundation for assessing each investment and for preparing OMB's Exhibit 300. Readers looking for more information on this topic can go to the following web sites: www.whitehouse.gov/omb/circulars/a11/current_year/

s300.pdf to access OMB Circular A-11 and www.cio.gov/index.cfm?function= speedoc&id=359 to access the Value Measuring Methodology.

The Role of the CIO

With IT representing about 70% of all capital expenditures estimated in total at over $1 trillion per annum in the United States, CIOs are expected to run IT like a business, maintaining specialized skills and expertise in:

- Providing utility services—keeping the lights on; and running operations, service, and support flawlessly
- Managing the IT architecture
- Driving and providing oversight to the discovery and development of new products and solutions
- Serving as a key strategist, offering art of the possible ideas and concepts in the formation of corporate strategy and balancing investments among various products, services, business units, and division
- Providing a venture capitalist approach in taking calculated risks based on potential IT solutions that could increase productivity, drive revenue growth, and decrease costs
- Managing and measuring the performance and alignment of the IT portfolio fund; serving a key role on the executive steering committee, translating and demonstrating complex ideas and solutions into a taxonomy that is meaningful, understandable, and demonstrates values
- Providing education; demonstrating marketing saavy and thought leadership skills; providing a balance between managing the status of IT investments, serving as an advocate for new and existing IT solutions, and promoting for the goodness and value created by the IT organization
- Assuring that the best and brightest are hired and retained within the IT organization
- Communicating key messages pertaining to IT throughout the company and overcoming cultural resistance
- Maintaining visibility and acceptable risk threshold levels across the IT portfolio and assuring that financial returns remain within the range of expectations

Given so many responsibilities, it is not surprising that many CIOs report to the CEO and are key members of the executive committee. In a survey completed by more than 100 top IT executives that was published by *CIO Magazine,* regular use of portfolio management or other project prioritization methodology ranked #1 as the most effective practice.[4] The use of IT portfolio management is paying off. According to research, CIOs who embrace IT portfolio management have an exemplar record of continuous IT efficiency improvements, with some companies able to reduce costs by 20% to 30%. Maintaining balance and stability within the many roles required of the CIO has been achieved through the use of IT portfolio management best practices. The positive results include better communications, management, alignment, and prioritization of IT investments within the business and the IT organization, and increased credibility and customer satisfaction with IT.

CIOs must develop business acumen and become skillful team players to win the continuing confidence of business managers. They must be able to orchestrate change, focus on business process, and be superb marketeers. This is not a trivial task in light of the transparency that both governance and IT portfolio management create. Eliminating pet projects, requiring business cases prior to selecting an IT investment, exposing performance measurements on a frequent basis, and holding people accountable for results is a change and can be a threat for some employees. The challenge for IT is to work as a full-fledged partner, providing justification of current decisions and communicating future directions and expectations. Maintaining confidence and trust is paramount to IT's success. According to *CIO Magazine,* two-thirds of CIOs indicated that IT projects are funded from business unit budgets.[5]

CIOs must be proficient at change management. What was once perceived as simple changes can have profound impacts on processes, partners, and integration points. CIOs rely on change management as an essential tool in the governance framework and in all areas of the IT portfolio. The impact of change management ranges from a single change that has no impact on other assets to changes that impact the homeostasis of external and internal conditions (corporate, business unit, and divisional levels). Change management and configuration management provide the common threads to maintain alignment, communication, and coordination in a heterogeneous ecosystem.

For leading CIOs, their engagement with IT portfolio management does not stop when projects are completed and their corresponding assets are in production. In fact, 75% of the top IT executives indicated that they conduct post-implementation audits.[6] Governance is full life cycle. Failing to do full life cycle IT portfolio management is akin to using investment portfolio management to acquire investments, then never looking at their performance again. Portfolio theory mandates that investments are proactively monitored, adjusted, and disposed of in accordance with investment objectives and tolerance for risk. Portfolio theory also mandates that interdependencies between components in the portfolio are identified and managed.

Thus, to further the investment portfolio management analogy, an effective CIO has the responsibility as the IT portfolio fund manager to monitor external conditions, recognize relationships between investments (which are often inverse), and balance the portfolio accordingly. If interest rates are expected to rise, an effective investment portfolio fund manager moves resources from bonds to cash quickly; after the rates rise, the investment portfolio manager reallocates from cash to bonds. Likewise, if the economy is expected to sour, it might be prudent for some IT portfolio fund managers to pull back on investing in systems, conserving cash. When the economy is expected to improve, the IT portfolio adjusts, investing capital in systems to support the expected release in pent-up demand, factoring in delivery times. One of the reasons the notion of on-demand or variable-priced computing resonates is that it supports the IT portfolio fund managers' requirement for rapid reallocation of computing resources.

IT will continue to increase in complexity, and the CIO's role will continue to evolve. Regulatory changes, globalization, access to unprecedented amounts of quality information, skepticism over silver-bullet solutions, and corporate memory will temper ill-thought adoption of unproven technological solutions. Corporate and IT governance will be the mechanisms by which this tempering occurs. Prescient organizations will adopt flexible and meaningful governance structures to incorporate new solutions into their IT portfolio and effectively contend with legacy solutions (i.e., those systems that fail to provide sufficient value to justify their supporting costs, or those that can be replaced by something with a more significant return).

Increasing Demand for Return on IT Investments

The third and final area of change that occurred both during the dot.com bust and the post-Enron era is the insatiable demand for return on investment. CIOs are tasked with two sets of expectations from shareholders, both with implications on return on investment:

1. Short-term expectations/goals for revenue and profits
2. Long-term expectations/objectives of the company for growth

In many companies, IT solutions expected to generate strategic/operational value or to simply be on time are failing to adequately deliver. Instead, the board is seeing costly overruns, investments not linked to the business objectives, scope creep, missed deadlines, and expected value falling short of planned objectives. Stakeholders are demanding greater levels of information, control, and accountability to ensure that limited resources are being optimally allocated and investments are being properly channeled to maximize returns. Many board members are looking more closely at investments made in security, business continuity, disaster recovery, infrastructure, and networking capabilities. Return on IT investments is being measured not in yearly increments but rather on a quarter-by-quarter basis (some on a month-to-month basis), with payback from investments expected to occur at a very accelerated pace. In 2004, a survey determined that 50% of organizations are planning to actually hold sponsors and IT accountable for attaining benefits originally outlined in their business cases. In prior years, less than 10% of organizations actually checked business cases for IT projects after their implementation.

Sarbanes-Oxley is just one data point toward a global expectation that organizations not only act with integrity but also have the controls in place around processes and information (or processing of information) to support integrity. Meeting this expectation will have a positive financial impact on the organization. According to Peter Weill and Jeanne W. Ross, "Firms with superior IT governance have at least 20% higher profits than firms with poor governance."[7] Stakeholders and customers alike will reward organizations capable of demonstrating excellence. In a study performed in 2002, a McKinsey Quarterly article showed that investors are willing to pay large premiums for companies that have sound governance practices.[8]

Disciplined governance, IT portfolio management, and enterprise architecture (inclusive of IT architecture) are no longer optional. Failure to integrate and optimize these three areas and accept the increased velocity of legislative mandates will put organizations and government agencies at a competitive disadvantage (bordering on managerial negligence). Governance must align the current state of IT with the desired future state to meet these requirements, achieve continuous improvement, and drive return on investment.

THE BUSINESS–IT ALIGNMENT

The organization chart for the vast majority of companies shows a distinct box for the information technology/information systems group. The criteria for employees within IT/IS are typically based on knowledge of specific technologies and systems or the ability to perform a specific type of IT role. Business expertise, strategic planning, trending and forecasting, metrics management, and interpersonal communication skills are not typical core competencies of the IT/IS group.

Business and IT have become inextricably linked and must collaborate closely, share complementary approaches, and jointly provide continuous insight and improvement to the company. Simply allocating a few resources to bridge business and IT is insufficient in optimizing alignment between business and IT.

Business management should own the IT portfolio because IT leveraged and used effectively to support the business maximizes value. There are also examples where co-ownership of the IT portfolio between business and IT management has been successful. Whether owned by business management or jointly controlled with IT, having business make decisions in selecting or sunsetting investments in the IT portfolio can be a major change for companies, and the loss of control may not be well received by some individuals in IT. Many within the IT organization will not view business managers as having the requisite training, skills, or expertise to make decisions in the best interest of the company.[9] There is some validity to this concern. Even with the growing importance of IT in businesses, many business managers only possess a cursory understanding of IT. IT knowledge and skills have not become embedded in a typical business manager's lingua franca, and this must change. Conversely, IT managers must become more strategic in their approach as they learn to work with the highest levels in the company in the formulation and execution of corporate business and strategic plans.

IT and business must remain closely aligned throughout the entire IT life cycle and in the development of the business and strategic plans. IT must provide input for business and strategic plans as opportunities to leverage IT, assessing risks and dependencies associated with IT. Business managers must have visibility across the entire IT investment portfolio, assuring IT investments are aligned with the business and strategic objectives and viewed in context with other investments and priorities.

Helen Pukszta presents nine challenges that need to be overcome for an organization to fully integrate IT with business strategy. The results of her findings, the key business IT model and characteristics (disjointed, adjacent, and integrated), and key challenges and suggested remedies are shown in Exhibit 3.1.

IT portfolio management and the alignment of business and IT is about people, communications, collaboration, partnership, and moving toward desired behaviors. There must be clear responsibilities and accountabilities assigned with an understanding of the culture of the company in mind and backed by training, consensus building, and buy-in to IT governance across the company. Only through this type of effort will the highest level of maturity be achieved.

IT GOVERNANCE

Overview

IT governance ensures that the right people make the right decisions in a timely basis to address the vital needs of a company. IT governance also helps eliminate rogue and duplicative spending, striving for reuse wherever appropriate. The MIT Center for Information Systems Research defines IT governance as "specifying the decision rights and accountability framework to encourage the desirable behavior in the use of IT."[10]

EXHIBIT 3.1   CHALLENGES OF IT ORGANIZATIONAL MODELS

Business IT Model and Its Characteristics	Key Challenges and Suggested Remedies
1. Disjointed Specifications for business applications are given to the IT organization, and the IT group responds with new systems and new applications. The interaction between the business and the IT group is minimal, and there is little understanding of each other's domains or challenges. Business managers and the IT personnel perceive the IT group as passive recipients of business IT wish lists, and technology considerations are not incorporated into business strategies. This outdated model still persists in many companies.	**Challenge 1: Little or no innovation in the strategic use of information technology** *Suggested remedies* • Institute massive education of business managers about IT • Reorient the role of the IT organization to becoming a partner in the strategic use of IT • Assign business manager the role of IT investment decision making • Provide incentives and rewards to employees who demonstrate a drive toward business innovation through information technology **Challenge 2: Central IT budget promotes a cost-centric view of IT investments** *Suggested remedies* • Fund IT investments by those deriving benefits • Do not fund a project without detailed business case (basic IT support and infrastructure management may be exceptions to this) **Challenge 3: IT is accountable for technical success of projects, but no one is responsible for business value** • Business managers maintain responsibility and accountability • Metrics and balanced scorecard track success and value delivered • Assign strong IT integration manager on each project
2. Adjacent There exists a closer collaboration between the business and the IT group facilitated by a few intermediaries between the two realms. IT delivery department and business strategies are facilitated by a few intermediaries perform the translating services of business needs to IT and of IT methods to the business—but meaning and nuances frequently get lost in translation. New techniques such as rapid application development, iterative development, and proactive involvement of business users bring the two realms closer, but they are still distinct and separate. This is the predominant model found in companies today.	**Challenge 4: Dilution of responsibility for IT investments—it's everyone's job** *Suggested remedies* • Define clear responsibilities for technology implementation and for business outcomes of IT investments • Define technical project management and business responsibilities for business value delivery • Assure that key roles are assigned to business-focused managers, whether the project is in the discovery portfolio, the project portfolio, or the asset portfolio **Challenge 5: Misaligned goals, where participants are not on the same page** *Suggested remedies* • Align financial incentives and career growth measures with IT investment goals • Empower business managers • Align functional affiliations of strategic IT with general business thinking; obliterate stovepipes **Challenge 6: Strategic IT opportunities fall through the cracks with business managers unwilling to undertake them** *Suggested remedies* • Communicate the business responsibility for IT investments • Assure risk policies are not too burdensome and too risk adverse
3. Integrated The IT group is dispersed into the business, and business managers are comfortable leveraging and managing information technology. IT demand strategies are included in business strategies, and there is a bidirectional and complementary relationship between business and IT supply strategies. A substantial number of business and IT leaders and managers are comfortable in both the IT and business realms. Even though the adjacent model may seem sufficient today for some businesses, to remain competitive, companies will have to progress to the integrated model.	**Challenge 7: In excessive fervor, IT is viewed and applied with abandon as the magic bullet** *Suggested remedies* • Assure the right people are in the right positions, and allow experience and good business judgment to develop with practice • Provide seasoned IT advisory support with a track record of rational and realistic assessments of technology • Put in place control and budgetary safeguards **Challenge 8: Focused on functionality, business managers ignore issues of IT architecture, maintenance, performance, scalability, and reliability** *Suggested remedies* • Educate business managers about all technology related costs of IT investments (Total Cost of Ownership, etc.) • Establish proactive IT advisory support **Challenge 9: Under pressure to deliver short-term results in their area of responsibility, business managers underinvest in long-term or organization-wide initiatives** *Suggested remedies* • Some IT investments will have to be sponsored, justified, funded, and managed independently of, but with participation from, individual business areas • Look for cross-correlations to jointly build and leverage buy-in that creates greater value

Published with permission from Cutter Consortium, www.cutter.com. © 2001 Cutter Consortium. All Rights Reserved.

IT governance provides the structure for making current and future decisions, and it employs many of the same governance principles found within other functional areas of a corporation, such as finance and human resources. Leveraging the excellent work from Peter Weill, director of the Center for Information Systems Research at MIT, an IT governance framework includes:

- Determination of specific areas requiring decision rights and input (e.g., architecture, infrastructure, applications, project management, IT investment and prioritization)

- Structure and interrelationships (mechanisms) of groups making decisions (e.g., boards, committees, review boards, written policies, councils, project management office)

- Desired policies, principles, and behaviors of the company (e.g., growth, profitability, costs savings)

- Composition of the members, decision-making guidance, and authority within these groups (e.g., consensus, majority, dictatorship, anarchy)

- Reliability, quality, source, dependencies, and variables associated with the information used to make decisions

- Criteria used for objective decision making (e.g., risk thresholds, financial return, architectural fit, and costs), business value, effective total cost of ownership, and IT asset life cycle considerations

- Regularly scheduled and out-of-cycle meetings regarding potential IT investments as well as status of existing investments

- Adherence to compliance, and meeting service-level agreements and other metrics and performance measurements[11]

For IT outsourcing, IT governance takes on additional responsibilities:

- Deciding what should be outsourced

- Weighting criteria to rank various outsourcer candidates

- Monitoring sourcing relationships and making adjustments where appropriate

In order for IT governance to be effective and efficient, the subportfolios (discovery, project, and asset portfolios) must have good tracking information. Much the way generally accepted accounting principles (GAAP), generally accepted auditing standards (GAAS), and securities regulations work in harmony to provide predominantly reliable information to make investment management decisions with various types of investments in a portfolio, IT must provide consistent and reliable information for all components within the IT portfolio.

Policy and Principles: The Foundation of Governance

Policy, a collection of explicit principles, effectively manages the inherent conflicts between the longer-term view of enterprise strategy and the shorter-term view of line-of-business tactics. Principles are statements resulting in consistent actions that a majority of concerned parties have agreed upon, and they form an important foundational element of IT governance. Achieving majority agreement (or consensus agreement) is critical; without it, companies will be dysfunctional. Articulation of principles and the act of attaining agreement should be viewed as a primary means to surface and manage value expectations. There are two important aspects of IT policy relating to IT portfolio management. First, IT policy is a best practice for managing the portfolio of IT investments. Second, the development of IT policy serves as an activity that IT can engage with the business, driving more universal views of the value of information and the technology within the business. Sound IT policies result in time and money savings due to quality and consistency in making decisions (all decision makers judge IT investments on a common set of principles). Characteristics of good policy include:

- Establishes solid business practices and promotes company strategy
- States preferred (architectural) direction and does not stand in the way of individual business units from achieving their respective tactical objectives, goals, and milestones
- Provides simple and direct statements of how a company will use information and technology over both the short term and the long term
- Establishes a context for design and operation decisions across the company
- Translates operations and mission requirements into fast decision-making parameters
- Provides an unambiguous basis for measurement
- Supports mandatory compliance requirement and exceptions
- Is enforced by process and organization

In order to ensure policies are meaningful and adhered to, executive management must support them. Without the support from top management, policy efforts will languish, causing participants to lose interest and start acting in their own interests, hastening the drift toward information anarchy. In addition, the formation of the policies must include input and directions from stakeholders, executive and business management, process owners, technologists, and users/customers.

EXHIBIT 3.2   BUSINESS, INFORMATION, AND IT POLICY

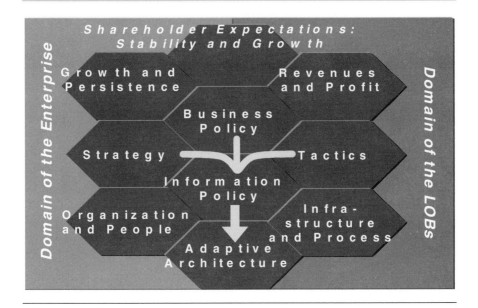

As Exhibit 3.2 shows, there are three types of policies: business policy, information policy, and IT policy (adaptive architecture). Business policy creates information policy, which creates IT policy. An example of how these policies were adopted by an electronic manufacturer is shown below:

- *Business policy:* provide a consistent way of doing business across the company [domain of the lines of business (LOBs)] and with others outside the company (domain of the enterprise).

- *Information policy:* information will only be captured once and validated as close to the source as possible.

- *IT policy:*
    - Applications will be independent of the technology platforms on which they are implemented.
    - Data will be independent of the applications.
    - Access to digital information required to perform one's job is possible via the user's workstation regardless of the location of the user.

The electronic manufacturer example shows how policy results in architecture and standards that positively reinforce governance.

Structure

There should be a governing body for approving and monitoring IT portfolio management—the board of directors. The board of directors is responsible for providing the strategic leadership and oversight aspects of IT governance: policies, measurements, and delegation of accountability. However, the level of understanding of IT at the board level and the allocation of sufficient time to evaluate and assess IT investments is limited, creating a suboptimal situation. Therefore, the tactical aspects of IT governance should occur at the executive level where decision-making authority and funding allocations are made.

The executive-level representation occurs through the executive steering committee (ESC) or IT investment committee, which is responsible for governing the ongoing operations of the company, including balancing the IT portfolio. This committee is responsible for translating business and strategic goals into actionable plans, providing the foundation for leadership, organizational structures, and infrastructure to facilitate the achievement of these plans. Staffed by business and IT leadership, the committee engages in all big IT decisions. Smaller IT investment decisions are usually made within subcommittees and governed by an individual investment threshold and/or a cumulative per annum expenditure amount. The ESC is tasked with taking direction from the board regarding risk threshold levels and setting control parameters at the business unit and divisional levels. In addition, the ESC ensures alignment, balance of investments, close coordination with other entities in the company, and delivery of relevant performance metrics according to plan.

With respect to IT governance, neither one size, nor one approach, fits all companies. The IT Governance Institute presents an insightful perspective of forming an IT strategy committee and an executive steering committee. The executive steering committee oversees the day-to-day management of IT and decides IT spending and cost allocations. The IT strategy committee provides direction and assures that IT is pointed in the right direction when aligning with business strategy. Both board and nonboard members are represented on this committee. They also serve as the watchdog for the board, assuring that IT is meeting plans. Exhibit 3.3 shows the responsibility, authority, and membership of each committee.

The executive steering committee interacts closely with the enterprise program management office, finance, legal, facilities, procurement, and the IT division. These entities work closely together to assure an optimal allocation of resources (people, facilities, infrastructure, data, applications, contractors, and outsourcers) in planning, scheduling, and implementing investment decisions.

The enterprise program management office (EPMO), which is both a project management center of excellence and the project portfolio management organization, serves an important role in IT governance. Most companies struggle with

EXHIBIT 3.3   IT STRATEGY AND EXECUTIVE STEERING
COMMITTEES

Level	IT Strategy Committee	Executive Steering Committee
	• Board level	• Executive level
Responsibility	• Provides insight and advice to the board on topics such as: — The relevance of developments in IT from a business perspective — The alignment of IT with the business direction — The achievement of strategic IT objectives — The availability of suitable IT resources, skills, and infrastructure to meet the strategic objectives — Optimization of IT costs, including the role and value delivery of external IT sourcing — Risk, return, and competitive aspects of IT investments — Progress on major IT projects — The contribution of IT to the business (i.e., delivering the promised business value) — Exposure to IT risks, including compliance risks — Containment of IT risks • Provides direction to management relative to IT strategy • Is driver and catalyst for the board's IT governance practices	• Decides the overall level of IT spending and how costs will be allocated • Aligns and approves the enterprise IT architecture • Approves project plans and budgets, setting priorities and milestones • Acquires and assigns appropriate resources • Ensures projects continuously meet business requirements, including reevaluation of the business case • Monitors project plans for delivery of expected value and desired outcomes on time and within budget • Monitors resource and priority conflict between enterprise divisions and the IT function, and between projects • Makes recommendations and requests for changes to strategic plans (priorities, funding, technology approaches, resources, etc.) • Communicates strategic goals to project teams • Is a major contributor to management's IT governance responsibilities
Authority	• Advises the board and management on IT strategy • Is delegated by the board to provide input to the strategy and prepare its approval • Focuses on current and future strategic IT issues	• Assists the executive in the delivery of the IT strategy • Oversees day-to-day management of IT service delivery and IT projects • Focuses on implementation
Membership	• Board members and (specialist) nonboard members	• Sponsoring executive • Business executive (key users) • CIO • Key advisors as required (IT, audit, legal, finance)

Includes text from *IT Control Objectives for Sarbanes-Oxley* and *Board Briefing on IT Governance,* 2nd Edition. Copyright © 2003 IT Governance Institute® (ITGI®). All rights reserved. Reprinted by permission.

complex, expensive, and difficult-to-manage IT projects. IT project management is a specialty skill requiring tools and templates and being responsible for determining the schedule, scope, resources, costs, dependencies, constraints, and deliverables from IT projects. In the case of IT outsourcing, the EPMO also monitors service providers and incorporates their information into the IT portfolio.

The EPMO has the expertise to filter many potential initiatives and projects, assessing the value and determining the impact of proposed investments, potential conflicts, and redundancies, and validating against the requirements and the architecture. The EPMO also serves as an important interface between local and regional business units and divisional needs to promote better alignment focus, reuse, improved efficiencies, and optimization of parallel initiatives. Specifically, the EPMO is responsible for:

- Establishing and standardizing project management policies, processes, tools, and methodologies
- Assigning and monitoring project resources and tracking project performance on a frequent basis; providing visual information in the form of a dashboard to the executive steering committee
- Scheduling resources and managing the prioritization of projects
- Monitoring change management and reporting variances
- Evaluating possible overlapping projects and consolidating efforts and resources where necessary
- Reprioritizing resources as per the directive of the executive steering committee
- Supporting the validity of business cases, and, in many cases, inputting data into portfolio management tools and providing their analysis and recommendations to the executive steering committee

The enterprise architecture (EA) group, in many models, serves as the IT asset portfolio facilitator—facilitating concurrent engineering with solutions delivery and operations. For the people component, the IT human resources (HR) department or IT resource manager serve as the people portfolio manager, aligning resource requirements with resource supply and ensuring IT human resources have an environment in which they can evolve their careers. Subcommittees and task forces such as the IT audit group ensure adherence to policies.

An academic model must be tempered with a dose of reality to be effective. In most companies, the enterprise architecture function is more mature than the enterprise program management office function, and the IT HR function is typically at a low level of maturity. The executive steering committee, which should be comprised of senior leadership, both staff and line, is actually staffed with their delegates. In addition, in most organizations, the board of directors is not involved in IT. In severely dysfunctional companies, application delivery groups and operations groups have extraordinary disdain for each other because of the perceived barriers and hardships each has placed on the other. The IT Governance Institute, as shown in Appendixes 3B and 3C, provides an excellent and detailed description of the top issues IT management face and the mapping of these top issues to key individuals and governance bodies.

Performance Management

The executive steering committee is responsible for monitoring and evaluating performance management. Performance management tracks discovery projects, project portfolios, and asset portfolios through service-level agreements, balanced scorecards, and status reports that show the evaluation, variances, and explanations of planned versus actual results. Performance management involves measuring and assessing both tangible and intangible assets. It can be difficult to measure without a comprehensive picture of the current architecture and associated IT asset inventories (showing critical versus noncritical systems and solutions, dependencies, users, associated processes, etc.).

Performance management can be impacted by the criteria on which employees are measured and rewarded. These criteria may not match the performance management metrics. Also, too many measures can be disruptive and lead to analysis paralysis in management and causing confusion-driven inertia in workers.

Developed in the early 1990s by Drs. Robert Kaplan and David Norton, the balanced scorecard is used by members of the executive steering committee as one of several performance management frameworks for measuring effective IT governance. The balanced scorecard assesses financial measures, but it also provides three other measures. It evaluates the objectives, measures, targets, and initiatives within:

- *Learning and growth perspective:* evaluates whether the company is sustaining the ability to grow, adapt, and improve
- *Business process perspective:* assesses the processes a company should excel at in order to satisfy customers and stakeholders
- *Customer perspective:* determines how the company should appear to customers and if the customer needs are being addressed
- *Financial perspective:* provides the financial targets that must be met[12]

The balanced scorecard approach allows the IT investment committee to assess intangible factors and integrate long-term goals and objectives with near-term actions. It translates the company's business and strategic objectives into a set of performance measures. For IT management, the balanced scorecard is essentially a navigation tool for managing IT performance against business objectives. Balance refers to cost and benefits, shareholders and customers, efficiency and effectiveness, long term and short term, as well as dependencies between investments and the priorities that drive success. More detail regarding the balanced scorecard is provided in Chapter 5.

Approaches

Throughout this chapter we have focused on how IT governance is primarily a top-down centralization approach. A top-down approach is the traditional, holistic view of the company, where strategic intent, business and strategic objectives, key performance indicators, and critical success factors drive needs and requirements. These needs and requirements are compared against the existing architecture, and identified gaps manifest into projects prioritized according to the IT portfolio management framework. Companies that utilize the top-down approach usually have a higher probability of simplification and standardization of applications and infrastructure.

A bottom-up decentralization approach tries to balance the needs of the local entrepreneur in order to maintain maximum agility, responsiveness, innovation, and attention to customer needs. In some cases, a merger or acquisition could result in the parent company allowing the merged or acquired company to maintain its independence from corporate IT standards and guidelines. In this decentralized governance structure, local divisions are empowered to develop and fund projects that will help shape and define the business and strategic objectives. Company-wide simplification and standardization are not priorities for a bottom-up approach, as this will come later in maturity. Communication with the corporate division becomes essential, as business units are given a great deal of latitude, authority, and authorization to spend IT funds. Although management and control is minimal in a decentralized structure, visibility into IT investments across business units and divisions, and adherence to a common and consistent process, is critical.

The extremes of centralization versus decentralization are manifested through decision making, management models (central versus autonomous), information imperatives (access versus sharing), and planning focus (entire enterprise versus line of business). On each end of the spectrum resides anarchy versus dictatorship (see Exhibit 3.4).

The challenge is how to develop an appropriate element of control. The real issue is one of trust. Governance helps bridge these issues by maximizing information use and strategically integrating technology with business units.

EXHIBIT 3.4 CENTRALIZATION VERSUS DECENTRALIZATION

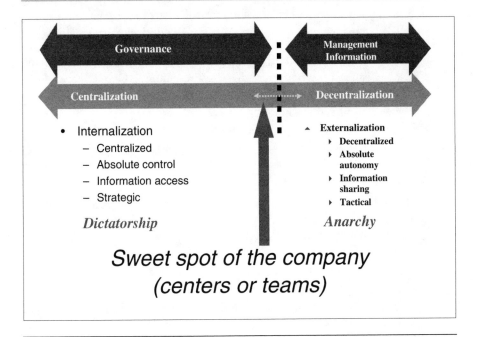

Sweet spot of the company
(centers or teams)

For many exemplar companies, IT governance is both a top-down and a bottom-up approach. This balance is called the federalism of IT—creating the ideal balance between the centralized and decentralized IT.[13] There must be a balance between being responsive to local customer needs and prioritizing company-wide integration. However, focus on alignment to the strategic intent, reuse, and balance provides opportunities to gain important economies of scale and scope, define and redefine value propositions across the company, and assure that the company is focused on moving in the same direction.

COBIT: MANAGING THE RISK AND CONTROL OF IT

Developed by the Information Systems Audit and Control Association (ISACA) in 1996, the control objectives for information and related technology (CobiT) were originally intended for IT auditing. However, the subsequent versions have expanded the applicability and scope of the CobiT. The CobiT manages the risk and control of IT, bridging the gap between business risks, IT technical issues, and control needs consisting of 34 IT processes and 318 detailed control objectives grouped across four critical domains: planning and organization, acquisition and implementation, delivery and support, and monitoring. Many companies are using the checklists contained in CobiT as a framework for Sarbanes-Oxley compliance. The CobiT model views risks and controls from three distinct vantage points:

1. Line of business issues: business managers focus on quality, fiduciary, and security issues. Questions that can be addressed using CobiT include:
   a. Does the system do what it is intended or designed to do, and does it meet or exceed the line of business expectations?
   b. Does it optimize the most economical and productive use of resources?
   c. Is the system compliant with laws and regulations?
   d. Does the system prevent the unauthorized disclosure, modification, or destruction of data? Are the data reliable and up-to-date?

2. IT resources: IT managers might focus IT resources in areas such as data repositories (internal/external, graphics, video, sound), application systems (manual and programmed procedures), technology (hardware, OS, DBMS, networking, multimedia), facilities (warehousing and supporting IT), and people (skills, awareness, and productivity). Questions that can be addressed using CobiT include:
   a. Is there an adaptable, scalable infrastructure in place to meet the line of business needs?
   b. Are the requirements better met through a selective sourcing agreement?
   c. Are adequate and trained resources available to code and support the business application?

3. IT processes: process owners, IT specialists, and staff members have a specific interest in a particular process or activity/task. Auditors and companies that must comply with Sarbanes-Oxley pay close attention to this area. Questions that can be addressed using CobiT include:
   a. Does the process employ control procedures in alignment with information policy and generally accepted IT best practices?
   b. Do the processes support control objectives?

Exhibit 3.5 shows a graphical representation of the 34 essential IT processes as identified by CobiT.

GETTING STARTED

It is not surprising that a chapter on any type of governance (which is a term derived from government) would be filled with excessive theory and rhetoric.

EXHIBIT 3.5 COBIT—MANAGING THE RISK AND CONTROL OF IT

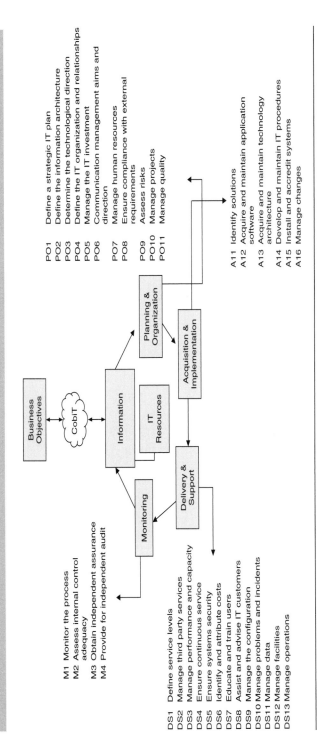

M1 Monitor the process
M2 Assess internal control adequacy
M3 Obtain independent assurance
M4 Provide for independent audit

PO1 Define a strategic IT plan
PO2 Define the information architecture
PO3 Determine the technological direction
PO4 Define the IT organization and relationships
PO5 Manage the IT investment
PO6 Communication management aims and direction
PO7 Manage human resources
PO8 Ensure compliance with external requirements
PO9 Assess risks
PO10 Manage projects
PO11 Manage quality

A11 Identify solutions
A12 Acquire and maintain application software
A13 Acquire and maintain technology architecture
A14 Develop and maintain IT procedures
A15 Install and accredit systems
A16 Manage changes

DS1 Define service levels
DS2 Manage third party services
DS3 Manage performance and capacity
DS4 Ensure continuous service
DS5 Ensure systems security
DS6 Identify and attribute costs
DS7 Educate and train users
DS8 Assist and advise IT customers
DS9 Manage the configuration
DS10 Manage problems and incidents
DS11 Manage data
DS12 Manage facilities
DS13 Manage operations

There are practical steps that can be taken to institute effective IT governance in support of IT portfolio management.

First, an organization must understand its business and strategic objectives and assess its portfolio management maturity. It is difficult to govern if processes are not governable and if current and future directions are not clear. Coordination of IT with goals, strategies, requirements, and priorities is essential. Thus, putting principles in place to steer appropriate behavior that align with strategy, investment objectives, and tolerance for risk is the first, albeit remedial, step.

Second, IT portfolio management should be leveraged to communicate the magnitude of the IT portfolio management opportunity. This will be a segway into IT investment governance.

Third, IT processes should be cleaned up and standardized. It is the IT processes that provide feedback into the IT portfolio. This will allow management and subsequent optimization of the IT portfolio.

Fourth, the existing business and IT processes, activities, and target areas that naturally fit into IT governance should be identified. These include areas such as:

- Budgeting
- Enterprise program management
- Architecture group
- Requirements committee
- Human capital management
- Purchasing
- Quality
- R&D
- Sourcing relationships
- Strategic planning
- Integrating product, project, and portfolio management

Fifth, the appropriate people and committees must be identified. The success of IT governance is contingent on active executive involvement. If acceptable committees exist, they should be leveraged. If not, they should be created. A simple exercise in stakeholder analysis involves identifying who are the key players and who will make IT governance and IT portfolio management successful. Establishment of a program office is an important component.

Sixth, these governing bodies should be chartered in writing. The charters should contain the purpose of the governing body, the scope, the participants, the processes, the policies and objectives, the expectations, specific roles and responsibilities, success criteria for measuring effectiveness, as well as documentation and definition of risks and assumptions.

Seventh, baselines for measuring effectiveness should be captured. Some examples include project spending as a percent of revenue, elapsed time to introduce new and innovative solutions, integrity and accuracy of data and information, and total IT costs per end user. Balanced scorecards are an effective tool for measuring the value of tangible as well as intangible assets. If the data does not actually exist, develop baselines by agreement. As an example, one company did not know its success rates on projects with precision because it never actually measured its projects. When key stakeholders knowledgeable in project execution were facilitated properly, consensus was that on average the company was three years late and 300% over budget. After instituting governance over project execution, it was only three months late and 30% over budget. The company attained an order of magnitude improvement, demonstrating the success of IT governance and a formalized IT portfolio analysis process. In the absence of a baseline, however, it would have appeared to be worse off with governance in place because the perception might have been that it was coming in on time and on budget previously and was now not only late but being burdened by governance overhead.

Eighth, improvements should be demonstrated and lessons should be captured. Leverage lessons learned from similar entities. It is common to adopt too much too quickly. For example, one company tried to implement full life cycle IT governance. As part of its initial effort, project team members had to capture task-level information. This was too much too quickly. It was rejected by the staff, particularly on smaller projects or projects with tasks having short durations. The CIO scaled back to activity-level tracking and the overall IT governance was deemed a success, improving resource utilization by 13% and increasing end user satisfaction from 40% to 70%.

Last, all of these steps should be evaluated, measured, monitored, and improved on a continuous basis. IT governance and IT portfolio management should use *keisen* principles. It is not advisable to continue rotating key individuals on IT governance committees.

IT governance is a critical capability and plays an important role in gating decisions made in the IT discovery, IT project, and IT asset portfolios as described in the next chapter.

NOTES

1. Win Van Grembergen, *Strategies for Information Technology Governance,* Idea Group Publishing, 2004.

2. "Management's Report on Internal Control over Financial Reporting and Certification of Disclosure in Exchange Act Periodic Reports," Securities and Exchange Commission, August 14, 2003, www.sec.gov/rules/final/33-8238.htm.

3. Michael Lester, "Supporting Sarbanes-Oxley Compliance with Enterprise Portfolio Management," Portfolio Knowledge, *www.portfolioknowledge./news/cio-perspectives.articles.asp?id =leste*

4. Richard Pastore and Lorraine Cosgrove Ware, "How to Run IT Like a Business—The Best Best Practices Finding," *CIO Magazine,* May 1, 2004.

5. Alice Dragoon, "Deciding Factors," *CIO Magazine,* August 15, 2003.

6. Richard Pastore and Lorraine Cosgrove Ware, "How to Run IT Like a Business—The Best Best Practices Finding," *CIO Magazine,* May 1, 2004,

7. Peter Weill and Jeanne W. Ross, *IT Governance,* Harvard Business School Press, 2004.

8. Roberto Newell and Gregory Wilson, "A Premium for Good Governance," McKinsey Quarterly, no. 3 (2002): 20–23; and Peter Weill and Jeanne W. Ross, *IT Governance*, Cambridge, MA: Harvard Business School Press, 2004.

9. Helen Pukszta, "The New IT Mindset," *Cutter Consortium, Executive Report,* Vol. 4, No 12, 2001.

10. Peter Weill and Richard Woodham, "Don't Just Lead, Govern! Implementing Effective IT Governance," MIT Center for Information Systems Research, CISR WP No. 326, April 2002.

11. Peter Weill, "Don't Just Lead, Govern! Effective IT Governance," MBS Alumni Thought Leadership Forum, October 2003.

12. Robert S. Kaplan and David P. Norton, *The Strategy-Focused Organization,* Cambridge, MA: Harvard Business School Press, 2001.

13. Peter Weill and Jeanne W. Ross, *IT Governance,* Cambridge, MA: Harvard Business School Press, 2004.

Sarbanes-Oxley Compliance Road Map

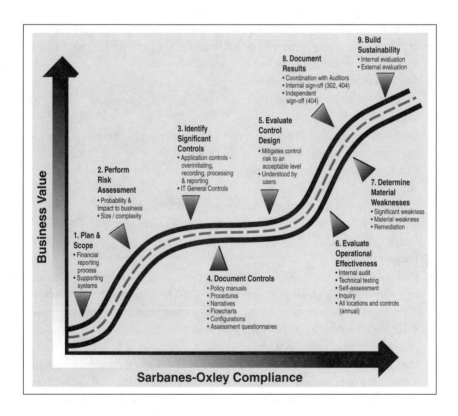

1. Plan and Scope: Gain an understanding of how the financial reporting process works and identify where technology is critical in the support of this process; key systems, subsystems.

2. Perform Risk Assessment: Performed for systems supporting the financial reporting process—for example, quality and integrity of information managed by IT systems, access controls, authorizations, availability and timeliness of information, recoverability controls, and so on. The probability and impact of possible failures at various locations, within business units, and so on, is critical.

3. Identify Significant Controls: Identify significant accounts and relevant application controls. Application controls are business processes designed within an application to prevent/detect unauthorized transaction, ensuring completeness, accuracy, authorization, and validity of processing transactions. Companies should assess the controls that support the quality and integrity of information.

4. Document Controls: Documentation is a unique aspect to the Sarbanes-Oxley compliance process and for many companies will present significant challenges. A company should document its approach to IT control, encompassing the assignment of authority and responsibility for IT controls as well as their design and operation.

5. Evaluate Control Design: Evaluate the ability of the company's control program to reduce IT risk to an acceptable level and ensure it is understood by users.

6. Evaluate Operational Effectiveness: After assessing control design, its implementation and continuing effectiveness must be confirmed. Initial and ongoing tests should be performed to check on the operating effectiveness of the control activities. Companies should consider how the IT control impacts financial and disclosure reporting processes.

7. Determine Material Weaknesses: Engage individuals with experience performing IT control audits to identify the weaknesses of IT internal control programs.

8. Document Results: Provide a comprehensive, easily understood summary of control effectiveness that is inclusive of all testing activities performed. This documentation should culminate in a management report that can be shared with senior executives and demonstrates the overall reliability, quality, and integrity of IT systems.

9. Build Sustainability: Ensure that internal controls are sustainable. IT management should be in a position to sign off on the IT internal control program effectiveness. IT has no option—control assessment and management competencies must become part of the IT department's core competency.

Note: This appendix includes text from *IT Control Objectives for Sarbanes-Oxley and Board Briefing on IT Governance,* 2nd Edition. Copyright © 2003 IT Governance Institute® (ITGI®). All rights reserved. Reprinted by permission.

Top Issues Faced by Management

- Strategic alignment: Focus on aligning with the business and strategic objectives with collaborative solutions—moving in the right direction and being better aligned than the competition both today and for the future. Consideration is given to the value/cost trade-offs of current and future technologies, capabilities required of IT to deliver current and future levels of service, cost versus benefit of current infrastructure to delivering measurable value to the company, etc. IT strategy is developed based on these considerations, and the board assures alignment of IT strategy with business and strategic objectives, ensuring delivery against the IT strategy, balancing the IT portfolio for investments that can transform versus run the business, and the focus of IT resources drive competitive advantage. Alignment also requires that IT maintains a role in the development of strategy, clarifying the role of IT (utility versus enabler), assuring that business maxims lead to IT guiding principles, and continuously monitoring and assessing the value of the discovery, project, and asset portfolios

- Value delivery: Concentrating on optimizing expenses and proving the value of IT—on-time, on-budget, delivering the quality solutions as committed. In business terms, this translates to competitive advantage, elapsed time for order/service fulfillment, customer satisfaction, customer wait time, employee productivity, and profitability. IT adds value through:
  - Meeting business requirements (delivering on time, with appropriate functionality and achievement of the intended benefits)

- Maintaining agility and flexibility to meet future requirements (rapidly integrate technologies, breaking into new markets, improving customer satisfaction, assuring customer retention, driving competitive strategies)
- Streamlining throughput and response times (timely, usable, accurate and reliable data and information)
- Providing ease of use, resiliency and security, and the integrity, accuracy, and currency of the information

IT balanced scorecards are an effective tool to establish value measures that are in concert between the business and IT. As opposed to the private sector that is concerned with financial measures like return on investment, payback periods, and internal rates of return, the public sector focuses on measures such as compliance and due diligence.

- Risk management: Addressing the safeguarding of IT assets, disaster recovery, and continuity of operations. Risks include areas such as operational and systemic risk, within which technology risk and information security issues are prominent. The board is responsible for ascertaining the risks, determining the risk-taking policies (the company's appetite for risk), assuring internal controls are in place to accurately measure and monitor risks, and having decision trees and rules in place on how to communicate and solve areas that present risk exposures. Risk management focuses on impacts to future investments in technology, extent to which IT assets are protected, and the level of assurances required.

- Resource management: Optimizing knowledge and IT infrastructure—optimal investments and assuring the best use and allocation of IT resources (people, applications, technology, facilities, data) in servicing the needs of the company and its value chain. The board assures that leadership, recruitment, retention, and training are in place and that appropriate facilities support the ability to meet requirements. This is an important area as human resources are the largest cost line item and the most valuable asset in most companies. The asset portfolio is the largest area of expenditure for most companies; therefore, effective control of the baseline operations through use of performance metric tools such as business-oriented service-level agreements provides the basis for effective oversight and monitoring of both internal and outsourced IT services, balancing the cost of infrastructure assets with the quality of service required. Effective management of the life cycle of hardware, software licenses, service contracts, and permanent and contracted human resources is a critical success factor.

- Performance management: tracking project delivery and IT infrastructure, pertaining to both tangible and intangible assets. Balance scorecards are an effective performance management system, providing a holistic short-term and long-term perspective of tangible and intangible value drivers that measure four perspectives, asking the following guiding questions in each perspective:

- Financial perspective: To satisfy our stakeholders, what financial objectives must we accomplish? IT enables the enterprise resource management solution.
- Customer perspective: To achieve our financial objectives, what customer needs must we serve? IT enables the customer relationship management solution.
- Internal process perspective: To satisfy our customers and stakeholders, in which internal business process must we excel? IT enables intranet, extranet, work-flow, and business process management tools.
- Learning perspective: To achieve our goals, how must our organization learn and innovate? IT enables knowledge management, collaboration, and web-enabled training solutions.

The balanced scorecard is an effective tool to aid the board and management to achieve IT and business alignment. The balanced scorecard establishes a vehicle for IT management reporting to the board and fostering consensus among key stakeholders regarding IT's strategic aims, added value, performance, risks, and capabilities.

Note: This appendix includes text from *IT Control Objectives for Sarbanes-Oxley and Board Briefing on IT Governance,* 2nd Edition. Copyright © 2003 IT Governance Institute® (ITGI®). All rights reserved. Reprinted by permission.

Top Issues Mapped to Key Individuals and Governance Bodies

1. Board of directors

	Strategic Alignment	Value Delivery	IT Resource Management	Risk Management	Performance Management
Board of Directors	• Ensure management has put in place an effective strategic planning process • Ratify the aligned business and IT strategy • Ensure the IT organizational structure complements the business model and direction	• Ascertain that management has put processes and practices in place that ensure IT delivers provable value to the business • Ensure IT investments represent a balance of risk and benefit and that budgets are acceptable	• Monitor how management determines what IT resources are needed to achieve strategic goals • Ensure a proper balance of IT investments for sustaining and growing the enterprise	• Be aware about IT risk exposures and their containment • Evaluate the effectiveness of management's monitoring of IT risks	• Assess senior management's performance on IT strategies in operation • Work with the executive to define and monitor high-level IT performance
IT Strategy Committee	• Provide strategy direction and the alignment of IT and the business • Issue high-level policy guidance (e.g., risk, funding, sourcing, partnering) • Verify strategy compliance (e.g., achievement of strategic goals and objectives)	• Confirm that the IT/business architecture is designed to drive maximum business value from IT • Oversee the delivery of value by IT to the enterprise • Take into account return and competitive aspects of IT investments	• Provide high-level direction for sourcing and use of IT resources (e.g., strategic alliances) • Oversee the aggregate funding of IT at the enterprise level	• Ascertain that management has resources in place to ensure proper management of IT risks • Take into account risk aspects of IT investments • Confirm that critical risks have been managed	• Verify strategy compliance, (i.e., achievement of strategic IT objectives) • Review the measurement of IT performance and the contribution of IT to the business (i.e., delivering the promised business value)

2. Executive management

	Strategic Alignment	Value Delivery	IT Resource Management	Risk Management	Performance Management
CEO	• Align and integrate IT strategy • Align IT operations with business operations • Cascade strategy and goals down into the organization • Mediate between imperatives of the business and the technology	• Direct the optimization of IT costs • Establish co-responsibility between the business and IT for IT investments • Ensure the IT budget and investment plan is realistic and integrate into the overall financial plan • Ensure that financial reporting has accurate accounting of IT	• Ensure the organization is in the best position to capitalize on its information and knowledge • Establish business priorities and allocate resources to enable effective IT performance • Set up organizational structures and responsibilities that facilitate IT strategy implementation • Define and support the CIO's role, ensuring the CIO is a key business player and part of executive decision making	• Adopt a risk, control, and governance framework • Embed responsibilities for risk management in the organization • Monitor IT risk and accept residual IT risks	• Obtain assurance of the performance, control, and risks of IT and independent comfort about major IT decisions • Work with the CIO on developing an IT balanced scorecard, ensuring it is properly linked to business goals
Business Executives	• Understand the enterprise's IT organization, infrastructure, and capabilities • Drive the definition of business requirements and own them • Act as sponsor for major IT projects	• Approve and control service levels • Act as customer for available IT services • Identify and acquire new IT services • Assess and publish operational benefits of owned IT investments	• Allocate business resources required to ensure effective IT governance over projects and operations	• Provide business impact assessments to the enterprise risk management process	• Sign off on the IT balanced scorecard • Monitor service levels • Provide priorites for addressing IT performance problems and corrective actions

2. Executive management *(Continued)*

	Strategic Alignment	Value Delivery	IT Resource Management	Risk Management	Performance Management
CIO	• Drive IT strategy development and execute against it, ensuring measurable value is delivered on time and budget currently and in the future • Implement IT standards and policies • Educate executives on dependence on IT, IT-related costs, technology issues and insights, and IT capabilities	• Clarify and demonstrate the value of IT • Proactively seek ways to increase IT value contribution • Link IT budgets to strategic aims and objectives • Manage business and executive expectations relative to IT • Establish strong IT project management disciplines	• Provide IT infrastructures that facilitate creation and sharing of business information at optimal cost • Ensure the availability of suitable IT resources, skills, and infrastructure to meet the strategic objectives • Ensure that roles critical for driving maximum value from IT are appropriately defined and staffed • Standardize architectures and technology	• Assess risks, mitigate efficiently, and make risks transparent to the stakeholders • Implement an IT control framework • Ensure that roles critical for managing IT risks are appropriately defined and staffed	• Ensure the day-to-day management and verification of IT processes and controls • Implement an IT balanced scorecard with few but precise performance measures directly and demonstrably linked to the strategy

3. Committees supporting the executives and the CIO, ususally coordinated by the CIO project office, chief architect, chief technology officer, etc.

	Strategic Alignment	Value Delivery	IT Resource Management	Risk Management	Performance Management
IT Steering Committee	• Define project priorities • Assess strategic fit of proposals • Perform portfolio reviews for continuing strategic relevance	• Review, approve, and fund initiatives, assessing how they improve business processes • Ensure identification of all costs and fulfillment of cost/benefit analysis • Perform portfolio reviews for cost optimization	• Balance investments between supporting and growing the enterprise	• Ensure all projects have a project risk management component • Act as sponsor of the control, risk, and governance framework • Make key IT governance decisions	• Define project success measures • Follow progress on major IT projects • Monitor and direct key IT governance processes
Technology council	• Provide technology guidelines • Monitor relevance of latest developments in IT from a business perspective	• Consult/advise on the selection of technology within standards • Assist in variance review	• Advise on infrastructure products • Direct technology standards and practices	• Ensure vulnerability assessments of new technology occur	• Verify compliance with technology standards and guidelines
IT Architecture Review Board	• Provide architecture guidelines	• Consult/advise on the application of architecture guidelines	• Direct IT architecture design	• Ensure that the IT architecture reflects the need for legislative and regulatory compliance, the ethical use of information, and business continuity	• Verify compliance with architecture guidelines

Note: This appendix includes text from *IT Control Objectives for Sarbanes-Oxley and Board Briefing on IT Governance*, 2nd Edition. Copyright © 2003 IT Governance Institute® (ITGI®). All rights reserved. Reprinted by permission.

CHAPTER 4

IT Portfolios and Their Content in Context

INTRODUCTION

Overview

The effectiveness and efficiency of IT portfolio management is dependent on the foundational processes (input, work activities, and outputs) from the phases of the IT life cycle. This chapter provides an overview of the IT life cycle, the IT phases, and the critical integration points with the IT subportfolios.

There are three phases to the IT life cycle: the discovery phase, the project phase, and the asset phase. These were introduced in Chapter 1 and are discussed in greater detail in this chapter. Accompanying these phases are three subportfolios that individually map into each one of these phases. These subportfolios comprise the entire IT portfolio.

- The IT discovery portfolio (i.e., opportunities, ideas, and concepts) is comprised of potential growth and transformative IT investments such as emerging technologies, new business and geographic expansion opportunities, mergers and acquisitions, and so on. Discussions regarding the IT discovery portfolio are focused on areas that pertain to innovative and emerging IT investments.

- The IT project portfolio (i.e., potential and funded projects) serves to expand, replace, or fix IT solutions.

- The IT asset portfolio (i.e., assets at work) functions to replace, reposition, maintain, or redevelop existing IT systems and solutions. The IT asset portfolio is also comprised of infrastructure and applications, human capital, information and data, and processes. The focus in this section of the chapter is primarily on the application aspect of the IT asset portfolio.

Stage-Gate® and the IT Life Cycle

Created by Dr. Robert G. Cooper, Stage-Gate® is a multidisciplinary, cross-functional, iterative process with defined concurrent processes and activities at each stage and decision points at each gate (www.stage-gate.com). Stage-Gate® forms a proven and seminal aspect of the IT portfolio management framework in that it provides the process discipline, structured oversight, and monitoring of IT investments at specific stages and gates during the IT life cycle. Depending on the technical and business/mission maturity, the criticality and impact, and the size of IT investments, there are opportunities to skip, accelerate, and/or consolidate stages and gates.[1] An example of the stages and gates in the IT project phase is shown in Exhibit 4.1.

Gates are interlaced between each stage and provide important control points, checks and balances for IT investments, improving the quality and success rate of IT investments while eliminating low value-added investments. Gates provide an assessment of the quality of IT investments, ensuring that a company is focused on the right projects and meeting commitments according to plan.[2] Gates are where the IT decision-making governance processes are often invoked. Decision makers representing cross-functional areas define standardized criteria at each gate and must be empowered to make and authorize decisions (i.e., go, cancel, hold, or recycle) regarding IT investments and to approve resources for the next stage.

The gates utilize the IT portfolio management framework, providing active and/or passive monitoring of IT investments. Passive monitoring occurs through predetermined milestones, deliverables, and exit criteria at each gate. However, decision makers can choose to select key variables, define boundary and threshold levels for these key variables, and actively monitor their status. If an IT investment crosses a defined boundary and thresholds are breached (e.g., rising costs, scope creep, risks), predefined triggers notify gatekeepers to take immediate action that could result in rapid changes to the IT portfolio. In some sense, gates are analogous to a stop-loss applied to individual financial investments (e.g., predetermined price at which an individual sells their stock).

Each gate contains a set of criteria that evaluate a project's performance from the previous stage, which should remain consistent for all IT investments. The criteria evaluated within each phase generally do not change to a great extent, but the inputs from projects assessed against the criteria should provide increasing

EXHIBIT 4.1 STAGES AND GATES IN THE PROJECT PHASES

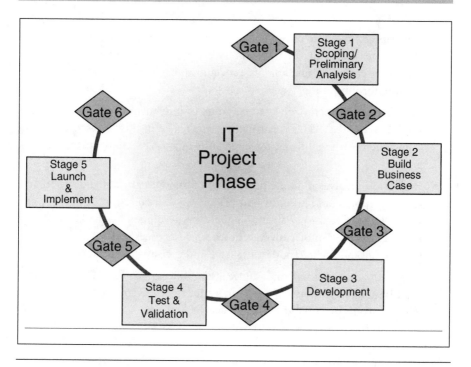

Source: Adapted from Robert G. Cooper, *Winning at New Products,* 3rd edition, Perseus Publishing, 2001.

levels of detail and accuracy at later gates. There are three common quality issues that should be evaluated at every gate:

1. *Quality of execution:* Have the steps in the previous stage been executed in a quality fashion? Have the project leader and the team done their jobs well?

2. *Business rationale:* Does the investment (continue to) look like an attractive one from an economic and business standpoint?

3. *Action plan:* Are the proposed action plan and resource requests reasonable and sound?[3]

Stages and gates are typically customized by companies with specific inputs, processes, and outputs. However, requirements for effective gates include:

- Each decision point (gate) is only a tentative commitment in a sequential and condition process. Gate decisions can be viewed as a series of option decisions.

- The gating procedure must maintain a reasonable balance between errors of acceptance and errors of rejection. Weak procedures produce evaluations that never cancel IT investments; procedures that are too strict never enable funding for innovations.

- Evaluation is characterized by uncertainty of information and the absence of solid financial data. This is particularly applicable in the IT discovery portfolio where early gates must accept both quantitative and qualitative data points.

- Evaluation involves multiple objectives and therefore multiple decision criteria. Corporate and business unit priorities, as discussed in Chapter 3, can differ. The criteria for evaluation should be developed by the key decision makers, and they must converge on these differences and reach consensus. Criteria should include both must-have and nice-to-have criteria.

- The evaluation method must be realistic and easy to use. The taxonomy must be understood by all participants, and the tools must be user-friendly. The ability to create and evaluate what-if and scenario planning must be simple to input, analyze, and view.[4]

The Stage-Gate® process has traditionally been applied to new product development. However, some companies are adding a discovery stage which occurs prior to the new product development.[5] As shown in Exhibit 4.2, the traditional application of Stage-Gate® can be extended to include the IT discovery phase and the IT asset phase.

Exhibit 4.2 shows the IT life cycle and associated stages and gates in a sequential manner. In reality, many of these stages and gates within a phase, particularly the IT discovery phase, occur concurrently, nonsequentially, and nonlinearly. In addition, depending on the technical, market, and business maturity, there are multiple points of entry to the IT life cycle. The IT life cycle is a closed-loop process, whereby now projects can be created based on input from the IT asset portfolio (i.e., the costs and limited features and functionality of legacy and heritage systems accelerate the need for new net- and network-centric alternative solutions. Exhibit 4.2 is not a single best practice approach as strategies, priorities, metrics, budgets, time, labor, financial, manufacturing and production, and other dependencies, constraints, and core competencies will vary from company to company and industry to industry. However, Exhibit 4.2 offers a viable starting point for companies to consider architecting their end-to-end holistic view of the IT life cycle, phases, stages and gates, and IT portfolio.

EXHIBIT 4.2   IT LIFE CYCLE

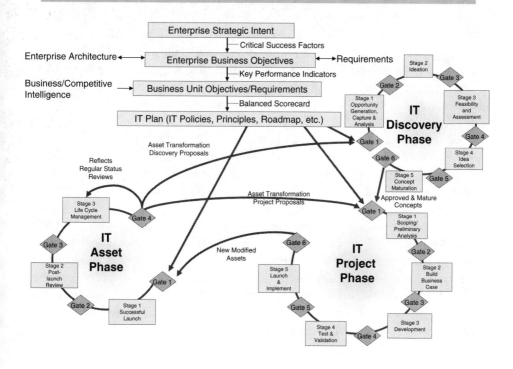

Adapted from: Scott Bittler; Peter Koen, "Understanding the Front End of Innovation—A Common Language and Structured Picture," The Front End of Innovation Conference, May 2004; Robert G. Cooper, Scott J. Edgett, and Elko Kleinschmidt, "Optimizing the Stage-Gate® Process: What Best Practice Companies Do—I," *Research-Technology Management*, Sept.–Oct. 2002, and; *www.stage-gate.com*.

The discovery phase, sometimes called the fuzzy front end, is comprised of a series of stages and gates for assessing, evaluating, and funding new opportunities, ideas, and concepts.[6] Assessing and evaluating new investments in the discovery phase is often difficult due to a high level of uncertainty created by incomplete data and a myriad of unsupported assumptions. Therefore, adhering to strict measures of return on investment and quantification of risks and benefits can be challenging. In the early stages of the IT discovery phase, the IT discovery portfolio relies on qualitative inputs to prioritize and rank IT investments.[7] At later stages, both quantitative and qualitative information and data are assessed.

The IT project phase is comprised of well-defined stages and gates for assessing, evaluating, and funding projects. Scoping and preliminary analysis determines the fit of the proposed IT investment with the strategic direction. The business case establishes the degree to which this alignment occurs, assuring minimum criteria are met. After completion of the business case in stage 2, rigorous financial and nonfinancial data and information are assessed in the IT portfolio framework. Stages 3, 4, and 5 are for the development, test and validation, and launch and implementation of the IT investment. During these stages the IT portfolio is assessed at each gate, monitoring the progress, performance, and priorities of these investments. Exhibit 4.3 shows the similarities and differences between the IT discovery phase and the IT project phase.

Last, the IT asset phase is comprised of a series of stages and gates for post-implementation launch status reviews, continuously assessing the value and life cycle of existing IT investments (e.g., hardware, infrastructure, applications). The IT asset portfolio also includes the human capital, information and data, and process portfolios.

The IT asset portfolio captures the age, utility, and total cost of ownership of investments in the IT asset phase and assesses and analyzes these inputs against possible alternative investments. Costs related to maintenance and support, enhancements, upgrades, and management are all factored into the total cost of ownership. The IT asset portfolio maps the business value against the technical quality of IT investments, assesses other factors, and recommends maintaining, reengineering, retiring, or reevaluating IT investments.

Commonality among the IT Subportfolios

There are many areas of commonality among the three IT subportfolios. First, all three portfolios must support the achievement of business and strategic objectives. This assumes business and strategic objectives are known, agreed to, measurable, prioritized, and achievable. This is not always the case. All investments in each of the three subportfolios should have a business case that shows the degree to which this alignment occurs. The objective is to assure that the right projects are assigned to the right resources focusing on the right areas within a company. The result is a sharper focus of resources combined with the elimination of low value-added investments. The ensuing savings are plowed back into the budget to fund priority investments. Managers must be held accountable to assure that these savings are realized and reinvested to fund additional projects.

As shown in Exhibit 4.4, through the use of its eBusiness Value Dial, Intel Corporation created a very effective thread showing the interface between business objectives (e.g., cash cycle, efficiencies, opening markets, satisfaction), value, metrics, descriptions, and specific applications. The x in the exhibit boxes indicates the intersection between value categories and applications.

EXHIBIT 4.3 SIMILARITIES AND DIFFERENCES BETWEEN THE IT DISCOVERY AND IT PROJECT PHASES

	Discovery Phase	Project Phase
Work	Experimental, often chaotic; "Eureka" moments; can schedule work but not invention	Disciplined and goal oriented with a project plan
Commercialization Date	Unpredictable	High degree of certainty
Funding	Depends; in the beginning stages many projects may be "bootlegged"	Budgeted
Portfolio Type	Discovery portfolio	Project portfolio
Revenue Expectation	Often uncertain with a great deal of speculation	Believable with increasing certainty as the release date gets closer
Activity	Individual or team emphasis in areas to minimize risk	Multifunction product/process development team
Measure of Progress	Strengthened concept	Milestone achievement

Source: Paul Belliveau, *PDMA Toolbook I for New Product Development;* Copyright © 2002, John Wiley & Sons, Inc. Reprinted with permission of John Wiley & Sons, Inc.

The second commonality is that many of the important pieces of information and data pertaining to IT investments are scattered among different locations and organizations in structured and unstructured formats with varying levels of quality and relevancy.[8] Effective implementation of the IT portfolio involves the creation of a centralized database that inventories and creates a standardized format for individual investments across an organization. The health, status, categorization, business case, and business value of ongoing IT investments are inventoried and constantly updated. Resource capacity and resource allocation are also inventoried. The centralized database enables common analysis between disparate investments giving visibility to governing bodies into the categories of investments as well as investments made in business units, divisions, product lines, and so on.

Mining the database should identify dependencies and redundancies among IT investments and show how limited resources are allocated among all three

EXHIBIT 4.4   INTEL CORPORATION'S EBUSINESS VALUE DIAL

Intersection of where IT (applications) helps to accomplish business objectives

Business Objectives	Value	Metrics	Description of Metrics	Inventory Management Systems (ex: CIBR, NWDW, IDT)	Planning Systems (ex: E2E)	Materials/Procurement Systems (ex: TW, WebPO)	Deliver Systems (ex: ASN)	Tech/Prod Doc Exchange Apps (ex: ePDM, eMark)	Employee Web Tools (ex: EASE, Exp Form)	Financial System (ex: EAP, G/L)	A/P, Payroll, Stock Programs (ex: SOP, Imaging)	Order Mgt & Customer Supt (ex: WOM, Supt.com)	Conveyance of Product Info (ex: FDBL, Chan.com)	Uptime/Reliability/Design	Remote, Down-the-Wire	Mergers & Acquisitions
Cash Cycle — WC		Days of Inv	$/Day Balance Sheet Impact. $ per Year Opportunity Value per Day Removed	X												
		Days of Rec	$/Day Balance Sheet Impact. $M per Year Opportunity Value per Day Removed				X									
	Exp	HC Reduction	Number of HC Reduced or Avoided x Avg Burden Rate for the Region & Job Type. HC may be converted into work transactions for calculation ease.	X	X	X			X	X	X	X			X	
Efficiencies		HC Productivity	% X (Number of HC Reduced or Avoided x Avg Burden Rate for the Region & Job Type). HC may be converted into work transactions for calculation ease.	X	X	X	X	X	X	X	X	X			X	
		HC Turnover	$ per Turnover Avoided	X	X	X	X		X	X	X	X			X	
		System EOL	Incremental Dollar Cost of Displaced System per each Actual Incident. Can apply to all, case-by-case.	X	X	X		X	X	X	X	X		X	X	X
		Mat'ls Discounts	Savings from (1) Direct contractual negotiated discounts, (2) Indirect (reverse auction), and (3) discounts from early payments to suppliers			X										
		Hdwr/SW Avoid	Actual Hardware & S/W Cash Avoidance from Infrastructure decisions, consolidations.	X	X	X		X	X	X	X	X		X	X	X
		Risk Avoidance	Intel Exposure times Probability of Occurrence	X	X	X		X	X	X	X	X		X	X	X
		Other Cost Avoidance	Actual Cost Avoided from Unique Automation Efforts (ex: Entex Tickets Avoided from Down-the-Wire Service)	X	X	X		X	X	X	X	X		X	X	X
	COS	Unit Cost	Material, OH, Conversion; product cost reduction via design collaboration					X								
		Factory Uptime	$k per Hour of Factory Downtime Avoided (unconstrained). $k per Hour of Factory Downtime Avoided (Constrained)											X		
		Scrap	% per year of Inventory (FG only)	X												
Opening Mts — Margin		Time to Market	$MM/wk TTM savings	X												
		Open New Mkts	Incr Volume times Appropriate ASP for Market and Product times appropriate Margin Rate									X	X		X	X
		Opt Existing Mkts	Incremental ASP or Vol times appropriate Margin Rate										X			
		Cross-Selling	Modeled Sales from Cross-Selling Products of Multiple Divisions & Acquisitions									X				X
Satisfaction	VOC	VOC	Qualitative VOC Score.	X	X	X	X	X	X	X	X	X	X	X	X	X

Source: Copyright © 2005 Intel Corporation.

114

subportfolios. The database begins to paint the picture of how vigorously each of these subportfolios competes for limited resources, time, and budgets. An example of an investment review scorecard from ProSight, Inc. showing a database of IT investments, their status, funding status, total forecast cost and benefits, and an application evaluation form is shown in Exhibit 4.5. Accounts receivable (ERP) is highlighted in the scorecard, and easy drill-down into the application evaluation forms database allows users to analyze detailed information (e.g., funding status, recommended action, financial plan). The needs of a company and its maturity in the IT portfolio management process will drive which models it chooses to use. Other multidimensional criteria that should be considered and balanced when assessing IT subportfolios are shown in Exhibit 4.6.

These views are usually provided in easy-to-digest reports and computerized interfaces, bubble charts, and graphs that help a decision-making committee (gatekeepers) determine and assess strategic alignment and the practicality of meeting key objectives against possible constraints (e.g., labor, budget, time, capacity). As shown in Exhibit 4.7, a bubble chart from ProSight, Inc. utilizing the account receivable from Exhibit 4.5 shows the account receivable (ERP) investment mapped according to the application priority index and budgetary unit. Totals for each budgetary unit is also shown. The bubble chart allows gatekeeps to quickly assess many variables and parameters. Bubble charts can be configured and easily manipulated for assessment.

It is also common that an investment is dependent on other investments and activities delivering business value. For instance, in some cases, measurable value is more aptly quantified according to the combined value of several related investments as opposed to a single isolated investment. It is important that readers keep in mind that the reliability of these models is dependent on the accuracy, timeliness, and relevance of the data and information used as inputs.

A fourth commonality is that all subportfolios are socialized through a decision-making committee as discussed in Chapter 3. Alternative options, sensitivity analysis, and trade-offs through the use of what-if and scenario planning provide the basis of the iterative process that occurs among gatekeepers in order to optimize limited resources. These discussions are complicated by the multiple goals of gatekeepers, assigning value to subjective and intangible factors, and reaching consensus on degree that each IT portfolio objective (e.g., balance, alignment, value, and practicality) should influence the final ranking and prioritization of investments. Reaching agreement on the weighting and scoring of criteria also provides the basis for assessing the impact of off-cycle priorities, easing the complexities associated with rapidly reprioritizing and revectoring resources to meet unexpected needs. As shown in Exhibit 4.8 from Mercury Interactive, scenario planning and web-based tools are effectively used for all subportfolios to analyze changes and assess impacts.

EXHIBIT 4.5   INVESTMENT REVIEW SCORECARD

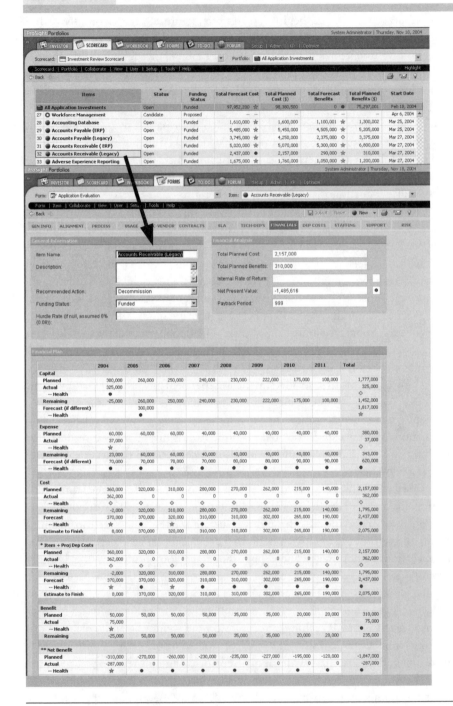

Source: Copyright © 2005 ProSight, Inc.

EXHIBIT 4.6   MULTIDIMENSIONAL CRITERIA

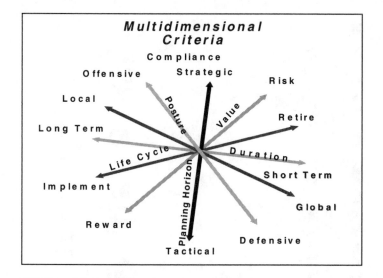

Last, continuous communication forms the most essential element of IT portfolio management. IT portfolio management is a people process, and communication and collaboration using the same language and vocabulary is an essential aspect of the process. Priorities, changes, risks, uncertainties, constraints, resource allocations, dependencies, time frames, criticality, benefits, and new requirements form a small fraction of the constant streams of communication that must occur within a company for IT portfolio management to be successful. The subportfolios must allow employees to easily drill down to granular levels of information and collaborate with others regarding issues or concerns. Priorities, critical tasks, and hot spots are visible and identified early, ensuring that they have the attention of executive management.

For some, IT portfolio management will be viewed as a large (and negative) change. For these employees, exposing data and information is viewed as a threat to decisions they have (or have not) made. In addition, it compromises their ability to procure IT investments on an ad hoc basis. Overcoming many of these ingrained behaviors can be very challenging. Incentives that tie the success of the subportfolio to compensation combined with rigorous training that addresses the IT portfolio management process and explains its impact on employees are effective ways to educate, change behaviors, and reach consensus and compliance.

Exhibit 4.9, Pacific Edge Software's selection dashboard, demonstrates how many of the areas identified in this section come together. Although the exhibit represents the IT project portfolio, all subportfolios could be reflected in the diagram. Indicators (circle, star, arrow) are highlighted that show the investment,

EXHIBIT 4.7 BUBBLE CHARTS FOR ACCOUNTS RECEIVABLE EXAMPLE

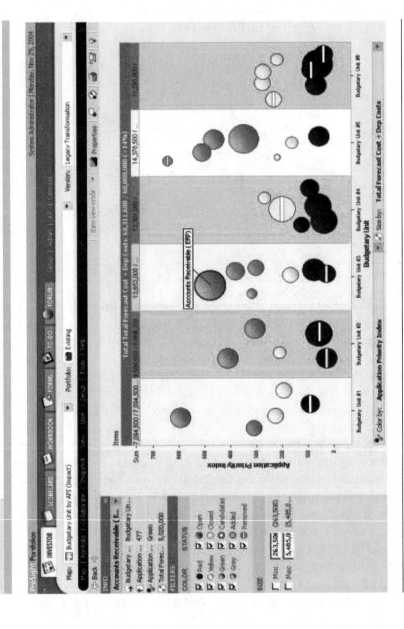

Source: Copyright © 2005 ProSight, Inc.

118

EXHIBIT 4.8 SCENARIO PLANNING AND WHAT-IF ANALYSIS

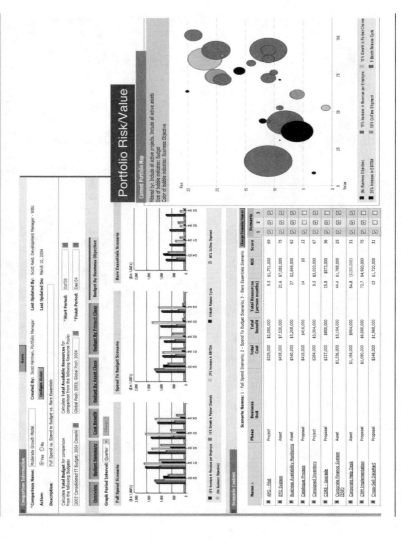

Source: Copyright © 2004 Mercury Interactive Corporation.

EXHIBIT 4.9 SELECTION DASHBOARD

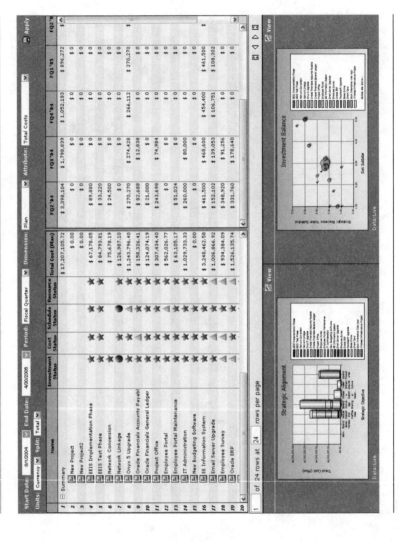

Source: Copyright © 2005 Pacific Edge Software.

cost, and schedule status for each IT project. The right side of the exhibit shows total costs. The bottom left chart shows allocation of project costs to strategic objectives (e.g., expand global markets, reduce operational inefficiencies, develop knowledge sharing).

The bottom right chart in Exhibit 4.9 shows the balance of investments. Strategic business value is represented on the y-axis and risk is represented on the x-axis, with the size of the bubbles representing total cost of the investment. This chart provides a user-friendly and easy-to-understand interface for decision makers, enhancing communications and allowing them to make changes to the investments and quickly analyze the impact of these changes. Results will also show changes to two important objectives of the portfolio: strategic alignment and balance within the portfolio.

IT DISCOVERY PORTFOLIO

Overview

For many companies, research and development occasionally develops, matures, and commercializes solutions. The front end of research and development traditionally has not been an area that is always closely aligned to a company's business and strategic objectives, therefore it has not produced a continuous and consistent stream of new value-added solutions. The fuzzy front end defines solutions that have high levels of technical and market uncertainty and are at a low technology readiness level (technology readiness level is defined in this chapter). Three important definitions within the fuzzy front end are:

1. *Opportunity:* a business or technology gap that a company or individual acknowledges between the current situation and an envisioned future in order to capture competitive advantage, respond to a threat, solve a problem, or ameliorate a difficulty.

2. *Idea:* the most embryonic form of a new solution or service. It often consists of a high-level view of the problem's preliminary solution identified by the opportunity.

3. *Concept:* has a well-defined form including both a written and a visual description including its primary feature and customer benefits combined with a broad understanding of the technology needed.[9]

Many companies still determine which fuzzy front-end initiatives to fund based solely on business unit or divisional stovepiped (isolated) strategies and budgets, fragmented and incomplete assumptions, panic/hype/wishful thinking, and, to a certain extent, the political clout of the initiative's sponsor. This myopic view of the enterprise strategy and the lack of the ability to prioritize investments through an IT discovery portfolio often means that potentially valuable opportunities, ideas, and concepts are not funded.

A major challenge faced by companies is not necessarily the ability to introduce sustaining innovation (e.g., incremental improvements, slight modifications and upgrades to existing solutions) but rather to implement a manageable and effective mechanism for introducing a repeatable process for the fuzzy front end of innovations. An enterprise with significant outdated business/technology infrastructures will spend its money on shoring up the cracks, resulting in a portfolio of initiatives slanted heavily toward tweaking the current baseline of investments. This approach creates the danger of obsolescence. Conversely, a hypercompetitive pharmaceutical company may overburden its IT discovery portfolio with potentially high-risk drug discovery initiatives. A balance between both spectrums must be reached.

Since 2000, changing economic conditions, the rise in importance of innovation, and the need for competitive differentiators have permanently altered the expectations of the fuzzy front end. All aspects of research and development have become essential elements to executing the business and strategic objectives and transforming the business. Without the ability and agility to constantly transform the business by creating new and breakthrough IT solutions, reach new markets and geographies, and rapidly gain first mover advantage, companies will have difficulty differentiating their offerings. Innovation and expansion opportunities are critical to growth, driving long-term sustainability and viability. In 1988, 65% of the current companies listed in the S&P 500 list would have been unrecognizable and unfamiliar entities to most investors.[10] "In the next 15 years, 75% of the S&P 500 will be composed of companies we don't know today."[11] Understanding how to transform the business through investment in the discovery portfolio is one of the primary drivers for growth and sustainability.

According to research, innovative companies are valued at 50% higher market capitalization than their peers. In addition, exemplar companies generally outmaneuver their competitors through well-thought-out innovative investments, especially during difficult economic times. In a study of 1,200 companies, McKinsey & Company found that many of today's industry leaders spent 22% more on R&D than their unsuccessful peers during the 1990–1991 recession. In contrast, the leaders spent just 9% more outside of the recession.[12] Intel Corporation spent aggressively during this period, delivering a total return to investors of more than 400% and dramatically outperforming the S&P semiconductor index.[13] A July 2003 *Business Week* article discussed how Intel spent "a staggering 45% of revenues" on R&D activities.[14]

However, because many innovations in the discovery phase are longer-term, and due to the need to produce short-term results in today's economy, management is faced with difficult decisions with respect to resource allocation, management attention, and so on. Managers must decide whether to fund short-term, low-value, incremental projects that have greater predictability from a cost-benefit perspective or invest in long-term, less certain, transformative, higher-risk investments. The evidence for investing in the discovery portfolio is compelling— breakthrough products offer the potential for a 5 times or greater improvement in performance combined with a 30% or greater reduction in costs.[15] But failures far exceed successes in innovation, and for risk-averse companies this presents a challenge to securing sufficient resources for the discovery phase. According to Stevens and Burley, every 3,000 unwritten ideas generate 125 written ideas, and only 1 (on average) leads to commercial success.[16]

With the importance and premium valuation that is being placed on innovation, it is interesting to note that according to the 2004 R&D Trends Forecast conducted by the Industrial Research Institute, more companies are reducing rather than increasing their R&D spending.[17] And, according to Standard & Poor's Compustat statistics, on average U.S. companies spend about 1.7% of sales dollars on research and development (internationally based companies with headquarters located outside of the United States—e.g., Japan, Sweden, Finland, and others spend more than twice this amount on research and development).[18]

Real options provide a means by which companies can invest in the IT discovery investments and limit their exposure. Ian MacMillan and Rita Gunther McGrath provide a categorization for real options as related to research and development investments that have a medium to high level of technical (e.g., timing to complete, skills required, technical barriers) and market (e.g., market demand, distributor/supplier support, probability and speed of acceptance) uncertainty:

- *Positioning options:* take into account that a company knows which markets it wants to serve but lacks the confidence in the feasibility of the technology; the company is uncertain about which technology road map to follow.

- *Scouting options:* technology will meet requirements, but there is uncertainty about which market segment will show the greatest uptake.

- *Stepping stone options:* a high degree of technical and market uncertainty exists in these underserved and niche customer segments. This option is staged and sequenced, and experience is gained as stepping stones to build increased features and functionality.[19]

While the categorization of real options helps management frame issues related to risk and uncertainty, the challenge of the discovery portfolio is the fact that innovation can be free-flowing, chaotic, and creative, where ah-ha moments are difficult to predict and nearly impossible to plan. Determining the compliance with the architecture, risks, benefits, total cost of ownership, target customers, and dependencies can be very challenging. Business cases and project plans are difficult to develop as assumptions and expectations are often based on guesswork and are highly unpredictable.

If an IT investment is ready to advance to the next stage, the deliverable from the discovery phase is a concept with an identified customer and market need outlined in a preliminary business case, requesting and justifying further resource requirements to transition to the IT project phase.

Technology Readiness Levels

Technology readiness level (TRL), an approach pioneered by the National Aeronautics and Space Administration (NASA), has become a tool frequently used by defense acquisition programs to select new technologies for development and maturation.[20] TRLs are based on a scale of 1 (lowest maturity level) to 9 (highest maturity level). TRL is a means to provide a common basis of communication within a company and among partners, suppliers, and distributors to assess the gaps that exist between a technology's current maturity and the maturity level required for incorporation into operations. Technologies reaching TRL 6 or 7 are usually deemed ready for consideration for the IT project phase; technologies less than TRL 6 are potential candidates for the IT discovery phase.[21] TRLs are used for hardware and software evaluations as shown in Appendix 4A. Readers who are unfamiliar with technology readiness levels may want to consider this taxonomy to classify the level of maturity for technology solutions.

Elements of the IT Discovery Phase*

As an investment within the IT discovery phase reaches higher technology readiness levels, the completeness and the quality of the information pertaining to each investment will mature. Financial information pertaining to each investment at early stages is especially difficult to assess with any level of certainty. Some of the criteria assessed at each gate might include:

- Opportunity fit with strategic objectives
- Originality of the opportunity (patent potential and other barriers to entry/exit); competitive alternatives
- Viability and feasibility of addressing unmet customer needs; market size and technology uncertainties, dependencies, complexity, and expertise

*The authors would like to thank Peter Koen for his excellent research and contribution to this section.

- Probability and timing of commercial and technical success
- Risks and financial criteria such as return on investment[22]

An example of scoring criteria used in ideas/concepts can be found in Exhibit 4.10. Xcel Energy, the fourth largest utility company in the United States, with over 11,000 employees, maintains a consistent set of metrics in its scoring of technology innovations. As shown in Exhibit 4.10, nine business values and seven technology innovation criteria are scored at each stage. In addition to these metrics, standard information is collected on the project, the sponsor, the classification of the idea, contact information, and attachments.

Depending on the technical, market, and business maturity of an IT innovation, there are multiple points of entry into the IT discovery phase. The planning and inputs that comprise the discovery phase and associated discovery portfolio are encompassed in key stages and gates:

- *Gate 1:* The first activity of the IT discovery phase is the evaluation in gate 1, which takes input from the IT plan and the IT asset portfolio and provides

EXHIBIT 4.10 XCEL ENERGY TECH INNOVATION SCORING CRITERIA

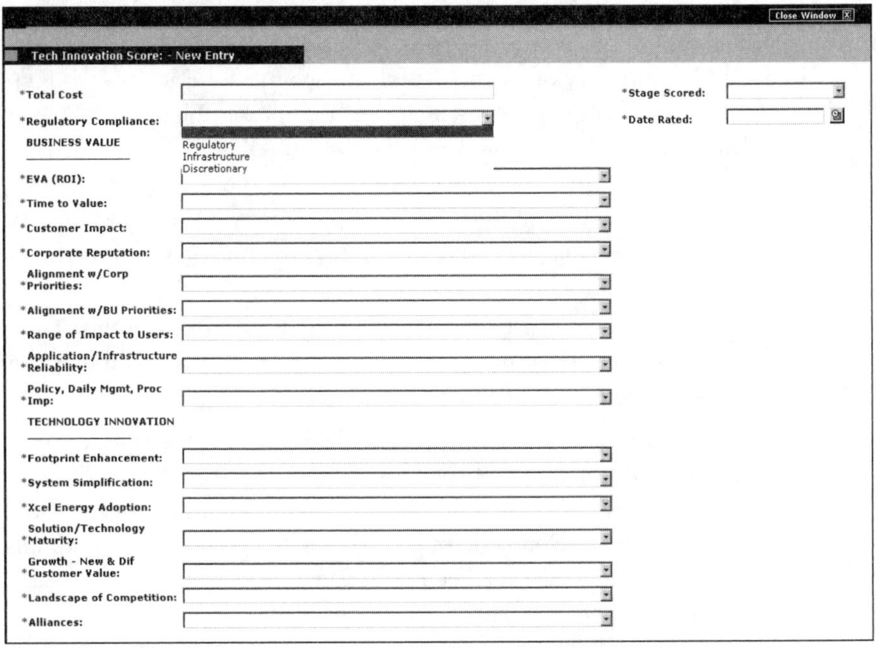
Close Window
Tech Innovation Score: - New Entry
*Total Cost
*Stage Scored:
*Regulatory Compliance:
*Date Rated:
Regulatory
Infrastructure
Discretionary
BUSINESS VALUE
*EVA (ROI):
*Time to Value:
*Customer Impact:
*Corporate Reputation:
Alignment w/Corp *Priorities:
*Alignment w/BU Priorities:
*Range of Impact to Users:
Application/Infrastructure *Reliability:
Policy, Daily Mgmt, Proc *Imp:
TECHNOLOGY INNOVATION
*Footprint Enhancement:
*System Simplification:
*Xcel Energy Adoption:
Solution/Technology *Maturity:
Growth - New & Dif *Customer Value:
*Landscape of Competition:
*Alliances:

Source: Xcel Energy Services, Inc. Copyright © 2005 Mercury Interactive Corporation.

direction and focus to stage 1. This gate also decides how many resources to commit to the opportunity generation stage.

- *Stage 1:* Opportunity generation, capture, and assessment are strategies used to generate potential new innovations from ideas, needs, and gaps.[23] Driven by the goals to transform and grow the business, opportunity capture defines opportunities such as a reaction to a competitive threat, a breakthrough opportunity to gain competitive advantage, or an opportunity to simplify, speed up, or reduce costs of operations.[24] Inputs to opportunity capture can come from mining business and competitive intelligence, addressing unmet customer needs, gaps in capabilities, extranet and intranet sites, partnerships with academia and venture capital firms, voice of the customer, and lead user input.[25]

- *Gate 2:* Opportunities are captured in a centralized repository. Inputs from the opportunity capture stage are analyzed, ranked, and prioritized in the IT discovery portfolio according to many of the criteria previously mentioned. Gate 2 concludes with a decision (e.g., go, cancel, hold, transfer) reached by a governing body. Members of this governance team must have an open mind due to high levels of uncertainty and lack of information.

- *Stage 2:* Ideation, meaning opportunities that go through many changes, iterations, and modifications are translated into ideas.[26] Creative tools such as mind mapping, lateral thinking, and problem-solving techniques such as scenario analysis, fishbone diagrams, process mapping, theory of constraints, TRIZ (theory of inventive problem solving—the acronym is Russian), and storyboarding are used during this phase. These tools try to stimulate creative thinking and enhance ideas. Observing customers in their environment and understanding their frustrations and challenges is effective during this phase.[27] Ideation and opportunity capture stages can be worked on closely together, and multiple passes and iterations through these stages is common.[28]

- *Gate 3:* The inputs from stage 2 are captured and the criteria in the IT discovery portfolio reach maturity. Gate 3 concludes with a decision (e.g., go, cancel, hold, transfer) reached by a governing body.

- *Stage 3:* Ideas are assessed, and the feasibility of each idea is evaluated.[29] Although the information and data available for the feasibility and assessment are still in an immature state, some elements evaluated as part of this stage include the development of a preliminary business case outlining potential customers, target market and potential barriers, technology gaps, fit with core competencies, risks, and approximate time frames.[30]

Ideas in the feasibility and assessment stage are still at a low technology readiness level; therefore, trying to pinpoint financials such as costs, cash flow requirements, expected returns, return on investment, break-even points, and so on, may be challenging. Also, a complete perspective of the risks and risk mitigation strategies may not be known. Action plans and future road maps are based on incomplete information due to the immature state of the initiative. As discussed earlier, real options are a viable tool to assess investments in the IT discovery portfolio. Real options encourage frequent decision points and incremental funding of initiatives until sufficient information is obtained to make a full fledged commitment.

When assessing feasibility, there are several best-practice methodologies that leading companies use (and they are also used in stages 1 and 2):[31]

- Road-mapping technologies facilitate the communication of strategy and planning by superimposing timelines for reaching desired levels of mission/business and technology maturity and capability levels. The goal is to assure that the desired future objectives within a company are in place at the right time.[32]
- Scenario modeling determines the feasibility and impact of candidate initiatives. Numerous targets of value will have surfaced during the discovery portfolio. For opportunities with the highest potential value, innovation scenarios are developed using techniques such as business scenario modeling and business event/process modeling.[33]
- Technology forecasting and technology adoption models are used by companies to determine at which point of the maturation and life cycle of a new technology a company should jump in and invest (the models can range from innovators and early adopters to laggards). Some of the more popular models include Everett Rogers's diffusion of innovation model, Geoffrey Moore's chasm model, Richard Nolan's S-curve, Clayton Christensen's disruptive technology curves, the Fisher-Pry model, and the Gompertz model.

- *Gate 4:* Information gathered from the feasibility and assessment phase is evaluated against the criteria shown at the beginning of this section. Gate 4 concludes by a governing body assessing and prioritizing investments in the IT discovery portfolio and making decisions (go, cancel, hold, or recycle).
- *Stage 4:* The translation of the ideation stage into a concrete and definable idea means ideas are evaluated, altered, redefined, and combined in unique ways as they go through many nonlinear experimentations, iterations, and spiral cycles. Customer interactions, cross-functional team participation, and collaboration with partners, suppliers, and other value-chain members are critical at this stage as conceptual designs, proposed specifications, and customer feedback are validated. The preliminary business case that was started in stage 3 is further developed.[34]

- *Gate 5:* Information collected from the idea selection stage is evaluated and assessed. The preliminary business case details the results of experiments, refinement of the solution specifications, and expansion on the information and intelligence related to the criteria identified in the feasibility and assessment stage. Gate 5 concludes with a governing body assessing and prioritizing investments in the IT discovery portfolio and making decisions (go, cancel, hold, or recycle).

- *Stage 5:* Concept maturation is the final stage of the IT discovery phase. The concept is matured, and a compelling case is prepared for investment consideration.

- *Gate 6:* Information collected from the concept maturation stage is assessed and evaluated. Inputs to the preliminary business case are finalized.[35] Gate 6 concludes by a governing body assessing and prioritizing investments in the IT discovery portfolio and making decisions (go, cancel, hold, or recycle). For those investments that receive a go decision, the data collected for gate 6 are used in the initiation form for gate 1 of the IT project phase (see Exhibit 4.11).

In addition to performing the tasks in the IT discovery portfolio, a readiness assessment should be conducted to assure that expectations are clear and the risks and blind spots related to transitioning concepts from the IT discovery phase into the IT project portfolio are identified. In some cases, the transition might involve a handoff from one set of team members to another. Assuring that the concept is positioned in the right entity, continuity from one or more members of the original team and completion of the preliminary business case, technical specifications, checklists, and other documentation are critical transition elements that will increase the probability of the continued success of an investment.

IT PROJECT PORTFOLIO

Overview

The Project Management Institute (PMI) defines a project as a temporary endeavor undertaken to create a unique product or service.[36] Projects make change happen. In many instances, projects are the vehicle by which an enterprise evolves into its business vision and manifests its strategy. Project management controls the change to improve the probability of success.

The IT project portfolio is a framework used to assess potential IT project candidates against a defined set of weighted, multidimensional criteria that maintain

EXHIBIT 4.11 PROJECT INITIATION FORM

Project Name:		Sponsor Name:	
Date:		BU:	

Project Description:

Scoring Dimension	Description	Score
1. Program Risk — The relative risk of implementing the initiative based on the complexity of the business/information/technology architecture. Success is defined as achieving the desired benefits of the project within the appropriate budget, time period, and scope.		
	(3) Low = Probability of success between 67-100% (2) Medium = Probability of success between 34-66% (1) High = Probability of success between 0-33%	
2. Financial Return — The projected impact of the initiative based on NPV		
	Return on Investment (ROI) (1) Low = < $100,000 (2) Medium = $100,000-$999,999 (3) High = >$1,000,000	
	Payback (3) Low = < 1 year (2) Medium = 1-3 years (1) High = > 3 years	
3. Discretion — The degree of discretion the enterprise has to implement the initiative. For example, regulatory requirements have the least discretion while innovative initiatives typically have the most.		
	(1) High = Innovative program, not part of business operations critical path (3) Low = Must do for regulatory reasons, business continuity, etc.	
4. Strategic Impact — The degree to which the initiative can be mapped to existing business strategies. *Note: Please check all strategies that apply.*		Please Check
	Increase customer loyalty	☐
	Increase market share	☐
	Recapture lost customers	☐
	Increase sales to affluent buyers	☐
	Increase civic responsibility image	☐
	Promote brand image	☐
	Develop personnel to maximize their satisfaction	☐
	(1) Low = Run the business (2) Medium = Build the business (3) High = Innovate the business	
5. Product Life — The useful life of the initiative once it has been implemented		
	(3) Short = < 2 years (2) Medium = 2-7 years (1) Long = > 7 years	
6. Scope — How many people are affected by this project? What is the impact on the organization?		
	(1) Local = Affects one business unit (2) Regional = Affects multiple business units (3) Global = Affects entire enterprise	
Total	*Highest Possible Score = 21, Lowest Possible Score = 7*	

alignment with business and strategic objectives, assuring that only projects that significantly contribute to sustained business success will be funded. Selecting the right projects based on criteria other than the single dimension of costs versus benefits, or simple financial calculations, is vital to supporting growth and transformation. The gatekeepers for the IT project portfolio develop, assess, and weigh criteria to evaluate each investment. Examples of criteria might include term of the investment, risk, duration, costs, scope, posture (offensive versus defensive), and life cycle.

Elements of the IT Project Phase*

As mentioned earlier in this chapter, Stage-Gate® roots are well established in the new product development process. The Stage-Gate® process can have a number of detours that skip or consolidate stages and gates. Changes to the traditional five-stage process are dependent on urgency and importance of a need and the level of risk a company is willing to absorb.[37]

The IT project phase leverages many of the Stage-Gate® processes, encompassing stages and gates. This section provides a high-level overview of the stages and gates in the IT project phase, showing where and how the IT portfolio management framework is utilized in this process. Best practices from various entities are shown. Due to the fact that companies tailor the IT project portfolio to meet their specific needs, there are variations in the exhibits, work activities, and outputs shown for stages and gates in this section. The authors hope these differences will stimulate ideas for best practices in tailoring the Stage-Gate® (or a similar gating) process to best meet your needs. Depending on the technical, market, and business maturity of a proposed IT project, there are multiple entry points into the IT project phase.

Gate 1:   This is the initial screening into the IT project phase. Many potential IT projects are evaluated at gate 1 based on how they score on the initiative request form (see example in Exhibit 4.11).

In addition to the project initiation form, some companies develop must-meet and should-meet criteria that are evaluated against each project. A no answer to must-meet criteria eliminates the potential IT project from consideration. Examples of must-meet criteria can include alignment to the business and strategic objectives, positive value (benefits exceed risks), and lack of significant barriers. A no answer to should-meet criteria is not necessarily a showstopper. Should-meet criteria include the degree to which the project aligns with the business and strategic objectives, market attractiveness (size, growth, competition, etc.), and solution advantages (unique differentiators, patent potential, etc.). Scoring models are used to weigh and score criteria (see Chapter 5 regarding further information

---

*The content for the text (not the exhibits) shown in gate and stage sections of the IT project phase is primarily based on guidance from Michel Delifer, Michael Booker, and from the following articles: *Portfolio Management for New Products,* 2nd edition, by Robert G. Cooper, Scott J. Edgett, and Elko J. Kleinschmidt, Perseus Publishing, 2001; *Winning at New Products,* 3rd edition, by Robert G. Cooper, Perseus Publishing, 2001; "Optimizing the Stage-Gate® Process: What Best-Practice Companies Do—II," by Robert G. Cooper, Scott J. Edgett, and Elko J. Kleinschmidt, Research-Technology Management, Nov.–Dec. 2002; "Stage-Gate Management in the Biofuels Program," National Renewable Energy Laboratory, September 2001, http://permanent.access.gpo.gov/websites/www.ott.doe.gov/biofuels/pdfs/stage_gate_management.pdf.

EXHIBIT 4.12   HIGH-LEVEL EXAMPLE OF CRITERIA AND VALUES ASSOCIATED WITH EACH CRITERIA

1. Strategic Tier/Time frame
   - (3) Dynamic — = 0–12 months (immediate threats and opportunities)
   - (2) Visible Horizon — = 12–36 months (perceived/expected threats and opportunities)
   - (1) Paradigm Pioneering — = 36 months out (unexpected threats and visionary market leadership initiatives)
2. Implementation Risk
   - (3) Low — = Probability of success between 61–100%
   - (2) Medium — = Probability of success between 34–66%
   - (1) High — = Probability of success between 0–33%
3. Revenue Margin Impact
   - (1) Low — = <2%
   - (2) Medium — = 3–5%
   - (3) High — = >5%
4. Discretion
   - (1) High — = Innovation type of program, not part of business operations critical path
   - (2) Low — = Must do for regulatory, operational necessity, political mandate, etc.
5. Strategic impact (fit to business drivers)
   - (1) Low — = Maintains competitive parity
   - (2) Medium — = Pushes the leading edge/provides competitive advantage
   - (3) High — = Bleeding edge/business invention/positions enterprise as market leader
6. Market Risk
   - (1) Volatile Market — = >25% chance of market for initiative changing
   - (2) Static Market — = <25% chance of market for initiative changing
7. Benefit Life cycle
   - (1) Short — = <3 years
   - (2) Medium — = 3–5 years
   - (3) Long — = 5+ years
8. Initiative Cost
   - (3) Low — = <$5 million   ( ) = score for dimension
   - (2) Moderate — = $5–25 million
   - (3) High — = >$25 million

Dynamic Portfolio Prioritization Matrix

Initiative	Risk Rating	Strategic Tier/ Time frame	Strategic Impact	Margin Impact	Implementation Risk	Market Risk	Lifecycle	Discretion	Cost	Total Score
Initiative 1	Low	Visible Horizon/2	High/3	Low/1	Low/3	Static/2	Long/3	Low/2	High/1	17
Initiative 2	Low	Visible Horizon/2	Low/1	High/3	Mod/2	Static/2	Long/3	Low/2	Mod/2	17
Initiative 3	Low	Dynamic/3	High/3	Mod/2	High/1	Static/2	Long/3	High/1	Low/3	18
Initiative 4	Moderate	Dynamic/3	Low/1	Low/1	Low/3	Static/2	Short/1	Low/2	Mod/2	15
Initiative 5	High	Paradigm Pioneering/1	Low/1	Low/1	Low/3	Volatile/1	Short/1	High/1	High/1	10
Initiative 6	High	Visible Horizon/2	Low/1	Mod/2	High/1	Volatile/1	Mod/2	High/1	Mod/2	12
Initiative 7	Low	Dynamic/3	Low/1	Low/1	Low/3	Static/2	Long/3	Low/2	Low/3	18
Initiative 8	Moderate	Visible Horizon/2	Low/1	High/3	High/1	Static/2	Long/3	Low/2	Low/3	17
Overall Risk	Moderate									15.5
Total Score Range = 8–22										
8–12 = High Risk										
13–17 = Moderate Risk										
18–22 = Low Risk										

on scoring models). The cumulative numbers are calculated for each IT project (the higher scores indicate more favorable characteristics in an IT project). An example of the scoring value and criteria are shown in Exhibit 4.12.

Projects can be categorized into one of the following three areas:

1. *Run the business:* required investments to keep the operations running
2. *Grow the business:* investments that expand the company's scope of product and services
3. *Transform the business:* investments involving project-based spending that creates new IT services to broaden an enterprise's reach to enter new, untapped markets (i.e., through new business ventures, mergers and acquisitions, new solutions, emerging and breakthrough technologies, new geographies, business process outsourcing)

These categories provide a guideline for companies to use in maintaining sufficient funding for each of these areas, assuring investments are balanced in all three categories according to the objectives and priorities of the company. The output from gate 1 is a categorization of the IT project, results from the initiative request form, and a decision made regarding the project (go, hold, cancel, or recycle).

The remainder of the stages and gates are described briefly using work activities and output. *Work activities* are the processes, analysis, and assessments that occur within each stage. *Outputs* are the deliverables, products, or services that result from the work activities. The descriptions and information should be treated as a possible reference or starting point in defining or maturing a Stage-Gate® process that would be appropriate for a particular company.

Stage 1: scoping/preliminary analysis. Identifies critical technical merits and customer appeal.

- Work Activities
  - Preliminary market assessment.
    - Perform Internet and literature research.
    - Determine market size, market potential, and competitive factors.
    - Engage customer in surveys and focus groups. Gather customer feedback, possible interest, and possibility of solution acceptance.
    - Approximate solution features and requirements.
  - Preliminary feasibility assessment.
    - Feasibility related to development and manufacturing, and technical and operations.
    - Evaluate time, cost, legal and regulatory risks and roadblocks (e.g., patents, licenses, etc.).

- Preliminary technical assessment.
- Preliminary build and/or buy (license) options assessment.
- Preliminary integrated product definition.
- Preliminary financial and risk assessment.
- Develop action items for the next stage.
- Output
  - Preliminary assessment results and recommendation to go, hold, cancel, or recycle the IT project.
  - Detailed action plan for next stage.

Gate 2: nearly the same process as in gate 1 but with the addition and refinement of information obtained in stage 1.

- Work Activities
  - Simple financial return models provide more depth to analysis within the IT portfolio.
  - Checklist and areas addressed from a quality and thoroughness perspective and calculation of the scoring model help facilitate the gate decision.
- Output
  - Results of IT portfolio management prioritizations and rankings.
  - Decision made regarding the project: go, hold, cancel, or recycle.

Stage 2: building the business case. Critical investigation stage that defines the solution and validates the appeal.

- Work Activities
  - Detailed market and customer assessment.
    - Target market definition/attractiveness.
    - Delineation of the solution concept.
    - Value proposition and positioning strategy.
    - Features, attributes, requirements, and specifications.
    - Competitive analysis.
  - Detailed technology and operations assessment.
    - Concept testing.
    - Technical appraisal or the achievability of the project based on customer needs and wish lists translated into technically and economically feasible solutions.
    - Development, integration, architecture compliance, and operations appraisal.
    - Source of suppliers.
    - Costs to develop and/or license and implement.
    - Total cost of ownership.

- Detailed financial and business assessment.
- Detailed business and financial analysis.
  - Discounted cash flow.
  - Sensitivity analysis.
- Legal, patent, and regulatory assessment.
- Detailed integrated risk assessment.
- Preliminary market launch assessment.
- Output
  - Business case containing many of the detailed assessments listed above. Also includes project definition, project justification, and detailed project plan.
  - Recommendation to go, hold, cancel, or recycle the IT project.

An example of a business case outline from Xcel Energy is provided in Exhibit 4.13. Additional information regarding business cases is provided in Chapter 5.

EXHIBIT 4.13   XCEL ENERGY BUSINESS CASE SUITE OUTLINE

- Program Structure (how project fits into other projects/programs)
- Purpose of Request
  - w/Summary of budget, amount spent, amount requested
- Financials Cost/Benefit Analysis
  - Spend to Date (Capital & O&M)
  - Total Project Cost
    - By Year, Capital, O&M, Total, Future O&M, Budgeted Y/N
  - Cost/Benefit
    - NPV, IRR, ROI, Hard Savings, Cost Avoidance, Soft Savings, Useful Life
  - BCS Valuation Scores
    - Overall, Financial, Value, Risk, Technical Viability
- Scope Summary
  - Purpose, Requirements, Options Considered, Ramifications if do nothing
- Functional Design
- Risk Management Summary
  - Risk Matrix (Impact vs. Probability), Risk Mgmt Plan, SOx impact
- Schedule Summary
  - Milestones, Stakeholders/Dependencies, Project Steering Committee
  - Resource Plan (PM, Business, Technical, Dates, Source, Rates)
- Major Assumptions
- Summary (free slide for any additional information)
- Attachment A: Costs by month (Labor, Hardware, Software, Travel/Exp, Other, Total)
- Attachment B: Benefits by year
  - BU Labor reduction, other hard, reduced future labor, other
  - Business Systems HW Maintenance reduction, SW Support, other hard, reduced growth HW/SW, other avoids

---

Source: Copyright © 2005, Xcel Energy Services, Inc.

Gate 3: heavy spending happens at this gate. Provides a detailed assessment of the project investment against the IT portfolio.

- Work Activities
  - Review activities and results from stage 2.
  - Evaluate and score criteria, with consideration for the detailed financial analysis.
- Output
  - Development plan and preliminary operations and marketing plans.
  - Results of IT portfolio management analysis, balancing, prioritization, and optimization.
  - Decision made regarding the project: go, hold, cancel, or recycle.

Stage 3: development. Translate business plan into physical deliverables that can be assessed.

- Work Activities
  - Updated market assessment.
    - Test and evaluate market and potential customer response (e.g., lead users, focus groups, user panels, partnerships) to determine continued need.
    - Develop market launch plans.
  - Prototype assessment.
    - Develop and demonstrate prototypes.
  - Technical and operational assessment.
    - Develop detailed test plans.
    - Develop transition/operations plan.
  - Update all mandatory/regulatory plans.
  - Update and finalize integrated solution definition.
  - Update financial analysis.
  - Preliminary solution life cycle outlook.
  - Detailed buy and/or build strategy.
  - Detailed market launch.
- Output
  - Customer (and other) assessments and analysis.
  - Documentation of all prototyping results.
  - Recommendation to go, hold, cancel, or recycle the IT project.

From stage 3 through the end of the IT project phase, both the project and program status (that ties to a particular project) can be monitored and tracked through a dashboard. Exhibit 4.14 from Mercury Interactive shows an example of the inputs that are tracked.

EXHIBIT 4.14 PROJECT AND PROGRAM STATUS SNAPSHOTS

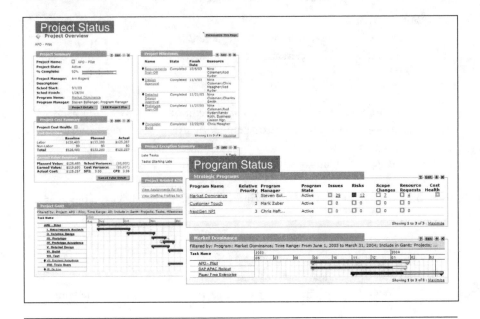

Source: Copyright © 2004 Mercury Interactive Corporation.

Gate 4: checks actual versus projected costs, schedule, milestones, and so on.

- Work Activities
  - Review activities and results from stage 3.
  - Evaluate and score criteria, with consideration for the detailed financial analysis.
  - Detailed marketing and operations plans are reviewed for probable future execution.
- Output
  - Monitor and track the IT project.
  - Decision made regarding the project: go, hold, cancel, or recycle.

Stage 4: test and validation. Validates feasibility, viability, costs, and benefits with more robust (commercial) solution.

- Work Activities
  - Extensive lab and field testing.
  - Limited rollout pilots, and user feedback taken into consideration.
  - Validate business and economic case.

- Finalized buy and/or build strategy and selection of industry providers/solution partners.
- Detailed solution life cycle.
- Output
  - Test and validation plan.
  - Monitor and track the IT project.
  - Decision made regarding the project: go, hold, cancel, or recycle.

Gate 5: go to launch.

- Work Activities
  - Evaluation and analysis of the test and validation plans.
  - Appropriateness of the launch and production/operational start-up plans.
  - Review marketing plans.
  - Evaluate solution life cycles.
- Output
  - Monitor and track the IT project.
  - Decision made regarding the project: go, hold, kill, or recycle.

Stage 5: launch and implementation.

- Work Activities and Output
  - Implementation of the plans (production, operations, marketing).
  - Execute the launch.

Gate 6: post-implementation review.

- Work Activities
  - Disband development/built/integration team.
  - Review performance: revenues, costs, expenditures, profits.
  - Assess project's strengths and weaknesses and lessons learned.
- Output
  - Monitor and track the IT project.
  - Provide lessons learned to appropriate personnel.

The Stage-Gate® process provides companies with an excellent framework from which to customize their particular strategies and objectives, design, management, and execution needs. A best practice in the area of phase-gate, which is very similar to Stage-Gate®, is shown in Exhibit 4.15. Teradyne, Inc., a manufacturer of test equipment for the semiconductor industry, uses a phase-gate framework to manage its projects. Each phase consists of a series of specific product and project deliverables (entry and exit criteria), laying out the resources required at each stage and the decision makers at each gate. Teradyne refers to each of the stages in its process as a phase.

EXHIBIT 4.15 TERADYNE'S PHASE-GATED PROJECT PROCESS

TERADYNE

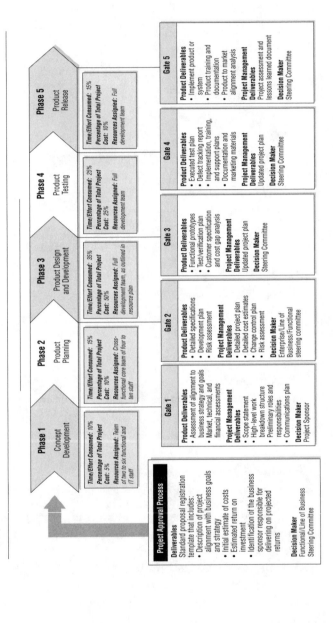

Phase 1 — Concept Development

Time/Effort Consumed: 10%
Percentage of Total Project Cost: 5%
Resources Assigned: Team of two to six functional and IT staff

Gate 1

Product Deliverables
- Assessment of alignment to business strategy and goals
- Market, technical, and financial assessments

Project Management Deliverables
- Scope statement
- High-level work breakdown structure
- Preliminary roles and responsibilities
- Communications plan

Decision Maker
Project Sponsor

Phase 2 — Product Planning

Time/Effort Consumed: 15%
Percentage of Total Project Cost: 10%
Resources Assigned: Cross-functional core team of four to ten staff

Gate 2

Product Deliverables
- Detailed specifications
- Development plan
- Risk assessment

Project Management Deliverables
- Detailed project plan
- Detailed cost estimates
- Change control plan
- Risk assessment

Decision Maker
Enterprise/Line of Business/Functional steering committee

Phase 3 — Product Design and Development

Time/Effort Consumed: 35%
Percentage of Total Project Cost: 50%
Resources Assigned: Full development team, as outlined in resource plan

Gate 3

Product Deliverables
- Functional prototypes
- Test/verification plan
- Customer specification and cost gap analysis

Project Management Deliverables
Updated project plan

Decision Maker
Steering Committee

Phase 4 — Product Testing

Time/Effort Consumed: 25%
Percentage of Total Project Cost: 25%
Resources Assigned: Full development team

Gate 4

Product Deliverables
- Executed test plan
- Defect tracking report
- Implementation, training, and support plans
- Documentation and marketing materials

Project Management Deliverables
Updated project plan

Decision Maker
Steering Committee

Phase 5 — Product Release

Time/Effort Consumed: 15%
Percentage of Total Project Cost: 10%
Resources Assigned: Full development team

Gate 5

Product Deliverables
- Implement product or system
- Product training and documentation
- Product to market alignment analysis

Project Management Deliverables
Project assessment and lessons learned document

Decision Maker
Steering Committee

Project Approval Process

Deliverables
Standard proposal registration template that includes:
- Description of project alignment with business goals and strategy
- Initial estimate of costs
- Estimated return on investment
- Identification of the business sponsor responsible for delivering on projected returns

Decision Maker
Functional/Line of Business Steering Committee

- *Project Approval Process (Phase Zero)*—Before project execution begins, project requestors complete a standard proposal template that describes the initiative's alignment with business goals and strategy, provides an estimate of costs, and identifies the business sponsor responsible for delivering on projected returns. After a proposal is approved, the project enters the phase-gate project execution process.

- *Concept Development (Phase One)*—Involves defining the market opportunity, gathering customer requirements, and examining product feasibility. Also includes an initial project scope statement, a communication plan, the formulation of an initial project schedule, and the initial assignment of roles and responsibilities.

- *Product Planning (Phase Two)*—Entails refining the product concept and the creation of a development plan, including a risk assessment and the definition of business success metrics. Also requires the creation of a detailed project schedule and focuses on the creation of an initial project business case, including an estimate of project costs and risks, and resource and change control plans.

- *Product Design and Development (Phase Three)*—Encompasses technical design and development of the proposed solution, a gap analysis against customer specifications and cost estimates, and a focus on the completion of any approved or required changes to the project plan.

- *Product Testing (Phase Four)*—Involves verification that the product meets customer specifications and preparation for customer shipment. This includes the successful execution of the test plan, preparation of the implementation, training, and support plans, and validation of business success metrics.

- *Product Release (Phase Five)*—Includes the rollout of the completed solution, the incorporation of additional approved changes, continued progress reporting, and the creation of "lessons learned" documentation for the entire project.

- *Phase-Gate "Lite"*—Smaller projects (those costing less than $50,000 and requiring less than 250 effort hours) are not subjected to the same level of rigor as larger projects. In this scaled-down process, phases and gates 2 through 4 are combined, with only the most significant deliverables required for successful advancement.

Sources: Teradyne, Inc., Internal document. All rights reserved; CIO Executive Board/Corporate Executive Board, "Governance and Prioritization for Agile IT Organizations," 2002.

Using a phase-gate approach, Teradyne's success rate for large projects jumped from 40% to 90%. In addition, many efficiencies were gained through execution of projects as well as early decommissioning of projects. This enabled Teradyne to fund off-cycle projects.

Key Take-Aways

IT project portfolio evaluations and reviews at each gate serve as a check and balance, ensuring the right balance of projects are strategically aligned to a company's priorities. Managing the IT project portfolio and IT project phases is dependent on many key factors, some of which are listed below:

- Program management discipline throughout all IT project phases (e.g., management, support, tools, processes, quality and standards, methodologies, mentoring, training, consulting).

- Ability to effectively and efficiently allocate limited resources. In the event of an off-cycle request, a company must have options to quickly tap into additional skilled and experienced resources.

- Efficient and effective processes such as change management, transition management, configuration management, project management, resource and capacity management.

- Alignment with business and strategic objectives, requirements, and architecture.

- Close collaboration and partnership with the enterprise architecture group and the enterprise program management office.

- Focus, focus, focus. Avoid stretching resources beyond their means; avoid the syndrome of treating most projects as must-do, constantly responding to customer input or sales and overloading the system with too many projects.

- Leadership commitment and active senior leadership support.

- Project management and monitoring tools that quickly sense when a project is not achieving its objectives, and providing a means by which changes can be communicated and rapidly acted upon.

- Policies, security, governance, and procedures that provide clear guidance, direction, accountability, and responsibilities.

- Core team of individuals engaged in all phases of the IT life cycle; switching the core team around opens too many avenues for plausible deniability when projects go south.

- Limited tolerance for schedule slips. Instead, consider increasing resources to a project that is slipping.[38]

- Development of clear and consistent criteria:
  - Achieving an effective equilibrium between:
    - Practicality, balance, alignment, risks, and rewards
    - Priorities of business units, product lines, and corporate
    - Tangible versus intangible, subjective versus objective, quantitative versus qualitative factors
  - Prioritizing growth projects
  - Consolidating and reusing components across the company
  - Willingness to cancel projects
- Analysis and assessment of constraints
- Development and execution of performance management and metrics

It is important that companies maintain a healthy balance of low-risk versus high-risk and short-term versus long-term projects in the IT project portfolio. A study by Edward McDonough and Francis Spital showed "that the more successful portfolios had a smaller proportion of projects with both low technical and low market uncertainty . . . portfolios that best meet their objectives have a higher proportion of uncertain projects."[39]

Transition to Operations

IT projects that graduate from the IT project phase are ready to launch into operations or be introduced into the commercial marketplace. A transition readiness list will help smoothen the transition from the IT project portfolio to the IT asset portfolio. This will also help IT investments achieve a greater probability of attaining their projected goals and objectives. Some of the checklist items that will help assure the continued success of the project are:

- The team working on the project during the IT project phase must be convinced that the project is operationally or commercially ready for release.
- The project has reached an acceptable technology readiness level.
- Detailed specifications, security, testing under real operational conditions, and scalability have all been validated.
- The business case is mature and approved; security, policy, regulatory, funding, and facility issues have been addressed and adequately resolved.
- Customers have been engaged throughout, and value of the project has been fully validated.
- Importance/urgency of the project and key dependencies/constraints have been sufficiently addressed and resolved.

- A well-documented, rollout plan has been vetted and approved.

- The business unit, division, and so on, that will be accepting this project are fully versed on the benefits, value proposition, and possible opportunities created by this project.

- They are resourced to take the project into operations and support the operations and maintenance tail.

- Appropriate and skilled resources have been identified to operate and sustain the project.

- Integration and process issues have been resolved. Production and manufacturing issues have been adequately addressed and resolved.

- Value-chain partners are aligned, committed, and in lockstep with next steps.

- Issues related to protection of intellectual property are at advanced stages of approval.

- Marketing, sales, training, HR, legal, communications, procurement, and other functional areas are educated as to the value proposition, competitive differentiators, benefits, and costs of the project, and they are prepared for full rollout. Most have developed plans within their respective functional areas detailing their expectations and obligations related to the successful release of the project.

- The executive steering committee oversees the success of the transition and dedicates sufficient resources where necessary to assure success.[40]

IT ASSET PORTFOLIO

Overview

The IT asset portfolio consists of investments that already reside within a company. The four primary elements of the IT asset portfolio shown in Exhibit 4.16 are:

- *Information and data:* customer data, product catalogs, corporate and business unit data, and so on.

- *Infrastructure and applications:* servers, storage, networks, desktops, phones, operating systems, databases, and middleware. Applications include commercial off-the-shelf (e.g., supply chain, ERP, CRM, etc.) and custom-developed applications (e.g., patents). Also includes help desk, data and command centers.

- *Human capital:* IT staff, knowledge, skill sets, relationship management, human resource processes (recruiting, training, career development, compensation, resource allocation).

EXHIBIT 4.16   IT ASSET PORTFOLIO

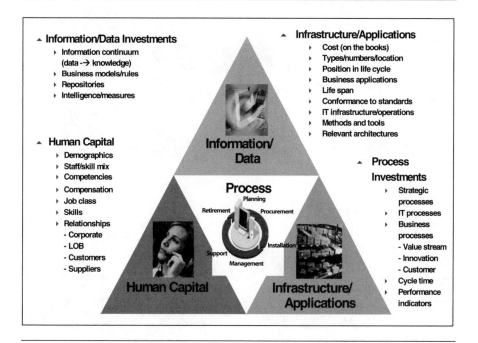

▲ **Information/Data Investments**
  ‣ Information continuum
    (data --> knowledge)
  ‣ Business models/rules
  ‣ Repositories
  ‣ Intelligence/measures

▲ **Human Capital**
  ‣ Demographics
  ‣ Staff/skill mix
  ‣ Competencies
  ‣ Compensation
  ‣ Job class
  ‣ Skills
  ‣ Relationships
    - Corporate
    - LOB
    - Customers
    - Suppliers

▲ **Infrastructure/Applications**
  ‣ Cost (on the books)
  ‣ Types/numbers/location
  ‣ Position in life cycle
  ‣ Business applications
  ‣ Life span
  ‣ Conformance to standards
  ‣ IT infrastructure/operations
  ‣ Methods and tools
  ‣ Relevant architectures

▲ **Process Investments**
  ‣ Strategic processes
  ‣ IT processes
  ‣ Business processes
    - Value stream
    - Innovation
    - Customer
  ‣ Cycle time
  ‣ Performance indicators

Information/Data

Process
  Planning
  Retirement   Procurement
  Support   Installation
  Management

Human Capital

Infrastructure/Applications

- *Processes:* work flow, business process management, network and system automation, process definitions and flows.

Creating an IT asset portfolio is dependent on developing a clear picture of the current as-is asset topology and architectural views, comparing these against a to-be desired future state, and identifying and prioritizing the associated gaps. Many companies lack detailed views related to both the as-is and to-be states, which will drive costs higher and promote duplication and tremendous inefficiencies. It should not be a surprise that costs to maintain existing infrastructure (inclusive of the associated labor) are under excruciating scrutiny, as they represent the largest IT expenditures within most companies.

Many companies are under pressure to have their existing IT assets aligned with business and strategic objectives, to perform better/faster/cheaper, and to maintain agility to change directions on a dime based on growing volatility in the marketplace. In addition, with the advent of web services, grid computing, virtualization, autonomic computing, and migration to an on-demand adaptive environment, companies will closely assess the benefits of these solutions and the variable (total cost is a direct function of consumption) versus fixed (total cost is independent of consumption) cost aspects. As shown in Exhibit 4.17, utilization rates for UNIX

EXHIBIT 4.17 HARVESTING UNDERUTILIZED FIXED ASSETS

Average Server and Storage Utilization

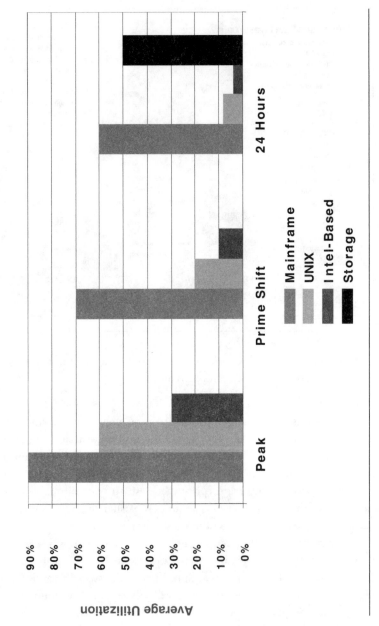

and Intel-based systems are very low; therefore, harvesting underutilized fixed assets through the creation of an on-demand or a variable cost model is attractive and will be closely evaluated by companies.

Elements of the IT Asset Phase

Each individual gate and stage in the IT asset phase is not isolated and described in this section. Rather, an overview of the seminal elements of the IT asset phase is presented in this section.

IT asset portfolio reviews should be conducted at least on a quarterly basis. The authors recommend that all IT asset investments should be reviewed at this meeting. The reviews should incorporate:

- Status (forecast versus actual) of costs, schedule, delivery, staffing, budget, technical, change orders executed
- Ties to the current business and strategic objectives
- Impact on business performance
- Effectiveness of meeting original objectives
- Evaluation of service-level agreements and key performance indicators
- Client involvement and satisfaction
- Skill availability
- Risk and risk mitigation strategies
- Assessment of the portfolio mix
- Time required for issues to be resolved and number of issues outstanding

The capability to review the status of IT investments should be available to all interested stakeholders. A dashboard enables executives and managers to view the health of IT investments, question and challenge key areas, track metrics, and intervene where necessary. Some companies use color-coded green, yellow, and red lights to show the health of existing IT assets:

- Red indicates that the defined boundaries of acceptable performance have been breached.
- Yellow indicates risk of falling outside threshold levels.
- Green indicates the IT investment is achieving performance within acceptable ranges.

Leaders in web-enabled IT portfolio management tools provide automated alerts in the event that an asset declines in the color rating, enabling drill-down capabilities to determine the root causes, issues, and problems. IT assets such as hardware, software, and infrastructure are scored against technical quality and business value. Based on how an IT investment scores against these two criteria, there are four quadrants that help decide the future of the IT investment: retire/consolidate, reengineer/modernize, reevaluate/reposition, or maintain/evolve. IT asset needs for new capabilities and identified gaps can filter into the IT discovery or IT project portfolio, thus creating a closed-loop process.

Infrastructure

Infrastructure is a confusing term in IT. In the early years of information systems infrastructure connoted hardware. As more hardware functions become virtualized, more infrastructure is software. For IT portfolio management, consider IT infrastructure as the underlying foundation of services that enable business applications. The value of the infrastructure comes from the translation of infrastructure and applications into business value. The goal of the infrastructure portfolio is to enable performance, agility, efficiency, and cost reduction while keeping the infrastructure and applications current, aligned and balanced with the business and strategic objectives.

The infrastructure portfolio helps to organize information required for infrastructure planning and assessment. It captures real instance information (inventory) in a structured way (the template or reference manifest of components and other information) along with standards. The standards define the external and internal structure of the class of entities stored in the portfolio (which should include links to other portfolios). The infrastructure portfolio is decomposed according to:

- *Components:* define individual technologies and actual products, including hardware and software. Often organized by technology domains or platform layers such as network, server, security, storage, and so forth.

- *Domains:* group individual component technologies and actual products by technology and organizational affinity. Same as architecture domains and include common domains such as network, database, integration, and so on.

- *Patterns:* facilitate rapid mapping from business requirements to infrastructure designs and end-to-end component set selections. End-to-end ordered sets of components and services that match classes of applications.

- *Services:* represent a set of components physically implemented and reused as a single unit but not all components required for any single application (not a full pattern). Sets of infrastructure components are implemented and shared physically by applications. Common services include storage, identity management, transactional integration, and enterprise application integration.

The infrastructure portfolio determines the right mix of projects and investments, assuring that mission critical and business continuity systems remain fail-safe, producing the optimal combination of risk reduction and value maximization. Categories assessed in the infrastructure portfolio include:

- Documenting the infrastructure portfolio using structured templates for patterns, services, components, and domains.
- Assessing as-is versus to-be status. Examples of areas to consider include:
  - Alignment of the investment with the business and strategic objectives and requirements
  - Number of users supported
  - Age, utility, importance, and criticality of the asset
  - Technical condition, longevity, and total cost of ownership
  - Perceived business value
  - User growth rate sustainability
- Ease of support.
- Service-level agreements.
- Dependencies and constraints: effect on applications, impact on other elements of the infrastructure.
- Ability to standardize, integrate, and interoperate with other systems.
- Number of features and functions supported.
- Duplication and redundancy associated with other assets.
- Historical, current, and future risks.
- Flexibility and agility to rapidly embrace change.
- Complexity, costs, and time associated with transition/migration options.

Creating and maintaining the infrastructure portfolio involves:

- Developing the infrastructure road map and transition plan showing the timing of migration, consolidation, integration, and so on, of infrastructure elements.
- Tying retirement, migration, outsourcing, and new infrastructure investments to the business and strategic objectives and to infrastructure value.
- Creating the categorization and prioritization of investments, and determining the optimal infrastructure investment portfolio to achieve minimal risk at the acceptable investment level.
- Performing what-if analysis and assuring balance.
- Linking new infrastructure implementations to the project portfolio. Requirements for breakthrough innovation would go to the discovery portfolio.
- Measuring, monitoring, and continuously evaluating results. Feeding best practices back into the system.

Processes

Processes are the work flows (interfaces), automation, roles/responsibilities, and measurements that enable integration and cross-process integration within a portfolio. The IT process management is a framework used to gather, measure, evaluate, optimize, and manage all available processes, and evaluate the impact on other resources. Processes are scored, and best-of-fit process modifications are identified. Setting attainable process improvements/measurement targets occurs in the management aspects of the IT process.

As part of ongoing modeling practices, the IT operations group should establish maturity baselines for processes critical to IT operational success. Some examples include:

- Asset management
- Business continuity
- Change management
- Configuration management
- Contractor management
- Cost recovery management
- Inventory management
- Operational readiness
- Problem management
- Service-level agreement management
- Systems monitoring
- Workload monitoring

Descriptions of the most widely used IT processes gathered from leading private- and public-sector entities can be found in the IT Infrastructure Library (ITIL). ITIL was originally created by the Central Computer and Telecommunications Agency (CCTA), a U.K. government agency, and it is the most widely accepted approach to IT service management.

It is not unusual to see companies focus on complex process work flows as the major indicators of IT operational success. It is important that IT operations groups capture the essence of process performance yet limit the number of individual process components measured. There are five key elements that in combination give a well-balanced view of operational process performance and maturity and serve as key inputs for the IT process portfolio:

1. *Process definition:* what is and is not included as part of the process
2. *Process integration points:* the inputs and outputs from each process and how they interrelate (e.g., integration points between companies' goals and

strategies, service requests, problems, and change management); identifying dependencies, timing, value/risk, and impacts on overall service delivery

3. *Skills and staffing:* the roles and responsibilities required to perform the processes (e.g., need for a change manager as part of the change management process)

4. *Process automation:* cross-platform performance of the process automation as it exists in the environment, with process tools that have been customized being measured according to their current state

5. *Process performance measures:* the operations group's ability to measure day-to-day performance of the individual process; analyzing activities, systems, or skills and watching for below-average performance and cost inefficiencies

Imitating Carnegie Mellon's Software Engineering Institute's capability maturity model (SEI CMM) maturity scheme, despite its traditional use for application development processes, helps in the communication aspects of the IT process portfolio. Operational maturity models must not only estimate process maturity on a particular platform, they must also weigh the importance of the platform to the company. The maturity models feed the IT process portfolio, where prioritization of process improvement activities based on performance levels and impacts occurs. Prioritization looks at many criteria, including business and IT. Maturity modeling also helps the IT process portfolio identify potential IT process performance risks. The inputs to the IT process portfolio will increasingly factor in the impact that business variables (e.g., organization culture, ability and willingness of the company to change, and process improvement priorities) have on the operational process performance and improvement efforts.

The IT process portfolio inventories and helps to identify related process grouping for which synergy between processes is demonstrated. The fields captured within the portfolio might include description of the process (e.g., activities, actors, dependencies, constraints), cross-process integration, and tool characteristics (e.g., open architecture, application program interface, intuitive graphic user interface).

IT operations groups identify possible process candidates that should be bundled and seek to prove performance returns. Processes are continually reviewed for modification and improvement opportunities. Six Sigma is a logical tool used by many companies for process improvement.

An example of a process within the IT portfolio that is critical to running operations is change management, which should be at a high level of maturity, particularly if the goal of a company is agility. Change management involves any variation to the current as-is state, with the goal of continuing to perform while effectively managing change. Change requires multiple levels of acceptance:

- Request for change is received (e.g., end users request alterations).
- Further due diligence of the nature (importance, criticality, etc.) of the request is assessed.
- Planning the change and analysis of impact of the change is determined (categorization, prioritization, risk, costs, benefits, etc.) using the IT process portfolio management framework.
- Approval from key constituents is obtained.
- Schedule of the change is solidified.
- Change is executed.
- Postmortem of the change occurs to assure that assumptions made in planning and analysis of impact were on track. Lessons learned are cataloged and fed back into the change process.

Change management integrates with many other processes:

- *Problem management:* if users do not feel they are receiving what they require, they notify the help desk, which opens a trouble ticket.
- *Configuration management:* assesses the risk, impact, and source of change. According to research, fewer than 1% of companies perform configuration management beyond simple desktop, server, and network configuration, significantly limiting the potential of the IT operations groups to effectively execute change management.
- *Operational readiness:* assesses the overall impacts of change beyond those related just to technology.
- *Request management:* closely communicating with the requestor (schedule, risks, impacts on other systems and processes, etc.).

Information and Data

Data is derived from the Latin word *datum,* which loosely translated is "something given." *Information* is derived from the Latin word *informare,* which is "to form." So it is that information is data that has been given meaning. Information is an abstraction of objects. Information represents patterns. Information influences actions. Information is communicated. Information is the foundation for knowledge. Knowledge, coupled with experience, leads to wisdom. The analogy could be drawn that data are the raw materials, and information is the finished goods. The letters in this book are data. Their structure within sentences provides information. If successful, this book will impart knowledge on the readers to enable them to perform IT portfolio management activities. The readers will have wisdom—we hope.

High-quality data and information provide organizations with knowledge to enable effective actions and decisions. Nonexistent data and information, or poor-quality data and information, lead organizations to either fly blind or fly into the side of a mountain. Research indicates that 90% of all business decisions are suboptimal because of data quality. Ironically, the biggest data quality complaint does not pertain to the accuracy of the data but the completeness of the data. Incomplete data translate into incomplete information, which leads decision makers to rely on intuition with greater frequency than desired. Most organizations do not know what data or information they have. They have no idea about the value of their data or information. Most organizations are aware that their data are important, valuable, and imperfect.

Organizations are making concerted efforts to improve data quality through cleansing and enrichment. There is, however, so much data and information that it is often difficult to determine where to focus data quality efforts. While it is simple enough to state that information and data should be treated as companies would treat financial and material assets, the fact is that most companies do not even know the difference between data and information. Most collapse data and that which the data represent. A few leading companies have formal methods to gauge and improve how they manage and leverage their information and data. They are in the minority.

IT portfolio management can be applied to making sense of the morass of data and information that flood organizations. It enables organizations to focus data quality and decision support efforts on what matters by identifying the entities that are critical to the business, their key descriptors, and the information maintained on these entities. It could legitimately be argued that the information subportfolio is actually metadata for the entire IT portfolio. Practically speaking, a portfolio of data is . . . impractical! Anything put into the information subportfolio, by definition, is information, making the information subportfolio ethereal and circular. Thus, the underlying theme of this book can be applied to make the information subportfolio both real and of immense value.

Objectives for IT portfolio management must be defined and attainable. These objectives must then be attained pragmatically. If the organization is awash with data stores, these data stores can be rationalized with IT portfolio management. If the organization is awash with reports, often referred to as information products, these reports can be rationalized with IT portfolio management. Data about the "information" that is the crux of the objectives are collected and compiled into information using the same IT portfolio management process that is used for project and asset portfolio management.

Those who have ventured into the information subportfolio through IT portfolio management have generally collected a list of the key entities that make the organization tick. These entities are usually smaller and simpler in nature than might be imagined. They consist of the basics—customer, employee, product, service, and a handful of basic descriptors of "things" that require tracking and decision support. For example, a multibillion-dollar U.S. retailer distilled the number of key entities that must be stewarded into 26 items. These 26 items were assigned basic attributes (e.g., name, description, synonyms) and mapped to other subportfolio items that rely on these entities (e.g., applications, processes, people). What became apparent in this instance was a lack of good stewardship with information. The most critical entities were tracked in multiple systems. No conscious coordination existed. No ownership existed. This enabled information management principles to be created. This enabled data quality efforts to be focused at the root cause.

In another instance, the key entities were collected in a portfolio view and assigned value based on the value of the processes that relied on that information and the costs to maintain that information—activity-based costing was applied to entities to provide an indication of their value. This enabled the organization to align the amount and types of effort stewarding the information to the relative value of that information. Other organizations that truly provide information products can assign actual value to the information products and fundamentally apply a BCG-like (i.e., Boston Consulting Group) portfolio management approach. Greater focus can be directed to those information products that will be providing greater market share or revenue. Information products that are mature or declining in market share or revenue receive less focus. This same rationale can be applied to internal information products.

The IT information and data portfolio helps management understand what entities must be monitored and how. Management can identify the value drivers behind information and data and direct the level and type of stewardship that must be given (e.g., accuracy, reliability, security, timeliness, integratability). The information and data portfolio helps management define the benefit of a specific unit of information or the contribution to revenues or margins, carrying costs/unnecessary inventory, latency, costs to obtain or generate that unit of information, as well as the costs to store and maintain it, and leverage and assimilate it into operations. Management can define key criteria and weighting factors that can be used within the entire IT portfolio. Management can optimize the benefits and minimize the risks associated with information and data (e.g., how information can flow more readily through information supply chains from the place where it is captured or generated to where it can be leveraged to optimize or maximize certain business processes). The stages to build and execute the information portfolio include:

- Identifying the objectives and scope of the information portfolio to prevent analysis paralysis
- Identifying the ideal future state of information in support of the enterprise's strategy, often through enterprise information architecture (i.e.,

future state models of information) and support of critical business processes (see Exhibit 4.18)

- Gathering current state metadata from credible sources (e.g., information systems documentation, subject matter experts, etc.) and assigning appropriate attributes to the metadata (e.g., value, cost, quality, useful life, density, velocity, etc.)

- Creating the information and data portfolio by transforming the metadata into meaningful decision criteria replete with weights and scores; assuring that information and data are in alignment with the business and strategic objectives

- Assessing and balancing the information and data portfolio through transformation efforts:
  - Optimizing information availability versus quality
  - Balancing accessibility versus security
  - Improving information supply chain performance and integration

EXHIBIT 4.18   HIGH-LEVEL INFORMATION FLOW DIAGRAM

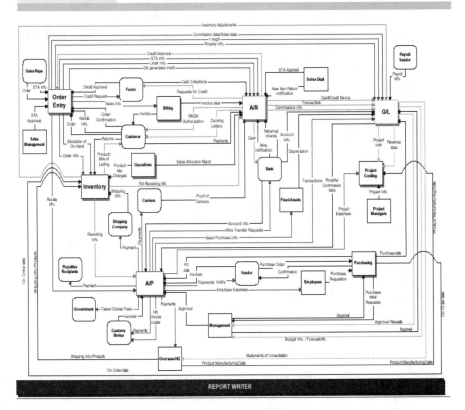

- Optimizing and eliminating enterprise processes
- Optimizing and eliminating applications that manage data and create information

Human Capital

The people included in the human capital portfolio are generally limited to those who create and manage IT investments—assets and projects. The objective of the human capital management portfolio is to ensure that IT human resources are optimized. IT staffing represents 42% of the IT budget. A study of IT project delivery resources within internal IT departments of Global 2000 organizations (i.e., people who are supposed to be actively working on projects) shows the average utilization is 66%. Full-time employees who are supposed to be working on projects are actually working on them 66% of their time; the other 24% of their time is not effectively utilized. Assuming 2,000 working hours in a year and a standard cost of $100 per hour, $48,000 per employee is wasted. Human capital management also includes managing the skills, experience, training, and availability of employee resources and external relationships.

IT portfolio management is almost always applied to human capital to optimize resource utilization. It can also be leveraged to facilitate project and asset portfolio optimization, identify and proactively manage retention risk, and assist with career pathing. Effective IT portfolio management applied to human capital requires an understanding of the available human capital, their skills and experiences, and the demand for their skills and experiences. Applying this technique enables better career pathing and retention risk identification.

Pairing IT human capital portfolio management with project portfolio management and asset portfolio management enables human resources to be optimally utilized by matching the supply of human resources and their skills and experiences with the demand for them. As asset management (i.e., operations) in most organizations is relatively stable, the focus is usually on the human capital portfolio in concert with the project portfolio to improve utilization of project delivery staff.

The human capital portfolio must link people management issues to the business and strategic objectives. These objectives are achieved when the company is using the right people in the right positions, with the added benefit of innovation and higher commitment levels (lower turnover, happier employees, better market position, etc.).

Developing the human capital portfolio includes identifying the desired portfolio of human resource capabilities and matching it against the actual case. The general steps in developing the IT human resources portfolio involve:

- Identifying the desired skills and experiences of the human capital portfolio.

- Collecting data on the existing human capital, often leveraging the skills database included in most portfolio management tools. Attributes for the human capital portfolio include:

- Competency/knowledge aligned with core business and technology processes
- Talent/skills for specialized areas or general problem solving
- Maturity level by process area or center of excellence
- Management skill level
- Business awareness skill level
- Technology-specific skills
- Communication skills
- Effectiveness/adaptability to respond to and enrich customer interactions
- Ability to learn
- Demographics of numbers of people by classification (job type), salary grade, geography, training, and title
- Assessing the current state of the human capital portfolio against the desired future state, paying careful attention to qualities and characteristics such as staff skills and experiences, utilization rates, and future demand for skills and experiences.
- Identifying portfolio gaps (e.g., skill shortages and overages, retention risks, etc.).
- Identifying gap-closing scenarios (e.g., training, hiring, outtasking/outsourcing, etc.).
- Creating a strategic resource management competency that focuses on the processes and skill sets of engaging internal and external resources.
- Assessing, monitoring, measuring, and reassessing actual versus projected performance, evaluating metrics and benchmarking data, and making changes to the framework as required. This may also include feeding important lessons learned and knowledge captured back into the system.

Leading-practice companies apply human capital management practices across the entire value chain and maintain the ability to staff up or staff down with internal or external resources for on-cycle and off-cycle needs. These companies understand that talent management is a critical differentiator. Attributes of these companies include:

- Higher retention rates and the ability to attract talent from top universities and leading companies
- A culture and organizational structure that embraces change, constantly empowering, challenging, and rewarding employees for attaining desired behaviors
- Reduced hierarchies and bureaucracies
- Development of a learning organization mentality

- Creation and sustainment of excellent relationships with employees and external entities

- Stellar communication, knowledge management, collaboration processes, and tools to change directions at a moment's notice

According to research, companies with highly mature human capital management processes have 50%+ greater commitment, productivity, and loyalty from their employees. Of extreme importance, however, is working through the human capital portfolio with the human resources department and possibly the legal department. Some information that is desirable to collect may not be lawful to collect. Some organizations benefit from diversity programs focusing actively on ensuring a balanced mix of such attributes as gender and ethnicity. Often, however, tracking this type of information is not lawful. While the potential benefits of an optimized human capital portfolio are enormous, careful attention must be paid to organization change management.

Application Portfolio*

Applications are the fulcrum of the IT asset portfolio (e.g., processes are automated and aggregated on applications). Research indicates that as many as 40% of existing applications can be retired in some way, and another 40% can benefit from reengineering, restructuring, or replacement. Exhibit 4.19 provides the definitions and elements of an application.

Accurately assessing the value/business benefit and total cost of ownership for an application is one of the more difficult challenges of the application portfolio as seen in Exhibit 4.20. The key to effective application portfolio management is to keep the overall goals in mind while continually questioning whether gathering information about a particular application attribute will enable a useful analysis. The long-term challenge is to perform this exercise regularly to keep information and analysis up-to-date with a high degree of automation. The overall goals include:

- Providing the basis for a consistent set of application-related discussions

- Communicating the status of the existing application set (including targets for decommissioning or sun-setting)

- Highlighting and aligning which applications support the business strategy and vision (and associated cost burden) and which applications are likely to constrain the business in the future

- Uncovering major issues associated with applications

---

*The authors would like to thank Val Sribar, Elizabeth Roche, and Willie Appel of META Group for their stellar contributions to this section.

EXHIBIT 4.19   APPLICATION DEFINITION AND APPLICATION
ELEMENTS

What Is an application?

An application is:
- An aggregation of software code impounding business logic and rules

- Transforming users or system input into data output

- For the purpose of automating and optimizing business functions, processes, tasks, and activities therein

But it could also be:
- A view of business processes at a point in time

- In the eye of the beholder

Today's view of an application finds that one person's application is another person's:
- Suite

- Module

- Procedure

- Function

Application origin:
- Custom built: any software application (in-house of bespoken or custom developed) built specifically to user

  requirements

- Configured: any commercial software package that has been upgraded or configured specifically to user

  requirements

- Commercial: any commercial software package that has been installed with only infrastructure configuration

Application types:
- Analytical: any application whose primary objective is to capture and store data in databases for query and

  analysis purposes

- Transactional: any application with its primary objective being the capture, exchange, or transfer of static data

  with standards or predefined reporting capabilities

- Collaborative: are across the company (e.g., e-mail, groupware, NetMeeting, web-based project planning,

  professional services). In the future, derivatives will extend the concept of applications to include extensions,

  modules such as composite applications and web services, that will further blur the definition of an application.

EXHIBIT 4.20   APPLICATION VALUE, BENEFITS, AND COSTS

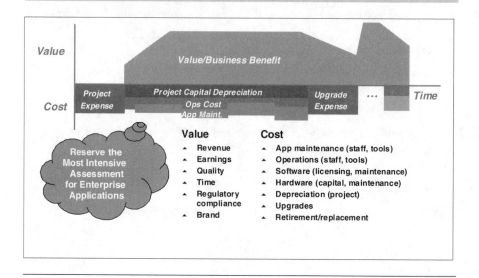

- Identifying how applications interact with each other to deliver key business processes
- Providing a "sanity check" framework to ensure that the current set of application-focused projects and programs is necessary, strategic, and not redundant
- Identifying potential new projects and programs
- Prioritizing the projects, programs, and maintenance activities that must be conducted to improve applications, delivering valued features and functionality faster
- Rationalizing and consolidating applications while aligning them to key business initiatives and strategies; driving decisions to possibly externalize applications
- Providing a detailed view of total application spending and identifying diminishing returns on investment, such as inadequate or high-cost infrastructure (trailing technologies), high core/nondiscretionary maintenance costs, large staff commitment to support legacy and heritage or end of life cycle systems
- Determining and forecasting staff skills and resource requirements
- Identifying applications that will be affected by new projects and other technology changes; balancing buy (commercial off-the-shelf) versus build (custom developed applications)

The first step in applying portfolio management to existing applications is to create a template of attributes that must be gathered and tracked for each application. Usually, this template is consistent for all applications, but there may be additional attributes for particular types. Similarly, company-wide infrastructure applications like e-mail may have different attributes or be included, instead, in the infrastructure portfolio.

Application attributes can be gathered into classes: general attributes, key business functions/processes/strategies enabled, overall business value, user information, technical condition, costs, and risk profile. General attributes are similar to those kept for any item in a portfolio. They are necessary to identify each application, understand its role, and catalog information such as whom to contact with questions about the application. They typically include:

- Name of application
- General description focusing on key capabilities the application provides, business processes it enables, user groups the application empowers, and how the application works at a high level
- Application type including details such as whether the applications is:
  - Business unit specific versus company-wide
  - Operational, analytical, collaborative, or hybrid
  - Customer-facing, internal, supplier–facing, or other external (e.g., contract manufacturer)
- Business owner(s) including the name(s) and contact information

Key business processes/functions enabled specify the business processes enabled by the application. More sophisticated organizations include information that is normally developed as part of a business architecture effort or the business process and functional requirements stage of a major business application project. This attribute information may include:

- Business process diagrams mapping how the application supports various processes and their interfaces
- Information maps highlighting how information is created and manipulated as well as who is responsible for various levels of information (e.g., the information steward)
- Data flows detailing how specific data types are defined, populated, stored, and managed throughout an application (or the creation of a centralized IT asset portfolio database as entire application portfolio)

Once the first two attribute classes are gathered, a diagram can be created (see Exhibit 4.21). Many companies that have large numbers of applications (>50) add

EXHIBIT 4.21 SAMPLE ENTERPRISE FRAMEWORK

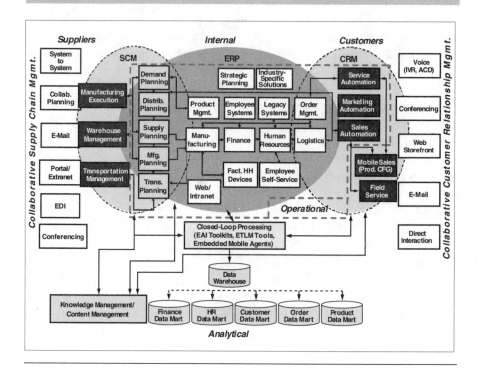

more details to the "application type" attribute to simplify the views, thus facilitating understanding and gaining consensus agreement. Applications can be aggregated into higher-level categories such as HR or finance. This diagram supports:

- Communication of what the application portfolio looks like and potential highlights of key issues/status (which applications need to be replaced or where gaps exist).

- Determining gaps by comparing a company's application portfolio diagram to a best-practice application model (e.g., for the CRM domain, comparing the diagram to the CRM Technology Ecosystem). Gaps can then be graphically represented and prioritized.

- In-progress application projects.

- The complexity of integration, showing some or all of the interactions among applications.

A more esoteric use for this type of diagram is as a sanity check during business continuity planning. Typically, this includes prioritizing the order in which applications will be recovered during a disaster. Because it is unlikely that all applications will come back up at once, the company can use this diagram to highlight functionality that will not be available in an application because of dependencies on other applications that may be lower on the restoration priority list.

Overall business value ideally focuses on a standardized (or agreed-on) set of value statements or categories. The most basic value statements associated with applications are that they empower users to do something with information or they automate a business process (resulting in specific value statements such as reducing costs, cutting cycle times, or improving quality). Best-in-class companies have developed value categories as part of how value is created and have captured them in an overall value management process. It is important to note that some applications will deliver on more than one value statement. Ideally, all types of value associated with an application are created and rolled into an overall value rating. Common value categories include:

- Increasing revenues, potentially with subcategories such as reaching new customers/markets, selling new products, upselling
- Reducing costs
- Reducing cycle times—for example, shortening sales cycles, reducing time to market for new products, accelerating delivery of products or services to customers, or shortening order-to-sales cycles
- Migrating risk by enabling or improving regulatory compliance, business continuity, and security

User information can range from basic descriptions to key user groups and number of users to feedback from the users on how well the application enables them:

- *User satisfaction:* The level of user happiness with a particular application is simply a litmus test that is often overlooked.
- *User competency:* Many application issues actually stem from users not being properly trained rather than core issues with the application. Simple questions to ask for this attribute include:
  - Does the application justify an investment in training?
  - Did users go through any training on the application?
  - How often do users go through a refresher or more advanced course?

User information attributes can lead to some interesting analysis:

- *Number of users:* One of the simplest ways to analyze existing applications is to identify which have the most users and which have the least users. Applications with the most users are usually worth analyzing in depth because anything that can be done to improve these applications is likely to have a dramatic impact on the portfolio. Applications with only a few users represent interesting targets for retirement, replacement by function from a more popular application, or application outsourcing to another party that may have a better economy of scale in this type of application (e.g., regulatory compliance applications that only one or two people actually use).

- *User satisfaction:* Applications that users are most frustrated with make a good target for replacement or major upgrades. An interesting way to corroborate finding from user surveys is to cross-reference results with help desk statistics on the number of trouble tickets associated with an application and application maintenance statistics on the number of change requests. It is often possible to create a compelling argument for addressing the root problem in the application simply based on savings in reduced help desk calls and application change requests.

Business process outsourcing impact is a much more sophisticated analysis that focuses on the impacts of outsourcing part of the business. Most companies spend little time analyzing the overall IT—and particularly application—impacts of outsourcing a part of the business (e.g., moving from internal distribution centers to a third-party logistics provider). If applications can be sorted by user group, this quickly creates an impact list of applications associated with outsourcing a particular user group:

- *Technical condition:* An applications technical condition can be viewed from the perspectives of strategic alignment with architectural principles and standards, operational condition, and overall technical condition.

- *Strategic alignment with architectural principles and standards:* Strategic alignment focuses on whether the application and its underlying components comply with the key principles and standards outlined in the enterprise solution architecture and enterprise technical architecture. In many cases, an application will comply with standards at a point in time. However, as a company's architecture evolves, the application can fall out of compliance, driving the need to upgrade or replace it. This reinforces the need to regularly update application attributes and conduct key analyses.

- *Operational condition:* Tactically focused, which often includes statistics gathered from the help desk or systems management software. These statistics often form the basis for particularly compelling arguments for application change. Indicators of an application's operational condition include the number of maintenance/service requests, average time to complete a service change, number of help desk trouble tickets, availability, and response time.

Applications with the highest numbers of service requests, trouble tickets, availability issues, and response time problems are all candidates for further analysis and investment. Sophisticated companies look across these attributes, identifying applications that have issues in multiple areas, and use this as the basis for a compelling argument to change the application.

Once an application's business value and technical condition have been determined, a higher-level portfolio analysis can be conducted as shown in Exhibit 4.22. Leading organizations periodically look at classes of applications and plot them based on their business value and technical condition:

- Applications ending up in the lower left quadrant have low business value and are in poor technical condition. They are candidates for retirement, consolidation, or replacement.

- Applications in the lower right quadrant have high business value but are in poor technical condition. They are candidates for reengineering and modernization.

- Applications in the upper left quadrant are in excellent technical condition but have low business value. They are candidates for reevaluation and repositioning.

EXHIBIT 4.22   VIEW OF TECHNICAL QUALITY AND BUSINESS VALUE FOR APPLICATIONS

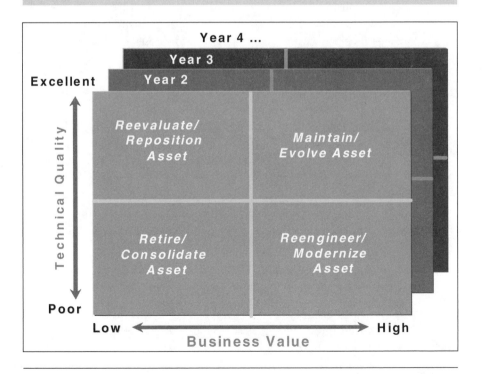

- Applications in the upper right quadrant have high business value and are in excellent technical condition. Counter to conventional wisdom, these applications are still worth worrying about. They must be carefully maintained and evolved; otherwise, they will end up in the lower left quadrant over time.

Cost is a key class of application attributes that must be tracked. Common cost attributes include:

- *Ongoing costs:* The expense required to keep an application running. These costs typically include:
  - *Operations:* Data center costs associated with running an application, such as personnel, systems management tools, facility costs (e.g., power), and process refinement.
  - *Maintenance:* Maintenance fees paid to the application software vendor as well as maintenance fees associated with underlying components such as databases, operating systems, servers, and storage.
  - *Licensing:* Costs associated with purchasing the application and periodically upgrading licenses as appropriate. These costs should also include any underlying infrastructure licenses (e.g., database licenses) that the application requires.
  - *Depreciation:* Some application project costs are capitalized, and their depreciation should be taken into account as part of the costs of the application. Financial Accounting Standards Board updates—FASB 1134—include capitalizing some or all of the costs to retire an asset.
- *Fixed versus variable costs:* A useful way to analyze costs to highlight for business executives which costs vary (and why) versus which costs remain fixed.
- *Direct versus indirect costs:* Some progressive companies recognize there are many indirect costs associated with an application, such as the revenue and productivity impacts of downtime. It is not worth calculating all these financials for most companies, but companies that need to be very complete may need to do this.
- *Costs to change/upgrade the application:* As upgrade requirements become better understood and scoped, these costs should be included in the overall cost of the application.
- *Replacement costs:* In some cases, it is important to know what it would cost to replace a system so that ongoing costs can be properly compared to replacement costs and effective decisions can be made.

Regarding the risk profile, business and IT executives are becoming increasingly aware of risk and are focusing on risk management. Applications exhibit many different kinds of risk, which should be identified, categorized, assessed, mitigated, and monitored. Primary application risk-related attributes include:

- *Security:* Applications vary widely in their security capabilities, which should be tracked as part of the overall portfolio. This attribute can be as basic as three levels: very secure, secure, and not secure. Companies with significant security concerns are much more sophisticated not only about application security but also about an overall information security program.

- *Business continuity:* Applications should be categorized from a business continuity priority–setting perspective. Ideally, a simple table showing applications that will be restored first versus later can be compared to the overall application portfolio diagram to ensure that proper priorities and expectations have been set. As with security, business continuity represents an entire set of disciplines and an overall program. Applications play a key role in business continuity planning but are only part of the picture.

- *Vendor viability:* The viability of the software vendor that created the application and any professional services firms that may be needed to maintain the application is of concern. In addition, some software packages are tightly tied to specific operating systems, databases, and hardware. The vendors of these underlying products must also be tracked from a business viability perspective.

- *Regulatory compliance:* Many application changes are driven by the need to keep up with regulators (e.g., FDA, FERC, FAA). The level of regulatory compliance is an important attribute to track for applications and information subject to regulations such as the privacy laws and guidelines of various countries.

- *Technical condition:* The technical condition attributes discussed previously feed into the risk analysis, since poor technical condition increases the risk of the application failing.

- *IT human resources:* Focuses on the fact that most organizations have a very small group of people who understand a particular business process well and understand how a particular application automates that process. As applications age, so do the people with these skill sets, creating a long-term risk that nobody will be around to support an aging application.

- *Project/program:* As applications require modifications, projects and programs are developed that carry their own risks of failure, running overbudget, missing deadlines, and possibly introducing defects into the operational ecosystem.

- *Privacy:* The increasing focus on privacy will likely drive many companies to raise this attribute out of the regulatory compliance bucket and make it a stand-alone attribute that is tracked.

- *Information risk:* The information created by applications has potential quality and legal retention issues that might need to be taken into account in a risk profile.

Rolling these risks into an overall risk rating is still very much more art than science. In fact, most companies have not gone far down the path of profiling the risk of an application. However, risk awareness at executive levels and regulatory issues will force many organizations to develop this aspect of their application portfolios.

Applying the Attributes

Analyzing the impact of moving to the next version of an application is an example of where a portfolio of existing applications is invaluable. The general attributes help anyone new to the environment quickly understand what the application does and who the key contacts are. The key business process/function-enabled attributes quickly identify which business processes, information types, and related applications will potentially be affected. The user information attributes identify which user groups must be consulted and managed through upgrade issues, potentially identifying training requirements or refining rollout timetables.

Technical condition attributes highlight the need for the new version of the application to conform to architectural principles and standards as well as specify operational shortcomings, which should ideally be addressed by the upgrade. Cost attributes are often invaluable in identifying the complete costs of a version upgrade, including changes in licensing and maintenance levels, as well as underlying component costs and operational impacts. Risk profile attributes effectively summarize many of the overall challenges associated with an upgrade by pulling together risks as disparate as regulatory compliance and project execution. Exhibit 4.23 shows an example of bringing these attributes together for a large customer service application.

Process assessment analysis demonstrates how well a particular application enables the types of processes that a business needs to go forward. The more an application is a barrier to driving the right business process changes, the more brittleness becomes an issue and should drive the retirement/decommissioning/major upgrade of the application.

Variations across business areas or geographies can lead to business process–level discussions addressing an interesting point: Should the process be consistent or are there reasons for local variations? This should lead to a pretty clear take on whether there should be multiple versions of a particular application.

Documenting and Balancing the Application Portfolio

The complexity of gathering, organizing, and analyzing the application portfolio will depend on the number of applications in the environment, the number of

EXHIBIT 4.23 SAMPLE ATTRIBUTES FOR APPLICATIONS

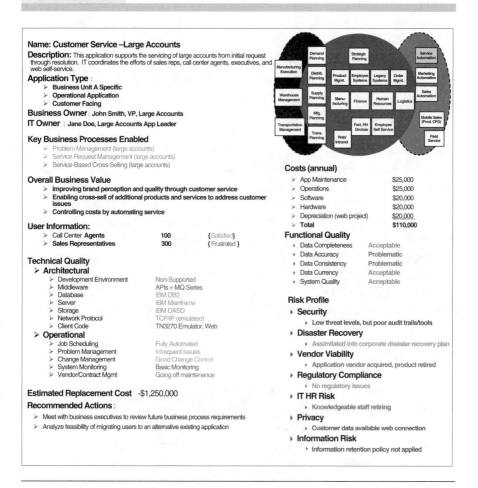

Name: Customer Service –Large Accounts

Description: This application supports the servicing of large accounts from initial request through resolution. IT coordinates the efforts of sales reps, call center agents, executives, and web self-service.

Application Type :
➢ **Business Unit A Specific**
➢ **Operational Application**
➢ **Customer Facing**

Business Owner : John Smith, VP, Large Accounts
IT Owner : Jane Doe, Large Accounts App Leader

Key Business Processes Enabled
➢ Problem Management (large accounts)
➢ Service Request Management (large accounts)
➢ Service-Based Cross-Selling (large accounts)

Overall Business Value
➢ Improving brand perception and quality through customer service
➢ Enabling cross-sell of additional products and services to address customer issues
➢ Controlling costs by automating service

User Information:
➢ Call Center **Agents**   100   {Satisfied}
➢ Sales **Representatives**   300   { Frustrated }

Technical Quality
➢ **Architectural**
   ➢ Development Environment   Non-Supported
   ➢ Middleware   APIs + MQ Series
   ➢ Database   IBM DB2
   ➢ Server   IBM Mainframe
   ➢ Storage   IBM DASD
   ➢ Network Protocol   TCP/IP (emulated)
   ➢ Client Code   TN3270 Emulator, Web
➢ **Operational**
   ➢ Job Scheduling   Fully Automated
   ➢ Problem Management   Infrequent Issues
   ➢ Change Management   Good Change Control
   ➢ System Monitoring   Basic Monitoring
   ➢ Vendor/Contract Mgmt   Going off maintenance

Estimated Replacement Cost -$1,250,000
Recommended Actions :
➢ Meet with business executives to review future business process requirements
➢ Analyze feasibility of migrating users to an alternative existing application

Costs (annual)
➢ App Maintenance $25,000
➢ Operations $25,000
➢ Software $20,000
➢ Hardware $20,000
➢ Depreciation (web project) $20,000
➢ Total   **$110,000**

Functional Quality
▸ Data Completeness   Acceptable
▸ Data Accuracy   Problematic
▸ Data Consistency   Problematic
▸ Data Currency   Acceptable
▸ System Quality   Acceptable

Risk Profile
▸ **Security**
   ▸ Low threat levels, but poor audit trails/tools
▸ **Disaster Recovery**
   ▸ Assimilated into corporate disaster recovery plan
▸ **Vendor Viability**
   ▸ Application vendor acquired, product retired
▸ **Regulatory Compliance**
   ▸ No regulatory issues
▸ **IT HR Risk**
   ▸ Knowledgeable staff retiring
▸ **Privacy**
   ▸ Customer data available web connection
▸ **Information Risk**
   ▸ Information retention policy not applied

---

attributes required for each application, and the types of analysis to be performed. In addition, the needs for ongoing updates and analysis must be considered. In the simplest case, and organization having relatively few applications (<10), wanting to assess relatively few attributes, and seeking only to "inventory" its applications (rather than perform sophisticated analyses) will be adequately served with a "low-tech" approach. Based on the answers to these questions, the options available are:

- *Unstructured manual* (e.g., Excel, Visio): manually gathering information, keeping it in spreadsheets, and performing analysis on spreadsheets. Any kind of dependency/relationship diagramming is done manually in Visio.

- *Structured manual* (e.g., database and Visio): manually gathering information and putting it into a relational database. Designing an appropriate schema to do the types of queries and analysis that need to be performed. Visio is used to manually produce diagrams.

- *Automated/advanced:* portfolio management software (see Chapter 6) from vendors can be configured automatically to collect data, automatically generate graphical diagrams, and make recommendations concerning portfolio balance.

The Big Picture

Many companies only have partial portfolio views of their applications—usually a by-product of some other analysis (e.g., during gap analysis for a top-down business initiative). The key is to take an iterative approach to applying portfolio management to existing applications. If the majority of application projects are already agreed to and well understood, the initial focus should be on just getting an accurate list of applications and some basic attributes (e.g., name, business process enabled, cost). As companies become more sophisticated in running IT as a business, the mapping of portfolio management disciplines to existing applications will become more sophisticated.

CONCLUSION

Portfolio management for the discovery, project, and asset portfolios categorizes investments in each of three phases of the IT life cycle, enabling decision makers to objectively inventory, evaluate, balance, analyze, align, and optimize investments according to defined criteria and scoring. For each portfolio there are processes for inventorying, analyzing, planning, tracking, and reviewing investments. There is no one-size-fits-all approach to IT portfolio management—the definitions of business and strategic objectives, value, risk, benefit, core dependencies, and priorities differ by company and by industry.

Chapter 5 discusses the overall process for doing IT portfolio management. Readers may want to refer back to Chapter 4 for descriptors of the IT life cycle processes and detailed information regarding the content and context of subportfolios.

NOTES

1. Robert G. Cooper, Scott J. Edgett, and Elko J. Kleinschmidt, "Optimizing the Stage-Gate Process: What Best-Practice Companies Do—II," *Research-Technology Management,* Nov.– Dec. 2002.

2. Robert G. Cooper, *Winning at New Products,* 3rd edition, Perseus Publishing, 2001.
3. Ibid.
4. Ibid.
5. Robert G. Cooper, Scott J. Edgett, and Elko J. Kleinschmidt, "Optimizing the Stage-Gate Process: What Best-Practice Companies Do—I," *Research-Technology Management,* Sept.–Oct. 2002.
6. Adapted from Peter Koen, Greg Ajamian, Robert Burkart, Allen Claman, Jeffrey Davidson, Robb D'Amore, Claudia Elkins, Kathy Herald, Michael Incorvia, Albert Johnson, Robin Karol, Rebecca Seibert, Aleksander Slavejkov, and Klaus Wagner, "Providing Clarity and a Common Language to the 'Fuzzy Front End,' " *Research-Technology Management,* March–April, 2001.
7. Ibid.
8. Ian S. Hayes, "Managing the Project Portfolio," Clarity Consulting, www.clarity-consulting.com.
9. Paul Belliveau, Abbie Griffen, and Stephen Somermeyer, *The PDMA Toolbook for New Product Development,* Chapter 1, John Wiley & Sons, April 2002.
10. Richard N. Foster, "Corporate Performance and Technological Change through Investors' Eyes," *Research-Technology Management,* Nov.–Dec. 2003.
11. Richard N. Foster, "Corporate Performance and Technological Change through Investors' Eyes," *Research-Technology Management,* Nov.–Dec. 2003.
12. Richard N. Foster, "Corporate Performance and Technological Change through Investors' Eyes," *Research-Technology Management,* Nov.–Dec. 2003.
13. Richard N. Foster, "Corporate Performance and Technological Change through Investors' Eyes," *Research-Technology Management,* Nov.–Dec. 2003.
14. Steve Roesenbush and Cliff Edwards, "Corporate Spending: Signs of Life," *Business Week,* July 14, 2003, p. 32.
15. R. Leifer, C. M. McDermott, G. C. Otonner, L. S. Peters, W. Veryzer, and M. Rice, *Radical Innovation.* Cambridge, MA: Harvard Business Press, 2000.
16. Stevens and Burley, "3,000 Raw Ideas = 1 Commercial Success," *Research and Technology Management,* May–June 1997.
17. Albert Johnson, "Industrial Research Institute's R&D Trends Forecast for 2004," Jan.–Feb. 2004.
18. www.compustat, October 2003.
19. Ian C. MacMillan and Rita Gunther McGrath, "Crafting R&D Project Portfolios," *Research-Technology Management,* Sept.–Oct. 2002.
20. Caroline Grattinger, Suzanne Garcia, Jeannine Sivly, Robert Schenk, and Peter VanSyckle, "Using Technology Readiness Levels Scale to Support Technology Management in the DoD's ATD/STO Environments," Carnegie Mellon Software Engineering Institute, Sept. 2002.
21. Ibid.
22. Peter A. Koen, "Understanding the Front End: A Common Language and Structured Picture," Stevens Institute of Technology, The Front End Innovation Conference, IIRUSA, 2004.
23. Ibid.
24. Ibid.
25. Robert G. Cooper, *Winning at New Products,* 3rd edition, Perseus Publishing, 2001.
26. Peter A. Koen, "Understanding the Front End: A Common Language and Structured Picture," Stevens Institute of Technology, The Front End Innovation Conference, IIRUSA, 2004.

27. Robert G. Cooper, *Winning at New Products,* 3rd edition, Perseus Publishing, 2001.

28. Paul Belliveau, Abbie Griffen, and Stephen Somermeyer, *The PDMA Toolbook for New Product Development,* Chapter 1, John Wiley & Sons, April 2002.

29. Peter A. Koen, "Understanding the Front End: A Common Language and Structured Picture," Stevens Institute of Technology, The Front End Innovation Conference, IIRUSA, 2004.

30. Paul Belliveau, Abbie Griffen, and Stephen Somermeyer, *The PDMA Toolbook for New Product Development,* Chapter 1, John Wiley & Sons, April 2002.

31. Ibid.

32. Richard E. Albright and Thomas A. Kappel, "Roadmapping in the Corporation," *Research-Technology Management,* Mar.–Apr. 2003.

33. Paul Belliveau, Abbie Griffen, and Stephen Somermeyer, *The PDMA Toolbook for New Product Development,* Chapter 1, John Wiley & Sons, April 2002.

34. Ibid.

35. Peter A. Koen, "Understanding the Front End: A Common Language and Structured Picture," Stevens Institute of Technology, The Front End Innovation Conference, IIRUSA, 2004.

36. PMBOK 1996 edition. Project Management Body of Knowledge, Project Management Institute, 1996.

37. Robert G. Cooper, Scott J. Edgett, and Elko J. Kleinschmidt, "Optimizing the Stage-Gate Process: What Best-Practice Companies Do—II, *Research-Technology Management,* Nov.–Dec. 2002.

38. Edward F. McDonough, III and Francis Spital, "Managing Project Portfolios," *R-Technology Management,* May–June 2003.

39. Ibid.

40. Adapted from Gina Colarelli O'Connor, Richard Hendricks, and Mark P. Rice, "Assessing Transition Readiness for Radical Innovation," *Research-Technology Management,* Nov.–Dec. 2002.

Technology Readiness Levels: Hardware and Software

Technology Readiness Level	Description (HW=Hardware; SW=Software)
1. Basic principles observed and reported	**HW:** Lowest level of technology readiness. Scientific research begins to be translated into applied research and development. Examples might include paper studies of a technology's basic properties.
	SW: Lowest level of software readiness. Basic research begins to be translated into applied research and development. Examples might include a concept that can be implemented in software or analytic studies of an algorithm's basic properties.
2. Technology concept and/or application formulated	**HW/SW:** Invention begins. Once basic principles are observed, practical applications can be invented. Applications are speculative and there may be no proof or detailed analysis to support the assumptions. Examples are limited to analytic studies.
3. Analytical and experimental critical function and/or characteristic proof of concept	**HW:** Active research and development is initiated. This includes analytical studies and laboratory studies to physically validate analytical predictions of separate elements of the technology. Examples include components that are not yet integrated or representative.
	SW: Active research and development is initiated. This includes analytical studies to produce code that validates analytical predictions of separate software elements of the technology. Examples include software components that are not yet integrated or representative but satisfy an operational need. Algorithms run on a surrogate processor in a laboratory environment.

Technology Readiness Level	Description
4. Component and/or bread-board validation in laboratory environment	**HW:** Basic technological components are integrated to establish that they will work together. This is relatively low fidelity compared to the eventual system. Examples include integration of ad hoc hardware in the laboratory.
	SW: Basic software components are integrated to establish that they will work together. They are relatively primitive with regard to efficiency and reliability compared to the eventual system. System software architecture development initiated to include interoperability, reliability, maintainability, extensibility, scalability, and security issues. Software integrated with simulated current/legacy elements as appropriate.
5. Component and/or bread-board validation in relevant environment	**HW:** Fidelity of bread-board technology increases significantly. The basic technological components are integrated with reasonably realistic supporting elements so that they can be tested in a simulated environment. Examples include high-fidelity laboratory integration of components.
	SW: Reliability of software ensemble increases significantly. The basic software components are integrated with reasonably realistic supporting elements so that they can be tested in a simulated environment. Examples include high-fidelity laboratory integration of software components.
	System software architecture established. Algorithms run on a processor(s) with characteristics expected in the operational environment. Software releases are "alpha" versions and configuration control is initiated. Verification, Validation, and Accreditation (VV&A) initiated.
6. System/subsystem model or prototype demonstration in a relevant environment	**HW:** Representative model or prototype system, which is well beyond that of TRL 5, is tested in a relevant environment. Represents a major step up in a technology's demonstrated readiness. Examples include testing a prototype in a high-fidelity laboratory environment or in a simulated operational environment.
	SW: Representative model or prototype system, which is well beyond that of TRL 5, is tested in a relevant environment. Represents a major step up in software-demonstrated readiness. Examples include testing a

Technology Readiness Level	Description
	prototype in a live/virtual experiment or in a simulated operational environment. Algorithms run on processor of the operational environment are integrated with actual external entities. Software releases are "beta" versions and configuration controlled. Software support structure is in development. VV&A is in process.
7. System prototype demonstration in an operational environment	**HW:** Prototype near or at planned operational system. Represents a major step up from TRL 6, requiring demonstration of an actual system prototype in an operational environment such as an aircraft, vehicle, or space. Examples include testing the prototype in a test bed aircraft.
	SW: Represents a major step up from TRL 6, requiring the demonstration of an actual system prototype in an operational environment, such as in a command post or air/ground vehicle. Algorithms run on processor of the operational environment are integrated with actual external entities. Software support structure is in place. Software releases are in distinct versions. Frequency and severity of software deficiency reports do not significantly degrade functionality or performance. VV&A completed.
8. Actual system completed and qualified through test and demonstration	**HW:** Technology has been proven to work in its final form and under expected conditions. In almost all cases, this TRL represents the end of true system development. Examples include developmental test and evaluation of the system in its intended weapon system to determine if it meets design specifications.
	SW: Software has been demonstrated to work in its final form and under expected conditions. In most cases, this TRL represents the end of system development. Examples include test and evaluation of the software in its intended system to determine if it meets design specifications. Software releases are production versions and configuration controlled in a secure environment. Software deficiencies are rapidly resolved through support infrastructure.
9. Actual system proven through successful mission operations	**HW:** Actual application of the technology in its final form and under mission conditions, such as those encountered in operational test and evaluation. Examples include using the system under operational mission conditions.

Technology Readiness Level	Description
	SW: Actual application of the software in its final form and under mission conditions, such as those encountered in operational test and evaluation. In almost all cases, this is the end of the last "bug-fixing" aspects of the system development. Examples include using the system under operational mission conditions. Software releases are production versions and configuration controlled. Frequency and severity of software deficiencies are at a minimum.

Special permission to reproduce Appendix . . . [4A] from "Using the Technology Readiness Levels Scale to Support Technology Management in the DoD's ATD/STO Environments," Copyright © 2002 by Carnegie Mellon University, is granted by the Software Engineering Institute.

Building the IT Portfolio

INTRODUCTION

Overview

There is no single best practice for building or improving the IT portfolio. IT portfolio management is a fluid and dynamic process of trying to create and maintain the perfect homeostasis between optimizing capacity and demand against a series of criteria and constraints whereby:

- New discovery initiatives and projects are evaluated, selected, and prioritized
- Priorities of active projects are constantly being updated and evaluated
- Existing assets may be maintained, reengineered, phased out, or repositioned[1]

Building and maintaining the IT portfolio is a balancing act that is both an art and a science. It is an art due to the nonnumeric, subjective, qualitative, intangible, and uncertain variables factored into evaluating and assessing IT investments and the IT portfolio. It is a science due to the numeric, objective, quantitative, tangible, and reliable information and data that are also used for evaluation and assessment. The importance and criticality, and thus the weighting and priority, of the art and the science vary by company and by industry. In addition, rankings of these factors are constantly being adjusted due to continuous internal and external changes and events. There are three critical factors to keep in mind throughout this chapter:

1. The IT portfolio management process and framework do not make decisions—people do!
2. All models shown in this chapter, however sophisticated, in and of themselves are only partial representations of the realities they are meant to reflect.

3. People with varying functional and disciplinary perspectives must buy in to the IT portfolio management process for it to be successful.[2]

Building the IT portfolio employs portfolio management techniques for investment, resource planning, and decision making to identify and select trade-offs involving costs, benefits, risks, and timing. Trade-offs for IT portfolio management are not limited to financial measures such as return on investment (ROI) and net present value (NPV) of a specific investment. Many other factors can and often should be included such as:

- Business and strategic fit
- User/customer needs
- Risks versus return
- Balance and diversification
- Trends
- Architectural impact
- Human resource capabilities and core competencies
- Intangible benefits
- Constraints due to costs, resource capacity, and scheduling
- Resource allocation
- Timing
- Practicality
- Interdependencies and correlations created between projects and existing investments
- Core capabilities

The IT portfolio management framework assigns weighting and criteria to these factors. An emphasis on one or a few of the factors at the expense of others will possibly lead to far different results. For instance, an emphasis on minimizing risks would lead IT investments (and the IT portfolio) to demonstrating poor shareholder returns (value) and many unhappy employees whose compensation might be tied to the performance of the company. The magic is identifying the critical parameters and obtaining the right emphasis and the right ranking of these factors, which are dependent on current and future internal and external priorities, conditions, trends, and events. Multiple iterations and trade-offs occur that require knowing which potential and existing investments are essential to meeting business objectives and which are undervalued, overvalued, redundant, and show diminishing rates of return. Research indicates that fewer than 10% of global 2000 organizations adequately measure indirect costs and benefits, confining their analyses to direct financial impacts.

A balance between the rigor in which a portfolio management process is applied (high accuracy) and the level of precision required to make a decision must be determined. The amount of data collected and time required to reach a decision should be determined by the impact, criticality, size, and duration of an investment. However, diminishing marginal returns can result from collecting and analyzing too much data over a long period of time.

IT investment decisions in the discovery and project phases can be based on reasonably accurate estimates. Although the authors present advanced modeling and simulation techniques for valuing investments, highly detailed financial modeling, granular project and task plans, and comprehensive revenue and cost estimates to assess each potential discovery or project investment can be inefficient and do not necessarily translate into better decision making.[3] Summary level data and estimates are usually reliable indicators, assuming that historical data are reasonably accurate, benchmarking data are attainable, and accounting systems and forecasts are kept up-to-date. However, if estimates consistently prove to be unreliable, assess the source of the information, the methodology behind the estimating techniques, and the assumptions used.

Before going into detail about the IT portfolio management stages and accompanying tasks, it is important to understand that business strategies drive company priorities. They might include improving productivity, expanding into new markets, transitioning from a product-based to a service-based entity, or developing new products and solutions. Strategic fit/alignment between an IT investment (or the IT portfolio) and business and strategic objectives are key factors in making portfolio decisions, so it follows that understanding business strategy is vital. In many instances, business strategy is not readily available or does not exist. This is why strategic drift, or the difference between actual strategy and intended strategy, is so wide and pervasive in many companies—all projects essentially fit the de facto strategy.

In their book *The Discipline of Market Leaders*,[4] Treacy and Wiersma maintain that there are only three real strategies: customer intimacy, operational efficiency, and product excellence. They assert that you must be excellent at one and good at the other two. In the absence of defined strategy, the Treacy and Wiersma hypothesis may be leveraged. Annual reports, internal communications, strategic intent, and interviews with key stakeholders are effective means to unearth and uncover business strategy. Beyond the shortfalls of not having a business strategy, there are other blind spots as shown in Exhibit 5.1 that can derail the IT portfolio management effort.

As previously indicated, the primary reasons IT portfolio management processes are not executed successfully are due to people aspects. At its bear essence, IT portfolio management is a people process—it is about gaining consensus and effecting change. Achieving the highest level of IT portfolio management maturity requires

EXHIBIT 5.1   AREAS THAT HAVE DERAILED PORTFOLIO
               MANAGEMENT EFFORTS

- Lack of support and failure of buy-in from key stakeholders and gatekeepers
- Inability to modify behaviors—people naturally resist change. Employees feel most confident when the status quo is being met. Changes such as new systems, measurement, and data visibility may not be readily accepted.
- Methods too complex. Users afraid to use them.
- Little to no education about the model given to users, who misinterpret its meaning and function.
- False sense of accuracy. IT portfolio management can only be as accurate as its estimates are.
- Too much reliability on the IT portfolio management output. IT portfolio management output should not be a substitute for strategic analysis and optimization discussions or common sense.
- Few in the company who truly understand how to use the IT portfolio management methods.
- Hard to acquire data and information (e.g., resource constraints).
- Models used in IT portfolio management are inadequate to fit the nature of the investments. This might originate from the wrong definition of model needs or from a changed environment that makes the models obsolete.
- People still try and game the system; therefore, IT portfolio management is used for political maneuvering.

Sources: Adapted from:

Archer N. P., and Ghasemzadeh F. (1996). "Project Portfolio Selection Techniques: A Review and a Suggested Integration Approach," *Innovation Research Working Group Working Paper No. 46,* McMaster University.

Felli J. C., Kochevar R. E., and Gritton B. R. (2000). "Rethinking Project Selection at the Monterey Bay Aquarium," *Interfaces,* 30/6, pp. 49–63.

Jackson B. (1983). "Decision Methods for Selecting a Portfolio of R&D Projects," *Research Management,* Sept.–Oct., pp. 21–26.

Lee J., Lee S., and Bae Z. (1986). "R&D Project Selection: Behavior and Practice in a Newly Industrializing Country," *IEEE Transactions on Engineering Management,* EM-33/3, pp. 141–147.

Levine, H. A. (1999). "Project Portfolio Management: A Song Without Words?" *PM Network,* 13/7, pp. 25–27.

Loch C. H., Pich M. T., Terwiesch C., and Urbschat M. (2001). "Selecting R&D Projects at BMW: A Case Study of Adopting Mathematical Programming Models," *IEEE Transactions on Engineering Management,* 48/1, pp. 70–80.

Martikainen, Juha (2002)."Portfolio Management of Strategic Investment in the Metal Industry," master's thesis, Helsinki University of Technology, January.

Steele L. W. (1988). "What We've Learned—Selecting R&D Programs and Objectives," *Research Technology Management,* Mar.–Apr., pp. 17–36.

a new mindset that is not pervasive in the majority of companies we have studied. The new mindset requires IT to run as a business, defining and widely communicating business strategies, providing measurable returns, and delivering business value and results.[5] In this chapter, the major steps in building and optimizing the IT portfolio are identified. Effectively building and applying IT portfolio management is discussed. The objectives for this chapter are to enable the reader to:

- Identify the business climate and major capabilities that must be in place to establish an IT portfolio management framework
- Present a high-level step-by-step road map of how to build and sustain an IT portfolio management framework, quantifying business value and risks
- Show how to assess the current as-is state, discuss the to-be state, and identify resulting gaps in each major phase of IT portfolio management
- Demonstrate processes, tools, practices, approaches, and metrics for each stage of IT portfolio management
- Discuss where to begin applying or improving IT portfolio management

Building the IT portfolio should result in:

- Institutionalized management processes that are defined, documented, and easily accessible for creating, assessing, and balancing the portfolio. These processes can be repeated and are consistent.
- Regularly validating costs, benefits, and risk data used to support IT investment decisions. The information and data are accurate, reliable, and up-to-date, forming the basis for grounded decision making.
- Focusing on continuously measuring and evaluating progress and results.
  - Assess the effectiveness of the IT portfolio management process.
  - Determine the impact on performance.
  - Evaluate efficiency of the generation of relevant data and decision-making processes.
  - Assess the completeness as to how faithfully the processes, stages, and activities are being followed across the company and how often investments are being revisited.[6]

Prior to discussing the stages and tasks associated with building the IT portfolio, three important staples of IT portfolio management are briefly described: value, risks, and costs. Companies must have a keen understanding of IT and business with respect to value, risks, and costs. Throughout this chapter, additional detailed information is provided in these three areas.

Value

Information about transactions has often become equal to if not more important than the transactions themselves (e.g., stock market performance, express package tracking, etc.). Technology enables specific information and performance attributes (e.g., timeliness, accessibility, quality, and accuracy), which in turn determines its value. IT management will increasingly be judged on its ability to increase information value.

Value is derived when the benefits of an investment exceed its costs. However, defining the benefits and costs for a future investment is subject to the interpretation of key stakeholders and gatekeepers. What might be valuable to one stakeholder might not be to another. Benefits can be based on intangibles (e.g., customer satisfaction, improvements to core competencies, etc.) that might not be obvious and highly visible to some decision makers. Gaining consensus as to what value means and how it is measured can be challenging. Often, individuals project their own value system onto their business and IT decisions. IT portfolio management is a technique that can be used to articulate the core values of the company so that decisions can be made that align with those values.

In order to optimize value in the IT portfolio, there must be agreement and alignment between IT and business regarding the definition of value and how each can mutually contribute to establishing value. IT portfolio management helps align IT efforts with business efforts to maximize value. However, if value is not understood within the enterprise, IT portfolio management will fail. A listing of value categories and value factors can be found in Appendix 5A.

It is not unusual to see differing opinions among senior management regarding their priorities of value drivers, as shown in Exhibit 5.2 from United Management Technologies. Risk tolerance, current trends, interpretation of data presented, personal and political agendas, and other potential blockers all impact the ability to reach consensus on value priorities as shown on the left side of this exhibit. The right side shows that senior management has reached consensus.

IT portfolio management must constantly drive and deliver value to succeed. Driving value means knowing what is valued at all times. Value must be approached from key stakeholder perspectives (this chapter addresses the key stakeholder assessment, which identifies key stakeholder values). Value must be communicated. IT portfolio management must not only drive value but communicate this value again and again. Thus, an integral part of the IT portfolio management process is understanding what the company values, what key stakeholders value, and ensuring that both the company and key stakeholders understand the value proposition set forth through IT portfolio management. The analog in the investment world is understanding the financial objectives of the individual investor prior to developing the investment portfolio. Some value

EXHIBIT 5.2   DIVERGENCE AND CONVERGENCE REGARDING
VALUE DRIVER PRIORITIES

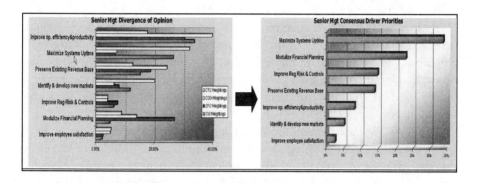

Source: Copyright © 2004 United Management Technologies (UMT), www.umt.com.

security and safety of principles over higher returns, whereas others value socially conscious investments.

Risks

Most people do not know what risk is. They just know they do not like it! And, according to research, less than 10% of global 2000 organizations proactively manage and quantify portfolio risk. For all intents and purposes, risk is the potential deviation from expected results. Risks can negatively impact the costs of investments through dramatic change in scope and unplanned funding requirements. They can impact other interdependent projects, therefore delaying value, influencing schedules, affecting performance, and causing a loss of trust, confidence, and competitive advantage. There is a correlation between identifying and mitigating risks and the probability for a successful outcome.

Positive risk can occur in IT. For example, projects can be ahead of schedule, or greater than expected e-business activity can occur. Both of these positive risks can result in negative risks downstream. If there are dependencies in project resources or if operational bottlenecks in supporting operational systems develop as a result of increased e-business activity, many negative risks such as resource contentions and customer dissatisfaction can occur.

Risk must be evaluated for individual investments and assessed across the entire portfolio. In IT, operational risk is usually managed via a business continuity plan or disaster recovery plan. For IT projects, however, only half of global 2000 organizations do a risk assessment prior to starting the project; of those, only 50% ever look at the risk assessment again throughout the life of the project. Thus, only 25% of IT projects proactively do risk assessment. An example of risk categories and risk factors is shown in Appendix 5B.

Business and IT management must reach consensus as to the allowable boundaries and risk thresholds. Companies evaluate risk based on a range of scenarios (high/medium/low, short term/long term, etc.), or for financial measures they adjust hurdle rates (the higher the hurdle rate, the less attractive the net present value) based on a multitude of parameters such as geography, business unit, or type of investment.

Exhibit 5.3 shows the steps for identifying risks, risk tolerance levels, and risk types; gathering and evaluating alternative risk mitigation/elimination strategies; and determining residual risks. Risk assessment and management processes within IT and the business must be standardized and instituted. Information stemming from the risk assessment and management processes must roll up into the IT portfolio and must be further consolidated into the enterprise risk management program. Leading organizations factor project risk into their budgets and plans as processes for risk assessment and risk management become more quantitative, incorporating historical metrics, much the way actuarial information is used in the insurance industry. Failure to incorporate adequate risk assessment and management into the enterprise solution portfolio will likely lead to undesirable outcomes as companies take on overlapping initiatives.

Costs

Financial constraints (i.e., IT budgets) are a major limiting resource facing companies when evaluating IT investments. Miscalculating the procurement, development, integration, and execution costs for a potential IT investment, as well as incorrectly estimating the total cost of ownership (e.g., upgrades, maintenance and support, management, enhancements, increase in rates) for new and existing IT investments, could have devastating consequences. Redundant investments, poor prioritization of investments, and unwillingness to retire existing investments or kill IT projects create a tremendous drain on IT costs, essentially suffocating IT investments that could add significant value and competitive advantage to a company.

As previously mentioned, costs are correlated with the value delivered by an investment. Business and IT must carefully monitor the cost aspects of the IT portfolio, assuring that cost savings (e.g., as a result of retiring existing assets or canceling IT projects) are accounted for and reinvested back into areas such as grow the business and transform the business. Employees must be held accountable to assure this reinvestment cycle is efficient and effective.

EXHIBIT 5.3 RISK AND IT PORTFOLIO MANAGEMENT

1. Determine the company's position on risk.
   a. Rate the organizations relative tolerance for risk that is consistent with the company's culture.
2. Identify risk categories. For example:
   a. Conditions—internal or external changes (e.g., geopolitical, legislative, economic) will occur in a manner that negatively impacts the portfolio.
   b. Culture—the culture of the company will not embrace change imparted through the portfolio.
   c. Complexity—complexity of the portfolio or its components will lead to higher probability for rejection of failure.
   d. Cooperation—questionable cooperation of key stakeholders, internal or external, leading to change in expected results.
3. Inventory IT risks, IT risk mitigation strategies, and impact of the IT risk.
   a. CobiT, described in Chapter 3, is a process used to audit risks.
4. Assess risks and validate alignment with company risk threshold levels (individual investments as well as entire portfolio).
   a. Risks are assessed based on evaluating the threat (deliberate or accidental), the vulnerabilities, and the business impact to the company.
   b. Identify all statutory and contractual requirements.
   c. Determine unique set of risks (security, other requirements) to the company's assets.
   d. Identify the nature, business purpose, and environment of business information and systems.
5. Evaluate IT risk mitigation strategies that could lower the IT inventoried risks.
   a. Diversification: share/consolidate, avoid, control, and accept.
   b. Balance IT risks with business rewards and prudent controls.
6. Assess the residual IT risks (the risks that remain after applying risk mitigation strategies). This is IT's equivalent to a financial stop-loss. For example:
   a. Determine the probability of the risk occurring (i.e., complete loss of data and information).
   b. Evaluate and determine contingencies for residual risk.
   c. If the risk occurs, what is the potential impact of the risk?
   d. Determine the degree of project risk the company is willing to accept: complexity, size, slippage, or even importance.
   e. Determine the amount of portfolio risk the company is willing to accept both on portfolio and subportfolio levels.
7. Determine risk goals, performance metrics, triggers, and communication. For example:
   a. Map risks into IT portfolio management processes.
   b. The types/kinds of events that trigger a risk, or elevated risk notification.
   c. The process of how risks are communicated and how are they managed/governed.

Achieving a balance between fixed- (i.e., in-house resources) versus variable- (i.e., outsourcing) cost strategies also drives cost efficiencies. Companies must become adept at quickly shifting their portfolio mix between fixed and variable costs, as their business postures shift between growth and contraction. Fixed IT costs are long-term expenditures (more than one year) to which an organization has committed. Typically, these costs include hardware depreciation/lease payments, capitalized development expenses, maintenance, long-term software licenses, and salaried personnel. Variable costs are expenditures that change in the near term (less than three months) based on changing business volumes, usage, or staffing levels. These costs typically include per-seat software licenses, training, and the incremental storage and server capacity required to support near-term growth. Many industry providers (e.g., hardware, software, networking) have been moving to on-demand options for technology products and services that will add new dimensions to variable-cost strategies.

Business and IT use many processes and tools within the IT portfolio management process to monitor and control costs and assure business alignment—for example:

- The business alignment scorecard, as shown in Exhibit 5.4, shows the relative cost % versus driver priorities % (as determined by the stakeholder assessment), strategic intent, and business strategy.

- Real options, a mathematical model used to create a series of decision points to buy, hold, or sell an investment, is an important method for assessing risks and cost exposures. This will be discussed further.

- The IT life cycle discussed in Chapter 4 is based on the practice of maintaining a series of decision points throughout the life span of investments, thereby frequently and continuously monitoring costs.

Key Stages in Building the IT Portfolio

Exhibit 5.5 shows the eight general stages for IT portfolio building: game plan, planning, creating, assessing, balancing, communicating, governance and organization, and assessing execution. They appear as a waterfall approach. However, there is a high degree of iteration that takes place between these stages, and, in practice, these processes are not linear or sequential. They are collaborative and spiral. This cyclical process provides feedback loops for continuous assessment, validation, and improvement.

The remainder of this chapter will describe each stage in building the IT portfolio and provide a description of the tasks and activities associated with each of these stages. The tasks and activities are flexible. If the tasks in the stages do not

EXHIBIT 5.4   BUSINESS ALIGNMENT SCORECARD

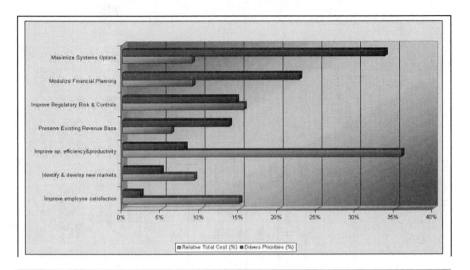

Source: Copyright © 2004 United Management Technologies (UMT), www.umt.com.

address the readers objectives, don't do them. If tasks need to be added in order to meet stated objectives for IT portfolio management, then add them to the plan.

STAGE I: GAME PLAN

The strategic planning aspects of the IT portfolio are created and solidified in the game plan stage. Goals for IT portfolio management should be identified:

- Outline how broad and deep the portfolio should be (objectives aligned with capabilities and maturity).
- Examine what measurable expectations and needs exist.
- Look at planned asset life cycles.
- List migration decisions.
- Identify risk/reward boundaries.

A common mistake is wanting to set the world on fire without any matches. Goals and objectives must be achievable. If goals are not attainable because of lack of resources, schedule or cost constraints, or cultural issues, change the goals. Changing goals is not an uncommon practice.

EXHIBIT 5.5 EIGHT STAGES OF IT PORTFOLIO BUILDING

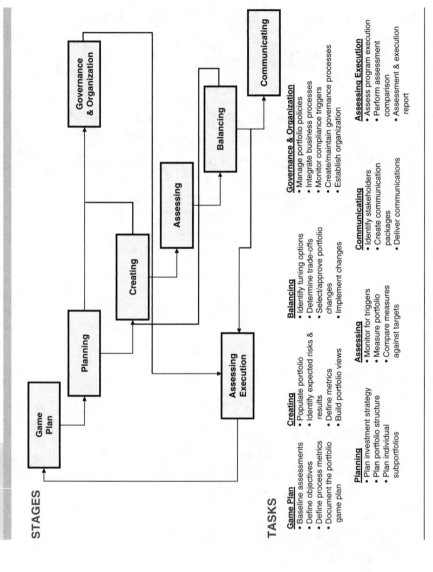

STAGES

TASKS

Game Plan
- Baseline assessments
- Define objectives
- Define process metrics
- Document the portfolio game plan

Planning
- Plan investment strategy
- Plan portfolio structure
- Plan individual subportfolios

Creating
- Populate portfolio
- Identify expected risks & results
- Define metrics
- Build portfolio views

Balancing
- Identify tuning options
- Determine trade-offs
- Select/approve portfolio changes
- Implement changes

Assessing
- Monitor for triggers
- Measure portfolio
- Compare measures against targets

Governance & Organization
- Manage portfolio policies
- Integrate business processes
- Monitor compliance triggers
- Create/maintain governance processes
- Establish organization

Communicating
- Identify stakeholders
- Create communication packages
- Deliver communications

Assessing Execution
- Assess program execution
- Perform assessment comparison
- Assessment & execution report

Exhibit 5.6 outlines the specific tasks and activities involved in developing the game plan. The critical activities of the tasks shown in Exhibit 5.6 that are addressed in this section include:

- Perform baseline assessments to develop an understanding of capabilities and resource constraints
- Define (or most probably refine) objectives for doing portfolio management
- Develop metrics and success criteria to demonstrate success
- Create the portfolio management game plan including the work effort, resources required (people, process, technology, tools, and facilities), steps and activities that need to be performed, key milestones, timetables, and goals

Refer also to Chapter 2 for additional information on the game plan.

Baseline Assessment

The activities assessed in this task are:

- Readiness
- Business–IT credibility and dependency
- IT portfolio management maturity
- Capabilities

The baseline assessment determines the current strategic and operational environment (assessing readiness and maturity), and it ascertains the readiness and commitment of the company to IT portfolio management (assessing capability and capability/dependency relationships). This assessment sets the foundational elements needed to identify many of the critical components of the subsequent stages.

Assess Readiness

A thorough readiness assessment can be very complex and time-consuming. Assessing readiness involves understanding the current as-is state of IT portfolio management and determining the future to-be goals of the business and IT portfolio management. The gaps between these two states and understanding what problems and issues IT portfolio management is trying to solve are critical to efficiently and effectively gauging readiness. Setting specific time-box goals and detailed work breakdown structures will help focus a company's efforts on achieving desired IT portfolio management maturity levels.

One of the most important tools for assessing readiness and evaluating the current as-is versus desired to-be states is the stakeholder assessment. This tool identifies and ranks an individual's priorities and values. The stakeholder analysis tool also identifies goals, objectives, and what will make a stakeholder successful (critical

EXHIBIT 5.6 DETAILED TASKS IN DEVELOPING THE GAME PLAN

Iterate Throughout These Tasks →

Baseline Assessments

Readiness Assessment As-Is State	Validate and Refine Readiness Assessment	Assess IT Portfolio Management Maturity Model	Gap Analysis and Assess Capabilities	Define Objectives	Define Process Metrics	Document the Game Plan

• Define information and analysis needs
• Collect information and data
  - Interviews
  - Baseline research
  - Benchmarking
  - Surveys
  - Focus groups
• Develop an understanding of some of the problems and issues
  - Identify potential low hanging problems that can be solved
• Level set on the definition, upper and lower limits, and parameters regarding value, cost, and risk
	• Present initial findings to executive management
	• Obtain concurrence on priorities and direction
	• Seek additional data and information
		• Evaluate readiness assessment against the IT portfolio management maturity model in Chapter 2
		• Determine optimal end state in the maturity model (e.g., level 3, level 4)
			• Identify specific gaps that exist between the results of the readiness assessment and the desired end state as determined by the maturity model
			• Assess capabilities as-is state and compare against gap analysis to determine if adequate resources currently exist to close gaps
			• For those gaps that do not close with current resources, determine options (and potential resistance) for closing gaps (buy, build, hire, lease, alliance, outsource, etc.)
				• Based on results of the gap and capability assessment, develop a list of priorities and focus areas to allocate resources
				• Evaluate importance and urgency of each element above:
				  - Perform customer segmentation
				  - Identify areas of low hanging opportunities to solve real issues and problems
				• Assure that defined objectives are traceable to the business strategy
					• Define metrics that measure and monitor the processes and improvements that are in-work as well as completed
					• Metrics should include both tangible and intangible assets
					• Process metrics should include incentives and rewards for employees in attaining goals and milestones as provided in the objectives
						• The plan captures and synthesizes the data and information obtained in the prior tasks
						• The plan contains the charter for IT portfolio mgmt and includes:
						  - Purpose
						  - Goals
						  - Scope
						  - Expectations
						  - Governance
						  - Policies
						  - Guidelines
						  - Processes
						  - Metrics
						  - Work effort and action plans with milestones and time-tables
						• Communicate with key stakeholders; seek consensus and approval to proceed to the next stage

success factors, key performance indicators, current state and desired state). An example is shown in Exhibit 5.7.

Unfortunately, it is not unusual to see companies that have not considered the strategic planning aspects and thus dive in head first. Performing a readiness assessment is the first step in laying the foundation and defining the basics of how much change can be effected based on the company's maturity in several dimensions. Exhibit 5.8 provides a simple assessment for companies to consider as they assess additional readiness factors for IT portfolio management. Appendix 5C provides a more detailed listing of three areas: business diagnostic, internal diagnostic, and operational diagnostic.

Assess Business–IT Credibility and Dependency

Performance is often taken for granted. As business executives see the swelling of the expense line item for IT, they continue to ask how to get more for less. "Better, faster, cheaper," and "free, perfect, now" have become the new buzzword phrases to express this sentiment. IT management must be prepared to manage value

EXHIBIT 5.7   STAKEHOLDER ASSESSMENT

Stakeholders	(Indicate specific stakeholders in column)	Critical Success Factors	Strategy	Key Performance Indicators	Current State	Desired State	Processes	Owners
		Enter the critical success factors (CSF) for each stakeholder	Enter the strategy that is the basis for achieving their critical success factors	Enter the key performance indicators that are indexes that measure the capacity to reach those critical success factors	Enter the current state (actual results of KPI)	Enter the desired state (desired results of KPI)	Enter the processes that impact current KPI	Enter the process owners who can provide additional information to align the solution to reach the desired state
CEO								
CFO								
CIO								
Sourcing								
Human Resources								
Legal								
BU Leads								
Cust1								
Cust2								
Cust3								

EXHIBIT 5.8 READINESS ASSESSMENT

1. Capability, maturity, and core competency: How ready is the company to adopt, mature, or increase the scope of IT portfolio management? How mature is the company's portfolio management process? What capabilities exist within the company to do IT portfolio management?
2. Value management process: How credible is IT in the eyes of the business? How dependent does the business feel it is on technology solutions?
3. Project prioritization process: How defined is the project prioritization process? Is it highly defined? Is it ad hoc? Nonexistent?
4. Program management: How mature are the project and program management processes within the enterprise? Do project managers require certification to be project managers? Do standardized project templates exist and are they in use? Are there standard program and project management processes?
5. Enterprise architecture: Is an enterprise architecture present? Is the enterprise architecture refined enough for analyzing portfolio components?
6. Governance: Is IT governed? Are consistent processes and policies in place and used? Do governing bodies exist to set and enforce policies and processes?
7. Measurement: Is an active metrics program in place? Is a formal estimating process in place? Do performance evaluation metrics exist and are they used for process improvement?
8. Product/Services Catalog: Does an IT products and services catalog exist to understand what is available within IT and its associated costs?

relationships (ultimately, to manage both perceived and real value) while quantitatively accounting for IT's contribution to key drivers that support business objectives.

Exhibit 5.9 illustrates how many IT management organizations within companies must change business perceptions from IT simply supporting the business to being a strategic partner and collaborating with business executives to drive business value. According to research, 70% of global 2000 companies view their IT organizations as a cost center—a necessary evil of questionable importance. If a company has a high perception of its dependence on information technology and a low perception of its IT organization's ability to deliver information technology, this could be viewed as a business risk. The IT organization becomes a candidate for outsourcing. Ideally, IT management wants to be placed in the upper right-hand quadrant—strategic partner—and move from cost and efficiency to investment and effectiveness.

In order to make it into the upper right-hand quadrant, however, the IT organization must understand the business and its issues, proactively suggesting solutions that address these issues and opportunities. Although this sounds straightforward, the head of IT strategy at a major studio once confided that "most

EXHIBIT 5.9 GROUP CREDIBILITY AND DEPENDENCY MATRIX

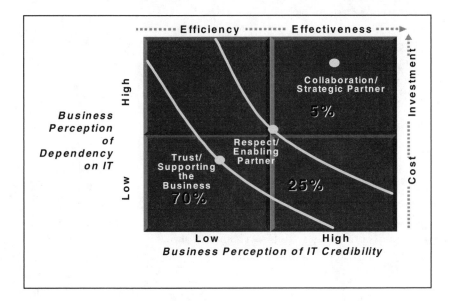

of the people in IT have never even been on a live set." Research indicates that 75% of IT operations groups do not understand business strategies and have not allocated resources to tackle business issues. IT management is usually focused on reducing costs, as well as providing maintenance and enhancements. In order for IT portfolio management to be successful, it must understand key business processes and business performance indicators and be able to respond to these indicators. Examples include:

- Financial/cost-reduction measures
- Customer service efficiency and effectiveness measures
- People productivity measures
- Marketing effectiveness indicators (e.g., time to market)
- Quality measures (e.g., defect rates)
- Regulatory and compliance metrics (e.g., government/legal risk avoidance)

For business and IT, value can best be driven by:

- Knowing value at all times and evaluating IT continuously.
- Approaching strategy from the customer's perspective.
- Making IT relevant and tangible.

- Creating a value taxonomy for business and IT. Focus on how value relates to:
  - Business issues
  - Revenue (cash inflow)
  - Costs
  - Risks
  - Capabilities
  - Value drivers/mission statements
- Reinforcing continuous improvement.
- Knowing customers needs and values better than the competition.

Assess IT Portfolio Management Maturity

The IT portfolio management maturity model, which is addressed in detail in Chapter 2, enables readers to determine their current and targeted profile for IT portfolio management. The model is based on practices the authors have noted within many companies—some based on ad hoc, random approaches and others on precision in optimizing portfolios. The model shows five maturity levels (from level 0, admitting, through level 4, optimizing) of the projects and assets subportfolios (i.e., applications, infrastructure, processes, and information). The overall IT portfolio is also assigned a maturity level. The discovery portfolio is often a chaotic process; therefore, trying to determine IT portfolio management maturity levels for this subportfolio is not included in the maturity model.

Portfolio maturity starts at the basic level of the model as a communication vehicle, evolves to the intermediate level of managing the portfolio within views, and graduates to the advanced level of holistically managing the entire set of IT investments as one portfolio. Managing the business and IT portfolios as one holistic portfolio achieves world-class performance. Research indicates that less than 5% of the Global 2000 companies currently apply the world-class best practice of managing business and IT investments as one portfolio.

To assess IT portfolio management maturity, each subportfolio represented by the columns in Exhibit 5.10 must be reviewed. The model helps to spot inconsistencies between subportfolios. For instance, it is possible to be at level 3 for projects and level 0 for applications. However, if the project subportfolio is at a vastly greater level of maturity than the people portfolio, it is likely being measured optimistically; it is difficult to have an optimized project subportfolio when those working on projects are not being managed optimally. Likewise, if the application subportfolio rates at a substantially higher level than the information subportfolio, the quality of application effectiveness is suspect. In addition, the portfolio management maturity model identifies weaknesses within the IT life cycle by surfacing areas devoid of governance, defined processes, role accountability, and feedback metrics.

The maturity model provides an excellent balancing mechanism for determining optimal readiness and advancing the portfolio management process. Each iteration

EXHIBIT 5.10 IT PORTFOLIO MANAGEMENT MATURITY LEVELS

	Projects	Applications	Infrastructure	People	Process	Information	Overall IT Portfolio
Level 0 Admitting	Collecting data on projects	Collecting data on applications	Collecting data on infrastructure	Collecting information on people and their skills	Determining processes and owners	Identifying primitive entities	Recognition of need for an IT portfolio
Level 1 Communicating	Aggregated and interrelated project information with standard business cases	Listing of all applications with basic characteristics	Listing of all infrastructure with basic characteristics	Listing of all IT professionals and their skills	All processes documented in similar fashion	Listing of key entities with characteristics to identify issues	All sub-portfolios must be at level 1
Level 2 Governing	People, processes, and policies are standardized to ensure governance and consistency around project management.	Application owners exist. Life cycles managed. Defined application portfolio process in place.	Basic asset management processes in place. Infrastructure owners identified. Defined infrastructure portfolio process exists.	Basic human capital management practices exist to proactively update skills. IT human resource manager(s) exists.	A business improvement methodology and team exist. Processes stored in common repository. Processes reconciled to reduce redundancies. Process owners identified.	Information management active to enable portfolio management. Governance around information use exists. Legitimate owners of information identified.	All sub-portfolios at level 2
Level 3 Managing	Metrics for governing processes and key supporting processes are identified and captured.	Metrics for governing processes and key supporting processes are identified and captured.	Metrics for governing processes and key supporting processes are identified and captured.	Metrics for governing processes and key supporting processes are identified and captured.	Metrics for governing processes and key supporting processes are identified and captured.	Metrics for governing processes and key supporting processes are identified and captured.	All sub-portfolios at level 3
Level 4 Optimizing	The project portfolio reflects and is balanced against near-real-time project information. The project portfolio is integrated with other portfolios, most specifically people, infrastructure, and applications.	Performance and life-cycle information is affecting the application and IT portfolio. Information from other portfolios is used to balance the application portfolio, feeding information to the process portfolio.	Asset management information is used to balance this subportfolio and associated to related portfolios, including the project, people, and process.	People sub-portfolio against the process, project, and infrastructure portfolio to ensure that the optimum mix of skills exists in sufficient quantities to support current and future needs. Skill and resource shortages are identified proactively.	Processes exist in a portfolio with supporting metrics and ties to the applications supported by these processes and the information touched by these processes. Processes can be adjusted based on information from other sub-portfolios.	Data quality flows up into the portfolio, enabling rapid corrective action to be taken through information management or operational processes in other related subportfolios.	All sub-portfolios at level 4

of IT portfolio management should be an improvement on its predecessor. Reasonably attainable goals toward improvement should be included in the task plan. It is logical to strive to move up one level or less in iteration; skipping levels is dangerously optimistic.

Assess Capabilities

Capabilities should be considered according to what a company needs to do to achieve its desired strategic position. Assessment of capabilities leverages the work and analysis performed in the baseline assessment and the IT portfolio management maturity model. It identifies the gaps and missing elements that exist between the baseline assessment and the desired IT portfolio maturity level—the difference of where I am today versus where I want to be tomorrow:

- What capabilities are needed to address the gaps?
- Are existing resources sufficient to fill the identified gaps? What is the level of expertise required within the company to address these capabilities?
- Should identified gaps be addressed by fortifying existing capabilities, or are new capabilities required?

Organizational change readiness and team ability are the most important capabilities to assess. Inventorying people resources within companies and providing detailed information regarding their skills, areas of subject matter expertise, prior experience, and so on, becomes important when assessing future required capabilities. Some additional capabilities needed as companies target more advanced levels in the IT portfolio management maturity levels include resource buffers for off-cycle events, training and incentive compensation (addressing some of the cultural issues), advanced analytical and evaluation methods, and key processes.

Define Objectives

Objectives are the reason for doing IT portfolio management. They are based on:

- Baseline architecture requirements
- Evaluating the gaps that exist between the desired capabilities and the targeted IT portfolio maturity level
- Stakeholder assessment
- Value versus cost analysis

Objectives are paired together and the strength of the relationship between objectives, as determined by the decision makers, is established. This creates an initial ranking. Then weights are assigned to each objective based on its strength, which can be determined by a number of factors including its criticality (timing) and importance, as shown in Exhibit 5.11.

EXHIBIT 5.11   SAMPLE CRITERIA USED TO SCORE
OBJECTIVES

Score	Criticality (Timing)	Importance
0	Low	Low
20	Medium	Low
40	Low	Medium
60	Medium	Medium
80	Medium	High
100	High	High

Each objective is given a numerical score, and the total of scores for the objectives is determined (cumulative score). Each objective is then assigned a percentage based on its score divided by the cumulative score. The sum of all percentages for all objectives should equal 100%.

An example of the weighting and percentages assigned to strategic and tactical objectives is shown in Exhibit 5.12. This framework is based on the Analytical Hierarchy Process, developed by Thomas L. Saaty (1990). There are three important points:

1. Defining objectives involves creating definitions that are unambiguous, relevant, achievable, and measurable.

2. Objectives must be categorized according to specific areas (Exhibit 5.12 includes customer, strategy, technology, and delivery categories). Each criterion contains subcriteria that are also weighted according to importance.

3. The degree or standards (strong, moderate-strong, moderate, low, none) that each IT investment meets an objective, and the weighting of these factors, provides a higher degree of accuracy in analyzing and scoring investments.

To further illustrate, Exhibit 5.13 shows the investment strategic map that evaluates each project against each objective. The resulting heat map as indicated by the various shadings in Exhibit 5.13 shows the strength of each of these relationships

EXHIBIT 5.12 DEFINING OBJECTIVES

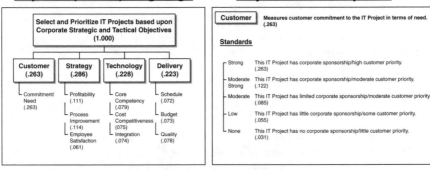

Source: Bruce Miller, "Portfolio Management: Linking Corporate Strategy to Protect Priority and Selection," *PM Solutions,* Expert Series, 2002. Retrieved from www.pmsolutions.com/articles/portfolio_mgmt.htm.

(low, moderate, strong, extreme) based on different shadings. The investment strategic map is an advanced IT portfolio management capability.

Accurately defining objectives provides a road map for business and IT management. Objectives drive critical success factors and key performance indicators that monitor and track specific parameters to assure a company is meeting its objectives and business strategy on a timely basis.

Define Process Metrics

According to research, 80% of IT measurement programs have traditionally failed because the technology solution was too rigid, too expensive, or did not improve

EXHIBIT 5.13 INVESTMENT STRATEGIC MAP

Drivers	001001	001002	001003	001004	001005
Projects	Improve reg risk and controls 14.5973%	Identify and develop new markets 4.9423%	Preserve existing revenue base 13.7142%	Improve employee satisfaction 2.3377%	Improve op. Efficiency & Productivity 7.9987%
001001001 Asset Management	Low			Low	
001001002 SLA Measurement System	Low		Low	Low	Moderate
001001003 IBM Server Strategy	Moderate	Low	Moderate	Low	
001001004 Compliance (C/O)	None				Low
001001005 EGTRRA Regulatory Compliance	Low		Low		Low
001002001 Internet Based IPSEC Rem Acc VPN	Moderate		Low	Moderate	Strong
001002002 Voice Over IP (VoIP)	Low	Strong	Low	Moderate	
001002003 Defining LAN Strategies				Low	Moderate
001002004 Network Mgt Tools Framework	Low			Moderate	Moderate
001002005 Storage Design - Large Data Center	Moderate	Strong		Low	

Objective · Weighting (Percentage) · Degree of Meeting Criteria

Source: Copyright © 2004 United Management Technologies (UMT), www.umt.com.

anything. However, defining metrics is the only way to demonstrate the effectiveness of IT portfolio management. If an objective cannot be measured at the end of the initiative, the initiative runs the risk of perceived failure.

There are five stages in developing a performance measurement program. The program must be tailored to the IT portfolio management baseline assessments, defined objectives, and maturity model. The outline in Exhibit 5.14 provides activities for business and IT management to build an effective program for evolving an IT portfolio performance measurement culture.

The performance management process cycle should be completed on a monthly basis, or quarterly if significant effort is required, for data collection and analysis. Ideally, a current scorecard (i.e., a dashboard) should be available to managers that is continuously updated as soon as performance indicators are known. External benchmarking should be conducted on an annual basis.

IT portfolio management emphasizes the alignment of IT strategy to business strategy. Companies continuously experience difficulty translating the traditional IT efficiency metrics (i.e., doing things right) and the business emphasis on IT

EXHIBIT 5.14   BUILDING AN EFFECTIVE MEASUREMENT
PROGRAM

- Identifying: laying the groundwork for effective IT portfolio performance management improvement
  - Identify team to evaluate current performance measures
    - Project management office
    - Business analysts
    - Process improvement team
  - Define performance goals – what is the vision and value proposition
  - Determine reporting requirements
    - What is reported?
    - How often?
    - Who is the audience?
    - What are their values? What are their value drivers? For example:
      - Alignment (e.g., goals, incentives, value, vision, strategies, effort, behaviors, measures)
      - Quality (e.g., product defects, process effectiveness, rework, leadership, customer satisfaction)
      - Innovation (e.g., patents, ideas and suggestions, process improvements)
      - Throughput (e.g., productivity, sales volume, service usage, bandwidth)
      - Cost reduction (e.g., reduced staffing, ease of maintenance, return on investments, reduced inventories)
      - Reuse (e.g., economies of scope, productivity, reduced testing and rework)
      - Speed (e.g., time to market, time to value, time to repair, responsiveness)
    - How are measurements defined? Are they obvious to both IT and business executives?
    - Prepare views that align with specific audience needs
  - Information structure
    - Formalize information and data infrastructure
      - Sources
      - Storage/repository
      - Identify information and data access rights
    - Select metrics
      - Conduct initial surveys and interviews
      - Document evaluation/interpretation methods
      - Review and revise metrics
- Positioning: determine as-is state versus to-be state
  - Compare performance to benchmarks – what are acceptable performance zones?
  - Establish business goals and IT alignment
    - Update targets and identify dependencies
  - Identify obstacles, issues and risks of potential performance changes (e.g., behaviors, accountability, targets, peer performance, customer perceptions, shared vision, information access)

EXHIBIT 5.14 *CONTINUED*

- Identify anticipated benefits
  - Deciding and implementing what to measure drives clarity on what people will focus on
  - Creating a clear communications framework to convey a company's targets
  - Checks and balances as to whether objectives are being met
  - Challenge the company's strategy
- Identify costs of reaching next targets
- Identify the effects of not implementing certain performance components
- Planning: planning specifics of how people reach their destination
  - Define and revise policies, processes, roles, and responsibilities
  - Communicate/educate – process buy-in
    - Communication plan with specific messages targeted to specific audiences
  - Monitor and manage resistance
  - Training for process goals, collection methods, reporting analysis
- Experimentation: test assumptions and casual relationships
  - Install required tracking tools
  - Collect and validate performance data
  - Analyze input
  - Validate impact
  - Report performance
- Evaluating: learn from the experience and improve the process
  - Solicit and review process improvements
  - Conduct user feedback and benchmarking
  - Use scorecards
  - Recognize and reward IT portfolio management performance improvements
  - Update training materials and documentation

effectiveness metrics (i.e., doing the right things). Organizational alignment and agility are the cornerstone of effective companies, but companies are struggling to bridge the gaps between these goals and implementation tactics. Determining value, goals, objectives, priorities, strategy, tactics, processes, and metrics involves disparate sources of input (e.g., IT management versus line of business, current versus target performance, individual versus group incentives, etc.). To simplify the details and tie them to objectives, companies must manifest their goals through identifying critical success factors (CSFs)—the core areas they must address in order to achieve their goals. Detailed progress toward achievement of CSFs is measured through key performance indicators (KPIs). Exhibit 5.15 shows an example of the linkage between a critical success factor, key performance indicators, and measurement validation.

In developing KPIs, the adage of "less is more" holds true to form. People will lose focus on key performance indicators if too much is measured. Achieving a

EXHIBIT 5.15   EXAMPLE OF A CRITICAL SUCCESS FACTOR, KEY PERFORMANCE INDICATORS, AND MEASUREMENT VALIDATION

Critical Success Factor	Key Performance Indicator(s)	Measurement Validation
Quality	• Product defect — detection, elimination	• Defect count — density
	• Process defect — detection, elimination	• Documentation quality
	• Quality assurance — defect avoidance	• Causal analysis

balance of measuring the right indicators with the right number of key performance indicators is critical.

Ideally, IT portfolio measures should reflect cross-company measures, essentially eliminating silos that exist between business units and divisions. Measures, as expressed through scorecards, dashboards, and other means, must be used by IT and business executives to reduce the probability of problems, gain earlier insight into potential problems, and anticipate opportunities. Thus, measures should not only provide the status of current conditions but should serve as leading and lagging indicators across the company. Measures should also be used to:

- Quantify the value of individual investments
- Quantify the value of the IT portfolio—show IT's value contribution to the business
- Incorporate subjective and intangible value

To be effective, measures must be managed, monitored, benchmarked, and communicated. Their use must be mandated as standard operating procedure, compared against industry norms, and they must provide valuable gap analysis to spur innovation. In addition, measures should be tightly linked to performance standards, as well as compensation and incentives (employee reward and recognition systems).

At this early stage in the process, measures are defined to demonstrate the effectiveness of the effort and identify areas for subsequent improvement of the process. The measures used to demonstrate effectiveness of the IT portfolio management process, however, will undoubtedly link to the measures of the portfolio content as the effort progresses. Keeping this in mind early will greatly increase the likelihood of success downstream.

One final note of caution around metrics: they are not always as quantitative as some people might think. IT measurement—and measurement in general—is as much art as science in analyzing and assessing objective versus subjective variables, tangible versus intangible assets, and reliable versus questionable data.

Document the Portfolio Game Plan

To the seasoned methodologist, this is fundamentally an assembly activity. Simply organize all of the information developed in previous tasks into a presentable deliverable for the sponsors and appropriate stakeholders. To the seasoned practitioner, this is the close of the sale. During this activity, the seasoned practitioner presents and gets approval for the approach, goals, objectives, and success criteria. This person also gets commitment for participation and funding for the effort. As with any other improvement approach, heads will nod up and down when the approach and benefits are presented. People nod off when the rubber hits the road, effort is required, change is required, and pain is perceived. Completing the game plan means nailing the key stakeholders down to do IT portfolio management. The portfolio game plan synthesizes the baseline assessments, defined, but attainable, objectives, metrics, and success criteria into a cohesive charter replete with a plan.

It is at this stage that software solutions (also called tools) used for IT portfolio management are selected or validated. Often a mismatch between a tool and its requirements are carried way too far through the process, generating rework or additional effort. In general, if the scope and objectives are light, simple office automation tools will suffice. If the scope is larger and the objectives are loftier, more robust tools are required. Requirements regarding tool selection are discussed in Chapter 6. At a minimum, the IT portfolio management charter should contain:

- The purpose, goals, objectives, and scope of IT portfolio management
- Work efforts, action plans, milestones, and timetables as appropriate
- The definition of the IT governance role, membership, and empowerment
- Policies, practices, principles, and guidelines for IT portfolio management
- Success criteria by which the effort will be evaluated
- Performance measures to support success criteria, goals, and objectives
- Defined threshold levels for risk and cost
- Funding and resource requirements
- Select portfolio management tools
- The communication approach
- A place for the signatures of key stakeholders to indicate they understand all of the aforementioned information and agree to support it fully

The charter is a living, breathing document—it will evolve over time. Set expectations accordingly. Ideally, the game plan and charter should be presented and signed at a kickoff meeting attended by the project sponsor and key stakeholders.

Above all else, IT portfolio management is a mechanism to communicate in support of decision making. Therefore, a communication plan should be created and put forth. Effective IT portfolio management includes communication throughout the entire process. This is not spam but the planned delivery of key messages via appropriate mechanisms replete with acknowledgment of receipt and demonstration of understanding. Key stakeholders, types of messages, and their corresponding delivery mechanisms should be identified. It is often worth the extra effort to identify events that would trigger communication, including issues that surface during the process and attainment of milestones. Communicating early and often allows for midflight course correction and minimizes the impact of surprises.

STAGE 2: PLANNING

In stage 1, the focus is on planning the overall portfolio management initiative and setting it up for success. Based on input from the game plan, a portfolio plan is developed to define the investment strategy and the structure of the IT portfolio. During stage 2, the subportfolios are determined. An overall portfolio categorization scheme is developed, and the target percentage of resource allocation within each category is agreed upon. A personal investment portfolio analog would note the distinction between bonds, various types of equities, and real estate, and would make a guesstimate of how much will be invested in each category. An overall portfolio strategy and the categories into which investments will be split are determined (e.g., run, grow, and transform; core, nondiscretionary, discretionary, growth, and venture; or discovery, project, and asset investments). The goals and target investment mixes across these categories are set. Exhibit 5.16 outlines the specific tasks and activities involved in developing the planning stage. The critical activities of the tasks shown in Exhibit 5.16 that are addressed in this section include:

- Plan investment strategy
- Plan portfolio structure
- Plan individual subportfolios

Plan Investment Strategy

The planning of investment strategy for the IT portfolio begins with the determination of investment categories. Establishing these categories provides defined

EXHIBIT 5.16 PLANNING STAGE TASKS

Iterate Throughout These Tasks ⟶

Plan Investment Strategy	Plan Portfolio Structure	Plan Individual Subportfolios

• Define specific investment categories
  - Based on business objectives and IT plan
  - Identify risk and rewards
  - Determine goals and metrics
• Determine appropriate mix of these categories
  - Alignment with business and IT goals
  - Risk tolerance
	• Determine hierarchy
	• Define how the portfolio is organized
	  - Highlight different parts of the portfolio
	• Define requirements
	• Define views of the portfolio
	  - Key investment types
	  - Risk/reward trade-offs
	  - Metrics
	• Select the set of subportfolios
		• Determine goals, metrics, and target mixes for each subportfolio
		  - Iterative and refine
		• Evaluate the portfolio impact
		• Package subportfolio information into the portfolio plan
		  - Highlight relationships and trade-offs between various subportfolios
		  - Gain initial feedback and iterate
		  - Prepare communication document
		  - Seek final approval

buckets for IT investments and reflects the company's business and IT strategy. In addition, the plan investment strategy takes into consideration the appropriate risk/reward balance and practicality (capacity, capability, costs, timing, and core competencies) of successfully aligning business and IT strategy. In a similar way to the financial portfolio manager starting with categories for investments (e.g., short-term liquid, medium-term stable, and long-term growth), the IT portfolio manager must develop categories for IT investments that resonate with the business. There are usually threshold levels (e.g., budget, risks, number of investments) associated with each category. Current and planned investments should be mapped into the categories to ensure appropriate resources are allocated to appropriate investment types. Categories can be defined by top-down, bottom-up, and hybrid approaches:

- *Top-down:* the business's vision, goals, and strategy drive investments, resource allocations, and therefore investment categories. Two approaches can be used (these are not mutually exclusive):

- *Product/service road map:* a series of milestones and deliverables in the development of a solution that defines what investments should be undertaken
- *Strategic buckets:* resource allocation across various markets, technologies, time horizons, business units/divisions, and project types

- *Bottom-up:* evaluates current and proposed investments, and a decision is made as to which best meets the goals and objectives of the business. These investments are rigorously screened against criteria (business/strategic fit is one of these criteria). The result is a portfolio of aligned projects with defined investment categories.

- *Hybrid* (top-down and bottom-up): utilizes the core characteristics of both approaches. The two approaches are reconciled through multiple decision-maker iterations.[7]

These approaches, also see similar discussion in Chapter 3, lay an important foundation for establishing categories of investments and can be tailored to the specific needs of a company. A starting point for companies to consider in investment categorization is shown in three parameters:

1. Run the business (keep the business operational).
2. Grow the business (expand the business within its current scope of operations).
3. Transform the business (break into new markets, expand beyond current scope).

As shown in Exhibit 5.17, ideally these broad categories can be applied consistently across all subportfolios and resonate within a company's strategy and tolerance for risk. Another slightly more advanced categorization scheme is:

- Core
- Nondiscretionary
- Discretionary
- Growth
- Venture

The run, grow, and transform parameters define the business classifications for the IT discovery, IT project, and IT asset portfolios. Exhibit 5.18 shows a detailed description of each of the investment classifications.

A significant challenge is deciding the depth to which these disciplines should be applied. For some companies, simply categorizing IT and using portfolios as a communication tool is a monumental event, whereas other companies must apply detailed portfolio management process disciplines replete with statistical analysis

EXHIBIT 5.17 IT INVESTMENT PORTFOLIO CLASSIFICATIONS

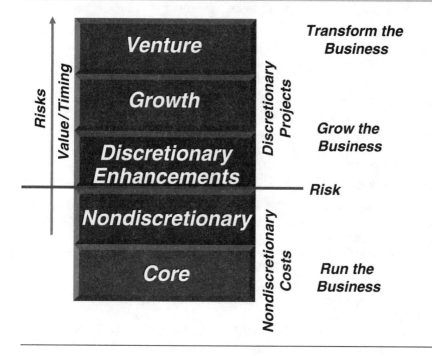

to engage the business. While there is no single right answer for the proper category breakdown and level of precision required, the answer should be apparent if the assessments are performed. The question becomes: How should the pie be sliced—that is, what percentage of resources should be allocated toward operations (i.e., run the business), revenue growth (i.e., grow the business), and transformation (i.e., expand into new markets/lines)? A common mix is:

- 60% allocated to run the business
- 30% allocated to grow the business
- 10% allocated to transform the business

One thing to watch for is a mismatch between allocation percentages and the organization's objectives. If an organization plans to grow its revenues 100% over the next three years and has determined that 80% of its resources should be allocated to run the business, there is probably a mismatch. It is also common to see time lags. In post-M&A situations, a firm's business will often want to stabilize; however, the IT infrastructure may require major surgery. This situation can be seen in recently deregulated industries (e.g., financial services in the United States).

EXHIBIT 5.18 DESCRIPTION OF IT INVESTMENT CLASSIFICATIONS

Run the business (RTB) investments involve keeping the business operational. Items falling under this category often include utilities, maintenance contracts, and disaster recovery, with the following metrics used to measure the effectiveness of such investments:

- *Budgeting:* account allocations, cash flow, project cost and schedule
- *Cost reduction:* rework, defect tracking, inventory
- *Maintenance fixes:* effort, staffing levels
- *Service-level agreements:* availability, downtime, mean time to repair
- *Customer satisfaction/retention*

The nature of RTB investments is broken into core and nondiscretionary:

- *Core:* Spending in this category provides mission and business critical services for the front office (sales order entry, customer service) and back office (payroll, accounting, HR). Common spending entities include network services, data center operations for specific services, IT vendor support, backup/restore, and disaster recovery.
  - *Business risk:* because assets in this category have instantiated processes and use does not typically change, the business risk potential is usually low.
  - *Business reward:* business reward potential in this category ranges from medium to high.
- *Nondiscretionary:* Spending in this category mitigates the impact of organic growth consumption of core/operational assets such as infrastructure (e.g., server, storage, middleware, database management systems, network), operations, and related processes on existing IT service performance. Typical external influences that modify spending decisions in this category include business climate changes and corporate events or activities (e.g., mergers, acquisitions, divestitures).
  - *Business risk and reward:* because spending activity in this category centers on expanding existing capacity to meet growth requirements (rather than to introduce new services), it represents an ideal investment to actually reduce business risk and stabilize business reward.

Grow the business (GTB) investments are made to expand the company's scope of products and services. Investments could be for upgrading software, adding incremental capacity, or developing skills within the staff through additional training or other efforts. Metrics to measure the success of these investments include:

- *Financial analysis:* return on investment, economic value added, capital, IT budget/revenue
- *Investment planning:* risk analysis, scenarios, portfolio planning (three-year model), supply-chain analysis
- *Enhancements:* project-phase analysis, cost of quality
- *Delivered information value*
- *Customer loyalty:* lifetime value

EXHIBIT 5.18   *CONTINUED*

Transform the business (TTB) investments involve moving into new markets. Sample TTB investments include new business ventures, mergers and acquisitions, new products, application package additions, outsourcing, and the hiring of employees with new skills. Possible metrics in this area include:

- New market share
- Future value

Grow the business and transform the business fall into three areas:

1. *Discretionary:* Spending in this category affords new levels of process efficiency and effectiveness that the business perceives it will need but that current assets (plus nondiscretionary enhancements) cannot justifiably deliver. Assets in this category influence business performance through process agility (effectiveness) or the ability to respond to new service requests much more quickly. Internal controls must be implemented along with new assets to ensure that integrity of all processes (particularly financial) remain intact throughout the changeover and post-changeover periods.
   - *Business risk:* moderate for this category. Although the new asset is intended to be a functional replacement, thereby minimizing process disruption, its architecture typically differs from the original. Therefore, it introduces business risks that have been known to make some businesses unviable.
   - *Business reward:* moderate potential for this category. Assets in the category provide a moderate increase in efficiency over the assets they replace (e.g., legacy services versus enterprise resource planning). This benefit is typically short-lived and therefore should not be a primary investment driver.

2. *Growth:* includes project-based spending that creates new IT services to deepen an enterprise's market penetration. Successful services in this category will logically align with established commerce chains.
   - *Business risk:* moderate to high, measured by the amount of brand recognition and levels of customer/partner relationships that can be or are being leveraged.
   - *Business reward:* moderate to high. Assets in this category provide incremental revenue streams from an established client base or similar market buyer.

3. *Venture:* includes project-based spending that creates new IT services to broaden an enterprise's reach to new, untapped markets. Emphasis is on the speed required to gain control of a new market via first-mover advantage.
   - *Business risk:* highest in this category; many existing processes will be exposed to unplanned events.
   - *Business reward:* potential ranges widely. Using the venture capital analogy, the rewards of successful venture initiatives should offset the relatively high rate of failure among other such initiatives.

EXHIBIT 5.18   *CONTINUED*

Metrics to measure the success of these investments include:

- Innovation value
  - Brand awareness in a new market
  - Product differentiation
  - Process innovation
  - Innovation capital
- Time to innovation
- Innovation results
  - Innovation activity
  - Innovation management
  - Innovation performance
  - Innovation yield

Under these conditions, an apparent mismatch between business objectives and IT investment strategies is plausible.

There can be differences between business units and divisions in the same company. For example, a company may adopt a strategic business unit (SBU) approach, whereby the life cycle of each SBU is monitored. Some SBUs may have unit-specific strategies that seem to fly in the face of the enterprise as a whole or other units competing for the same scarce resources. These business unit or divisional differences must be considered. Divisional investment categories will be rolled up to reflect the total company portfolio.

Enterprise optimization of IT investment is the overall goal of IT portfolio management. Business alignment must always be a priority. A larger business unit may be a mature one in a mature market where IT investments would primarily be in the run-the-business category. A smaller business unit might be the growth engine of a firm. IT investment in this business unit would probably be mostly in the grow-the-business (or even transform-the-business) category. Care and attention must be paid to this dynamic. If 10% of the IT budget is devoted to transforming the business, should not this 10% be allocated to the business unit that is poised to transforming the business? Have these types of dialogs early to avoid friction and minimize politicking downstream.

As previously mentioned, with whom you do IT portfolio management is as important as how you do IT portfolio management. Determining investment categories and target investment mixes without the understanding, buy-in, and support of the senior leadership of the organization (e.g., IT investment council) will provide suboptimal results. If the CEO, CFO, and IT investment council all buy into the core categorization scheme and target percentages, the chances of success are much greater. Determining the categories and target investment percentages should be done by a trained facilitator. This is a critical decision. In addition, it is worth the time to do benchmarking to see what others in your industry and related industries or companies are doing and how they are determining and allocating monies to investment categories.

Plan Portfolio Structure

Designing the structure of the portfolio up front will allow it to be changed to meet the needs of the stakeholders. Different stakeholder groups have different concerns. The finance group is concerned with cost, risk, return, and possibly issues around legislative compliance (e.g., Sarbanes-Oxley). Project managers may be more concerned with project dependencies than legislative compliance. Different views of the portfolio will have different meanings and varying levels of importance depending on the constituency being addressed.

Defining a flexible portfolio structure allows for adaptability. The focus of this activity is on the hierarchical relationships of the subportfolios and the interrelationships of the portfolio components. The critical success factor is capturing enough structure to maintain relationships and hierarchy without creating unnecessary complexity or work. The primary tasks in this activity are:

- *Defining the portfolio requirements:* defining the requirements for the portfolio to be able to maximize the value of the portfolio in the context of the scope and objectives.

- *Planning the portfolio views:* Based on the stakeholders' needs and objectives and scope (largely identified in the game plan stage), initial subportfolios are identified; however, they are subject to subsequent refinement. Bubble charts, as discussed in Chapter 4, provide visual representation of a number of key parameters that can be analyzed. Exhibit 5.28 represents another example of a bubble chart.

- *Determining the portfolio characteristics:* refinements are made to the portfolio structure to enable the desired views.

- *Refining the subportfolios:* the subportfolios that will be optimized are finalized after careful consideration to objectives, requirements, and needs of key stakeholders.

A few rules of thumb must be reiterated at this point. If work does not address requirements, do not do it. However, in some exceptions, create a new requirement. For example, a line of business view might be added if a key stakeholder shows interest during the process. A new portfolio requirement would subsequently be reverse engineered. Likewise, if requirements are not being addressed by the structure of the portfolio, a misstep has occurred. Many companies have success using prototypes of subportfolios, showing samples from tool vendors to key stakeholder groups for feedback. However, building up the power of portfolios over an extended period, which culminates in the parading of a bubble chart or two, can be a letdown. Provide samples ideally based on similar structures to those required for your objectives, and obtain feedback from key stakeholders. Also, accept that this process is iterative and imperfect. In the financial portfolio world, it is exponentially easier to reach precision (e.g., the efficient frontier) than in IT—most IT numbers are suspect. Accept this ambiguity and work with it.

Plan Individual Subportfolios

At this point, you are probably wondering when we are going to stop planning and start doing. Soon. Individual subportfolios have unique characteristics and potential requirements. In Chapter 4, three subportfolios were identified: the discovery portfolio, the project portfolio, and the asset portfolio (infrastructure and applications, processes, information and data, and human capital). Enterprise goals and objectives must be translated into goals and objectives for each subportfolio. These goals and objectives may translate into slightly different target investment mixes. Usually, run the business, grow the business, and transform the business will work well in all subportfolios.

Some subportfolios will simply be deemed out of scope. Few organizations have successfully tackled the information subportfolio. To a large degree, this is due to the dependencies between the information subportfolio and virtually all other subportfolios and the ethereal nature of information. The information subportfolio presently exists primarily in theory. Other portfolios, however, will be deemed either directly in scope or will be impacted indirectly. If the focus of the IT portfolio management effort is on infrastructure assets, application assets will be impacted, and vice versa. It is imperative that companies recognize the mapping of the portfolios and their interrelationships and interdependencies to support the goals of the business. For example, a customer relationship management application has multiple dependencies and can be mapped to multiple portfolios:

- CRM application (application portfolio)
- Personalization aspects and rules engine of a customer relationship management system (process portfolio)
- Service and support (human capital portfolio)
- Hardware to support the CRM application (infrastructure portfolio)

The impact to the subportfolios and overall IT portfolio must therefore be called out. Document the expected changes to the IT portfolio based on stated goals and interdependencies. Validate these impacts with key stakeholders (e.g., owners of the assets, sponsors of the projects).

While the contents of the planning stage are developed in an iterative manner, time boxing is advisable. It is easy to get caught in analysis paralysis early on. At certain milestones, the elements of the plan are shared with and approved by executive management and other key stakeholders. They also approve the final contents of the planning stage. The plan should be communicated to all key staff. Information and feedback from employees and customers will drive continuous change to elements in the planning stage. Similar to the way project plans change throughout the life of a project, the portfolio plan will also change.

STAGE 3: CREATING

After the portfolio has been planned, you finally have the pleasure of building it. The moment you have been waiting for! It is at this point that you use that slick silver bullet tool replete with collectors and agents to grab every modicum of data about all things IT, right? Wrong! Sure, this is the time when you collect data about the portfolio; however, there is a minor catch-22. Most of the pain points in IT are not cleanly structured to make data collection a breeze. Most of the time, target areas are identified for a reason. They are a mess.

Many of the tools on the market have collectors and agents. Some have built-in enterprise application integration (EAI) tools. While these are helpful, they are by no means silver bullets. Even if they were silver bullets with respect to the data they collect, those data are suspect. IT organizations have a tendency to be the cobbler's stepchildren with regard to maintaining good-quality operational data. In fact, most successful IT portfolio management initiatives approach this stage with extreme pragmatism—the collected data are either readily accessible or reasonably estimated and assessed in a rapid manner. Too much time spent collecting and analyzing the data can have rapidly diminishing returns. As mentioned previously, there must be a balance struck between being directionally accurate and precision.

The IT portfolio and subportfolio structures are to be populated with data and descriptors that will allow the previously defined views to be generated and the articulated objectives to be met. Lists of active and proposed projects are captured. In most organizations, a lack of standardized project processes generates "abnormalized" data. Often the data must be manually "cleansed." Some assets are measured and tracked with greater accuracy and precision than others. It is common for infrastructure asset data to be readily accessible and in relatively good shape. Standards that exist for management of these assets are mature and allow collectors or agents to bring back data in a standardized format. The lion's share of the pain within IT organizations, however, does not rest in mature infrastructure. It rests in discovery initiatives and projects. It rests in applications. It rests in information. It rests in human capital. When populating subportfolios with their components and assigning descriptors to enable views, this reality must be accepted.

Exhibit 5.19 outlines the specific tasks and activities involved in developing the creating stage. The critical activities of the tasks addressed in this section include:

- Populate the portfolio
- Identify expected risks and results of the portfolio
- Define or improve on the portfolio metrics
- Build the portfolio views

Populate the Portfolio

The population of the portfolio can be a slippery slope. Most companies derive maximum benefit by leveraging the Pareto principle: 20% of the effort or data provides 80% of the value, which tends to be enough to get the job done. Most success stories of IT portfolio management involve the 80/20 rule. Leverage existing inventories whenever possible. When inventories do not exist, identify the bare minimum required to meet the previously articulated objectives. Do not drown yourself in data.

The inputs to populate the portfolio are from existing IT inventories and their associated component information. In addition, the population of portfolios should include investments in the pipeline and wish lists. In some cases, the inventory of information will include detailed business cases, project plans, and work breakdown structures. In many cases, none of this will exist. Interviewing key stakeholders will help fill in many of the missing pieces. The inventory of new and existing IT investments must have sufficient documentation, size, and cost analysis. The recycled or collected information must match the portfolio structure. Critical decisions include:

- Determining the accuracy, relevancy, timeliness, and completeness of existing inventories, new projects and initiatives, and proposed investments
- Achieving a balance in assessing qualitative versus quantitative, and subjective versus objective data and information
- Identifying legitimate sources of portfolio component information
- Identifying reasonable attributes or descriptors of portfolio components to provide views and linkages/dependencies/constraints (e.g., windows of opportunities)

EXHIBIT 5.19 TASKS IN THE CREATING STAGE

—— Iterate Throughout These Tasks ——

Populate Portfolio

- Identify investments that are in each part of the portfolio
  - Map investments into subportfolio
  - Map investments back to investment categories

Identify Expected Results and Risks

- Determine individual investment and subportfolio expected results
  - Determine desired portfolio risk and return for entire portfolio
  - Determine desired subportfolio risk and return
  - Determine desired individual investment risk and return

Define Metrics

- Define metrics for each area of the portfolio
  - Identify behaviors specific to meeting goals for overall portfolio, subportfolios, and individual investments
  - Assign metrics to behaviors for overall portfolio, subportfolios, and individual investments
  - Determine assessment cycle for each level of the portfolio; schedule cycles and determine what constitutes an off-cycle triggering event
- Communicate to appropriate parties to gain consensus and approval

Build Portfolio Views

- Design views for analysis by multiple constituents
  - Decisions must have risks and returns documented
  - Dependencies, relationships, impact, and key characteristics of parts of the portfolio must be identified
  - Develop models and views to capture these dependencies, impact and key characteristics, and continuously update

IT Portfolio

- Identifying the financial value, quality and status, life span and life cycle costs, and risks
- Validating appropriateness of selected tools
- Associating portfolio components with investment categories.

Key lessons learned include:

- There will be more data than you know what to do with, but they will not necessarily be the right data.
- Collecting the data from their owners is usually challenging. The job can be somewhat mitigated with sponsorship support and interpersonal skills. Allocate more time than you think is necessary.
- Debates will ensue over inclusion of components in a portfolio or subportfolio (e.g., inclusion of Microsoft Office in the application portfolio). Keep a coin handy to make these difficult decisions.
- Relative accuracy will almost always win out over precision.
- Arguments may ensue over the category assigned to an investment (e.g., whether a new order-entry system is run the business, grow the business, or transform the business).
- Evaluations and findings should be compared against industry benchmarks.

The core portfolio management team will be responsible for collecting the data; however, the data are frequently owned by those outside this team. Thus, those seeking the knowledge must work closely (and cautiously) with those possessing the knowledge. When populating the portfolio, the key tasks that must be performed are:

- Gathering investment information and mapping into the appropriate subportfolio
- Mapping the investments to their appropriate investment category

These steps generally happen in parallel. The portfolio facilitator/team will work with the owners of the investments that are to be analyzed to capture pertinent characteristics of the investments and the appropriate investment category. If the focus is on applications, the goal is to work with the application owners to capture the application names, information that will help ascertain the quality, costs, risks, and benefits of the application, and the investment category with which it fits most closely (e.g., run the business, grow the business, transform the business). Often, a finance expert is brought in to contend with these issues and minimize friction. Even though portfolio management is a proven technique for optimizing investments, stakeholders are generally aware that it will be used for allocating scarce resources. It is common to see attempts at gaming the system at this juncture. Careful attention to the organization's culture is critical, and often a legitimized expert in finance can expeditiously work through cultural issues and minimize politicking.

It is incumbent on the portfolio facilitator/team to also work closely with the IT portfolio decision makers during this entire process to assure that the data and information being collected will be useful in their selection processes. There are many interdependencies between portfolios. These interdependencies become an important element when mapping investments. Each investment will likely have touch points with more than one portfolio.

The Business Case

Populating the portfolio is much easier if each IT investment has a business case detailing the value, costs, requirements, risks, target markets and customers, and link to current and future business and strategic objectives. In the past, less than 10% of companies ever checked the business case for validity after a request for funding an IT investment was approved. However, a research study of 40 CIOs conducted in 2004 suggests that this dynamic may be changing. In this study, 50% of CIOs stated their companies plan to check business cases for accuracy and validity after projects are completed. Whether this really occurs remains to be seen; however, it is a shift in thinking about accountability.

The business case, which is detailed in Chapter 4, should serve as a baseline, outlining the risks, value, strategic alignment, and architectural fit of a proposed initiative. It should transfer into a project charter, which is a dynamic document that should be evaluated, refined, and assessed throughout the life of a project. When a project is complete and it becomes an asset, information from the business case and project charter should be transferred to a monitoring system (e.g., fixed assets, asset management) that tracks against the costs of the assets, measures against the value of the assets, and enables feedback and lessons learned to be incorporated back into the business case development process. Although this dynamic does not happen with great frequency, it should. It is a natural evolution of the maturing discipline called IT service delivery.

Whenever possible, include this information in the IT portfolio. It will be most readily available for initiatives being proposed and existing projects. In most organizations, however, it will not be readily available (or relatively accurate) for assets in use. If this is the case in your organization, an opportunity for improving the IT service delivery process now exists. The business case should enable appropriate analysis for or against doing something that will expend resources. IT portfolio management and business cases work together:

- Business cases standardize the information about initiatives being proposed so that the portfolio comparisons are fair.

- Project information and business case information can be compared through IT portfolio management to ensure that differences between the two are in line with the organization's culture.
- Business cases feed asset management systems, allowing life cycle, value, and cost expectations to be validated through asset portfolio management.
- IT portfolio management raises discrepancies between business cases and reality, enabling positive changes to be made in IT processes (e.g., project estimating, ROI calculation).

There is no universally accepted standard template for a business case; therefore, the following points are suggestions for companies to consider as they build or mature their business cases. The essence or spirit of the business case is to make it legitimate and actionable, so avoid getting mired down in too much detail and analysis. The business case is an evolving document and matures along the life span of each investment. Information pertaining to specific IT investments includes:

- Name
- Description of the investment
- Current state and status
- Requirements addressed
- Owner, sponsor, and customer(s)
- Division/business unit
- Business and strategic imperatives
- Benefits
- Financial models and financial returns
- Costs
- Risk and risk profiles (probability of success, vendor, customer, impact, size, complexity, etc.)
- Project attributes (milestones, schedule, scope)
- Resources required
- Deliverables
- Dependencies and constraints (labor, material, facilities, costs, schedule, and timing)
- Portfolio name/center of excellence (e.g., process and change management)
- Business processes impacted or enabled
- Related technologies and tools
- Cycle frequency review

- Replacement dates and cost
- Value and value index (dollar range of value, business value)
- Vendor/provider (e.g., internal IT or vendor)
- Portfolio maturity rating (see Chapter 2 for a description of maturity ratings and associated criteria)
- Communication and reporting matrix (responsible, accountable, consulted, informed)
- Outstanding actions
- Risk profile
- Market and competitor intelligence
- Architectural technical analysis
- Operational technical analysis
- Availability of applications
- Data integrity
- Problem resolution time
- Classification (e.g., for applications, whether it is transactional, analytical, or collaborative)
- Workload classification (e.g., high, medium, or low)
- Origin (e.g., purchased, custom built, or configured)

Identify Expected Risks and Results

Most of the time, those responsible for approving funding simply want to know if they give you money, what they will get in return, and they want to be told about the chances of things not playing out as expected. During this activity, the expected returns for the portfolio as a whole, the individual subportfolios, and the individual investments are articulated. Also, there is an agreement on the risk tolerance. Seemingly simple, portfolio management is a technique to maximize the risk/return trade-off by balancing investments of various types and within various categories. It is completely allowable to have a higher tolerance for risk and greater expectation on returns for investments in the transform-the-business category than in the run-the-business category. By predefining the percentage of resources that will be allocated to the various categories, the optimum mix of risk and return can be generated.

The Risk/Return Trade-off

Portfolio management is about balancing risk and return of related items. For financial investment portfolios, a top-down approach is usually where things start.

Investment objectives are defined. Tolerance for risk is defined. Groupings of investments are identified that have relationships to balance, and diversify risk and return.

By now, the notion that all things roll up into an IT portfolio should be understandable. The IT portfolio, much like a financial investment portfolio, needs to have articulated objectives, acceptable returns, and diversified (and tolerable) risks. Each subportfolio may or may not mirror the overall IT portfolio. It may and usually is the case that projects have a higher threshold for return and tolerance for risk than assets. Assets in production are expected to work with stability, which implies predictability. Some assets may have a higher tolerance for risk than others based on the subportfolio within which they exist. Individual investments may also have differing levels of acceptable risk and return. A run-the-business project probably has lower risk and lower expected return than a transform-the-business project. The desired return and acceptable risk must be defined for:

- The overall IT portfolio
- Each subportfolio
- Individual investments

The desired return and tolerable risk for the overall IT portfolio can generally be determined rather quickly by facilitating agreement with key stakeholders. The key stakeholders, or roles, for making this determination are usually:

- Representatives from the business
- The CIO
- The risk management expert(s)
- The IT finance expert(s)
- A scenario planner
- Other members of the executive steering committee
- In some instances, the board of directors

Risk and Investment Categorizations

In the financial world, investments are described statistically in terms of their expected long-term return rate and their short-term volatility. This volatility is equated with risk. Translating this to the IT portfolio evaluation shows that organizations should select the optimal mix of IT assets through a beta risk factor that takes into account the company's level of risk tolerance. A beta factor measures the relative volatility of an investment against the portfolio; a beta of greater than 1 indicates that the investment category is more volatile than the overall IT portfolio, whereas a beta of less than 1 indicates that the investment category is less volatile than the overall IT portfolio. Paralleling with financial categories, consider this high-level aggregation hierarchy to define the components of the portfolio mix:

- Run-the-business items = cash
- Grow-the-business items = bonds
- Transform-the-business items = stock (equities)

A cash asset (run the business) is no risk, highly liquid, and flexible, assuming a stable geopolitical environment and manageable inflation. Its main characteristic is that it can be quickly upgraded into a more risky category or replaced with an alternative choice within the same category, or it can be substituted with a peer item. Besides expenses that enable IT operations to run and that replace outmodeled or worn-out hardware, mission-critical software should also fall into this category. A company must be able to manage mission-critical business through the most appropriate software solution available. Having ascertained that the software can be plugged into the IT backbone (e.g., an ERP system) via market standards, the organization will decide to install a best-of-breed niche solution. The plug-in capability characterizes the liquidity nature of this "cash" IT asset. Its interchangeability denotes the flexibility expected from a cash asset. Therefore, when assessing run-the-business candidates in the portfolio, business risk potential should be low, and the rewards for these investments should be medium to high.

Key points for a bond asset (grow the business) are long-term stability and well-accepted safeness. However, these investments generally have functioning par value and are less liquid than cash assets. Transposing this model to the IT world, expanding IT products and services can be considered safe and guaranteed when the company masters the business processes that the IT solution covers within the current scope of business operations. An investment in the basic component of a financial suite package (e.g., accounts receivable, accounts payable, general ledger) from one of the large ERP vendors can be considered safe or risk-free. The technology maturity of the offered solution shields it from the pitfalls in the medium to long term. This parallels the long-term stability nature of a bond asset investment.

With stock (transform-the-business) investments, companies will start forging their IT investments around a model not dissimilar to the financial capital asset pricing model (CAPM), although some fundamental differences apply. The beta risk factor will measure how the company will be intrinsically liable to the impact of the investment. Unlike the financial CAPM framework, where higher returns are expected from higher-rated beta assets, companies will work to transform their IT business with minor disruptive changes. Typically, low-risk IT investments implicit with low beta values will be preferred to those that show a higher beta factor. It is therefore relevant to factor in the relative beta risk factors when gauging the potential business advantages for transformative solutions from which a company can benefit.

Risks are associated with the potential impact on value (a potential risk causing a sizable impact on revenues) and costs (extra resources required to operationalize an asset). There are unidentifiable risks that can sometimes result in adverse conditions. Aligning value with investment risks and understanding the cost implications of risks allow companies to gauge their impact.

To systematically compare investment risks, many companies employ a scorecard that identifies and documents all known risks. Although elaborate scorecards can be devised, a relatively simple one that reflects common risk situations and factors endemic to a particular industry or organization is usually sufficient. Business cases and status reports from the past two years can be used to identify common risks. Within operations, risks can be located in business continuity plans that provide risk categories and relevant comparison factors. Residual risk identifies the amount of known risk that exists after exhausting risk mitigation strategies.

Exhibit 5.20 shows the technology risk category and a small subset of risk factors (more detailed risk categories and factors can be found in Appendix 5B). Companies using scoring methods (analytic hierarchy process is a commonly used scoring method) assign weights to risk categories and to each associated risk factor, which is scored according to high, medium, or low risk exposure (defined as a combination of probability of a risk and impact of a risk). A score of 100 is indicative of the highest level of risk probability and impact; a score of 0 is for the lowest level.

To further illustrate Exhibit 5.20, technology risk is shown as a risk category in Exhibit 5.21 with a percentage indicating its weight or relative importance when compared against other risks. Note these things from the scoring process:

- The total additive percentage for all categories (technology risk, business risk, etc) should always add up to 100.

- The percentages of the risk factors within a risk category should always add up to 100.

- The scoring range should be based on predefined, unambiguous, measurable, and agreed-to criteria. Each component of risk is then assessed against these predefined definitions and a score is placed against the risk factor.

- The weighted score is determined by multiplying the risk category percentage by each risk factor percentage by the scoring range.

- The total weighted score is the sum of the total weighted scores for each category.

- The sum of all the total weighted scores provides a numerical figure for this particular investment. The higher the score, the higher the risk associated with a particular investment.

The total score in Exhibit 5.21 should be measured against a range of allowable risks for an investment. It would appear that from measuring only the technology risk category, a score of 34.4 is very high.

EXHIBIT 5.20 ILLUSTRATIVE EXAMPLE OF RISK SCORING METHOD

Risk Category	Risk Factors	Risk Mitigation	Residual Risk	Percentages (also called weights)	Scoring Range	Weighted Score
Technology Risk	• Security • Availability • Architecture	Actions taken to mitigate risks	Remaining risk after risk mitigation	Identifies the relative importance of residual risks when compared against the business and strategic objectives, enterprise architecture, and requirements. Percentages are applied to both risk categories and risk factors — the higher the percentage, the greater degree of importance.	The probability of the risk occurring and the impact of the risk (on both value and cost) are evaluated on a scale basis, typically on a scale of 0 (low) to 100 (high).	The results of multiplying the percentages by the scoring range

Risk – Failure Probability	Score	Probability	Impact
1. AVOID PROJECTS THAT HAVE *High – probability* *High –negative impact and no long-range options improvement*	100	High	High
	80	Med	High
	60	Med	Med
	40	Low	Med
	20	Med	Low
	0	Low	Low

EXHIBIT 5.21   NUMERICAL EXAMPLE OF RISK SCORING METHOD

Risk Category	Risk Factor	Scoring Range	Weighted Score	Total Weighed Score
Technology Risk (40%)				
	Security (20%)	60	=(40%)*(20%)*60=	4.8
	Availability (30%)	80	=(40%)*(30%)*80=	9.6
	Architecture (50%)	100	=(40%)*(50%)*100=	20.0
				34.4
Business Risk (50%)				
Project Risk (3%)				
Resource Risk (5%)				
Customer Risk (2%)				
TOTAL 100%				

Many companies are augmenting their risk assessment with success probability. They define the probability of technical success (e.g., maturity, feasibility, architecture compliance, complexity, etc.) or the probability of end-user acceptance (e.g., pricing, differentiation, competitive advantage, integration/use, maturity) as well. This is an excellent measure for determining the risk-adjusted costs and returns of an investment.

Risk scores from individual investments are prioritized and ranked. Scoring methods allow users to easily view and assess the criteria and definitions related to the scoring ranges. Decision makers can modify weighting, enabling a what-if type of analysis and providing logical comparisons (see the section in this chapter on stage 5 for more details). Alternative investments might be considered and scored to evaluate the most optimal choice for a company. The risk of not making an investment also needs to be factored into the analysis.

Each risk applicable to the portfolio is factored into the overall portfolio. It is not unusual to find that risks associated with a particular investment may be mitigated or exacerbated by existing assets. Within each portfolio, boundaries should be established to assure that risks remain within threshold levels. Exhibit 5.22 shows a minimum, actual, and maximum number of risk investments.

Return and Value
In concert with capturing risks at the portfolio, subportfolio, and investment levels, return and value must be captured to create the IT portfolio. The value

EXHIBIT 5.22   MINIMUM, ACTUAL, AND MAXIMUM NUMBER
OF RISK INVESTMENTS

Enterprise Portfolio by Risk				
	Minimum	Actual	Maximum	Status
High	0	5	7	
Medium	0	25	30	
Low	20	70	100	
Legend		Within Range		
		On Range		
		1–10% out of range		
		11+% out of range		

generated from an investment, a portfolio, or a business unit can include tangible and intangible elements. When compared against costs, the value can generate positive (value > costs), neutral (value = costs), or negative returns (value < costs). Since so much value is bottled in intangible assets in today's technology-driven environment (customer satisfaction, quality, competencies, processes, relationships, etc.), calculating the true value can be difficult. Also, value from an investment may be dependent on the combined value generated from multiple investments that may not demonstrate their real value for some time. For example, implementing enterprise application integration (EAI) might cost more than using point-to-point integration. The value is derived over time after more investments leverage this shared infrastructure. Much of the value derived in implementing an EAI solution is intangible (e.g., more flexible IT architecture).

Value categories and value factors can be applied in a similar manner to the same scoring method shown in the last section for risks. Potential value categories and value factors are shown in Appendix 5A. For the portfolio, the value factors typically fall under four business drivers:

- *Strategic* (alignment): alignment with business drivers and strategic goals, and fiduciary responsibilities
- *Tactical* (attractiveness): return on investment, internal rate of return, economic value added, assessment against profitability and financial indexes, net present value, growth opportunities, payback period, market share potential, intangible value, diversification of risks, intellectual property rights, synergies with other areas in the company, process improvements, achievability

- *Life cycle:* reliability, conformance to standards, total cost of ownership, life span expectations
- *Regulatory:* cost to comply being less than fines for noncompliance

Categories of return, which can include tangible and intangible assets, are identified (e.g., financial, strategic importance, tactical importance, and regulatory mitigation). Weights are assigned to value categories and value factors, adhering to rules similar to those defined in the previous section on risk. Examples of scoring ranges for potential value factors are shown in Exhibit 5.23.

When capturing the value of investments and rolling them up into subportfolios and the IT portfolio, risk must be considered. When calculating the value of an investment, we recommend that companies add a column for risk and the impact that it might have in calculating the total weighted value score (as discussed

EXHIBIT 5.23 SAMPLE SCORING RANGES FOR VALUE FACTORS

Revenue Growth	Score	Value (Dollars)
Annualized net growth on a corporate basis over a three-year period	0	<$0
	20	$1–$500,000
	40	$500,001–$1,000,000
	60	$1,000,001–$1,500,000
	80	$1,500,001–$2,000,000
	100	>$2,000,000

ROI Percentage	Score	Value (Percentage)
Percentage returned as calculated by Corporate Finance.	0	<0%
	20	1–4%
	40	5–10%
	60	11–15%
	80	16–20%
	100	>20%

Accuracy	Score	Value (# of Errors)
Reduction in number of errors occurring on a monthly basis (intangible value)	0	0
	20	1–7
	40	8–14
	60	15–22
	80	23–29
	100	>29

Compliance	Score	Value (Yes/No)
Meets corporate, contractual, regulator, or auditory requirements (i.e., agent plans, accounts, providers, governmental, audit)	0	Is not compliant
	20	
	40	Meets some requirements
	60	
	80	
	100	Does meet requirements

previously in this chapter, this figure should be based on the probability of success). Identifying risks by value factor also provides a more detailed understanding of their impact.

Inventorying and Allocating Resources
Identification of expected risks and returns includes inventorying and allocating resources. While this is a more advanced maturity level, inventorying resources determines the capacity of the company to support projects and operations within the portfolio and includes:

- Defining primary roles (detailed task assignments are not required)
- Standard cost estimates (granular cost estimates are not necessary)
- Skills profiles and nonlabor resources (e.g., facilities, equipment, etc.)[8]

IT investment and operation requirements must be assessed against resource capacity of the company and availability of personnel (by skill type, experience, and subject matter expertise) to support projects and operations. Allocation of personnel should be based on the phases of an investment to avoid low utilization rates. At this level, dates and level of commitment are needed, and generic—not named—resources should be allocated based on full-time-equivalent resources.

A project plan typically defines the time element factors and resource loading aspects of investment needs. The impact of moving labor from other projects and priorities must be assessed, and, in the event that internal resources are insufficient to provide the needs of an investment, alternative options should be quickly considered (e.g., contracting and outsourcing).

IT portfolio management frequently evaluates the opportunity to optimize limited resources, assuring proper sequencing of priorities against possible resource allocation constraints. This is the fundamental genesis of the human capital portfolio. Rapidly responding to an unforeseen event, reprioritizing personnel and resources to act, is competitively advantageous. Integrated and advanced knowledge management systems, business intelligence, document management, portal and collaboration solutions, IT portfolio management, and program management solutions are key to maintaining flexibility and agility to meet changing conditions and assure good communications and optimal resource allocation.

Define Metrics

As previously mentioned, metrics tend to direct behavior. The assumption is that if it is being measured, it must be important. If it is important, you should focus on it. IT and business often have different perceptions of measurement, particularly with respect to precision and quantity of metrics. Business tends to want to measure as little as possible as quickly and easily as possible. IT tends to want to use calipers to measure the size of every gnat within a 5-mile perimeter of the building!

A set of desired behaviors for the overall IT portfolio, each subportfolio, and individual behaviors must be defined. Metrics must be identified that will generate the desired behaviors when measured. As few metrics as possible should be focused on. Too many overt metrics confuse things, leading to unpredictable behavior.

Metrics within IT portfolio management must link to business and strategic objectives, critical success factors, and key performance indicators. The specific metrics and corresponding desired behaviors should be formed based on the company's needs and priorities. Some of the metrics used to assess the IT portfolio management processes include:

- Actual versus planned performance of the IT portfolio
- IT budget allocated to decisions as a result of the IT portfolio management framework
- Revenue/profitability increase due to IT
- Percent decrease in run-the-business expenditures
- Change in the amount spent in transforming the business
- Reduction in redundant projects
- Staff productivity improvements (higher utilization)
- Percentage of IT investments that have an accompanying business case
- Amount of time spent on strategic versus tactical projects
- Customer satisfaction surveys
- Time through the cycle
- Accuracy in alignment with business and strategic priorities

Examples of the value propositions and metrics used by the U.S. Department of Treasury in its project portfolio are:

- Improved process capabilities for internally selecting and prioritizing investments
  - *Metric 1:* ability to capture baseline of treasury and bureau portfolio balance across key mission areas and strategic goals and to measure how this balance improves over time
  - *Metric 2:* ability to score and rank investments according to value, alignment, health, and risk criteria
  - *Metric 3:* ability to derive an optimized portfolio of investments
- Improved Office of Management and Budgeting (OMB) submissions for budget formulation

- *Metric 1:* increase in pass rate for OMB 300 business cases and related scores, as measured by an increase in the number of OMB 300s with scores of 4 or higher
- *Metric 2:* fewer number of OMB 300 business cases targeted for funding cuts
- Improved ability to identify duplicate investments and find opportunities for application consolidation
  - *Metric 1:* reduce number of applications per EA business area and line-of-business subfunction
  - *Metric 2:* improved target architecture compliance, as measured by an overall compliance score
- Improved ability to manage and control investments in build-out/acquisition phase
  - *Metric 1:* improved ability to identify high-risk and low-health investments targeted for funding delays or funding cuts as measured by percent decrease of investments in poor health/high risk
  - *Metric 2:* Reduction in percent of investments with cost overruns
- Improved overall compliance management environment
  - *Metric 1:* Higher percent of investments in compliance with enterprise architecture and security standards[9]

For those new to IT metrics, they can be classified in one of four categories:

1. *Economy* in business terms translates into cost savings and effort reduction in IT terms.
2. *Efficiency* relates to time in IT terms.
3. *Effectiveness* demonstrates the business impact of IT product and process quality.
4. *Empowerment* relates to the impact of employee decision making on output and productivity.

The four E's of business value align nicely with the four categories of the balanced scorecard (e.g., economy for financial performance, efficiency of business processes, effectiveness in customer relationships, and empowerment for employee growth). Exhibit 5.24 shows these measurement candidates.

In addition to performance, companies must evaluate effective measurements that encourage vision and collaboration, enable process tracking, and communicate improvements in overcoming problems and realizing opportunities. The definitions of these methodologies can be found in Exhibit 5.25.

These methods may already be in place and can be leveraged to demonstrate effectiveness of IT portfolio management and feed the portfolio. Exhibit 5.26 lists

EXHIBIT 5.24 SAMPLE OF BUSINESS IT MEASUREMENTS

Business Goal	Measures	Balanced Scorecard Category	IT Contributing Factor	Initiative Example
Economy	Market share, ROI, value-added cost/unit of output, backlog ratio, financial ratios	Financial	Cost savings, effort reduction	Activity-based costing (ABC) programs
Efficiency	Process cycle times, productivity, cost of poor IT quality	Business processes	Time to market, transaction response time	Software Engineering Institute's Capability Maturity Model® integration program
Effectiveness	Quality, satisfaction, performance, IT yield, business impact	Customer relationships	Quality	Total quality management, Six Sigma
Empowerment	Degree employees are empowered to act, exception handling time, percentage of innovative solutions	Employee growth	Volume of output and outcomes, productivity	Software process improvement (SPI) programs, functional point counting

the most common measurement methods and their characteristics as they relate to IT portfolio management.

Build the Portfolio Views

Once the portfolio and subportfolio data have been defined and collected, views must be created to enable the key stakeholders to make decisions. They are represented graphically as bubble charts, pie charts, and bar charts. These views should show how well the IT portfolio aligns with the stated goals and objectives (see Exhibit 5.27). They should articulate whether IT was successful in achieving the expectations, value, and risk reduction expected by management. The views should address all potential risk exposures and demonstrate risk mitigation strategies. The tasks in this activity include:

- Identifying decision points and risk/return scenarios—that is, views that identify the types of decisions to be made up front
- Identifying the characteristics and relationships that will be used in analysis to enable the recognition of interdependencies and ripple effects when what-if scenarios are tested
- Building models and views such as charts for use in analysis and decision making

EXHIBIT 5.25 DEFINITIONS OF ADDITIONAL MEASUREMENT
METHODS

- *Function point:* classifies components by breaking systems down. Systems are measured from a perspective; therefore, the variable is the amount of effort required to create and execute a collection of function points (the tools or languages can be assessed and a determination is made as to which option produces the greatest efficiency with the least or lowest function point, effort). For project development, function points can help spot scope creep.
- *Balanced scorecard (BSC):* provides a cohesive balance sheet, enabling executives to link intangible assets, strategic drivers, and outcome-based performance measures for easier decision making. Cost and nonfinancial information join forces to provide a strategic view of the work done. Additional information pertaining to the balanced scorecard is covered later in this chapter.
- *Earned value analysis (EVA):* tracks budgeted cost of work performed. EVA utilizes task criteria (e.g., objective measurement of completed tasks), as opposed to defect elimination, to indicate progress. This avoids the tendency to estimate tasks as 90% complete when actually only 50% is finished and not to quality levels. EVA is well deployed by military organizations and is applicable to larger-size projects.
- *Activity-based costing (ABC):* tool for detailed cost management, but variation of activity costs and duration often result in statistical noise. ABC enables an improved understanding and localization of cost drivers to eliminate low-value/high-cost activities, but adjustments for unused capacity (e.g., downsizing) can lead to revenue reductions. ABC is rigorous, expensive, and not pragmatic for most dynamic IT environments. Standard IT budget categories and staff roles do not exist to enable cost comparisons. If IT management intends to remain a cost center, ABC would be an appropriate accounting tool.
- *Six Sigma:* more of a goal than a process. Originally introduced by Motorola as a quality performance measure, Six Sigma has evolved into a statistically oriented approach to process improvement. It is deployed throughout a company using experts called black belts.
- *SEI capability maturity model:* originally a framework to evaluate IT contractors' process maturity. It has been applied more broadly to IT management and is widely imitated.
- *Total quality management (TQM):* an influential management theory. TQM brings the discovery that quality improvements must be integrated into the organization by aligning organizational systems and practices to support integrated teamwork and improved quality.

EXHIBIT 5.26   MEASUREMENT METHODS AND THE IT
PORTFOLIO

Criteria for Value Management Methodology	Function Point	Balanced Scorecard	Earned Value Analysis	Activity-Based Costing	Six Sigma	Total Quality Management
Enables management drill-down capability to pinpoint poor performance causes and to identify the interdependencies among IT assets	1	4	3	3	5	4
Integrates smoothly with ongoing enterprise-wide initiatives to minimize disruptions	4	3	3	3	2	2
Supports communication and education of the IT and business unit area processes	2	5	2	4	5	4
Encourages participation in the planning process	4	4	4	4	4	4
Establishes individual, team and organizational goal setting that mobilizes the company	2	4	3	4	4	4
Links incentives and rewards to performance as companies mature	2	5	4	3	4	4
Aligns IT and business units (e.g., competencies, structure, resources, goals)	2	5	2	3	4	4
Leverages performance feedback and facilitates continuous assessment and reporting	2	5	4	3	5	5
1= weak contribution; 2= minor contribution; 3 = moderate contribution; 4 = strong contribution; 5 = core methodology strength						

Most of this work is done by the portfolio management team, probably with the help of a financial expert. This is fundamentally an assembly activity, preparing portfolio information for key decision makers to poke, prod, and act upon. This activity is also where the portfolio team begins to discover whether the selected tools are appropriate, inadequate, or overkill. Unfortunately, in the absence of a good method for IT portfolio management, it is all too common to see efforts hindered at this point because the team:

- Went on the cheap, using a spreadsheet and graphics program, when a more robust portfolio management solution should have been implemented.

EXHIBIT 5.27 THREE DIFFERENT (BUT RELATED) VIEWS OF THE IT PORTFOLIO

Decision View
- ROI
- Business Impact
- Price/Performance
- Risk/Opportunity...

Management View
- Costs/Budget
- Schedule/Effort/Delay
- Standards
- Resource Availability...

Operational View
- Process/Activities
- Products/Specs
- Policy/Procedures
- Constraints/Guides...

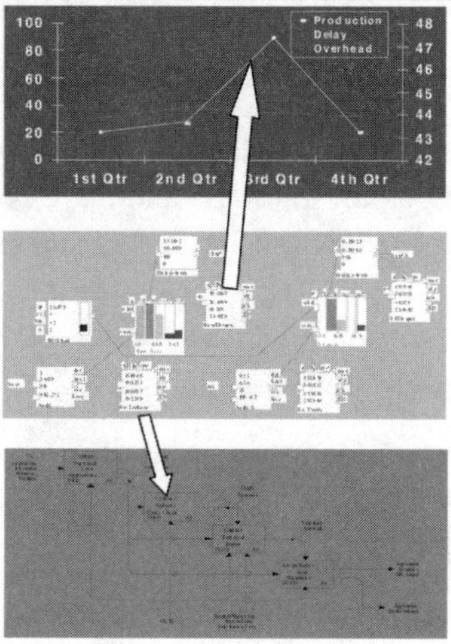

- Purchased a shotgun to kill a fly, buying an expensive portfolio management application and overpopulating it with every conceivable piece of datum only to discover that key stakeholders wanted something quick and dirty.
- Did not have a good grasp of processes prior to making an IT portfolio management software purchase. Therefore, the logic of the IT portfolio software program dictated the actual business logic of the management process, resulting in severe mismatches between the needs and demands of IT portfolio management and the capability delivered.

Portfolio views should enable:

- Identification of redundant investments, since there are typically many redundancies in applications within most large companies (e.g., multiple CRM, portal, ERP). The views should identify many of these duplications. In addition, advanced views will isolate covariance and correlations between various investments. Determining these elements provides insightful detail into the impact of accelerating, downsizing, halting, or eliminating an investment.
- Isolation of areas of synergy, sharing lessons learned and looking to reuse components wherever possible. This is an underestimated benefit of IT portfolio management.

- Identification of constraints and interdependencies such as infrastructure, costs, schedule, labor, timing, alternatives, technologies, and core competencies.

- Assessment of how the expected outcome of an IT investment or a sub-portfolio meets short-term and long-term objectives, to what degree, and how this might close out gaps identified in the enterprise reference architecture and requirements.

From the stakeholder assessment that is part of the game plan (baseline assessment), it is important to understand the views that are of most interest to each stakeholder segment and design the analysis and graphical presentations around these needs. For instance, financial personnel might be interested in the views in Exhibit 5.28.

In addition, financial and IT managers are interested in knowing actual versus budget costs, value, and risk (current month and year-to-date) figures for:

- Investment categories (run, grow, or transform the business) versus IT portfolios (discovery, project, asset)

EXHIBIT 5.28   FINANCIAL VIEWS

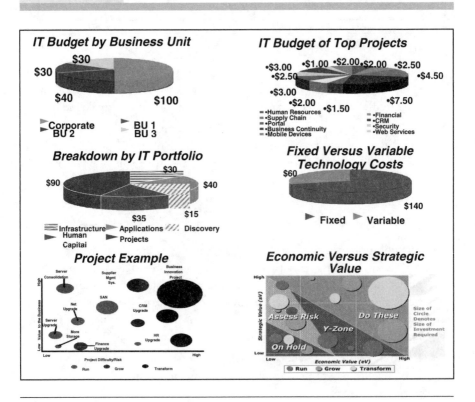

- Mandatory versus discretionary investments (by investment category)
- Risk versus reward
- Value percent versus cost
- Spending allocations and total cost of ownership for run versus grow versus transform the business (by quarter, by year, by division/business unit, by product line, by geography, etc.)

As a starting point, companies should consider simply defining the portfolio pie by spending to facilitate a dialog between business and IT. Good candidates are:

- *Projects* (programs): show how much of the overall IT budget is spent on projects and programs.
- *Run* (base): show how much of the overall IT budget is spent on base activities in operations.
- *Upgrades* (application maintenance): demonstrate the amount of effort going into supporting incremental changes that are part of the basic operations activities.

Pulling It All Together

At this point, there is an assembly of all deliverables from stage 3. The collected information and its mapping back to objectives must be clearly communicated to the key stakeholders of the IT portfolio management effort. Generally, the executive steering committee, IT steering committee, or IT investment council must approve the work, understanding not only what has been done but why and how the information will be used. If the effort misses the mark and the IT portfolio management team pushes forward, results may lead to a failed initiative. The portfolio views are used to make hard decisions about resource allocation, asset disposal, and funding. If the underlying data within these portfolio views are inappropriate for the stakeholders making these decisions, the validity of the effort will be called into question.

The contents of the creating stage are developed in an iterative manner. At certain milestones, the elements are shared with and approved by executive management and other key stakeholders. Their approval is also needed for the final contents. The last thing the IT portfolio management team wants to discover is that it missed the mark after expending much effort. Communicate and validate early and often. Information and feedback from key stakeholders and gatekeepers will drive continuous positive change.

STAGE 4: ASSESSING

This stage is generally where the real fun begins. All of the previous efforts come together to generate the ah-ha factor. The actual performance of the portfolio is compared with the expected performance. Guess what? They almost never match, which is where the ah-ha factor comes in. It is common to identify 25% waste in project portfolios during the assessment and to discover that IT assets are being utilized at only half of their practical capacity.

Exhibit 5.29 outlines the specific tasks and activities involved in developing the assessing stage. The critical activities of the tasks shown in Exhibit 5.29 that are addressed in this section include:

- *Monitoring for triggering events:* looking at internal and external events and their impacts on the portfolio
- *Measuring the portfolio:* quantifying the risks and returns of the portfolio contents

EXHIBIT 5.29   ASSESSING STAGE TASKS

Iterate Throughout These Tasks →

Monitor for Triggers	Measure Portfolio	Compare Measures Against Targets

Observe external and internal events that impact the portfolio
  - Evaluate and quantify significance of triggering events based on validated portfolio
	• Quantify the risks and returns for the views and changes that drive portfolio assessment cycle
	  - Assemble actual and expected return and risk on investment for portfolio analysis views
	  - Update portfolio decision points and risk/return based on new analysis and impact of triggering events
		• Evaluate and contrast portfolio actual and expected results and actual and target investment mix using populated portfolio totals
		  - Evaluate and contrast actual and expected result gaps and compare to target investment mix

- *Comparing measures against targets:* analyzing expected and actual results of the portfolio to identify areas where balancing should occur

If tools, investment attributes, and views were appropriately selected and applied, this stage can be relatively easy. It will get tripped up if key data elements were not collected, inappropriate tools were selected, or views were not chosen well.

The major players in this stage are the portfolio team and manager, the metrics expert(s), and the key stakeholders for specific views. Each view is assessed with the view owner. In the previous section, a sample view for financial personnel stakeholders is highlighted. During this phase, the view is assessed to see how well actual data align with expected results. Careful attention must be paid to showing the right information to the right stakeholder groups without superfluous information.

Monitor for Triggers

This step involves monitoring triggers, analyzing the impact of external and internal events, and determining the relevance of triggers. It includes actual performance of the portfolio views against results on a periodic and event-driven basis to identify when the portfolio needs to be reevaluated, rebalanced, and reprioritized.

Triggers are predetermined events that could have an impact on IT portfolio investment mix. They are driven by timing, the economy, relationships, and specific business/industry events. Triggers help determine the company's tolerance for risk and desired return levels. They are set when investments have high associated risks or potential for high returns.

In a stock portfolio, a trigger could be a stock price hitting a predetermined buy or sell point, announcement of a change in the fed funds rate, or even a major news announcement about the company. In IT portfolios, triggers include periodic activities (annual budget review, customer satisfaction surveys, status reviews), life cycle events such as an investment that has reached total cost-of-ownership thresholds (desktop refresh cycles), and environmental events (emerging technologies or competitor moves). What makes an event relevant as a trigger is its potential impact on risk or reward within the IT portfolio. Predetermined actions, also known in IT as road mapping, prepare IT portfolio managers for quick decisions in the event that a trigger event occurs. Advanced consideration of potential actions prepares IT management with options for a quick decision. When business agility means competitive advantage, such decision enablers provide an edge. Establishing triggers without developing reaction plans can waste time and resources in determining an appropriate tactic.

Once triggers are defined, IT management monitors the environment for triggering events. When one occurs, portfolio performance is assessed against targets to determine whether acting on the trigger will improve the reward or reduce risk. Rebalancing investments may occur.

Changes affect the possible risks faced by companies (i.e., on projects, within processes, and for asset purchases) or the achievable returns (i.e., from system replacement). When the potential risk or return is significant, companies establish measurement thresholds—variances or limits at which they will consider reacting to the changes by rebalancing the investment mix in their IT portfolio. Associating triggers with actions that may be taken if the threshold is met is an important IT portfolio management decision-making step.

Evaluating triggers involves risk/reward impact analysis. The question is whether event repercussions are sufficiently consequential to warrant assessing and potentially rebalancing the portfolio. Risk evaluation can be simple (judging impact and probability on a low- to high-risk scale) or highly complex (statistical processes weighting various situational factors). Based on their risk tolerance, most businesses have a risk evaluation process that IT management can employ. Reward assessment is specific to the investment and the trigger. For instance, vendor price reductions as a trigger on infrastructure investments may signal the opportunity to expand storage capacity within acceptable capital purchase limits (reduced risk), enabling data warehousing expansion (increased reward).

Temporal event triggers (cyclical, periodic) are drawn from fiscal calendar dates and business milestones. Annual or quarterly planning and budgeting activities and status reports would naturally trigger IT portfolio managers to assess and potentially rebalance the portfolio. Life cycle triggers, although potentially viewed as event based, require special consideration. Realizing the life cycles and refresh rates of other investments in the IT portfolio will greatly enhance portfolio benefits.

The assessment cycle of each level of the portfolio (i.e., entire portfolio, subportfolio, and investment) should occur on an as-needed or at a minimum on a quarterly basis. For an off-cycle event, the assessment would be based on an event trigger. So it follows that events must be defined that would trigger assessments. Triggers can be generated from:

- The entire portfolio
  - Changes in customer demands that are sensed by online analytical (pattern recognition) tools
  - Major changes in business detected through business and customer intelligence systems
  - Major shifts detected through scenario planning processes
  - Major economic or regulatory changes
- The subportfolio
  - Significant deviations from revenue projections and corresponding adjustments required in variable operational spending (e.g., projects, people, on-demand asset pricing)

- Investment
  - Early warning system detecting a project calamity
  - Significant deviations from expected costs or returns on an investment or asset
  - Departure of key staff based on skills

IT portfolio management is about alignment with business strategy, which should view change as an opportunity. Establishing triggers requires advanced thinking by portfolio managers about changes and potential impacts on risks and returns. Using triggers involves:

- Determining what is sufficiently important to warrant a trigger

- Setting limits, thresholds, or ranges beyond which a trigger evokes portfolio assessment action

- Monitoring for triggering events

- Evaluating the impact and relevance of an event that occurred

- Developing scenarios to consider in the event of each trigger

Measure the Portfolio and Compare Measures against Targets

Measuring the portfolio and comparing measures against targets involves:

- Assuring that accurate, reliable, and timely data are collected. A centralized repository is a best practice in this area.

- Processes used to collate the data and measurement tools to help pull the information together and provide relevant information to the appropriate stakeholders.

- Metrics and gauges (dashboard) to provide the interface for stakeholders to view and analyze the data.

- Storing the history of the data for future possible access.

The IT portfolio scorecard, as per Exhibit 5.30, maps:

- The desired target ranges—investment categories juxtaposed against strategic, tactical, life cycle, and regulatory categories—of each business unit. They are rolled up to reflect the total company perspective.

- Portfolio duration (life cycle) categorized according to short term versus long term.

- Portfolio risks.

EXHIBIT 5.30   IT PORTFOLIO SCORECARD

	Transform			Transform			Transform			Transform			Transform						
	Division 1			Division 2			Division 3			Corporate			Total Company						
	Run	Grow	Trans form	Run	Grow	Trans form	Run	Grow	Trans form	Run	Grow	Trans form	Run	Grow	Trans form	Actual Total	Minimum	Maximum	Status
Strategic	32		4	60			14	3	18	64	3		42.5	1.5	5.5	49.5	10	30	
Tactical	20	20	1	2	15		22	6	7	2			11.5	10.25	2	23.75	25	60	
Lifecycle	8			3			12	3		14			9.25	0.75	0	10	5	15	
Regulatory	15			20			15			17			16.75	0	0	16.75	5	15	
Maximum	70	42	8	90	25	0	60	35	30	100	7	0	80	20	15				
Minimum	50	20	0	75	10	0	30	15	10	95	0	0	65	5	0				
Actual	75	20	5	85	15	0	63	12	25	97	3	0	80	12.5	7.5				
Status																			

Company Portfolio by Risk				
	Minimum	Actual	Maximum	Status
High	0	5	7	
Medium	0	25	30	
Low	20	70	100	

Portfolio by Duration				
	Minimum	Actual	Maximum	Status
Long	40	75	60	
Short	40	25	80	

Legend	
	Within Range
	On Range
	1-10% out of range
	11+% out of range

To determine high, medium, and low risks, a decision-making scoring method is used. Criteria and factors are weighted, scored, and prioritized in much the same manner as the scoring methods for risks and returns discussed earlier in this chapter. Range limits are usually set, and a shading shows actual status juxaposed against range limits (e.g., within range, on range, 1–10% out of range, and 11+% out of range). Examples of ranges and limits might include these parameters:

- Strategic or long-term investments: 10% to 50%
- High risk: maximum 20%
- Life cycle (reengineering/retrain/retire): 10% to 35%
- Locally focused: maximum 15%
- Short-term or tactical: maximum 20%

From this analysis, multiple views are created and communicated to the appropriate stakeholder.

The subsections that follow show the methods, models, and approaches used to assess investments:

- Scoring methods
- Standard financial models
- Advanced modeling and simulation
- Nonnumeric models

The maturity of companies in using IT portfolio management will dictate whether they use two or more models. Companies at the highest maturity level may use a combination of most of the models, while companies that are just beginning tend to use the financial and the nonnumeric models. The key is not to get bogged down in analysis paralysis and to make decisions based on the best information available.

Scoring Methods

Scoring methods provide a structured framework that allows comparison of qualitative and quantitative criteria to derive weights and establish priorities of alternatives used within the decision-making process.[10] Multiattribute value tree (MAVT) analysis is a scoring methodology that gives meaning to multiple tangible and intangible objectives that may have conflicting goals and priorities in support of the decision-making process.[11] The analytical hierarchy process is a commonly used scoring model for value tree analysis. The advantages and disadvantages of using scoring models in assessing investments and the IT portfolio are shown in Exhibit 5.31.

Standard Financial Models

Many financial models address the time value of money, translating costs and benefits into offsetting streams of discounted cash flows. The most commonly applied financial models are shown in Exhibit 5.32.

Return on investment (ROI), productivity index, profitability index, and payback periods are examples of additional financial models to assess the IT portfolio. Sensitivity analysis is an effective adjunct to financial models, offering a range of perspectives based on various scenarios. The advantages and disadvantages of using financial models in assessing investments and the IT portfolio are shown in Exhibit 5.33.

Advanced Modeling and Simulation

Advanced modeling and simulation approaches are explained in Exhibit 5.34. Unlike the scoring method or the financial models, the modeling and simulation approaches examine more than one single score or value. These models require

EXHIBIT 5.3 | ADVANTAGES AND DISADVANTAGES OF SCORING METHODS

Scoring Methods Used to Assess IT Investments	
Advantages	Disadvantages
• Accepted practices, standard definitions	• Result is a relative measure that has no real value or utility
• Easy to use	• Weights may be based on subjective criteria
• Based on standardized weighting of company priorities and objectives	• There is independence between factors
• Considers both quantitative and qualitative inputs	• It does not result in multiple decisions or possible timing of options
• Factors risks and uncertainties through incorporating the probability of success	• Assumes that the highest scored investments should be given higher priority of consideration than lower-scoring investments — it does not answer the fundamental question: Is this a good investment?
• Produces scores for individual investments	
• Allows users to adjust weights and parameters to enable what-if scenarios and analysis	

Sources: Adapted from:

Archer, N. P., Ghasemzadeh, F. (1996), "Project Portfolio Selection Techniques: A Review and a Suggested Integration Approach," *Innovation Research Working Group Working Paper No. 46,* McMaster University.

Henriksen, A. D., Traynor, A. J. (1999). "A Practical R&D Project-Selection Scoring Tool," *IEEE Transactions on Engineering Management,* 46/2, pp. 158–170.

Martikainen, Juha (2002). "Portfolio Management of Strategic Investment in the Metal Industry," master's thesis, Helsinki University of Technology, January.

Matejcik, F. J. "TM 665 Project Planning & Control," South Dakota School of Mines and Technology.

Meredith, J. R., Mantel, S. R., Jr. (2000). *Project Management—A Managerial Approach,* John Wiley & Sons.

Steele, L. W. (1988). "What We've Learned—Selecting R&D Programs and Objectives," *Research Technology Management,* Mar.–Apr., pp. 17–36.

expertise for evaluating many scenarios and variables. The advantages and disadvantages of using modeling and simulation approaches in assessing investments and the IT portfolio are listed in Exhibit 5.35.

Nonnumeric Models

Nonnumeric models are based on must-have investments where the cost of not investing in a particular project or ongoing investment far exceeds the cost of the investment. These include investments that address mandatory/regulatory

EXHIBIT 5.32 COMMONLY APPLIED FINANCIAL MODELS

Net present value: discounts outstanding cash flows at a suitable cost of capital (hurdle rate or weighted average cost of capital). The net present value is positive if an investment earns a rate of return above the cost of capital (or hurdle rate). Since projects can have varying degrees of risk, the hurdle rate should take this into account and be set higher for riskier projects. Since net present value only assigns one specific figure, it might not be applicable to analyze investments that may have a range of possible outcomes.

Internal rate of return: related to net present value, internal rate of return is the rate at which the net present value is zero. If the internal rate of return is greater than the hurdle rate, the net present value must be greater than zero. There is a chance that a project could yield multiple internal rates of return. Internal rates of return provide the same discount rates to both costs and revenues, which in some cases is undesirable.

Expected commercial value: determines the commercial worth of an investment by considering the future stream of costs and benefits, the probability of technical and commercial success, and the strategic importance of an investment.

Economic value added: is equal to the after-tax operating profit generated by an investment less the dollar cost of the capital employed to finance the investment.

Sources: Adapted from:

Eric Burke, "Portfolio Analysis, Key Metrics, and Techniques for Analyzing the Portfolio," *Portfolio Knowledge.*

Alastair L. Day, *Mastering Financial Modelling,* Financial Times/Prentice-Hall, 2001.

Gabriel Hawawini and Claude Viallet, *Finance for Executives,* 2nd edition, South Western, 2002.

Joel G. Siegel, Jae K. Shim, and David Minars, *The Complete Book of Business Math,* McGraw-Hill, 1995.

requirements, operational necessities whereby sizable losses will occur if investments are not made, and competitive responses in order to at least remain on par with competitors.

Assess the Performance of the IT Portfolio

The balanced scorecard created by Robert S. Kaplan and David P. Norton[12] is essentially a navigational tool for managing performance against business objectives. A balanced scorecard translates business and strategic objectives into a set of performance measures. The use of the word *balance* refers not only to cost and benefit, shareholder and customer, efficiency and effectiveness, and/or long and short term but also to dependencies between investments and the priorities that drive

EXHIBIT 5.33   ADVANTAGES AND DISADVANTAGES OF FINANCIAL
MODELS

Financial Models Used to Assess IT Investments	
Advantages	Disadvantages
• Accepted practices, easy to use, standard definitions	• Do not account for intangible value (except for risk)
• Variable can be altered for what-if analysis	• Timing of cash flow needs not considered
• Leverage accounting data	• Multiple gating decision points not considered
• Primarily a single numerical output	• Can be biased toward short-term investments
• Risk is incorporated in some models	• Criteria based on financial return/profitability

Sources: Adapted from:

Archer, N. P., Ghasemzadeh, F. (1996), "Project Portfolio Selection Techniques: A Review and a Suggested Integration Approach," *Innovation Research Working Group Working Paper No. 46,* McMaster University.

Henriksen, A. D., Traynor, A. J. (1999). "A Practical R&D Project-Selection Scoring Tool," *IEEE Transactions on Engineering Management, 46/2,* pp. 158–170.

Martikainen, Juha (2002). "Portfolio Management of Strategic Investment in the Metal Industry," master's thesis, Helsinki University of Technology, January.

Matejcik, F. J. "TM 665 Project Planning & Control," South Dakota School of Mines and Technology.

Meredith, J. R., Mantel, S. R., Jr. (2000). *Project Management—A Managerial Approach,* John Wiley & Sons.

Steele, L. W. (1988). "What We've Learned—Selecting R&D Programs and Objectives," *Research Technology Management, Mar.–Apr.,* pp. 17–36.

success. The word *scorecard* implies measurement against goals and targets. Unlike dashboards that monitor progress and key indicators on an ongoing basis, balanced scorecards act as lenses for seeing targets and navigating the best course of action.

For some companies, the traditional four focused quadrants of the balanced scorecard (finance, customer, internal process, and learning/innovation) provide reasonable visibility to make strategic decisions. For others, the focus might shift more to specific or narrow targets involving close links with operational measures. For example, simple financial measures are not sufficient to manage the outcomes of many aggressive e-business initiatives. The lessons learned from world-class firms often include:

• The scorecard is not as important as the performance planning and management activity itself

EXHIBIT 5.34   ADVANCED MODELING AND SIMULATION
APPROACHES

Monte Carlo simulation: emerged from the sciences and engineering fields, having been deployed in domains for which the algebraic complexities are effectively unsolvable. In IT portfolio management, Monte Carlo simulation is not used in algebraic problems but rather in an incomprehensible spectrum of possible future outcomes as they affect a present decision. Unlike the scoring or many of the financial models, Monte Carlo does not produce a single value. Monte Carlo analysis results in a distribution of the present value of many possible future outcomes. Monte Carlo simulation is emerging as a modeling tool in IT portfolio management.

Real options: provide the right but not the future obligation to acquire an asset with its associated physical and intellectual capital assets. Real options are the present value of the future right to make a choice involving the full investment in a project. Most financial options have an established extant market, allowing buyers and sellers to readily determine value and volatility. For IT investments, value and volatility are not always as obvious, with little history on which to perform traditional valuation assessments. The key for using real options in valuing IT investments is knowing that at a future point additional information will be available to make a more economically intelligent decision.

Scenario planning: more expansive and more comprehensive than performing what-if analysis. Scenario planning is developing the ability to view and assess what happens if certain worlds are realized—the discrete classifications of the wide range of future possible business outcomes. Using Monte Carlo, there are elegant ways of incorporating scenario planning and modeling.

Decision (probability) trees: show the sequence of possible outcomes of an investment. Cash flows and net present value of a project under different circumstances can be highlighted in a decision tree. The advantage of this approach is the visibility into possible outcomes of the investment, which makes decision makers more cognizant of adverse possibilities and depicts the nature of short- and long-term cash flows. Decision tree analysis is complicated and requires reasonable knowledge of the complexities associated with an investment over the period of time it is evaluated.

Efficient frontier curve: economic concept developed by Dr. Harry Markowitz. The efficient frontier curve displays all possible combinations of optimal values at minimal risks (the impact of a dollar investment juxtaposed to the value received) that can be generated with resources in an unconstrained mode.

Sources: Adapted from:

Richard Razgaitis, *Dealmaking Using Real Options and Monte Carlo Analysis,* John Wiley & Sons, 2003.

Jae K. Shim and Joel G. Siegel, *Handbook of Financial Analysis, Forecasting, & Modeling,* Prentice-Hall, 1988.

United Management Technologies, www.umt.com.

EXHIBIT 5.35   ADVANTAGES AND DISADVANTAGES OF MODELING
AND SIMULATION APPROACHES

Modeling and Simulation Approaches Used to Assess IT Investments	
Advantages	Disadvantages
• Evaluation of multiple stages and decisions; limited downside risk	• High level of expertise to input, operate, and assess is needed
• Identifies good investments	• Detailed and accurate information and data are required
• Focuses management on considering multiple options and scenarios	• Determining probabilities can be highly subjective

Sources: Adapted from:

Archer, N. P., Ghasemzadeh, F. (1996), "Project Portfolio Selection Techniques: A Review and a Suggested Integration Approach," *Innovation Research Working Group Working Paper No. 46,* McMaster University.

Henriksen, A. D., Traynor, A. J. (1999). "A Practical R&D Project-Selection Scoring Tool," *IEEE Transactions on Engineering Management,* 46/2, pp. 158–170.

Martikainen, Juha (2002). "Portfolio Management of Strategic Investment in the Metal Industry," master's thesis, Helsinki University of Technology, January.

Matejcik, F. J. "TM 665 Project Planning & Control," South Dakota School of Mines and Technology.

Meredith, J. R., Mantel, S. R., Jr. (2000). *Project Management—A Managerial Approach,* John Wiley & Sons.

Steele, L. W. (1988). "What We've Learned—Selecting R&D Programs and Objectives," *Research Technology Management,* Mar.–Apr., pp. 17–36.

- Arbitrary setting of targets and performance zones results in poor performance management (not to mention the angst of those responsible for the performance)
- A systematic goal/question/metric approach focuses the balanced measures on essential performance management issues and results in better visibility

Exhibit 5.36 is a balanced scorecard for IT, with the goals, questions, and key metrics displayed.

An assessment report is created at the conclusion of this stage to compare the investment mix and results against the target and to show all gaps and residual risks. This report is shared with and approved by executive management and other key stakeholders. Approval of the final contents of the assessing stage also occurs by executive management (e.g., IT investment council) and key stakeholders (e.g., portfolio view owners). The elements of this stage should be communicated to all

EXHIBIT 5.36   BALANCED SCORECARD FOR IT

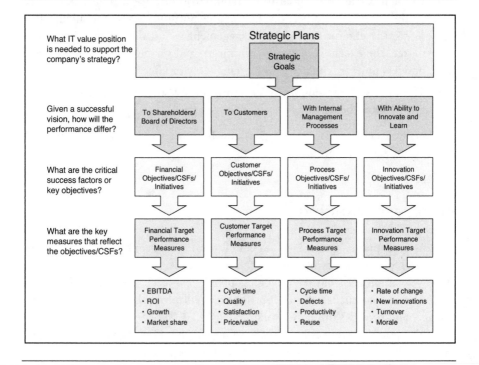

key staff. Information and feedback from employees and customers will drive continuous change to assessment elements.

Gaps can usually be seen at this juncture of the process. Some of the gaps between the target and the current investment mix might show these areas need to be addressed:

- Current investments do not support achievement of future business and strategic objectives.

- Measurement and monitoring processes are insufficient to track progress of achieving critical success factors.

- Portmortem analysis of projects after they are inserted into operations is not sufficient.

- The mix of investment according to the categorization of investments does not align with future strategies.

- Too many projects are underway that are being supported by too few resources. The allocation of the company's best resources are not targeted to the most important projects.

- Intangible assets are not factored into the value of the portfolio.

- Cultural barriers are harder to overcome than originally estimated. Collaboration and communication among the portfolio team, the architecture teams, the enterprise program management teams, the requirements committee, the executive steering committee, and various functional areas and business units are not yet working efficiently or effectively.

- The results of assessing financial returns of investments do not support the growth story being told by executives.

The next stage evaluates these gaps and fine-tunes the portfolio to bring it closer to the target IT portfolio.

STAGE 5: BALANCING

Systems are supposed to tend toward equilibrium . . . but only in thermodynamics. The IT portfolio is by no means a thermodynamic system. It is a complex mix of new technologies, old technologies, people, projects, and ideas. Without a framework to rationalize the IT portfolio, it will probably decay. IT portfolio management provides this framework.

To this point, objectives have been defined for the IT portfolio. These objectives have been tempered with the realities of the organization's culture and abilities. The structure of the portfolio has been designed. The portfolio structure has been populated. The populated IT portfolio has been analyzed and assessed against the goals, desired returns, and tolerance for risk. There is most likely a gap between the existing IT portfolio and the desired one.

Using the portfolio performance report, the validated portfolio, and the various views from stage 4, balancing the portfolio involves creating a set of repeatable processes for adding, subtracting, repositioning, and performing what-if trade-off analysis to maximize IT value. During the assessment phase, the performance of the portfolio should have been well documented; a list of gaps should have been made to enable portfolio tuning. Stage 5 is fundamentally the tuning phase, along with the refinement of the tuning processes. Of the various options, the optimal ones are selected and acted upon. Depending on the selected portfolio tuning options, balancing could be as simple as changing the list of funded projects, or it could kick off a large transformation initiative to revamp the portfolio of applications in production. Along with a balanced portfolio, the outputs of this stage include:

- A list of approved portfolio changes and associated change recommendations (e.g., shifting resources from one project to another, developing new skills, providing user training)

- Portfolio reassessment requests when the balancing activities require that additional assessments be conducted
- Approved updates to various portfolio views and associated prioritization based on the new metrics and assessments

Exhibit 5.37 outlines the specific tasks and activities involved in developing the balancing stage. The critical activities of the tasks addressed in this section include:

- Identifying tuning options
- Analyzing portfolio options to determine trade-offs
- Selecting and approving portfolio changes
- Implementing portfolio changes

Balancing, like the other stages discussed in this chapter, is a highly iterative process. One of the most important outputs of IT portfolio management, however, is the ability to create a set of repeatable processes for dynamically adding, subtracting, reprioritizing, and repositioning portfolios and investments to maximize IT value at minimal levels of risk (while satisfying these within schedule, labor, funding, and other constraints). The IT portfolio balancing capability is one of the key competencies that must be ingrained in the fabric of the organization. Ideally, IT portfolio management should not be a one-time event. It should be an

EXHIBIT 5.37   BALANCING STAGE TASKS

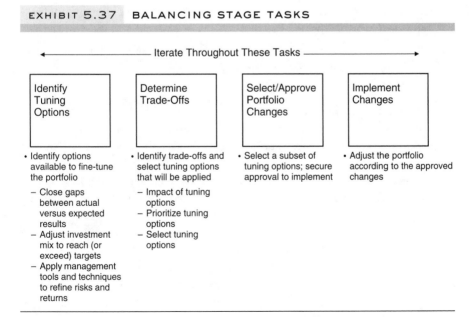

ongoing balancing of the IT portfolio to match change requirements of the business. The ultimate impacts of not balancing the IT portfolio dynamically are:

- Overspending for value received
- Not aligning resources optimally
- Uncontrolled hardware base growth, driving the need for more personnel
- Accumulation of noncompetitive technology, necessitating tying associated costs to goods and services
- Inability to invest where investment is really needed because capital is tied up where it should not be
- Loss of leverage for IT investments and therefore a reduction of potential return on assets

Balancing is nothing new to investment managers at money management firms who have developed sophisticated portfolio optimization tools that explore the most advantageous risk-adjusted returns for investments. Balancing the IT portfolio is the result of:

- Identifying gaps (e.g., investments and portfolios not meeting expectations, projects or existing assets that should be retired, comparison against benchmarks) with the portfolio performance report
- Spotting inefficiencies (e.g., redundant solutions, solutions showing diminishing returns, lack of reuse)
- Identifying changes in current conditions (e.g., competitor announces a new product that threatens a company's market share) and their impacts
- Performing what-if analysis (e.g., adjusting key variables in service levels or analyzing alternatives and performing sensitivity analysis on each of these variables)

Many companies base their IT investments on annual budget cycles, allocating the entire budget to run-the-business, grow-the-business, and transform-the-business opportunities. The expectation is that all of these investments will stay on track, avoid scope creep, and continue to align with company priorities. This static approach does not leave room for off-cycle IT investments, rebalancing priorities, or accelerating, delaying, or canceling investments in light of changing conditions. Often, it also fails to leave contingency for errors in estimating. Estimates, by definition, are inaccurate. For some odd reason, however, there is a belief that estimates are accurate. IT portfolio management, especially at the balancing stage, allows organizations to contend with differences between estimates and actuals. Mapping of resources, competencies, and capabilities to investments is a leading practice. Balancing these mappings or relationships assures allocation of resources is in line with the needs of the business.

Identify Tuning Options

The first activity in this stage is to identify the various options that will lead to an optimal portfolio. IT portfolio management is as much an art as a science. The identification of portfolio tuning options involves leveraging work from previous stages, including the assessment of portfolio performance from stage 4. Portfolio tuning also requires consideration of the validated future-state portfolio and the impact of internal and external events. Given these inputs, several things occur:

- Identification of options for eliminating differences between actual and expected portfolio results
- Identification of options to meet investment targets if they differ from expected portfolio results, which after going through this exercise, they often do
- Scenario analysis or what-if analysis to determine an optimal list of options

Most of this effort is done behind the scenes. The portfolio manager, the portfolio team, and the owners of the various subportfolios are involved, but the senior leadership is usually kept out of the loop. This is an analytical exercise that uses methods and approaches discussed in the previous stage such as scoring methods, standard financial models, and advanced modeling and simulation tools. Senior leadership tends to want well-thought-out bottom-line solutions to approve or reject.

The identification of portfolio tuning options should culminate with a first cut of the actions required for balancing. It tends not to be the final list, and it has not been approved or funded.

At this point, it will undoubtedly be known whether the tools used to support the IT portfolio management effort were appropriate. If the initial scope of IT portfolio management was small, simpler tools may get you through an entire cycle. If, however, the scope or quantity of data being analyzed is great, the what-if analysis will justify the cost of a tool designed to do IT portfolio management. It will also bring the office automation tools to their knees.

Determine Trade-Offs

Trade-offs usually exist because of resource constraints. They must be analyzed to generate a list of prioritized actions against the portfolio replete with supporting analysis, which will come in handy as invariably some will not be pleased with the outcome of the analysis (e.g., the son-in-law of the CIO who no longer gets funding for his "sticky" web thing). The major steps in this activity are:

- Performing impact analysis on tuning options
- Prioritizing tuning options
- Identifying risk/return trade-offs

These steps require business representation. Someone with IT financial expertise should also be part of the process. Scenario planning is another skill required to get through these activities. This role can be filled by anyone who has done scenario planning before. The portfolio manager acts as a fund manager, balancing the risks and benefits of IT initiatives to manage IT investments.

Scenario planning is an important capability that decision makers use in developing multiple alternatives and assessing the viability and achievability of each alternative. Often, each scenario is mapped visually, and impacts of the scorecard are evaluated based on value, risk, balance, alignment, and capacity. The discussions for the discovery, project, and application portfolios are also applicable to subportfolios.

Trade-offs in the IT Discovery and IT Project Portfolios

After identifying the tuning options against defined and weighted criteria that have been vetted and approved by the decision makers, the portfolio is scored. A prioritized ranking of investments is shown based on a numeric scoring value, and the cost of the investment is also shown. A dynamic rank-ordered list shows the prioritized rank order of investments based on concurrent assessment of several criteria such as net present value, internal rates of return, strategic importance, probability of success, etc.[13] Investments can be bucketed according to percentage allocations in such areas as:

- In investment categories (run, grow, transform the business)
- By business unit
- By product line
- By geography

For smaller, singularly focused companies, a single portfolio showing all of these investments may be appropriate. In addition, each of these allocations can be further broken down according to risk versus return, portfolio types, and so on.

Typically, there are more investments than a company can afford. The highest-scoring to the lowest-scoring investments are usually shown in order. A cutoff point is reached when cumulative investment costs equal the budgeted amount. Investments that fall above this line have a high likelihood of being accepted; those falling below the line will probably be canceled or put on hold.

And now the fun begins. Tools alone do not make decisions; people do! So on first impression, you may think that the perfectly balanced, aligned, achievable, and

valuable portfolio has been built. The prioritized ranking was built on the foundation of decision maker input on the development, definition, and weighting of the
criteria. But variables such as uncertainty and subjectivity in some of the data and
information, interdependencies, constraints (costs, resources,.capacity, timelines of
value creation, acceptable risk and return levels), changing conditions and priorities, and other factors can result in multiple iterations and adjustments by the decision makers to optimize the portfolio. Alternatives range from adjusting a few
variables through what-if analysis (e.g., testing the sensitivity of the portfolio to
adjustments made to risk threshold levels, budget plus-ups or cutbacks, or alterations to strategic scenarios) to scenario planning, where multiple-value dials are
adjusted. In addition to the bucket method, there are other approaches, examples
shown in Exhibit 5.38, that companies can use to assess portfolio balance.

**EXHIBIT 5.38   ADDITIONAL MODELS USED TO ACCESS THE
BALANCE OF THE IT PORTFOLIO**

- *Mathematical programming:* produces an optimal set of investments based on
  objectives and constraints. Mathematical models use detailed sensitivity analysis
  through many models and methods such as integer, linear, nonlinear, dynamic,
  and goal programming.
- *Contingent portfolio programming (CPP):* recent approach to portfolio balancing,
  combining decision trees with mathematical programming. Utilizes uncertainties
  with certainty equivalents.
- *Pictorial diagrams:* two-dimensional bubble charts, histograms, line and pie charts
  graphically showing investments under consideration.

Sources: Adapted from:

Archer, N. P., Ghasemzadeh, F. (1996). "Project Portfolio Selection Techniques: A Review and
a Suggested Integration Approach," *Innovation Research Working Group Working Paper No. 46,*
McMaster University.

Gustafsson, J., Salo, A. (2001). *Managing Risky Projects with Contingent Portfolio Programming,*
unpublished manuscript.

Henriksen, A. D., Traynor, A. J. (1999). "A Practical R&D Project-Selection Scoring Tool,"
IEEE Transactions on Engineering Management, 46/2, pp. 158-170.

Lockett, A. G., Gear, A. E. (1973). "Representation and Analysis of Multi-Stage Problems in
R&D," *Management Science,* 19/8, pp. 947-960.

Martikainen, Juha (2002). "Portfolio Management of Strategic Investment in the Metal Industry," master's thesis, Helsinki University of Technology, January.

Matejcik, F. J. "TM 665 Project Planning & Control," South Dakota School of Mines and
Technology.

Taha, H. A. (1997). *Operations Research—An Introduction,* 6th edition, Prentice-Hall.

Trade-offs in the Application Portfolio

The application portfolio is one of the more active portfolios that is frequently balanced. Many applications paid for the infrastructure needed to run the application, leading to ad hoc infrastructural growth and maintenance of unique components in support of aging applications. Adding to this chaos is the fact that applications may be added and not retired, so the actual portfolio grows and becomes a burden that inhibits change as opposed to enhancing agility.

Determining how to balance the application portfolio should begin with a firm understanding of the objectives and key performance indicators a company is trying to deliver over the short term, medium term, and long term. These are mapped against the as-is and to-be business processes, and a gap analysis is developed. Existing applications are analyzed to determine their (also see Chapter 4):

- Functional quality
  - Data completeness
  - Data accuracy
  - Data consistency
  - Data currency
  - System quality

- Technical quality
  - Architectural (development, environment, middleware, database, server, storage, network protocol, client code, etc.)
  - Operational (job scheduling, program management, change management, system monitoring, vendor/contract management)

- Costs (application maintenance, operations, software, hardware, depreciation)

- Risk profile (security, disaster recovery, vendor viability, regulatory compliance, IT HR risk, privacy, information risk)

- User information (customer satisfaction)

- Support and dependencies of other portfolios as well as of other applications

- Business value (supporting business and strategic objectives, revenue, quality, time, regulatory compliance, cross-selling opportunities, controlling costs)

- Business processes that are enabled (e.g., problem management, service-request management, service-based cross-selling)

The information collected regarding the application is assessed against the business process gap analysis. The business value and technology assessment provides information for migration strategies and trade-offs for application portfolio decisions. Possible alternative investments are considered if the gap analysis does not close with the existing application.

The portfolio manager acts as a fund manager, balancing the risks and benefits of IT initiatives to manage IT investments. Each investment scenario is mapped, and impacts on the scorecard are evaluated based on value, risk, balance, alignment, and capacity. The mapping of scenario planning and migration patterns can occur over many years as shown in Exhibit 5.39.

EXHIBIT 5.39   APPLICATION PORTFOLIO MIGRATION PATTERNS

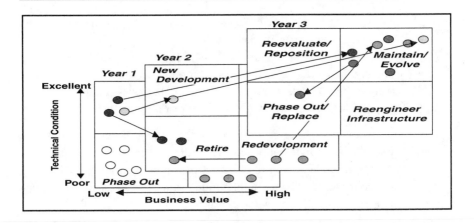

Phase out/replace: low business value, low technical condition: these applications are candidates for replacement/retirement, although many may be legacy or back-office systems that may not justify replacement due to replacement costs or the limited business value to be added. Value alternatives include
- Retire
- Outsource
- Replace
- Delegate to another entity

Reevaluate/reposition: low business value, excellent technical condition: these applications typically have been implemented in the near past following architectural guidelines but with such a limited scope or silo-oriented design that significant business value is not achieved. The key is to identify and analyze opportunities for reuse of these applications or their components across the enterprise. Value alternatives include:
- Productize
- Focus
- Innovate

Reengineer/modernize: high business value, poor technical condition: these applications serve the business well but create significant problems when there is a need to share information or integrate with other applications. A more adaptive application infrastructure (component-based, event-driven, n-tier, with message-based interfaces) is the prescription. Value alternatives include:
- Wrapper — leave core untouched, add surrounding flexibility
- Restructure
- Centralize
- Rehost

Maintain/evolve: high business value, excellent technical condition: these applications deliver value and have been architected for adaptability. Care must be taken to ensure high business value and excellent technical condition are attained when optimizing the application portfolio to accommodate change. Value alternatives include:
- Partner
- Streamline
- Collaborate
- Fix/repair

In the Exhibit 5.39, a simple application portfolio is phased over a multiyear period. This graphic, however, may be one of many to facilitate the selection of the optimal set of actions against the application portfolio. Companies use a variety of portfolio optimization views, including:

- *Arthur D. Little life cycle approach:* assesses an industry's life cycle (i.e., embryonic, growth, maturity, and aging) against competitive positions (i.e., dominant, strong, favorable, tenable, weak). Companies assess the life cycle of an investment versus the strategic position in the marketplace. Also, investment categories are compared against the industry life cycle, providing very useful analysis.[14]

- *Boston Consulting Group's growth share matrix:* a quadrant chart comparing relative market share versus market growth rate. Categories are:
  - *Question mark:* low relative market share, high market growth rate
  - *Rising star:* high relative market share, high market growth rate
  - *Cash cow:* high relative market share, low market growth rate
  - *Dying dog:* low relative market share, low market growth rate[15]

Recall that in identifying portfolio tuning options, the goal was to identify the various options that led to an optimized IT portfolio. This activity analyzes the cross-portfolio impacts, identifying the changes that could be made and selecting those that will be made. It generates a multitude of graphics and a wealth of supporting analysis to create and receive approval for a list of doable action steps to optimize the portfolio. Spreadsheets are generally used to support financial analysis. Advanced risk analysis tools can be used for risk assessment in complex situations involving high-risk transformation. While advanced techniques such as Monte Carlo simulation might be called upon, they are not typically used in practice. The value derived from the effort must exceed the cost. Project and program management skills are also leveraged to build an actionable plan that includes dependencies.

Select/Approve Portfolio Changes

Select/approve portfolio changes is a task that selects a subset of the tuning options and secures approval to implement changes. Chapter 6 discusses software tools that allow business and IT to rapidly analyze many variables and parameters in the portfolio in order to quickly assess, alter, rebalance, and optimize the mix of investments. Examples of variables and constraints that can be adjusted when balancing the portfolio are:

- Analytic hierarchical structure
- Weighting factors assigned to each investment

- Hurdle rates used to calculate net present value
- Scoring criteria for each factor
- Acceptable range of the probability and the impact of risks
- Resource constraints
- Schedule
- Labor
- Budget
- Dependencies
- Allocations in investment categories
- Percentage of long-term versus short term investments
- Local versus global allocations
- Offensive versus defensive investments

The portfolio is optimized for generating the highest level of value (mandatory investments may not generate return, but are value added for companies) at acceptable levels of risk. Many companies are benchmarking their balance of investments against the competitors and leading companies in other industries. In balancing the portfolio, there are other subsets of tuning options that can be changed to alter the costs, risk, and ability to reach goals of the portfolio:

- *Fixed versus variable costs:* As a means to possibly gain efficiencies, companies may look to turn fixed costs into variable costs. On-demand offerings, insourcing versus outsourcing, and reassessment of the value chain are options for companies to explore.

- *Repositioning of service levels:* Service levels define the level of costs versus the availability for an offering. In the example in Exhibit 5.40, understanding the right number of nines and the value per increment dollar per 9 is essential to understanding how to balance and optimize the IT portfolio. The investment in availability is made to decrease the risk of downtime (which can have adverse revenue impact consequences).

- *Alternative investments:* When analyzing new investments and looking at trade-offs such as value, risk, and cost, there are times when the right functionality of a particular solution is an exact match to the capabilities needed. However, while the right solution may look like a perfect match, the costs of the solution greatly exceed the costs of an alternative solution (one that may have 80% of the capabilities needed). Balancing the portfolio means that IT and business work together and optimize based on a variety of variables.

EXHIBIT 5.40   BALANCING THE PORTFOLIO: AVAILABILITY

Availability	Minutes of Outage per Year
99.9999	0.53
99.999	5.26
99.99	52.56
99.95	262.80
99.9	525.60
99.5	2,628.00
90	52,560.00

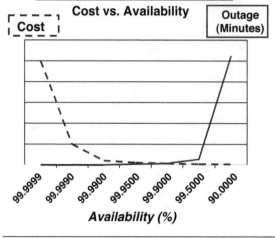

- *Consolidation opportunities:* Balancing the portfolio enables the company to look across various portfolios and investments to see where opportunities for consolidation may reside. Exhibit 5.41 shows a company with multiple divisions, each maintaining its own independent human resources application, and associated infrastructure and staffing. Depending on the unique business rules associated with the HR applications, this appears to be a likely candidate for portfolio balancing.

- *Life cycle and asset relationships:* Portfolio management occurs throughout the life cycle of an asset. Knowing the useful life of an asset, understanding the features, functionality, dependencies, and relationships of the asset, knowing when an asset has overengineered its target, having visibility across the company regarding other possible asset relationships, and being able to assess whether the asset is delivering on the initial assumptions (see Exhibit 5.42) are critical to balancing the portfolio. There are instances where new technology will displace an existing asset, and the decision to make these changes is difficult for many companies. Knowing when to retire or replace

EXHIBIT 5.41 BALANCING THE PORTFOLIO: MULTIPLE
AND REDUNDANT APPLICATIONS

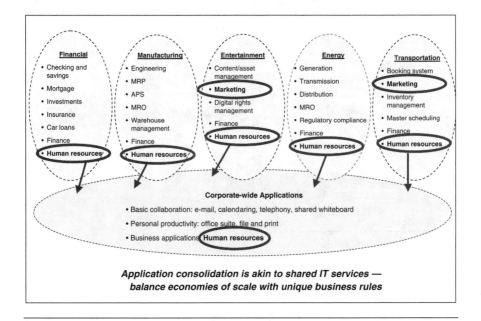

Application consolidation is akin to shared IT services —
balance economies of scale with unique business rules

an asset, even before the end of its life cycle, is critical to balancing the portfolio. Modeling the life span of investment and understanding the various milestone dates is also important.

Views to Select/Approve Portfolio Changes

The impacts of each of these possible options can be illustrated through views and characterized graphically. The trade-offs of each option being considered (and the result of combinations of options) can then be discussed with business leaders by showing the impacts to schedules, costs, risks, and value, and describing the business impacts resulting from each case. Each option and change to a variable produces a scenario illustrating the value/risk repercussions. Changes are made to one (or more) of the three models shown in the assessing stage: the scoring method, standard financial models, or advanced modeling and simulation approaches.

As shown in a screen shot from United Management Technologies (UMT) Portfolio Optimizer, the Efficient Frontier Curve in Exhibit 5.43 shows how tuning a subset of variables and constraints such as costs, resources (labor and nonlabor), and schedule (time and duration) could lead to dramatic improvements. In the exhibit, through tuning the variables and constraints associated with the Efficient Frontier

EXHIBIT 5.42 BALANCING THE PORTFOLIO: LIFE CYCLES AND LIFE SPANS OF APPLICATIONS

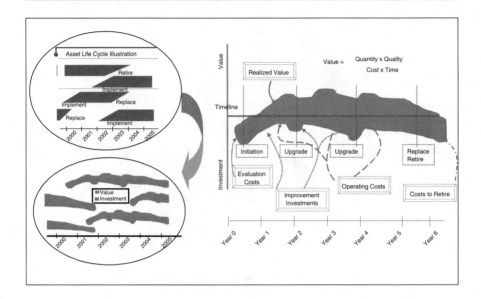

Curve, a UMT client experienced a 24% strategic value gain and $137 million EBIT (option 3) at the same budget level as the original selection (option 1).[16] As shown in Exhibit 5.43 in the subsection labeled Efficient Frontier:

- Portfolios that are below the curve reflect inefficient portfolios
- Portfolios that are on the curve are maximizing value from limited budgets
- It is impossible to have portfolios that are above the curve.[17]

The table on the left side of the chart in Exhibit 5.43 reflect investments, priorities as ranked against business drivers, and cost associated with each investment. Options 2 (optimal selection) and 3 (recommended solution) are what-if scenarios performed against option 1. Option 3 was the chosen portfolio. For many reasons, including mandatory investments that may not rank as high as other investments, the optimal solution, option 2, was not chosen.

Implement Portfolio Changes

Evaluating, prioritizing, and balancing IT investments is an emotionally charged activity. People are naturally attached to the merit of their project or operational

EXHIBIT 5.43 EFFICIENT FRONTIER CURVE

#	Portfolio	Strategic Value	Total EBIT
1	Original Selection	51%	$389 M
2	Optimal Selection	82%	$564 M
3	Recommended Selection	75%	$526 M

Efficient Frontier

Strategic Value Gain = 24%

EBIT Increase = $137 MM

Projects	Priorities	Total Cost	Original Selection Decision Variables	Optional Selection Decision Variables	Recommended Selection Decision Variables
Customer Relationship Management	11.8677%	3,495.62			
ATS APPLICATION Target Arch	8.6192%	1,386.29			
IBM Server Strategy	8.2821%	963.98			
SLA Measurement System	7.6460%	1,388.01			
Storage Design-Large Data Center	7.5780%	635.87			
Internet Based IPSEC Rem Acc VPN	6.2649%	914.18			
Service Delivery Project	6.2071%	1,200.91			
Tech Direction for Office Printing	6.0849%	500.82			
Asset Management	5.0562%	3,000.08			
Blades	3.9634%	1,989.83			
Storage Design-Mid Size Data Cent	3.3496%	2,427.77			
Windows 2000 Rollout	3.2832%	2,492.27			
Voice Over IP (VoIP)	2.7845%	1,799.45			
Technology Direction for Mass Print	2.3195%	3,270.62			
Oracle/Linux	2.0566%	473.85			
Tablet PC/PDA	2.0566%	50.79			
Email	2.0566%	1,827.85			
Network Mgt Tools Framework	1.9544%	1,090			
Quality of Service	1.8143%	617.89			
EGTRRA Regulatory Compliance	1.5560%	2,459.76			
CA Brightstor Storage Mgt	1.3088%	1,303.64			
Defining LAN Strategies	1.1289%	726.5			
BrightStore Vantage ROI Analysis	1.0283%	863.09			
IBM MVS Tools	1.0283%	1,177.81			
Application Security (Comp)	0.3428%	1,124.99			
Compliance(C/O)	0.3428%	3,155.02			
Limit Vector					

Source: Copyright © 2004 United Management Technologies (UMT), www.umt.com.

area. However, armed with predefined categories, criteria, and a balanced portfolio based on business and strategic objectives, IT investment decision making becomes easier.

Companies must compare the impacts and trade-offs of each alternative against the goals to be achieved when making final decisions. Risk tolerance, business strategy, and economic and industry trends will affect final choices; having the ability to model the effects of certain variables on the business fabric increases the probability of making the right decisions. The need for decision-making speed and accuracy exacerbates the decision maker's struggle for obtaining sufficient, useful information on which to base the decision within the available time. Being able to model the environment via a portfolio and generating scenarios that illustrate the alternatives' impact through a portfolio analysis and balancing process greatly increase the probability of making high-value decisions.

At the conclusion of the balancing stage, the portfolio is adjusted based on the approved recommendations. Approval of the final contents is also given by executive management and key stakeholders. The elements of this stage should be communicated to all key staff. Information and feedback from employees and customers will drive continuous change.

STAGE 6: COMMUNICATING

If you wait until the portfolio has been optimized to communicate, you will fail. We have tried to make this message loud and clear. We have tried to incorporate communication tasks in each stage. There is, however, a structured approach to communication.

The communication stage is not part of a sequential stage in portfolio building. Communicating happens throughout all stages of the IT portfolio management process. As previously mentioned, technology does not make decisions; people do! This includes identifying key audiences and key messages and measuring communications success. Mapping communication content to each audience is based on the results of stakeholder analysis and assessment. It involves understanding the best way to communicate to each audience, how often, and how to address people's needs and concerns, the medium that should be used, and knowing who should do the communicating. Above all else, IT portfolio management is about:

- Identifying the need for change and communicating that need to the right people
- Enabling analysis now and in the future, and communicating the need for change
- Driving support to make agreed-upon changes to the portfolio

- Setting up a structure to communicate changes to the portfolio that may require adjustment, balancing, or resetting of expectations
- Setting up a structure to communicate changes in the environment that will affect the portfolio
- Enabling a constant dialog between IT and business to improve effectiveness and reduce tensions

The communication stage should be treated much the way project management is treated. The traditional phases of project management are start-up, managing, and closure. You do not simply wait until the system is complete to start project management. Conversely, you cannot do all project management at the first stage. You must intersperse project management and communication tasks throughout the IT portfolio management plan.

The very first step in any initiative should be stakeholder analysis. This is certainly true of IT portfolio management. Yet all types of initiatives devoid of stakeholder analysis are common. This is simply wrong and must be corrected. Many excuses exist (e.g., I did it in my head, we don't need that at our company, it's so easy). They are unacceptable. Stakeholder analysis will help frame the issues and communication styles of those who can make or break IT portfolio management.

Another common mistake is to fixate on one type of communication. Many IT portfolio management initiatives have fixated on bubble charts. Clearly bubble charts enable understanding of the portfolio view, but they do not serve as very good invitations to key meetings. In general, a communication plan must exist and must be refined throughout the evolution and maturation of IT portfolio management. The plan must be acted upon and must at least contain these core components:

- Stakeholder analysis
- Communication methods
- Communication timetable
- Communication goals and metrics

Early in the portfolio management process, the communication focuses more on communicating the value of portfolio management to solicit support. As portfolio management understanding and adoption increase, communication focuses on sustaining support, eliciting participation, minimizing criticism, setting expectations, and demonstrating progress. Further along, communication tends to shift to support management of change and expectations.

For example, the changes and results of the balancing stage are communicated to all stakeholders of that stage. These stakeholders include representatives from the business, the executive steering committee, and possibly a program or project office. The key messages are identified, as well as a mechanism for measuring communications success. For the balancing stage, the communication tasks added to the overall communication plan might include:

- Mapping communication content to each audience based on the results of stakeholder analysis and assessment. This involves understanding the best way to communicate to each audience or individual and knowing who should be doing the communicating

- Delivering the actual messages to various parties

- Identifying acknowledgement of receipt of the messages surrounding changes to the portfolio and making suggested adjustments or receiving general acceptance

- Communicating back to key stakeholders about the value received during the balancing stage, possibly coupled with a message relating the value to preceding stages and the involvement and benefits expected in succeeding stages

For many companies, implementing IT portfolio management is a large change from the current status quo. Changes must be communicated in a consistent manner. The rationale for how objectives are defined, metrics existence and purpose, and the scoring approach must be clearly communicated and agreed to by personnel responsible for feeding and managing the IT portfolio management process. Relating these areas to employees asking, "What is in it for me?" conveys the need for information to be transparent. Training also plays a significant role, especially during times of massive changes. In addition, accountability, authority, responsibility, and related incentives and rewards must be in place and supported by employees.

Exhibit 5.44 outlines the specific tasks and activities involved in developing the communicating stage. The critical activities of the tasks addressed in this section include:

- Identifying stakeholders
- Creating communication packages
- Delivering communications

Identify Stakeholders

Communicating the portfolio creates a consistent approach for driving awareness, goals, status, and what needs to change. The awareness needs to be driven by a communication plan that tailors messages to specific audiences and makes sure they are received and acted upon.

EXHIBIT 5.44   COMMUNICATING STAGE TASKS

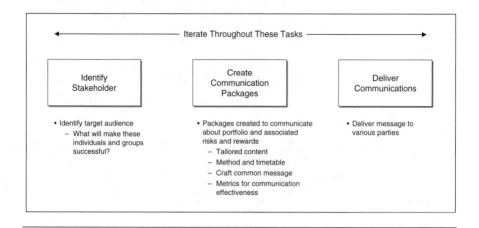

As Exhibit 5.45 shows, different stakeholders will have different pain points and different priorities. Therefore, the communications plan will need to take into consideration the varying criteria of what messages are conveyed, the frequency of the messages, and the media that should be used. Determining what will make the stakeholders in Exhibit 5.45 successful and tailoring communications and results through a dashboard and other media are seminal aspects of communications.

Create Communication Packages

Communicating the plans, goals, objectives, policies, procedures, and guidelines of IT to the entire company is essential. Communication of IT portfolio management to key stakeholders is equally necessary. A reasonable balance to who gets what message to manage expectations is critical. Care must be taken not to position IT portfolio management as another silver bullet approach that will solve all company issues without change pain. Conversely, enough potential and actual value and benefits must be communicated to keep people engaged.

Communicating the achievement of critical requirements and attainment of business value must occur. This has a positive impact on keeping employees vectored in the same direction and provides valuable information regarding the priorities of the company, creating alignment in the rank and file. Often this is done with some of the visual tools mentioned throughout this book. These tools must constantly be updated. Examples include:

EXHIBIT 5.45   UNDERSTANDING KEY PAIN POINTS AMONG
STAKEHOLDERS

Stakeholder	High-Probability Pain
CEO	Business units losing market share; overhead killing profits; information quality varies widely, confused debate among business unit IT directors; strategic planning fast (or nonexistent), implementation slow; business units do not innovate; each business unit has unique IT story
CFO	IT ROI impossible to calculate; IT budget is expense, not investment; corporate revenue declining; logistics costs rising; business unit financial data unreliable; business unit cannot answer financial questions promptly; business units vary in responsiveness
Business Unit VPs	Slow time to market; competitors innovate faster; need/cannot get new intelligence; corporate/third-party information not reusable; sales dropping
CIO	Multiple similar but unleverageable development projects; maintenance, not innovation; line IT directors on separate planets; one site — one IT vision; IT budget is being slashed, not treated as an investment; new processes cannot be computerized
Line IT	Firefighting and code maintenance; local systems unique; need offbeat skills
Third-Party Service/Outsourcers	All work is custom; cannot buy software components; each site unique; must use old development tools; IT strategy debates
End Users	Green screens; information in database but unavailable; information only one form; rekeying information; no mobile computing
Trading Partners	Poor e-commerce linkage; logistics information missing or inaccurate; systems cannot communicate; every site is unique

- *The balanced scorecard:* Discussed previously, the balanced scorecard is a performance measurement system that quantifies tangible and intangible assets, aligning with vision, business, and mission requirements. It displays a comprehensive view for executives, managers, and employees.
- *Key performance indicators:* These metrics are specifically related to achievement of objectives. Key performance indicators include productivity, customer satisfaction, budget and costs, resource management, quality (defects), agility (e.g., change management, configuration control, mean time to repair), and maturity.
- *Detailed reports:* Key aspects of project and operational metrics are reported, such as schedule status, life span, resource allocation status, budget and cost status, earned value status, variances, achievement of milestones, customer satisfaction survey results, performance status and accomplishments, open issues, and concerns.
- *Summary reports:* Whereas some prefer detailed reports, others, especially those in the executive leadership, just want the bottom line.

Beyond the reporting aspects of communicating the IT portfolio, employees will want to:

- Understand the business and strategic objectives of the company.
- Have insight into new proposed investments and criteria for new projects, including how they are evaluated and scored. In the event that resources

need to be rebalanced, transparency into proposed investments and new projects provides justification to employees regarding the prioritization of investments. In addition, it provides supporting evidence of why a current IT investment may need to be put on hold or canceled.

- Gain insight into the maturity of the IT portfolio, with specific goals and objectives for achieving the next level of maturity (assuming this is important to the company).

- Understand key metrics, what their specific contribution is to these measurements, and how they are calculated.

As shown in Exhibit 5.46, these performance and reporting mechanisms convey the business/IT value proposition to the executives, line managers, and operating staff (along with their IT peer groups).

Deliver Communications

The communications plan should articulate value and risks as well as scenarios and options. The who, what, how, and how often are related to the communications plan as shown in Exhibit 5.47. Other media for communicating performance of the IT portfolio include portals, newsletters, bulletin boards, reports, presenta-

EXHIBIT 5.46   PERFORMANCE AND REPORTING MECHANISMS

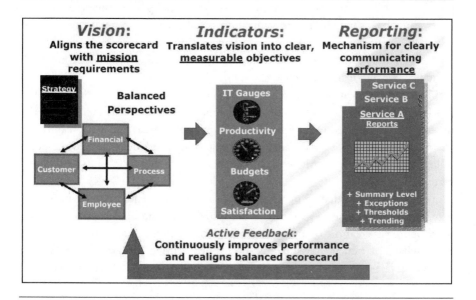

EXHIBIT 5.47 COMMUNICATION PLAN OVERVIEW

Who	What	How	How Often
CEO	Overview	Meetings	Quarterly
Execs	Strategy	Meetings	Quarterly
IT Staff	Tactics	Meetings	Monthly
Suppliers	Purchasing	Seminar	2x per year
Customers	Web Service	Webinar	Quarterly
Everyone	News & Status	Web & E-Mail	Weekly/Daily

tions, focus groups, letters, the IT annual report, the executive marketing plan, IT and corporate strategic plans, and even brown bag lunches.

STAGE 7: GOVERNANCE AND ORGANIZATION

The term *governance* often trips people up. Cognitive dissonance often occurs. Good governance is enabling. It identifies responsibilities of individuals, specifies processes to follow, and puts down principles and policies to eliminate ambiguity. Does it involve change in most organizations? Yes! Is change generally painful and met with skepticism? Yes! Thus, governance is an efficiency and effectiveness enabler. Too much too quick is bad. Appropriate governance will still be met with resistance because it involves change.

Like communication, refining governance should occur throughout the process. Governance should evolve as the process evolves. In fact, given the maturity model presented in Chapter 2, IT portfolio management can only get so far in the absence of governance. The underlying processes that feed the portfolio and are impacted by it require governance for the portfolio to evolve and mature.

The key skills needed to perform IT portfolio management are identified. A determination is made as to whether they represent additional tasks for existing roles or merit creation of new positions. This includes determining the rules about what a particular individual can do to the portfolio (or one of its parts) and who needs to be involved in the approval of changes in the portfolio management process. The board of directors provides the charter and oversight to the IT portfolio. More and more organizations are moving to this model as boards are being held more accountable and IT's importance is being recognized. A governing body (e.g., the executive steering committee, IT steering committee, IT investment council) is named that includes senior IT, business unit leaders, and corporate executives. This governing body governs the IT portfolio management principles, processes, guidelines, and policies. The development of the IT portfolio management governance mechanisms must, however, be done by the IT portfolio management team and includes the following steps:

- Determining the roles, responsibilities, and processes for governing the IT portfolio management process; evaluating the organizational model to establish and sustain portfolio management.
    - Determining portfolio management responsibilities by identifying the portfolio management tasks necessary to put the process in place, as well as tasks to execute the process over and over
    - Determining portfolio management roles by grouping the identified portfolio management responsibilities that could logically be performed by a group or an individual
    - Assessing current versus desired organization structure, roles, and competencies; determining gaps and a plan (training, reskilling, hiring, etc.) to fill the gaps
- Defining the principles for guiding portfolio management decision making, and providing the rationale/justification and implications for each principle.
- Identifying and defining business process integration between portfolio management and other business/IT processes to maximize portfolio value (e.g., budgeting/capital planning, strategic planning, enterprise architecture, enterprise program management, enterprise needs, capabilities and requirements, human capital management, and any other areas impacted by portfolio management).
- Identifying governance compliance triggers.
- Developing and maintaining the roles, responsibilities, and processes required for governing the portfolio management process. This should be consistent with and influence overall enterprise and/or IT governance processes already in place.

Exhibit 5.48 outlines the specific tasks and activities involved in developing the governance and organization stage. Chapter 3 covers both of these areas in great detail. Refer to Chapter 3 for an in-depth perspective of these two areas as well as an understanding of:

EXHIBIT 5.48 GOVERNANCE AND ORGANIZATION OVERVIEW

Iterate Throughout These Tasks

Portfolio Management Policy	Business Process Integration	Governance Compliance Triggers	Governance Processes	Establish Organization

Portfolio Management Policy
- Define the principles for portfolio management decision making

Business Process Integration
- Identify/define the process integration between portfolio management and other business/IT processes
  - Identify processes that will be impacted by or have an impact on the portfolio management process
  - Define what information should be exchanged, decisions to be made, approval steps, and dependencies

Governance Compliance Triggers
- Identify areas for compliance

Governance Processes
- Identify and maintain roles, responsibilities, and processes required for governing the portfolio management process
  - Define roles and responsibilities
  - Define and model sequence and dependencies of events
  - Identify metrics

Establish Organization
- Define and refine the organizational model for supporting and sustaining the portfolio management process
  - Identify appropriate tasks
  - Identify individual versus group tasks
  - Assess as-is organization structure, roles, and competencies
  - Develop the IT portfolio management charter

- Portfolio management policy
- Business process integration
- Governance compliance triggers
- Governance processes
- Organization establishment

When applying governance to the IT portfolio management process, the first step is to define the principles and corresponding policies under which IT portfolio management will operate. These can usually be derived from information provided in the game plan stage (e.g., portfolio goals, portfolio investment strategy). If corporate or IT principles exist, they may be used as a foundation as well. We recommend including the reason for abiding by a principle. Devoid of rationale and justification, principles can seem like academic fluff to a change agent in the field. Principles are subsequently decomposed into policies. Initially the policies are around IT portfolio management. As the recognition of the relationship between the underlying operational processes that feed the portfolio occurs, governance expands to operational processes, and IT portfolio management is integrated with other business processes.

In a perfect world, a wand could be waved and all processes that feed the IT portfolio would be standardized, documented, and provide accurate information to the portfolio near real time. We do not live in a perfect world. The business and IT processes that have direct linkage to the IT portfolio must be identified. Some of the most probable candidates are:

- Strategic planning
- Budgeting
- Program/project management
- Solution delivery
- Human capital management
- Purchasing
- Quality
- Research and development of emerging technologies
- Sourcing relationship management
- IT operations

For each process—ideally those that tie back to the scope and objectives—identify the integration points, and define the integration and its interactions.

Governance does not just happen. There are generally triggers that start one form of governance. Individuals or groups need formal accountability for governing IT portfolio management. Often this occurs through formal bodies of senior executives, much the way a city council meets to refine the policies of a community. Sometimes, however, this occurs as an audit. Extending the city government metaphor, the equivalent of a cop with a radar gun checks speed limits of drivers. When a person exceeds the speed limit greatly, a triggering event occurs: someone gets a ticket. So, too, with IT portfolio management. For governance to be effective, it must be interspersed with existing processes. Project management methods must explicitly call out when to touch the IT portfolio management process (e.g., update with new information). Governing triggers are identified. Some will be temporal in nature (e.g., the start of a planning cycle). Some will be exception driven (e.g., legislation passed requiring a supporting technology or system). Regardless, and probably most importantly, all obvious triggers are recognized that would require the IT portfolio to:

- Adopt changes in assumptions, investment criteria, or tolerance for risk
- Be updated
- Be rebalanced

The governance information must be assembled into a usable and digestible format. Generally, integration into existing processes may be desirable. Things that must be called out explicitly are included in the IT portfolio management charter. Key stakeholders, including senior business and IT leadership, must approve the governance information as well as the charter.

STAGE 8: ASSESSING EXECUTION

Objectives were set at the onset of the IT portfolio management process. The assessing execution stage asks if the results of the current iteration of the IT portfolio management process meet the expectations defined in the game plan. More and more, IT initiatives must live up to the business cases that funded them. Do the costs of IT portfolio management outweigh the benefits? Stage 8 is often left out, but it is crucial for enhancing readiness, maturing capabilities, and improving. It is a closed loop of information and communication flow that feeds back into prior stages of the process and helps modify, improve, and enhance future decisions and iterations.

Prescient IT portfolio managers know better than to wait until the end of a cycle to demonstrate value and success. If metrics and objectives attainment have been part of the process all along, communication of successes can occur throughout the process. This is important for maintaining support and involvement. Assessing execution involves:

- Collecting portfolio management process metric measurements necessary to reflect the outcomes of the current iteration of the portfolio management process.

- Comparing planned objectives with the actual program plan (comparing the actual outcomes of the portfolio management processes with objectives established during the game plan stage of the current iteration).

- Determining program lessons learned by identifying the improvements that need to be made and the successes that should be continued during the next iteration.

- Creating a program execution report that documents the finding of the current iteration's execution assessment.

- Performing an assessment comparison of the overall ability of the enterprise to support and sustain the portfolio management process at the end of an iteration. This is compared to the assessment done at the beginning of the current iteration (portfolio management maturity, portfolio management readiness, portfolio management capability, and credibility/dependence). Recommendations and findings are provided in the assessment and execution report.

Exhibit 5.49 outlines the specific tasks and activities involved in developing the assessing execution stage. The critical activities of the tasks addressed in this section include:

- Assess program execution
- Compare performance assessments
- Prepare assessment and execution report

Assess Program Execution

Assessing program execution entails reviewing the game plan versus the current activities, and assessing the activities and decisions made that influenced the outcome. Aggregating information such as measurements and evaluating actual versus desired objectives help management determine areas within the portfolio that were successful at developing and executing it, as well as areas that were deficient.

Assessing program execution helps refine and improve the various stages in the process. For instance, criteria, performance metrics, and tuning options developed in the creating, assessing, and balancing stages might be refined and improved based on evaluating the results. Problems should be identified, and the specific areas of weakness should be corrected. Areas that met their expectations also provide valuable input for highlighting important lessons learned and reinforcing aspects of the IT portfolio management process and framework.

EXHIBIT 5.49   ASSESSING EXECUTION TASKS

```
┌─────────────────────────────────────────────────────────────────┐
│  ◄──────────── Iterate Throughout These Tasks ──────────►         │
│                                                                   │
│  ┌──────────────┐   ┌──────────────┐   ┌──────────────┐           │
│  │ Assess       │   │ Performance  │   │ Assessment & │           │
│  │ Program      │   │ Assessment   │   │ Execution    │           │
│  │ Execution    │   │ Comparison   │   │ Report       │           │
│  └──────────────┘   └──────────────┘   └──────────────┘           │
│                                                                   │
│  • Assess the actual    • Reassess the overall  • Identify and report all │
│    performance of the     ability of the company   enhancement from areas │
│    current portfolio      to support and sustain   identified in the game plan │
│    management process     the portfolio            stage, and identify areas for │
│    - Collect              management process       further refinement and │
│      measurements         and compare to the       improvement │
│      necessary to         assessment in the        │
│      reflect and          game plan stage          │
│      measure the IT         - Evaluate maturity,   │
│      portfolio              readiness,             │
│      management             capability,            │
│      process                capability /           │
│    - Compare actual         dependence,            │
│      versus desired         peer benchmarks        │
│      objectives                                    │
│      established in the                            │
│      game plan stage                               │
│    - Determine lessons                             │
│      learned and                                   │
│      incorporate into                              │
│      the process                                   │
│    - Create program                                │
│      execution report                              │
└─────────────────────────────────────────────────────────────────┘
```

Compare Performance Assessments

The performance assessment comparison reassesses and evaluates the maturity of
the IT portfolio, determines strengths and weaknesses in the readiness assessment,
and evaluates the relationship between IT and business. Areas evaluated as part of
this activity include:

- Customer survey and user satisfaction levels to determine where the process
  excelled and where possible improvement can be made.

- Impacts of IT portfolio management based on the information and data collected, and whether the actual impacts were in line with the intended ones.
  Assessing and evaluating whether key deliverables, timelines, and milestones
  were met and aligned with business and strategic objectives is critical.

- People and culture aspects of performance, including evaluation and assessment of the extent to which the workforce complied with IT portfolio management, determination of the effectiveness of the collaboration efforts used to define criteria and weightings, and effectiveness of incentives and training in driving desired behaviors.[18]

Peer benchmarking is also used as part of this process to assure that the company is assessing and comparing its portfolio management process with other entities.

Prepare Assessment and Execution Report

All companies should have policies and procedures in place to document the findings from the assessing execution stage.[19] The assessment and execution report documents all enhancements made from areas identified in the game plan stage and those areas that require further refinement and improvement. Knowledge and insight are gained from the positive and negative aspects learned during the stages and activities, and it is imperative to memorialize both the success and failures in order to learn from mistakes and minimize the chances of reoccurrence.

There should be a mechanism to ensure that the information and data collected in this report are aggregated, fed back to decision makers and process owners, and acted upon to improve the IT portfolio management process. For instance, the criteria may need to be rethought, the weights recalibrated, or the balancing exercise readjusted to better meet business and strategic objectives. Not to overstate, but communication plays a vital role in this effort. The assessment and execution report should include this specific information:

- An assessment of the portfolio's effectiveness in meeting original objectives as defined in the game plan
- An identification of ways to modify or improve the IT portfolio management process to better maximize results and minimize risks
- An identification of benefits that have been achieved, an assessment of whether they match projected benefits, and a determination of reasons for any discrepancies
- An evaluation of whether original assumptions used to justify the portfolio and investments were valid
- A comparison of actual costs incurred against projected costs
- A determination of how well the IT portfolio and investments met time schedules and implementation dates
- Management and user perspectives on the IT portfolio and investments

- An evaluation of the issues, changes, and modifications that still require attention
- Benchmarked competitors and unrelated companies.

It is important to document and archive all decisions, changes, actions, and results that occur throughout the stages and activities. Also included are changes made to the business case or analyses that are created or revised during the process, as well as recommendations to change and improve the process.

CONCLUSION

The IT portfolio management process and the stages and activities presented in this chapter should always be assessed and evaluated for continuous improvement. This is not a static process. Management within companies should always challenge and question the current processes by asking:

- Are the current IT portfolio management processes, criteria, weighting, steps, and activities in line with the company's needs?
- How can the processes be modified to better meet these needs?
- Are the right members and the right mixture present at decision-making investment review and evaluation meetings?
- Are the right triggers and performance measurements in place for event notification and monitoring of project and existing operational investments?
- Are the time frames for the stages and activities taking too long and serving as blockers to effectively execute the process?
- Are there reoccurring problems that continue to manifest in the process? Are corrective actions being taken to address both the symptom and the core problem?

NOTES

1. Edmund M. Ziegler, ISBM Net Product Development Consortium Meeting, DuPont Consulting Solutions, March 2001.
2. Frank Joseph Matejcik, "TM 665 Project Planning & Control," South Dakota School of Mines and Technology.
3. Eric Burke, "Portfolio Analysis, Key Metrics, and Techniques for Analyzing the Portfolio," Portfolio Knowledge.
4. Treacy, M. and Wiersma, F., *The Discipline of Market Leaders: Choose Your Customers, Narrow Your Focus, Dominates Your Market,* Perseus Book Group, Jan. 1997.
5. Helen Pukszta, "The New IT Mindset," *Cotter Consortium Executive Report, Vol. 4, No. 12,* 2001.

6. U.S. General Accounting Office, "Assessing Risks and Returns: A Guide for Evaluating Federal Agencies' IT Investment Decision-Making," Accounting and Information Management Division, February 1997.

7. Robert G. Cooper, Scott J. Edgett, and Elko J. Kleinschmidt, *Portfolio Management for New Products,* 2nd edition, Perseus Publishing, 2001.

8. Eric Burke, "Getting Started with Portfolio Management," Portfolio Knowledge.

9. Harry Alton Lee, Director, U.S. Department of Treasury, Enterprise Solutions, 2004.

10. Bruce Miller, "Portfolio Management: Linking Corporate Strategy to Project Priority and Selection," PM Solutions.

11. Mari Poyhonen, "On Attribute Weighting in Value Trees," Helsinki University of Technology, 1998.

12. Robert S. Kaplan and David P. Norton, *The Balanced Scorecard: Translating Strategy into Action,* Boston: Harvard Business School Press, 1996.

13. Robert G. Cooper, Scott J. Edgett, and Elko J. Kleinschmidt, *Portfolio Management for New Products,* 2nd edition, Perseus Publishing, 2001.

14. Management Guru, www.mgmtguru.com/mgt499/TN9_5.htm.

15. Ibid.

16. United Management Technologies (UMT), www.umt.com.

17. Ibid.

18. U.S. General Accounting Office, "Assessing Risks and Returns: A Guide for Evaluating Federal Agencies' IT Investment Decision Making," Accounting and Information Management Division, February 1997.

19. A significant amount of content from this section was adapted from U.S. General Accounting Office, "Assessing Risks and Returns: A Guide for Evaluating Federal Agencies' IT Investment Decision Making," Accounting and Information Management Division, February 1997.

Value Categories and Value Factors

- Financial
  - Net present value: the sum of the annual net savings and other tangible benefits, which have been discounted by an estimated interest or hurdler rate that is commensurate with the risk (grow, run, and transform investment categories should have different hurdle rates to reflect their varying levels of risk). The value in using NPV is that the effects of time and the cost of money are made consistent, thus enabling products of different-length development times and variable payback periods to be compared.
  - Return on investment: the sum of cash inflows divided by the sum of all cash outflows for a given period of time.
  - Payback period: the amount of time that must pass before the benefits exceed the costs of the investment. When the payback period is expressed in years as the development cost divided by the annual benefit, it is the reciprocal of the investment's return on investment. Most companies have established payback period requirements. Companies are looking for accelerated payback periods of less than a year.
  - Cost avoidance: expressed by avoiding payment to external entities
  - Revenue growth
  - Cost reduction
- Strategic importance
  - Business/strategic fit
  - Customer retention
  - Customer growth

- Customer upselling and cross-selling
- Strategic alignment
- Compliance
- Revenue growth
- Ease of doing business
- Fulfill commitments
- Expand into new markets
- Provide revenue growth
- Improve competitive positioning
- Increase market share
- Improve negotiating power
- Improve brand
- User satisfaction
- Patent potential
- First to market
- Tactical importance
  - Improve performance
    - Reliability
    - Responsiveness
  - Improve quality
  - Reduce cycle times—for example,
    - Shortening sales cycle times
    - Reducing time to market for new products/services
    - Accelerating delivery of products or services to customers
    - Shortening order-to-cash cycles
  - Longevity
  - Competency-enhancing
  - Improve productivity
  - Other competitive impacts
  - Economic value added (business value added): used to assess the qualitative aspects of an investment through providing a numerical figure to IT investments' contribution to attaining business and strategic objectives
  - Strategic value: an index of customer satisfaction with the degree to which the operational product meets strategic business goals
  - Tactical value: an index of customer satisfaction with the degree to which the operational product meets tactical business goals
  - Risk mitigation
    - Regulatory compliance
    - Business continuity
    - Security

Risk Categories and Risk Factors

Category (Examples shown below)	Risk Factors (Examples shown below)
Technology Risk	Security
	Availability
	Architecture
	Business processes
	Applications
	Development
	Disaster recovery
	Complexity
	Information
	Performance
	Integration
	Feasibility
	Maturity
	Existing assets
Business Risk	Strategic
	Regulatory/compliance
	Financial
	Customer satisfaction

	Meeting objectives
	Brand
	Privacy
	Alignment
	Balance
	Business continuity
	External risks: environment, competitors, vendors, suppliers/partners, etc.
	Costs
	Asset protection
Project Risk	Milestones
	Schedule
	Budget
	Scope
	Complexity
	Costs
	Other projects
Resource Risk	Staff availability
	Skills
	Experience
Customer	Price
	Performance
	Quality
	Satisfaction
Operational	Facility
	Quality
	Defects

Readiness Assessment: Business, Internal, and Operational Diagnostics

- **Business Diagnostic**
  - Do business and/or strategic objectives exist? Are they unambiguous, actionable, and readily available to IT management and other areas within the company? Does IT management participate in the formation of these objectives? How well does the IT strategic plan mirror or link to the corporate strategic plan? Are there key performance indicators, critical success factors, and balanced scorecards that provide metrics and monitoring capabilities, translating IT performance metrics into business benefit? Are future business needs and a technology road map available to business and IT management?
  - Are there regulatory or legislative actions that are driving IT portfolio management?
  - What are the expectations of the benefits of IT portfolio management?
  - Is the implementation and maturation of the capabilities of IT portfolio management critical for the company to meet its goals? Can the business goals be reached without IT portfolio management?
  - What are the drivers creating the need to mature the company's capability in IT portfolio management?
    - What are the critical areas management hopes to resolve with maturing IT portfolio management capabilities?
    - Are there many IT projects that made it through the process but failed to deliver value? Conversely, are there technology candidates

that are failing to make it through to operations, and have these roadblocks been identified (e.g., skills, funding, politics)?

- How engaged are key customers, stakeholders, and end users in developing and monitoring IT portfolio management?
  - Are the value propositions of each of these entities understood?
  - Is there a customer segmentation analysis that shows the prioritization of customers and their needs?
  - Has a stakeholder readiness assessment been completed?
  - How are current and future priorities incorporated in the process?
- Is there funding available for establishing full-time positions focused on IT portfolio management? Is there funding available to assure that investments can transition from the discovery portfolio to the project portfolio and to the IT asset portfolio (operations and sustainment)?
- Are expected financial returns based on models such as return on investment, internal rate of return, payback period, and so on, used when evaluating investments? Is total cost of ownership calculated?
- Are there benchmarking data points to assess IT investment competitiveness? Are best practices from other companies and industries considered and leveraged?
- Has the impact of not investing been considered?
- Are competitors using IT portfolio management to create a sustainable competitive advantage?
- Are economic, IT, and other trends and competitive intelligence factored into the criteria used for prioritizing investments?
- Do partners, vendors, and suppliers have insight into future needs and requirements of the company? Does the company have influence over its future road maps and investments? Does the company have insight into the obsolescence and other risks associated with its solutions?

- **Internal Diagnostic**
  - Is there an IT governance framework with committees/boards that have defined areas of responsibility, accountability, and decision-making authority? Are business and IT management represented on these committees/boards? Is there a strong relationship between corporate governance and IT governance? Do the IT governance committees/board have purview over all IT portfolios (discovery, project, and asset portfolios)? How engaged are the members of the board of directors in IT portfolio management?
  - What current IT portfolio management processes exist? Are they working, and how are they governed, managed, and measured? Do clear prioritization criteria exist, and are they consistent with business and strategic objectives? What are the lessons learned from these business

units/divisions, and can they be leveraged and communicated across the company? Is IT portfolio used for internal as well as external (e.g., out-sourcing) purposes?

- Does the company have people, processes, and technology in place to rapidly and agilely respond to unexpected, unplanned, and unscheduled events?
- How well is IT portfolio management understood by employees and sen-ior management? How committed is the company to maturing its IT portfolio management capabilities? Is senior leadership fully engaged?
- Does an IT architecture board, a requirements committee, and a pro-gram management office exist? Are their strategies, plans, and insights linked to the business? How adaptable are their processes in sensing and responding to unanticipated needs? Are their capabilities at a level 2 or above on the maturity scale? What is their role, function, and input to the IT portfolio management framework? Do enterprise-wide archi-tectural standards exist? Are they enforced, and is there an exceptions-handling process?
- Is there a team assembled to study and provide recommendations regard-ing maturing the IT portfolio management efforts? Who is championing, sponsoring, and supporting this effort? How knowledgeable are they in IT portfolio management? What support are they receiving from leader-ship, business units, divisions, and so forth? How well represented is the functional and business unit leadership on this team? What will be their commitment to implementing, monitoring, and managing IT portfolio management after their engagement is complete?
- Do standardized business cases exist? Are they monitored, measured, and matured throughout the entire life cycle of an investment?
- Is there sufficient funding, time, and resources available to perform a complete internal diagnosis?
- How detailed are processes defined that affect or impact IT portfolio management?
  - Which steps have the greatest impact, and which have the poorest performance on key process measures?
  - Which processes require the greatest rework?
  - What systems or solutions support the process? Are they flexible to handle off-cycle requests? Are outputs measurable?
  - Which divisions/business units are engaged in the process? Are they the right personnel, are these processes required, and do these personnel add value to the process?
  - Are there bottlenecks, delays, missing, out-of-sequence, or redundant steps? Are there overly burdening manual and paper-based steps?

- Is there training for the processes? Are the processes well documented?
- Is there a common nomenclature to how information and data are defined?
- Are employees incentivized and rewarded for reaching specific milestones and achieving well-defined performance targets?
- Is management willing to make possible transformational changes to assure the success of IT portfolio management?
  - Has management given consideration to changes to the organizational structure, alterations to people practices and processes, new measures, reorganizing, and establishing a performance culture?

- **Operational Diagnostic**
  - Are there knowledge capture, sharing, and knowledge repositories detailing aspects of all investments and portfolios (or subportfolios) that is up-to-date and accessible by employees?
  - Are IT investment dependencies on other existing or new investments mapped and well documented? Are IT portfolios mapped to other related portfolios?
  - Does a centralized IT asset repository exist? Are any of the following fields captured in this repository?
    - Age?
    - Impact of the system or solution?
    - IT system dependencies?
    - History of failure rates?
    - Supportability, maintenance, and operations?
    - Current and future state processes (project, development, maintenance, change management, demand management, operations management, others)?
    - Is there a series of checkpoints (Stage-Gates®) to evaluate IT investments? Are investments that provide little to no value to the business strategy identified and halted early in the process? Are systems that provide little to no value to the business strategy frequently sunsetted?
    - Key users?
    - Service-level agreements?
    - Training and knowledge management?
  - Are there facilities that enable experimentation, proof of concept, piloting, and prototyping activities?
  - Is there a postmortem performed on IT initiatives and projects? How often are investments in IT assets assessed?
  - How often is the IT portfolio process reassessed?

CHAPTER 6

The IT Portfolio Management Market and Industry Provider Assessment Methodology*

INTRODUCTION

The IT portfolio market evaluation and software provider selection process has never been more critical. Success requires a combination of speed, accuracy, and thoroughness. To meet business and mission demands, companies need a consistent process by which they can develop and evaluate a short list of candidates and rapidly determine an industry provider's ability to meet IT portfolio management requirements.

Companies employ fire-drill tactics to collect, sort, and evaluate information from multiple sources. Too many companies begin the search for an IT portfolio management software solution (also referred to as tools) with a management imperative to buy something with little or no understanding of their internal organizational, process, and functional needs. Perhaps a recent disastrous miscalculation fuels the urgency of the "just get me a tool!" approach.

Most companies have little visibility into their IT portfolios, resulting in major redundancies. For instance, one utility company was using two identical data warehouse programs simultaneously without knowing it. When the CEO found out, the company initiated a search for an IT portfolio management software solution

* The authors would like to thank Melinda-Carol Ballou for her many superb contributions to this chapter.

immediately. As discussed in earlier chapters, you need to know where your company sits on the IT portfolio maturity scale and assess the greatest pain points to make good tool choices.

Some of the primary questions companies ask when evaluating and assessing an IT portfolio management software solution are shown in Exhibit 6.1. This chapter provides answers to these questions, as well as an understanding of the market, future areas of development, and criteria for rating and ranking industry IT portfolio management software providers. Vendors, ratings, and quantitative rankings for the criteria related to specific IT portfolio management software providers are not provided. However, a framework, detailed criteria, and capabilities are included for consideration.

IT PORTFOLIO SOFTWARE MARKET

The portfolio management software market is eclectic, dynamic, and complex, and has recently seen enormous movement. A host of new entrants have emerged from

EXHIBIT 6.1   IMPORTANT CONSIDERATIONS IN EVALUATING IT
PORTFOLIO MANAGEMENT SOFTWARE PROVIDERS

enterprise resource planning (ERP) vendors (leveraging their existing base in HR and financial management), application life cycle management vendors, and other vendors with significant capital to capture market share, as well as new releases from existing vendors with roots in enterprise project management, stand-alone portfolio management, and other niche areas. The IT portfolio market is converging into suites of capabilities that include not just portfolio creation for decision support but also related functional areas of project and resource management. In addition, the IT portfolio market is integrating with operational support solutions.

The market is divided into three areas: niche portfolio management–targeted solutions (typically with stand-alone portfolio analysis capabilities), project portfolio management tools (with suite capabilities), and asset portfolio management tools. We have not seen any IT portfolio management software solutions specifically targeting the discovery portfolio but believe that many of the features and functionality contained in niche and project portfolio management solutions could address this area. To further elaborate on the three market areas:

- The initial entrants into the IT portfolio management space, niche portfolio management software solutions, tend to opt for a best-of-breed approach, including advanced features into their software (e.g., Efficient Frontier). Many of the companies in this category provide portfolio management solutions with views across both the project and application portfolios.

- The project portfolio management suite vendors, many of which have their roots in enterprise project management or the dwindling professional services automation (PSA) space, tend to support five core areas of functionality: project, program, people/resource, portfolio, and process management. Other functionality is emerging (financial management, demand and opportunity management, etc.).

- Asset portfolio management tools, focusing on hard assets such as systems and infrastructure, are beginning to encompass other capabilities such as application portfolio management. Asset portfolio solutions exist in the category of automated solutions, to which both the general portfolio management solutions and project portfolio management suites are beginning to provide integration.

The project portfolio market is the most mature of the three areas. The niche portfolio and project portfolio markets are converging into suites, either through integration with existing project and resource management tools or through acquisition (we call this market portfolio management tool suites or PMTS). Drill-down asset portfolio management capabilities have remained distinct so far, with lesser depth and portfolio management capability. Yet integration with assets (particularly the application portfolio) is increasingly prevalent from the suite vendors and is beginning to be in high demand from mature users across the asset portfolio. Recent surveys show a growing importance for this type of asset portfolio coordination.

Longer term, we believe that both consolidation of vendors and greater levels of integration will drive additional levels of features and functionality. Evidence to suggest that this is already beginning to occur can be seen through an amalgamation of the enterprise project management with the application life cycle areas, exemplifying additional features of combining qualitative data from application development life cycle players (e.g., testing, change management) to better evaluate the project/program portfolio. In addition, an increasing drive for innovation within companies suggests that the IT discovery portfolio will be part of the holistic IT portfolio management solution. Over time, convergence will offer customers IT portfolio management software solutions with:

- A single repository with appropriate views to categorize, assess value and risk, and score investments in the context of business imperatives (financial, resources, competitive position, etc.)
- The ability to provide analysis by ranking investments, performing what-if and scenario analysis, and assessing the impact and interdependencies of changes across all portfolios
- The ability to perform scheduling, planning and resource management, enterprise program management, process and change management
- Full integration with other systems and processes (financial, capital planning, HR, procurement, risk management, asset management, enterprise program management, scheduling, architectural views, configuration management, resource management, change management, etc.)

Precedence for convergence of related features and functionality are prevalent throughout IT. For example:

- Customer relationship management, enterprise resource planning, financial and HR management, and supply-chain management are offered under one software package by leading vendors
- Application server companies have rapidly expanded their offering through migration into the enterprise application integration and portal spaces

The writing is on the wall for convergence and close integration to occur across all three areas of IT portfolio management, although less mature asset portfolio management capabilities should be expected for some time.

IT PORTFOLIO SOFTWARE SELECTION PROCESS

Exhibit 6.2 depicts the IT portfolio management software selection methodology. Objectives for acquiring and using a comprehensive IT portfolio management software solution must be articulated and agreed to by all stakeholders. This means assessing and understanding where the organization sits from the perspective of the portfolio management process and organizational maturity. For example:

- Does your organization have poor or nonexistent project/program management processes and inventories?

- Is there a governance body (with excellent executive sponsorship) that coordinates business and technology staff to support criteria creation and application of criteria to make portfolio decisions?

- Are resources shared across divisions or siloed, and how current and comprehensive is information about staff experience levels?

These are examples of initial questions to ask in order to establish maturity assessments. Mapping appropriate maturity with sufficient functionality to address

EXHIBIT 6.2   IT PORTFOLIO MANAGEMENT SOFTWARE
SELECTION PROCESS

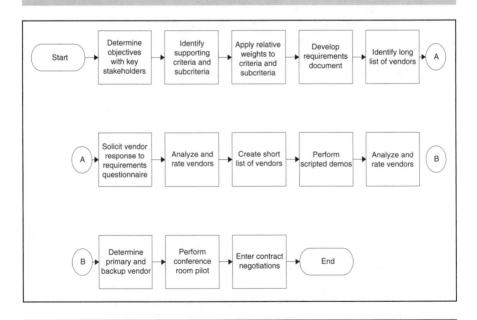

pain points, while addressing the level of difficulty of adoption and need for sufficient training and mentoring, are key considerations. Most failures for portfolio
management tools adoption occur due to human barriers, including the inability
to change culture to adopt tools consistently. As has been made clear in earlier
chapters, you need to know where your organization resides on the IT portfolio
maturity scale and assess the greatest, most acute challenges to make good tool
choices. Limiting your tool options to the handful of products that are listed as
"leaders" in an analyst report without factoring in your requirements, organizational structure, and culture is a big mistake. Understand your maturity.

Once the maturity level is established, the objectives must be translated into
requirements for vendor presence and performance by focusing on the greatest
current pain points. Typically, technology plays a significant role in this area
(which is part of the performance area discussed in the next section of this chapter). Also, high-level conceptual and detailed domain-level architectural principles
must be included as screening criteria; principles can either be converted into
requirements or left as is, requiring the vendors to demonstrate their support. Each
of the aforementioned criteria under presence and performance must be decomposed into germane subcriteria and weighted or ranked. The content for the
enterprise technical architecture must be included in the decision criteria; selecting a comprehensive IT portfolio management software tool that violates the
enterprise technical architecture erodes the credibility of the tool and the portfolio team.

The resulting deliverable is a requirements document that will be the basis for
an initial screen of vendors. Some vendors may be eliminated if they do not provide critical or technical design requirements. The requirements document can be
subsequently converted into a questionnaire or proposal (e.g., RFI, [request for
information], RFQ, [request for quotation], RFP, [request for proposal]) and sent
to the remaining vendors. The responses by the vendors should allow for further
refinement of the candidate list. Once the candidate has been culled, scripted vendor demonstrations ensue. Vendors should be invited to demonstrate their software, but companies should ask to see the functionality that it requires. Often,
taking the functional requirements outlined in the requirements document and
generating scripted scenarios for the software vendor to enact is effective. Software
vendors should have copies of the scripts well in advance to enable preparation. A
good demonstration can make the suboptimal product look optimal, and a poor
demonstration can put the favored product in a negative light.

Once vendors have demonstrated their product, a selection is generally possible.
A primary and a backup vendor should be selected. For negotiation and evaluation
purposes, we typically see organizations opting to have a third vendor in play,
although this needs to be balanced against the additional effort involved. Companies should begin negotiating prices with both (or all three), check references on

the primary vendor, and (if feasible) perform a conference room pilot to actually test the product's abilities and usability. If the primary vendor is viewed in a positive light, the contract can be negotiated, leveraging pricing information from the secondary vendor. However, if the primary vendor did not pass reference checks or survive the conference room pilot, the backup vendor should become the primary vendor, having its references checked and possibly performing a conference room pilot with its offering as well.

A comprehensive selection approach is the key to success and dramatically increases the probability of selecting a solution that will meet current and planned requirements. Failure to adequately analyze business goals and requirements up front will always produce suboptimal results and significantly increase the risk of the solution not meeting a company's intended goals and objectives.

As outlined in Chapter 5 and as shown in the previous steps, a need is determined. Requirements are developed to address the need. This chapter covers many of the steps that occur in the middle of the process, namely,

- Providing a set of questions and areas for consideration as vendors are identified that meet the requisite requirements. Organizational maturity, level of required training, complexity of the analysis, small versus enterprise deployments, and scale of portfolio analysis requirements are key factors in determining whether a high-end, more expensive solution or a lower-end, less functionally rich solution (but easier to use and easier to implement) will be required.

- Analyzing vendors to determine which provide the best overall solution to meet the defined needs. Companies with pressing needs for project management and the project portfolio may opt to choose vendors that provide highly focused and specialized expertise in these areas.

- Scrutinizing vendors with such techniques as initial high-level screenings, RFIs, RFQs, RFPs, scripted demonstrations, conference room pilots, and reference checks.

It is up to the company to determine the final rankings, prioritization, and weightings of the criteria, and the selection of primary and backup vendors. The final leg of the process, which is not addressed in this book, is negotiating and signing a contract. However, to justify the cost of this book, one piece of advice in this space is offered—ask for a discount! Most of the vendors in this space will discount their prices. The economics of software support discounting.

It is important to keep in mind that even the best IT portfolio management solutions will not help create effective governance and business adaptability if the data and information used as inputs are inaccurate, incomplete, irrelevant, or outdated. It is vital to address cultural change and invest appropriate amounts of resources in training, mentoring, and establishing effective process and organizational strategies for adopting portfolio management tools. Without this investment, tools implementation is likely to fail.

INDUSTRY PROVIDER ASSESSMENT METHODOLOGY

A proven methodology serves as the primary framework in this section for evaluating IT portfolio management software solutions. As shown in Exhibit 6.3, the approach consists of a category of functional capabilities followed by two dimensions: presence (ability to deliver value to the customer) and performance (ability to provide value to the customer).

These categories and criteria must be used in the context of the company's specific business environment, requirements, strategies, and priorities. They vary in importance across companies and among industries. Appendix 6A identifies more detailed and advanced categories, criteria, and questions.

Functional Capabilities

When selecting software, we recommend performing a vendor functional capabilities assessment encompassing a suite of related areas that are key to understanding the overall portfolio.

Project Management
Most portfolio management tools have either project management functionality or linkages to project management tools. A project is a time-bounded endeavor undertaken to create a unique product or service, or to modify or retire an existing asset, product, or service. *Time-bounded* indicates a fixed beginning and a fixed end. The requisite functionality sought in a solution should include project scheduling and planning, scope and change management, optimization, and value.

Program Management
Program management focuses on the ability to define and manage the interdependencies between projects, technology assets, people, and business processes dedicated to a specific mission (e.g., CRM, supply chain, etc.). Most portfolio management solutions should be able to bundle projects into programs. It is a straightforward, albeit not necessarily simple, rollup. The program management functionality generally sought should include:

EXHIBIT 6.3   IT PORTFOLIO MANAGEMENT SOFTWARE
SELECTION FRAMEWORK

Categories of Functionality
- Project management
- Program management
- Portfolio management
- Resource (or people management)
- Process management
- Opportunity management

Presence
- Vision/strategy
- Channels/partners
- Awareness/reputation
- Geographic coverage
- Business drivers
- Industry focus
- Investments
- Share

Performance
- Technology
- Services
- Pricing
- Execution
- Agility
- Financials
- Personnel

- Tracking budget, timing, risk, value, resources, and requirements to achieve program success and to support portfolio analysis
- Viewing capabilities to understand the interrelationships across projects, resources, and assets to provide a higher level of abstraction and relevant business information

As single projects become multiple projects, which are then grouped into programs, complexities inherent in coordinating and managing them together grow astronomically. This functionality is useful to manage ongoing program support (e.g., maintenance) and to evolve the business forward. While there are other views across the portfolio, the program view is significant to be called out separately.

Portfolio Management

Portfolio management provides a framework for understanding and evaluating the portfolio and alternative scenarios. Some technology vendors may claim to provide portfolio management capabilities. While in fact they may contribute to the "management" of "portfolio" investments, they are not IT portfolio management tools. True IT portfolio management tools provide for the intuitive categorization, valuation, and assessment of the discovery, project, and asset portfolios (and views) to optimize business impact. Functionality to look for includes:

- Risk, timing, and reward valuation techniques
- Budget control/impact, resource forecasting, user-definable, multiple views that highlight key comparisons (e.g., cross-portfolio interdependencies)
- Data import into a repository from relevant sources
- Ability to develop and compare scenarios (e.g., what-ifs) to enable the selection of appropriate changes

Resource (or People) Management
How the use, prioritization, and management of people and/or individuals impact the selection, initiation, and ultimate delivery of the overall IT portfolio within the organization is a key in successful forecasting and current portfolio management. This includes managing:

- Demographics
- Skills and proficiencies
- Work experience
- Location
- Career path
- Succession
- Resumes
- Roles
- Project work
- Time and expense entry

Process Management
The ability to create and manage an inventory of best-practice methodologies or processes to ensure the execution of consistent, targeted outcomes that are in line with business imperatives (e.g., the processes for portfolio assessment itself, application delivery processes, CobiT, ITIL) is important. Core functionality includes:

- Procedural and event-based work flow
- Intuitive editors
- Nested work flows
- Autoescalation
- Conditionals
- Versioning

Companies should leverage methodologies to model future initiatives against past successful initiatives. A tool should not only allow this but should support honing of these methodologies by providing data to enable process optimization.

Opportunity and Demand Management

A key feature is the ability to manage business opportunities and prioritize them by which ones are the most beneficial to the organization and why. This feature should take into account internal demand for project-related activities.

You may want to review the questions in the presence and performance criteria sections when creating requirements documents. What might be important criteria to one company may be irrelevant to another. However, basic guidance is provided on which subcriteria should be low, moderate, or high priority.

Presence Criteria

Presence criteria pertain to an IT portfolio management software company's ability to *deliver* value to the customer. This area is of lesser importance in a young, dynamic market than in a mature one. The subcriteria discussed in this section are:

- Vision/strategy
- Channels/partners
- Awareness/reputation
- Geographic coverage
- Business drivers
- Industry focus
- Investments
- Share

Vision/Strategy

Vision/strategy is of key importance when selecting a vendor. Is the vendor going to stay fixated on one thematic portfolio? Does the vendor have lofty visions of (portfolio) managing the world? Hopefully, it's somewhere in between. The vendor's vision for IT portfolio management will impact the direction of its product offering(s) and company structure. Due diligence should be applied to ensure the company's vision and strategy match plans on evolving IT portfolio management.

This area is typically not given as much weighting as other subcriteria, but it is important because it reflects the role that vision and strategy have in terms of corporate focus and direction. Success is driven by manifesting vision and strategy into successful business and product development. Areas that are evaluated include:

- *Messaging:* external, visible communication to the market about vision, views, expectations, priorities, and values
- *Differentiators:* quality of the top three differentiators for the company
- *Success/progress toward goal achievement:* demonstrable success and progress toward achieving vision/strategy

Channels/Partners

Strong channels and partners are helpful to technology vendors. Direct sales channels can rapidly become bottlenecked. If this is the case, most probably the vendor's ability to support the product and its client base is also in a logjam. Supplementary technologies and relationships, which extend functional capabilities and support for integration initiatives, process, organizational strategies, and training demand support from a rich, complimentary ecosystem of technology and service partners. The more established vendors tend to have the broadest range of partnerships. Additional partnerships enable stronger technology offerings and help to extend the reach of smaller niche players while offering training and support to facilitate successful implementations. Look for vendors with intelligent channel partners.

This subcriterion is typically given moderate weighting and emphasizes a key presence driver: channel development and performance. With so many service organizations needing software to implement IT portfolio processes at client sites, the dominant, fastest, and lowest cost distribution is through indirect channels. Areas that are evaluated include:

- *Percentage of revenues through indirect channels:* revenues generated through indirect versus direct channels.
- *Program scale:* scale (size and number) of active partners with which IT portfolio management solution providers have transacted business in the past 12 months.
- *Count and average selling price:* number of transactions and average transaction size through indirect channels.

Awareness/Reputation

This category describes the market awareness of the vendor and its capabilities and offerings, as well as its reputation generally as a technology provider and specifically related to this category of solutions. Information on the reputation can be found on the web, through analyst firms, and through reference checks. When checking references, ask about the entire experience from sales to post-implementation support. Ask open-ended questions. Ask for lessons learned. Check the most frequented chat sites and news groups for users actually implementing the tool and ask questions. This subcriterion is typically given moderate weighting. Areas that are evaluated include:

- *Top venue:* publicity, sales, marketing, service, and development events that build positive perception in the market and extend visibility above and beyond the company's size and/or share
- *Industry recognition:* measured achievement of visibility as demonstrated by direct and indirect activities, including publications, press engagement/coverage, and analyst/key influencer visibility
- *References:* measured, relative awareness on the part of existing and potential customers about capabilities, offerings, vision, and focus

Geographic Coverage

The explosion of the Internet has rapidly made geographic coverage less important. Vendors are offering services over the Internet with greater frequency—from training to enhancements. During the implementation of the solution, however, hands-on vendor assistance will be needed. Some consideration for geographic coverage is therefore warranted. Additionally, for international companies, geography-specific regulations and language support may be issues. If capabilities like multilingual support or support for financial requirements across geographic boundaries are required, these requirements should be factored into the decision accordingly. Additionally, more scalable product architectures may become key requirements that larger global companies should consider. Coverage should not include evaluation of channel/partners. This subcriterion typically includes:

- *Regional distribution:* extension of business reach, availability, and delivery via directly controlled entities
- *Distribution impact:* consistency, repeatability, integration, and effectiveness of the distributed organization to function efficiently
- *Customer mix:* account growth across geographies
- *Localization/globalization:* ability to accommodate local language, currency, and so on

Business Drivers

Business drivers include core competencies, value propositions, trademarks, licenses, intellectual property, capital, and other less tangible assets that act as competitive barriers to sustain business momentum and differentiation. This subcriterion is typically given a moderate weighting and involves the industry provider's exposure to competitive barriers. Actual and perceived barriers are considered because both influence competitor and buyer thinking. Areas that are evaluated include:

- *Core competencies:* underlying people, process, or technology-based business capabilities that are defensible, unique, and sustainable
- *Intellectual property:* internal processes, communication methods, leader-sponsored philosophies, or other dynamics that enable better client centricity, speed, responsiveness, efficiency, or market effectiveness
- *Patents, trademarks, and copyrights:* owned and protected patents, trademarks, copyrights, licenses, or trade secrets that reflect unique ideas, methods, technologies, and processes, and that offer tangible competitive advantage tempered by the ability to actively enforce such documents as well as how market players respond to the existence of such agreements

Industry Focus

Industry focus is the ability to direct resources, skills, and offerings to meet the specific needs of individual market segments, including verticals. This subcriterion is typically given moderate weighting. It examines the industry provider's ability to develop horizontal process and/or vertical industry business drivers. As the IT portfolio management solutions market matures, focus on specific industries or horizontal processes becomes a critical discriminator. Areas that are evaluated include:

- *Dedicated employees and stand-alone products:* vertical industry focus with dedicated employees (>50% of working time)
- *Vertical coverage:* the scope, depth, and relative strength within a given market as demonstrated by market share, expertise, tailored technology/service, sales coverage, and marketing activities

Investments

Investments are direct, related, complementary, and synergistic layouts of resources, expertise, and capital for investment, consolidation, defensive, or preemptive purposes. This subcriterion is typically given a low weighting. It reflects management's commitment to supporting and enhancing the IT portfolio management solution through maintenance revenue, allocating revenues to actively expand the business (e.g., channels, marketing, acquisitions). Continuously delivering new functionality through aggressive R&D investments and supporting the product in a timely, high-quality manner are important attributes. Areas that are evaluated include:

- *Percentage of revenue into R&D:* investment interest in product/service improvement
- *Other investment facts:* secondary investment interest in product/service improvement

Share

Share is the relative and absolute share of total market or market segment held by a specific vendor. It is measured by market share relative to competitors, mind share in terms of market awareness, and/or wallet share in terms of percentage of IT budget obtained relative to competitors. Although the weighting for this subcriterion is typically low, it reflects the importance of customer base growth and attraction for an industry provider's value proposition. Areas that are evaluated include:

- *Percentage of existing/new clients:* business mix between existing and new customers
- *Customer growth:* customer base growth over time

Performance Criteria

This section outlines criteria for evaluating an IT portfolio management software company's ability to *provide* value to the customer. The subcriteria are discussed in this section are:

- Technology
- Services
- Pricing
- Execution
- Agility
- Personnel
- Financials

Technology

Technology refers to the physical goods offered by IT portfolio management solution providers as part of a market portfolio. This subcriterion is typically given a high weighting, reflecting the importance of robust, mature functionality and performance. Areas that are evaluated include:

- *Product architecture:* the solution's functional technical architecture as it relates to the infrastructure
- *Development language:* development language support
- *Technology support:* support for generally available infrastructure products and brands
- *Functional components:* tools that support IT portfolio management primary functions

- *Portfolio analysis methods:* methods to perform the analysis
- *Scenario simulation methods:* methods to perform scenario simulations
- *Optimization methods:* methods to determine optimized portfolio performance and what needs to change to achieve optimal value
- *Simulation output analysis:* ability to analyze simulation output as the means to drive optimization
- *Templates:* approaches, techniques, methods, tools, and services that accelerate value realization of software and ensure quality decision modeling
- *Risk management:* framework to cohesively include risk as a scenario and portfolio optimization driver
- *Quality/quantity of information assimilation:* ability to consistently and cohesively render qualitative and quantitative data into scenarios and optimization plans
- *Financial analysis methods:* financial analysis features and functions

Services

Services range from support to consulting and all points in between, assisting customers through the implementation and delivery of skills, processes, methodologies, business templates, systems, and expertise. This subcriterion is typically given a moderate weighting. The services necessary to implement the software and the dependency of customers on the industry provider to perform this implementation work are examined. Industry providers who are the sole installers of their products rate low. Areas that are evaluated include:

- *Services purchased:* most commonly purchased services
- *Implementation accelerators:* services that accelerate implementation
- *Percentage of implementation/integration:* by the industry provider's internal professional services organization

Pricing

Pricing includes policies, procedures, methods, and standards that enable customers to effectively purchase IT portfolio management industry provider offerings. This subcriterion is given a moderate weighting. The economic components of each industry provider's product line are evaluated. Future pricing mechanisms will change the strategy of how IT portfolio management industry providers charge for their offerings. Areas that are evaluated include:

- *Pricing methods:* price models provided to customers that enable flexibility in the purchase and/or use of products and services

- *Value measurement:* demonstrated methods that enable customers to see break-even points, return on investment, or other important value metrics that help justify expected and actual costs

- *Implementation/license ratio:* ratio of implementation versus licenses to uncover sources of bigger cost versus value

- *Maintenance:* maintenance as a percentage of selling cost, providing critical revenue to further enable more significant product/service development

- *Average selling price:* average selling price to help understand base market differences between IT portfolio management providers

Execution

Execution refers to processes, systems, methods, or procedures that enable IT portfolio management industry providers to be efficient, effective, and positively impact revenue, retention, and reputation. This subcriterion is typically given a moderate weighting and represents an industry provider's ability to deliver new products, change business internally, and win sales. Areas that are evaluated include:

- *New product features:* demonstrated ability to keep pace with market demand from a product perspective

- *Top three improvements/efficiencies:* demonstrated ability to keep pace with market demand from an organizational perspective

- *Win/bid ratio:* performance in closing competitive business

- *Percentage competitive:* percentage of sales that are competitive versus non-competitive.

Agility

Agility reflects the vendor's ability to respond to change. Also important is the ability of vendors to pursue external solutions (e.g., acquisitions and alliances) to better match customer demand. The smaller organizations tend to be more nimble than larger ones. Without strong capabilities to respond to user and prospect demands, cogent development processes to deliver stable code with consistent quality, and the ability to flexibly incorporate additional functionality, it is challenging to gain and retain a leadership position. Look for a vendor that has a history of successful strategic alliances. A vendor that has an eye on the future and can turn on a dime should also be viewed very positively. This subcriterion is typically given a moderately low weighting. Reactive capabilities to identify, harness, and capitalize on changing market and customer dynamics are evaluated.

Personnel

Personnel is the organizational mix of skills, experience, expertise, capabilities, and leadership within each vendor. Vendors should have a good balance within their employee base of leadership/management, engineering/development, and marketing/sales. It is usually not the best technology that winds up owning the market but the most adaptable. The organization structure must support adaptability for it to be reflected in the product. This subcriterion is typically given a moderate weighting. Areas that are evaluated include:

- *Training:* professional development, certification, knowledge about specific technologies, verticals, services, processes and methods that are transferred into higher-value technologies and solutions with improved results for the customer
- *Voluntary turnover:* employee satisfaction and control over own direction
- *Workforce changes:* speed at which the business moves to keep pace with market conditions
- *Number and distribution:* impact that staffing and physical distribution have on the vendor's ability to execute
- *Experience:* intellectual capital potential

Financials

Most purchasers want to be assured that the vendor they select is stable and has the financial resources to continue operations and investments for the foreseeable future. Yet while financial viability is significant as it impacts vendor longevity, some vendors may not have achieved profitability in emerging markets or may be challenged financially, but they may still have strong product offerings. In a market in which vendors have widely varying degrees of obvious financial viability, financial performance should be tempered by a weighting that balances in execution, agility, and personnel, with a much stronger weighting toward technology and services across the performance category as a whole. This subcriterion is typically given a moderate to low weighting. Areas that are evaluated include:

- *Revenue growth:* growth of revenues over the past four quarters
- *Number and type of transactions per year:* number of business transactions with current and new customers over the past four quarters; new versus incremental license revenues; software versus development versus maintenance revenues
- *Future financial goals:* guidance regarding the company's financial goals for the next four quarters and beyond

- *Investor exposure:* degree of industry provider risk based on the number of investors and the position relative to the firm
- *Customer exposure:* degree to which the industry provider is exposed based on revenues generated by one or a small number of customers

CONCLUSION

The processes, criteria, and questions in this chapter should provide a more thorough list of requirements to consider in evaluating and assessing IT portfolio management software providers. Consider where your greatest process and organizational challenges are as you advance your capabilities in portfolio management.

The IT portfolio management tools and technology choices are rich, broad, and improving. High-end IT portfolio management solutions with deep functionality across the suite are easier to use than previously. More intuitive, broad products that are more easily implemented (but with shallower functionality) are ratcheting up capabilities somewhat and/or being acquired by vendors with synergistic products in related areas (and deeper pockets to evolve the technology further). Enterprise IT portfolio management software deployments remain costly and require sufficient training, effective process, and organizational frameworks. Yet the benefits accrue on a smaller scale and are now leading to greater maturity for those 20% to 30% of global 2000 companies that have established limited, midrange IT portfolio management adoption.

The key is to attack the biggest pain point within one of the three portfolios and begin implementing incrementally; establish successful departmental deployments, and mentor others to build the best foundation for benefits from automated tools.

Advanced IT Portfolio Software Provider Evaluation Criteria

The following section poses questions to ask vendors and is more detailed and advanced than the material covered in Chapter 6. If you are not familiar with some of the terms, you may want to seek the advice of an IT specialist or a market research analyst.

ARCHITECTURE

- What hardware platforms are supported (e.g., Windows NT/2000/XP, Sun Solaris, HP-UX)?
- What client operating systems are supported?
- Is the logic maintained on the server or is client software necessary?
- What language is the application written in?
- Is the software two-tier, three-tier, or *n*-tier?
- Is 24/7 online help available? Is 24/7 human help available?
- Is the online help context sensitive?
- Are patches electronically distributed?
- Are patches pushed or on demand?
- How often are patches sent?

- What types of APIs are fully embedded (i.e., how would other applications call into the application): Java (API), Java (EJB), XML, COM, C++, HTTP, other?
- What languages are used in the IT portfolio management software product regarding Internet functionality (i.e., Java, etc.)?
- Are all data accessible via corporate intranets?
- Are all data accessible via the Internet?
- Is it possible to enter data offline and synchronize at a later time?
- Do all users receive a personalized view of their projects/portfolios?
- Which databases are native and which are ODBC?
- Does the system support the entire portfolio from a single database?
- Is the application web service enabled?
- Does the application support load balancing? Failover?
- Are these features of enterprise portfolio management analysis sufficiently represented in the IT portfolio management solution:
    - Base portfolio evaluation separate from projects (i.e., the ability to place value on existing assets)?
    - Project evaluation and selection using base portfolio analysis (i.e., the ability to build a project portfolio imposing base portfolio metrics)?
    - Value calculation tied to organizational financial metrics (i.e., portfolios are linked to company financials—revenue, headcount, productivity, etc.)?
    - Bounding of asset values using financial (and other) metrics as root values (e.g., portfolio value cannot exceed company revenue)?
    - What-if capabilities of specific actions and changes (e.g., what if I remove an application from the portfolio)?
    - Is the software easy, fast, intuitive? Can I get results quickly?
    - Value base, peer benchmark comparisons embedded into the tool?
    - Heuristics to allocate IT budget and staff by line item across assets?
    - Extremely cost-effective?
    - Ability to perform both relative and absolute value comparisons?

INTEGRATION

- Does the software provide prepackaged integration with:
    - Enterprise resource planning?
    - Knowledge management?

- Project and scope management?
- Synchronous and asynchronous communication tools?
- Scheduling management?
- Resource management?
- Document and content management?
- Business intelligence and other software?
- Professional services automation (PSA) packages? Which ones?
- Scheduling tools (e.g., MS project)?
- Enterprise project management solutions?
- Help desk tools (e.g., Remedy, Peregrine, others)?
- Enterprise or IT asset management solutions (e.g., CA, Remedy, Peregrine, others)?
- Import/export files created in common office automation products?
- Groupware/e-mail systems (e.g., MS Exchange, Lotus Notes)?

- Which functions are supported in the integration (e.g., reporting, resource leveling, project hierarchy)?

- For third-party packages that do not have prepackaged integration provided, how is integration achieved (e.g., open API, professional services, etc.)?

- What existing partners/alliances are in place for integration with consulting or implementation partners?

SECURITY

- Is the security scheme role based, user based, customizable?
- How are specific user functions controlled?
- Can access be read-only or read/write?
- Does the application enable autogenerated user names and passwords?
- Are user names and passwords created manually?
- Can user names and passwords be pulled from an HRMS system, LDAP, or some other system?
- Can user names be reused?
- Does the application have the ability to permit users to change their own passwords?
- Are any restrictions placed on passwords (e.g., passwords cannot match last name, passwords must be changed after specified period)?
- Are passwords stored in an encrypted format?

- Can a user's access rights be suspended if a user fails to identify correctly after a configurable number of attempts in a single session?

- Can the system provide a configurable automatic maximum inactivity time-out?

- Is user activity logging available?

DATA MANAGEMENT

- Does the system support unlimited investment types in a single enterprise portfolio?

- Does the system include multiple standard investment types?

- Does the package support discovery, project, and asset (including application) investments?

- Does the package support services such as help desks and operational activities?

- Does the package support application inventories and license requirements? Are there service levels and support requirements?

- Does the application support platform and hardware inventories? Does this include service levels and support requirements?

- Does the application support supplier/industry providers and the information required to manage them? What types of information can be tracked and managed?

- Does the application support products including information needed to develop and eventually decommission end-of-life products?

- Does the application support any other investment types?

- Does the application allow unlimited user-defined investment types?

- Does the application allow any portfolio to contain multiple investment types?

- Does the system support unlimited numbers of independently owned portfolios from within a single enterprise portfolio (e.g., IT, R&D, sales, marketing, HR)?

- Does the system allow definition and enforcement of global attributes that will roll up across independently owned portfolios?

- Does the system enable each portfolio to maintain a unique set of attributes, processes, data, and models?

- Is the software capable of accepting multiple portfolio management methodologies?
- Does the software enable management of investment items from a top-down or bottom-up approach, or both?
- Does the software support internal business processes and approval cycles for commonly used forms and documents (e.g., business cases, status reports, staffing requirements)?
- Does the software enable users to specify their own company-specific formulas for computing priority, risk, quality, service level agreements, return on investment, economic value added, net present value, productivity, or financial indices?
- Does the software enable use and collaboration across geographic and business unit boundaries in a variety of platforms (e.g., desktop, mobile devices), supporting text and voice recognition?
- Is it possible to define baselines?
- Is it possible to archive data?
- Does the software have the ability to retain and access historical information for trend analysis?
- Does the application support a flexible dynamic filtering, grouping, and comparison user interface to identify redundant and duplicate investments?

VIEW MANAGEMENT

- Is it possible to search the portfolio by organization, division, and business unit?
- Is it possible to search the portfolio by people associated with the project, program, innovation, asset, initiative, and so on?
- Is it possible to search the portfolio by application, hardware, processes, information and data, and human capital?
- Is it possible to conduct a global search and replace?
- Is it possible to market table entries as inactive?
- Is it possible to identify currency?
- How many currencies are supported and maintained?
- Does the application support localized date formats, and can these be customized by location, by user, and so on?

- Is it possible to search architectural views and provide markups that are impacted by IT portfolio management?
- After an investment is made, is there a link to the technology road map to close a requirement and/or need?
- Does the application enable building hierarchies of investment types (e.g., parent–child relationships)?
- Does the application enable dynamic reconfiguration of the hierarchy?
- Does the application enable movement of any investment to any location in any portfolio? Does the software enable one investment to reside either in whole or in pieces in multiple portfolios simultaneously and still maintain traceability to all the parts?
- Does the system maintain roll-ups in all hierarchies for all investment types?
- Is the software able to organize portfolios for different organizational and business needs (e.g., business units, executive sponsors, product managers, markets, corporate strategies)?

INITIATION AND CATEGORIZATION

- Can the application categorize initiatives, programs, projects, assets, applications, and so on, by:
  - Portfolio?
  - Categorization (e.g., core discretionary)?
  - Phase?
  - Impacted organization?
  - Type of project?
  - Target organization for execution?
  - Business plan versus nonbusiness plan?
  - IT versus non-IT?
- Is it possible to define data about initiatives with associated programs and programs with associated projects?
- Is it possible to restrict initiatives being linked to other initiatives?
- Are programs linked to initiatives?
- Can projects be linked to programs or initiatives?
- Can projects be included without requiring linkage?
- Does the system enable investments to be managed based on relative priorities to the key business and strategic objectives?

- Does the software enable investments to be evaluated for selection or cancellation before, during, and after the funding decision?

- Does the software enable reviewing investments multidimensionally by health, risk, value, alignment, or any other factors to determine where investment gaps exist?

- Does the software enable the prioritization of investments based on specified prioritization criteria and analytics?

- Does the software help categorize investments and show where there are redundancies?

- Can projects or ideas be input into the system at any stage of their life cycle?

- Does the application support the creation of automated portfolios (i.e., defined and maintained automatically, putting projects with specific characteristics into a certain category)?

- Does the application support the creation of manual portfolios (i.e., user manually highlights specific project to place in a user-defined portfolio)?

- Can projects be made confidential? If yes, can certain fields of data be made public to users (i.e., is security access defined down to individual data elements)?

- Can projects or activities be set up as recurring (i.e., they do not have a defined timeline, but still need to be prioritized for resource scheduling purposes)?

- Does the solution support the creation of a project, asset, or other investment and integrate with an asset management system?

- Does the solution support investment classification by unlimited user-defined attributes?

- Does the solution support investment life cycle management (e.g., requested, approved, active, implemented, maintained, canceled)?

PRIORITIZATION

- Can the package support multiple contributors to metrics to see who contributed what?

- Can the application keep history/version of changes to metrics?

- Can the application assign modified permissions to categories of metrics to different users?

- What arbitration features are available when multiple providers have different opinions on metrics?

- Can variables be created and assigned to metrics instead of a discrete value?
- Can metrics or final scores be overridden manually to accommodate qualitative input?
- Can rules/flags be set that will lower or raise priority?
- Can projects be linked where dependencies exist (i.e., if a high-priority project is dependent on a low-priority project, the low-priority project will be reevaluated)?
- Can project scores be normalized based on project life cycle phases (i.e., an early stage idea will consistently score lower due to higher uncertainty than fully mature ideas)?
- Does the software enable the user to select the highest value or most critical investments based on any number of company-identified constraints?
- Does the software enable the user to set specific portfolio goals that are consistently retained for multidimensional analysis during portfolio analysis?
- Does the software enable the user to utilize multiple methods of gap analysis to determine the balance of investments within the portfolio and how well they align with goals?
- Does the software enable what-if analysis and modeling to show the outcome of changes in assumptions before funding decisions are made?
- Can users control what investment items (e.g., candidate, active, on-hold, closed) they want to aid in the selection of the portfolio?
- Does the software enable the user to drill down on any investment or investment candidate to get more detail?
- Does the software enable developing a project plan with a detailed work breakdown structure and resource allocations that tie back to a resource capacity system?
- Does the software track operating and capital expenditures over the life of initiatives?
- Does the solution support top-down estimating of time-phased resource requirements by skill set (i.e., using full-time employees or hours)?
- Does the solution enable setting multiple targets (e.g., conservative, default, stretch), capturing multiple baselines, and capturing multiple plans?
- Does the system support a flexible multi-level sort to rank and prioritize investments?
- Does the system show the resource load by investment (e.g., over-/under-loaded charts and reports)?

PERFORMANCE MEASUREMENT

- Can the software manage risk/reward trade-offs?
- Does an efficient frontier-based model exist that demonstrates tuning variables and constraints and impact to the portfolio?
- Does the software enable users to review the performance of multiple investments and cross-correlate the data? Does the software spot potential correlations and covariances among investments?
- Does the software track and measure the dependencies, constraints, and support for each investment in the portfolio?
- Can users select subjective ratings and specify criteria functions and analytics?
- Can users set up their own critical success factors, key performance categories and indicators as well as their own scorecards, investment maps, forms, dashboards, and so forth?
- Can users override the default calculations to handle unique situations?
- Can users toggle among portfolios that address different domains like applications, systems, projects, vendors, and customers?
- Can users toggle among key performance categories for color and size on a bubble chart?
- Does the software enable the user to automatically send an e-mail message to the manager of the investment plan when it is not performing according to plan?
- Does the software enable users to make changes to the portfolio and communicate the impact of these changes via e-mail to the other decision makers?
- Are the life cycles of projects customizable (i.e., do they consist of multiple stages or phases that are customizable)?
- Can each phase or stage be defined to have standard deliverables and/or milestones that are automatically established when the life cycle is chosen for a project?
- Can deliverables and milestones be added to any project or discovery investment?
- Is it possible to define multiple life cycles?
- Are there defined analysis stages for the application portfolio to determine course of action (retire, migrate, reengineer, etc.)?
- Can the system display status of current spending versus budget/forecast and associated timelines?

- Is it possible to define alerts based on project or existing asset health (i.e., project health is in jeopardy)?
- Is there a postmortem analysis for innovations or projects once they enter operations or commercialization? Did expectations meet reality?
- Are different categories of estimates available?
- Can estimates for a variety of groups or other classifications that roll up into a higher level total be tracked independently?
- Can the system display/report on projects that show a jeopardized status (in terms of dollars, scope, timeline, etc.)?
- Can estimates be shaped to reflect nonlinear spending during the timeline of the project?
- Does the system provide the ability to capture actual project costs (e.g., hours, costs, time sheets, expenses), operating costs, estimated benefits, and so on?
- Does the system enable the calculation of key performance indicators related to schedule, deliverables, costs, strategies, and so on?
- Does the system enable the calculation of variances related to schedule, deliverables, costs, strategies, and so on?
- Does the system calculate user-defined indicators with editable ranges (e.g., red, yellow, green status)?
- Does the system enable the generation of exception reports against key performance indicators along with configurable indicators?
- Does the system enable the generation of exception reports against variances along with configurable indicators?
- Does the system support distribution of an unlimited number of predefined dashboards, charts, and investment maps (e.g., bubble charts, scorecards, key performance indicators, roll-ups, predefined queries)?
- Can the system assess different mixes of investment objects for effectiveness, achievability, strategic fit, and so on, based on user-defined settings?
- Does the system enable capacity analysis by comparing top-down estimates with labor and budget constraints?
- Does the system automatically calculate time-phased resource costs using variable rates?
- Does the system support top-down estimating of time-phased benefits?
- Does the system support top-down estimating of time-phased costs?
- Does the system calculate net present value, return on investment, productivity and financial indices, payback period, internal rate of return, economic value added, and other financial ratios?

- Does the system have the means to calculate real options?
- Does the system calculate a Monte Carlo simulation?
- Does the system calculate risk with user-defined algorithms and weighted risk attributes?
- Does the system calculate expected costs and returns and have a mechanism to calculate risk-adjusted costs and returns?
- Can hurdle rates be adjusted for multiple variables (by division, geography, product line, etc.)?
- Does the system calculate value using user-defined algorithms mixing qualitative and quantitative measurements and balanced scorecards?
- Does the system support time-phased roll-up analysis of hours, full-time employees, costs, and benefits?
- Does the system support flexible roll-up and summary of investments to assess an investment's contributions to business and strategic objectives? Can this be done by:
  - Initiative?
  - Organization?
  - State?
  - Region?
  - Classification?

PORTFOLIO ADJUSTMENT

- Does the software help balance the portfolio when adjustments are required?
- If a key business objective changes or the priority among objectives changes, can the portfolio be reevaluated immediately?
- Does the software enable for collaboration in a common language to make adjustments due to rapidly changing business and mission conditions?
- Is it possible to add new metrics and change the prioritization model with minimum effort?
- Does the software provide an automated way to update portfolios dynamically, keeping the emphasis on interpreting and evaluating the portfolio?
- Does the software enable for a comparison of promised return on investment versus delivered return on investment?
- Does the software enable the user to easily spot deviations from goals by setting thresholds for balance and capacity based on stoplight indicators?
- Does the software automatically highlight deviations from goals?

- Does the software incorporate scenarios in the event of anticipated deviations?
- Does the system support what-if analysis and enable users to assess the impact of:
  - Including/excluding investments on budgets?
  - Including/excluding investments on value (i.e., benefit roll-up)?
  - Time shifting (i.e., pull, push, extend, or delay) an investment on resource capacity?
  - Time shifting (i.e., pull, push, extend, or delay) an investment on budgets (i.e., months, quarters, years)?
  - Time shifting (i.e., pull, push, extend, or delay) an investment on value (i.e., benefit roll-ups)?
  - Optimization of portfolio investments based on a number of possibilities including value, risk, strategy, and so on?
- Does the system support dynamically created ad hoc graphical charts based on what-if scenarios for easy visualization of changes?

REPORTING AND VISUALIZATION

- Is it possible to generate and publish reports to individually specified target groups?
- Does the system support user-defined embedded charts?
- Does the system support interactive charts with variable properties (e.g., axis parameters—x, y, bubble size, color, texture)?
- Does the system ship with a library of stand chart types (e.g., bar, line, bubble, pie, multibar, stacked bar)?
- Does the system support drill-down charts (i.e., navigates to detail view or secondary chart)?
- Does the system support 3D chart types?
- Does the system display an embedded Gantt style timeline of investment life cycle milestones?
- Does the system support export to Microsoft Office suite products (e.g., Excel, Word, Power Point, etc.)?
- Is the system able to produce hard-copy output, simple web-based reports, and interactive web-based reports (e.g., drill-downs)?
- Is the table structure open for standard reporting tools to utilize the data?
- Can raw data be output from a report in MS Excel format?
- Are normalized features across different metrics provided?

- How does the system support what-if scenarios?
- What executive summary reports are available?
- Does the system support multidimensional analysis (e.g., risk versus value, strategic versus tactical, planned versus actual, target versus planned, baselines versus planned)?
- Does the system display time-phased roll-up of any attribute at the top level or any sublevel of the hierarchy?
- Does the system support Sarbanes-Oxley compliance requirements?

COLLABORATION AND WORK FLOW

- Is it possible to set up work flow so that the completion of one step in the portfolio creation process initiates the second step?
- Does the software automatically send e-mail alerts based on predefined criteria?
- Does the software leverage data from other systems (e.g., project management, asset management, requirements database, architectural views, financial and accounting, knowledge management, document management, CRM, etc.)?
- Does the software enable users to collaborate with other team members using embedded collaboration features?
- Does the software provide a specific URL of each page for use in documents, presentations, e-mails, or web pages?
- Does the software enable users to obtain URLs to various pages and bookmark them?
- Does the software enable users to obtain URLs to various pages and save them as favorites in their browser?
- Can users modify analytics or add their own?
- Does the software allow algorithmic, script-based, user-defined analytics?
- Does the software enable criteria to be weighted, providing management of the investments based on the user's unique requirements?
- Does the software provide an early warning system highlighting when investments are exceeding performance boundaries?
- Does the software enable the user to drill down into an investment to make a change at a tactical level and have that change immediately reflected at the strategic level?
- Can the user enter annotations about information to document assumptions and other comments?

- Is it possible to attach documents to portfolio entries?
- Does the system support the ad hoc definition and publishing of an unlimited number of predefined queries?
- Does the system maintain a history of predefined queries and their results that may be securely stored and shared for stakeholder visibility and analysis?
- Does the system support distribution of approved portfolios to operational staff?
- Does the system support BPEL?
- Does the system support extensible markup language and extensible business reporting language?

RESOURCE MANAGEMENT

- Does the software allow you to adjust the rates and margins of each individual proposed resource?
- Can the resource search provide capacity information by skills to support skills pipeline management and gap analysis?
- Do the results of the search provide information on the resource's organizational breakdown structure (OBS) to see who manages the resource in case a different manager needs to borrow it?

PLANNING AND SCHEDULING

- Does the software provide a native scheduling tool or is a third-party package required?
- Does the software package include a standard built-in automatic project task-generation function and a library of project templates?
- Does the software package enable backward scheduling (backward from the project's scheduled finish)? If yes, is it possible to return to normal planning at any moment?

SCOPE MANAGEMENT

- Does the software support the process of managing and tracking changes in scope to a program and its component projects? If yes, is it delivered with prepackaged processes and analysis capabilities?

- Can all scope changes and analysis/approvals for a project be documented and audited?
- Can the business rules for scope change analysis/approval be defined without programming?

OPTIMIZATION AND PROGRESS MANAGEMENT

- In the resource histogram, does the software package display underuse?
- To resolve conflicts, can the system automatically shift tasks while respecting time constraints and priorities?
- Can the system automatically lower the percentage allocation of the resource in a constant or nonconstant manner over the duration of the tasks?

ESTIMATION

- Does the software enable estimation of costs?
- Does the software enable estimation of risks (both qualitative and quantitative)?
- Does it take into account the profiles of the resources involved with the project (skills, experience, subcontractor)?

TIME MANAGEMENT

- As a standard feature or as an option, does the software package include a module to track actual duration and work per resource?
- Is it possible to track actual duration and work on unscheduled tasks?
- Can time sheets track service, maintenance, vacation, and other nonproject work?

EXPENSE MANAGEMENT

- Can the application track billable versus nonbillable expenses?
- Can nonemployee project costs (e.g., training manuals, software) be added and billed to the client?
- Can the time and expense tracking be mapped to a charter of accounts to support capitalizing project costs to comply with GAAP SOP 98-1?

BILLING AND INVOICING

- In its standard configuration, can the software package manage contracts, work orders, invoicing, and payment tracking? Please specify.
- Does the software enable the creation of invoices?
- Is the creation of invoices done according to a fixed schedule, or can users customize the process?

PROJECT COST/ACCOUNTING

- Can the software package manage direct costs on resources (proportional to how long they are used)?
- Does the software package support earned value reporting?
- Are changes to the baseline automatically logged?

CHAPTER 7

Final Thoughts

If you have made it to this portion of the book, you have passed a previously unmentioned baseline assessment: the tenacity assessment. Positive change is often met with resistance, and implementing it requires tenacity. There is a high likelihood that you have the requisite tenacity to successfully lead an IT portfolio management effort within your organization.

IT portfolio management is a proven framework for better decision making regarding new and existing IT investments. IT portfolio management has helped businesses reduce IT costs by up to 30%, with a 2x–3x increase in value. IT portfolio management can and has been applied to infrastructure and networks, data and information, hardware and applications, processes, people, and supporting foundations. Used by internal and external constituents, it synthesizes seemingly complex information in terms and taxonomy that business and IT leadership understand. In coordination and collaboration with IT personnel, business executives provide supervision and monitoring of the IT portfolio, its underlying optimization process, and its overarching charter. IT portfolio management is first and foremost a people issue. Its effectiveness and evolution are largely dependent on:

- Well-defined organizational objectives and culture that drive the approach and deliverables
- Having objectives that are attainable and grounded in reality, which is something that is often achieved only by using baseline assessments that determine the fit, feasibility, capabilities, and expectations of portfolio management, providing a road map of current and future gaps and opportunities
- A laser-like focus on the objectives of the process, avoiding getting mired in superfluous information
- A commitment from executive leadership, with sufficiently allocated resources to this effort including participation of executive leadership

- Incorporating IT portfolio management with the underlying operational processes that generate data used to create the portfolio itself and to create a self-sustaining closed-loop improvement process

In rank and prioritized order, the IT portfolio shows an inventory of all IT investments that best meet key criteria (e.g., mission criticality, value, cost, risk, budget, maturity of the investment, impact, organizational readiness, alignment, and balance) agreed upon by a cross-functional leadership team. The IT portfolio is aligned to the operational, tactical, and strategic objectives. It highlights information regarding alignment, achievement, and manifestation of these objectives through tracking investments and their associated performance throughout their life cycle. Through the IT portfolio framework, investments are viewed holistically in context rather than as discrete groupings of isolated or individual investments. The IT portfolio also contains information regarding the inter- and intrarelationships between individual investments, the fit and feasibility of potential new investments, resource allocation, organizational capabilities, adherence to standards, the technical infrastructure, and the operational baseline.

IT portfolio management identifies mission-critical versus low value-added investments and investments at various levels of maturity (e.g., investments at their tail end of usefulness). It provides optimized return on investment by identifying low-value and redundant investments, supplying the decision-making framework to reevaluate/reposition, maintain/evolve, phase out/replace, or reengineer existing IT investments. Value is also created through early identification of investments in the IT discovery and IT project portfolio not aligned to objectives or not meeting expectations. Important investments receive the proper focus and resources to assure success. IT portfolio management serves as an important and ongoing audit trail for companies to adhere to new legislation and compliance requirements (e.g., Sarbanes-Oxley).

Active IT portfolio management is an iterative and continuously changing process serving as a common reference point for:

- Providing insight into the development of strategic and tactical planning
- Evaluating security risks and controls, as well as disaster recovery plans
- Synthesizing potential business opportunities, assessing value, feasibility, risks, costs, and other parameters
- Coordinating with budgeting and funding, providing a more accurate gauge of costs and exposures, assuring scarce capital is allocated to the optimal mix of IT investments
- Enabling reviews and reports, assessing important performance measurement parameters and reporting requirements
- Promulgating the use and adherence to guidelines, standards, and policies

Many of the quantitative/qualitative tools and best practices applied by money managers to investments in stocks and bonds have been leveraged in the creation of the framework for IT portfolio management. These same tools are applied to the IT discovery, IT project, and IT asset portfolios, providing a view of investment options based on value, cost versus return, alignment and balance, risk and risk diversification. Fundamentally, both the financial approach and the IT approach to portfolio management are grounded in the notion that all investments require active stewardship to maximize and protect value against adverse circumstances and events. From the perspectives of individual investments and the entire portfolio, maintaining investment integrity is paramount. There are many challenges and complexities that are similar between the financial and IT portfolios:

- Investment decisions are based on current information and assumptions created for future events and activities. This drives a level of uncertainty and unpredictability in decision making, producing a level of subjectivity in the assessment of investments.

- Dynamic and changing internal and external events produce portfolios that never stand idle. Reprioritizing, rebalancing, and reallocating resources at the turn of a dime are critical capabilities.

- Balancing diversification of different investment types as well as understanding and assessing the correlations, covariance, and dependencies among investments are important.

- Determining the achievability of projections based on optimization of limited resources is as much art as science.

- Sensitivity analysis, what-if factors, and scenario planning must be leveraged to manage uncertainty.

In contrast to the financial marketplace, there are many elements of the IT portfolio that are not as well understood or established. For instance, widely available archives of historical information based on a common set of standards (e.g., GAAP) for IT investments do not exist. IT investments are not always as liquid as financial investments. While killing a project that has "gone South" may have liquidity characteristics similar to equity shares in a defunct dot.com, unwinding an IT investment in production can be complicated—impacting multiple systems, databases, and operational and divisional capabilities, some related to mission-critical elements of the enterprise. Retiring IT investments can also impact a networked web of communities of partners, suppliers, distributors, and customers. Issues such as scalability, availability, functionality, reusability, interoperability, maintainability, and portability for IT investments become paramount. Rigid architectures and processes, unrealistic readiness assessments, and treating

IT portfolio management in an ad-hoc manner will sabotage the value that can be driven by IT portfolio management.

Due to the fact that the IT portfolio touches and affects many constituents, governance boards must be represented by a cross-functional group of decision makers under the guidance of a well-defined set of standards, policies, guidelines, and criteria. This coordinated, collaborative, and shared commitment from a cross-functional decision-making body ensures accountability and authority to make enterprise-wide decisions. Business and IT objectives and mandatory requirements are the leading criteria for assessing the merit and risks of IT investments. Decisions must also be tempered based on organizational capabilities, availability of qualified resources, and the culture of the organization. Transparent and successful governance is created through:

- Development and execution of standardized processes
- Objective investment criteria with executive, business, and IT management support and participation
- Visibility of the allocation of resources and the alignment of these resources to the business and strategic objectives
- Creation and full life cycle use of standardized business cases that validate new investments from idea inception to asset disposal; identification of retirement candidates from existing legacy systems
- Adherence to standards and integration protocols
- Providing simple and easy-to-use tools for decision makers to perform their own what-if analysis, taking into consideration alternative investments, adjustments to proposed investments, and/or alterations to current investments
- Identification and monitoring of risks, and mitigation of risks to acceptable and controllable levels
- Readily available reporting on performance and statutory requirements, showing adherence to service-level agreements, metrics, and compliance obligations
- Avoiding large exposures by decomposing sizable investments to smaller units with interim metrics and milestones (e.g., real option approach), and briefing progress and achievement to the decision makers on a frequent basis

Many of the aforementioned factors are captured, managed, and evolved in a centralized database (or system). Standardized business cases are developed for each investment, continuously updated, and fed into the centralized database. Data mining and analysis tools assess key artifacts within the business case, providing keen insight into hidden risks and value within each investment and across the entire portfolio. These tools also cater to the needs of the decision makers. Lessons learned from leading companies show that a limited set of analysis parameters is usually better and more efficient than an exhaustive list of views and graphical representations—less is more! In addition, it is critical that IT portfolio management objectives and culture drive the approach and deliverables for the IT portfolio, which in turn enables the appropriate tool choices.

The database feeds dashboards, which display warning signs, status reports, risk thresholds, adherence to return-on-investment assumptions, new investments, impacts, and constraints. Investments are evaluated, scored, ranked, and prioritized based on many criteria, including adherence to requirements, impact to business value and business rules, risk and risk mitigation strategies, influence on mission-critical systems (e.g., productivity, efficiency, reduction in cycle time), capability enhancement, mandatory investments, financial justification, impact of not investing, and so on. Many companies often get too bogged down in collecting too much information and overanalyzing too many factors and variables. While Chapter 5 provides an important and detailed step-by-step approach to developing and implementing the IT portfolio, there is no single approach that fits all companies. Achieving the right balanced approach and set of metrics that will be embraced by available resources, organizational objectives and capabilities, and the culture within a company is the optimal approach. Determine the trade-off between the need for speed and agility and the requirement for rigorous and detailed analysis. One size does not fit all.

IT portfolio management is typically initiated within the IT project portfolio. Lessons learned from leading companies show that for companies new to IT portfolio management, incremental approaches with attainable goals and objectives deliver rapid benefits and are deemed successful; conversely, organizations attempting big-bang approaches to full life cycle IT portfolio management invariably fail. Successful IT portfolio management initiatives identify low-hanging candidate projects (e.g., solutions that meet gaps in the baseline assessment), look for quick wins, and communicate early and often, which results in a few early and foundational success stories. The most common mistake companies make at the beginning of their IT portfolio management process is biting off more than they can chew!

As companies progress in their IT portfolio management capabilities, detailed business cases are cataloged within the centralized database. Business cases are vetted through a committee comprised of a representative from the project management office, IT management, architecture, and finance, which collectively validate assumptions, ensure the accuracy of the information presented, cluster related investments, and eliminate duplicate investments. In many instances, a preliminary evaluation occurs prior to developing a detailed business case. The committee scores each investment against a set of established weighted criteria and provides a numerical indexed value for each investment. Each investment is categorized into an investment bucket—run the business, grow the business, or transform the business.

Once the business case, ranking and prioritization, and categorization have been deemed complete, investments are presented to the governing body, which evaluates the numerical value assigned to each investment and assesses the ratio of investments within each category. The governing body also performs multidimensional analysis such as what-if trade-off analysis based on alternative scenarios, cost, budget and resource limitations, risk thresholds, technical feasibility, impact on the existing infrastructure and on organizational capabilities. Impacts to the prioritization of investments are analyzed. The governing body makes go, hold, and cancel decisions regarding IT investments.

IT portfolio management is an evolving process. The IT portfolio maturity model presented in Chapter 2 establishes specific goals and objectives to advance to higher levels. Practitioners of IT portfolio management should note that each level of the maturity model presents additional levels of complexity and commitment. Lessons learned from leading companies indicate that trying to jump maturity levels can be destructive to the IT portfolio management effort. Stretch goals are encouraged but at a pace that is absorbable with the resources, capabilities, and culture of the organization. Each iteration of the IT portfolio process presented in Chapter 5 will result in gaining valuable insight and expertise into the strengths, weaknesses, gaps, and opportunities of the portfolio. Benchmarking other entities is also a key for learning and growing capabilities and processes.

Frequent post-implementation reviews of investments constantly revisit assumptions made within the process of business case creation, thereby refining that process. These reviews identify the root causes of project drift, changes to assumed risks and benefits, unexpected costs, and impact of new technologies. Important feedback loops provide information about the key processes to decision makers so that continuous improvement occurs.

IT portfolio management provides the view and visibility across the enterprise, enabling better decisions to optimize resource use and reduce cycle time—that is, doing more with less. Knowing which investments will produce significant value-enhancing capabilities and which investments can leverage and reuse artifacts produced by previous IT investments creates an environment where the percentage of successful investments is increased. In addition, the targeting of these investments toward meeting specific goals and objectives is greatly enhanced. Investments made in low value-added areas are eliminated or minimized, freeing up important resources to focus on core issues and opportunities.

THE FUTURE VISION

"Seven-Eleven Japan Co. collects sales and other data several times during the day via satellite from its 10,000 stores and makes decisions—incorporating information such as weather data—up to a few hours before products are distributed to stores. Many of the items it sells are influenced by the weather, so having the right product available at the right time has a dramatic impact on its inventory turn. Seven-Eleven, now the largest retailer in Japan, turns its inventory an impressive 48 times a year"[1]

Companies such as Seven-Eleven, Cisco Systems, Xcel Energy, In-Q-Tel, Wal-Mart, Federal Express, Dell Computer, and others understand the power of IT in creating and sustaining competitive advantage. Seven-Eleven leverages IT portfolio management to maximize agility and adaptability—it is redefining the meaning of adaptability.

As IT becomes more commoditized, or as Nicholas Carr's *Harvard Business Review* article states, "IT Doesn't Matter,"[2] adaptability in light of increasing change becomes a paramount competitive advantage. Adaptive companies commit to:

- Multiple options, essentially supporting perpetual insurance policies to maximize certain events that might occur in the marketplace.
- Constantly monitoring the environment, creating detailed mappings of multiple scenarios and alternatives that could lead to action and implementation plans.
- Perfecting a keen sense of where value is derived, and how value is measured and assessed.
- Maintaining a corporate culture that exhibits an uncanny ability to radically change direction and redefine business models. Accountability and incentives that reward taking calculated risks are also aspects of the company culture.
- Simplicity, reusability, and leveraging of standards.

Adaptive companies leverage IT portfolio management to:

- Create efficiencies and maximize the use of IT investments
- Leverage information from the portfolio to create new innovations
- Gain powerful savings, focus, and alignment of costs on demand as a result of shifting resources outside the confines of the company (e.g., outsourcing)

There is a series of adaptive technologies that will continue to mature the concepts of the IT portfolio. Technology on demand is introducing new levels of flexibility through service-oriented architectures, model-oriented architectures, grid and autonomic computing. These technologies provide standards-based, reusable and modular components with automated reconfiguration, autoprovisioning, and virtualization of the infrastructure to adapt to changing business and user needs. Process changes are becoming composable. On-demand business models promise to create variable consumption choices for companies, essentially achieving higher utilization rates. The IT portfolio framework will incorporate these new service models, as well as their requirements for modularity, to maintain complex inter-relationships through standards.

As virtually everything becomes a node, as collaboration and communication continue to span beyond internal business processes and organizational structures, and as information and information value continue to increase, the half-life of information value will become dramatically shorter. Portfolio management will continue to serve as an important decision-making tool, providing a framework for rapidly collecting information and determining the impact of IT decisions on the operational baseline. Impact on resources (e.g., allocation, capacity, scheduling, and utilization), possible reprioritization and rebalancing of current projects in the pipeline, and the associated impact on other investments and resources will be rapidly assessed. More expansive integration into enterprise resource planning, customer relationship management, supply-chain management, and financial systems will provide immediate assessment of the impact of changes within the IT portfolio.

Well-established efficiencies, controls, market information, and automation seen in the financial marketplace will become the next generation of standard operating processes and procedures for IT investments. Advances and integration of key aspects within IT portfolio software products as identified in Chapter 6 will help this transformation.

We hope this book proves a valuable resource toward evolving your organization, its IT portfolio, and associated management. While all possible efforts have been made to provide a step-by-step approach, capturing lessons learned, and offering real-world guidance, this book is not a substitute for thinking or common sense. Through our research, many common threads have surfaced, which we have highlighted. Above all else, however, is the cardinal rule: apply common sense. Identify meaningful and attainable objectives, and work thoughtfully and expeditiously toward those objectives—nothing more, nothing less. Successful IT portfolio management is not reliant on luck. It is reliant upon planning and execution. Luck has been defined as a state "when planning meets with opportunity." We've provided both an approach to planning and an approach to opportunity creation. The only component missing is an introduction of planning and opportunity. This, we leave to you. Good luck!

NOTES

1. Cathleen Benko, "CIO Insight," *Best Intentions,* November 15, 2003.
2. Nicholas G. Carr, "IT Doesn't Matter," *Harvard Business Review, Vol. 81, No. 5,* May 2003.

Case Studies

This book concludes with three case studies from exemplar companies actively using all or some aspects of IT portfolio management. Each case study follows the same format: description of the company and the situation, the approach, the results, and the lessons learned.

The first case study is from Cisco Systems, Inc., the worldwide leader in networking for the Internet. The case study provides valuable and important insight into Cisco's IT project portfolio. The second case study is from In-Q-Tel, a private, nonprofit enterprise funded by the Central Intelligence Agency (CIA). The case study shows how In-Q-Tel engages with entrepreneurs, established companies, researchers, and venture capitalists, identifying and investing in companies that develop cutting-edge information technologies. In-Q-Tel exemplifies best practices in the IT discovery and project portfolios. The final case study is from Xcel Energy, which provides a comprehensive portfolio of energy-related products and services to 3.3 million electricity customers and 1.8 million natural gas customers through its regulated operating companies. In terms of customers, it is the fourth largest combination natural gas and electricity company in the United States. The case study provides details of the step-by-step leading practices of IT governance and IT portfolio management.

Cisco Systems, Inc.

Cisco, almost a common household name for a company that until 2003 didn't exactly sell household products, has enjoyed tremendous growth and success almost uninterrupted since its inception in 1984. The quintessential Silicon Valley garage startup, Cisco grew from $1.5 million USD in 1987 to $22 billion USD in 2004. Much of this growth came through acquisition.

Since 1993, Cisco has acquired over 80 companies; 2000 accounted for 20 acquisitions alone. Acquisitions tend to lead to revenue growth, vertical or horizontal market expansion, or deeper penetration into existing markets. One of the challenges inherent in most acquisitions, however, is achieving economies of scale through reuse. It is estimated that 70% of acquisitions fail to provide expected benefits because of the challenges of postintegration merger. Cisco, however, has managed to acquire and assimilate with seemingly relative ease.

One contributor to this relative ease of acquisition was the growth and margin in the markets in which Cisco . . . participates. Cisco, however, has a high organizational IQ. As such they recognized that their margins and growth would decline as time passed. 2000 was also an awakening for Cisco as the "Dot Com Bubble" burst. During 2001, Cisco reorganized, shedding 15% of its workforce. Cisco also adopted a host of tools to improve efficiency and effectiveness. One of these tools being used by Cisco is IT portfolio management.

Simple analysis of Cisco's current state showed the following:

- 9 order entry systems
- 16 customer relationship management systems
- 9 Siebel implementations
- 900 databases with 9,000 schemas
- 40 active call center initiatives

- 28 active order management initiatives
- 22 active operational reporting initiatives
- 55 active program/project management improvement initiatives

This is just but a small sampling of the low hanging fruit that can be plucked by even whispering the words "IT portfolio management." Cisco, however, is not one to whisper. Cisco, presciently recognizing that operational efficiency would be key to their future success, adopted IT portfolio management as an approach to balance supply for IT services and resources with demand for IT services and resources.

While many an organization has been known to rampantly adopt en vogue improvement approaches in an uncoordinated manner, Cisco adopted a targeted handful of approaches and coordinated their efforts. These approaches included:

- Six Sigma
- Enterprise architecture
- Project life cycle improvement
- IT portfolio management
- IT governance
- IT human resource management

Aside from identifying the opportunity to improve their IT service delivery before it was deemed a problem and carefully selecting and coordinating selected improvement methods, Cisco also worked to deal with some of the most critical issues in succeeding with IT portfolio management upfront.

First and foremost, Cisco ensured appropriate sponsorship for their IT portfolio management efforts. The primary sponsor was, and still is, the CIO, Brad Boston. Secondary sponsors exist throughout the finance and IT departments; a key secondary sponsor is the Vice President of Financial Planning. One of the common threads for successful IT portfolio management appears to be enrollment of support from those controlling the purse strings!

The approach and its value were also communicated and socialized heavily at the onset. The IT portfolio management initiative, which was an outgrowth of the project support office, had the buy-in from the project management community. Others within IT and business needed to understand the value proposition. For this, Cisco communicated heavily with key stakeholders in language they understood. Cisco developed a process internally that fit their culture and needs. While this book presents an approach to IT portfolio management, tailoring that approach to the needs and culture of the organization at hand is a critical success factor. Cisco also developed the process prior to selecting supporting technology. Cisco eventually selected Mercury Interactive's IT Governance Solution.

Cisco paid careful attention to articulating the goals of doing IT portfolio management. Cisco aligned IT portfolio management with other improvement initiatives within the enterprise, as well as existing processes. Of particular note is the alignment between project management, program management, IT portfolio management, and the business' planning process (see Exhibit A).

Cisco fundamentally matured out their project governance and management functions into IT portfolio management. The bulk of their IT portfolio management efforts, to date, have focused on project approval and execution with a mindset toward full life cycle IT portfolio management and governance.

After finding sponsors, socializing or selling the concept, and developing the approach, the project support office then tried the process out for a funding cycle. A standardized form for funding requests was created along with guidelines for its use. In addition, prior to aggregating funding requests and presenting them to senior management for decision making, the project support office scanned the funding requests to ensure that the data for each initiative under consideration was entered based on the guidelines published. In essence, the project support office served as a "filter." Once initiative request data was "normalized," the project

EXHIBIT A   THE BIG PICTURE

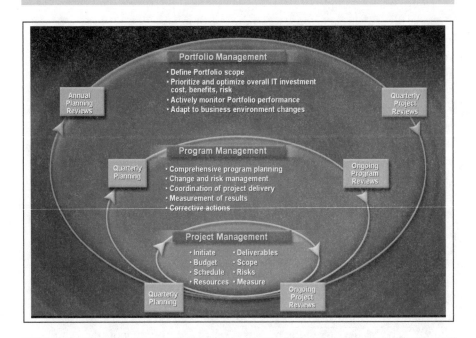

Source: © 2005 Cisco Systems, Inc.

support office assigned attributes to the proposed initiatives that primarily related back to stated business imperatives and key performance indicators.

Portfolio views of proposed projects were presented to management in a manner that allowed for identification of redundant initiatives as well as pet projects that didn't strongly tie to business imperatives. The apparent success of this approach strengthened the support of senior management and enabled IT portfolio management to serve as a project monitoring approach. The project support office was subsequently empowered to govern to the point that the can kill projects they deem wasteful. See Exhibit B for the Cisco IT portfolio management approach.

The payback for institutionalizing the IT project portfolio is greater confidence that capital is being allocated to projects efficiently and in a manner that supports legitimized business imperatives. At Cisco, results like these are adequate to continue with an initiative or approach, again speaking to their high organizational IQ.

While the IT portfolio management approach continues to evolve at Cisco, several lessons learned were cited. First, while it was obvious from the start, Cisco cannot understate the importance of retaining and maintaining sponsorship from

EXHIBIT B   OVERALL RELEASE PLANNING FRAMEWORK: INTEGRATING SIX SIGMA (DMAIC) AND PRODUCT LIFE CYCLE

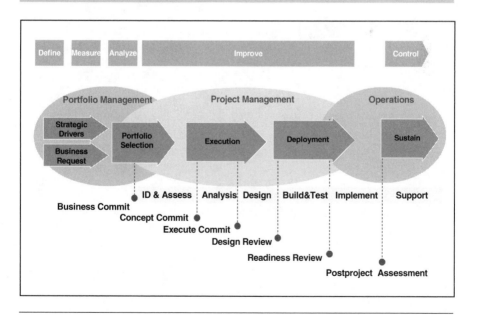

Source: © 2005 Cisco Systems, Inc.

both business and IT leadership. Second, it is of key importance to clearly articulate stated goals and approach. A charter for IT portfolio management is an imperative that states the goals, approach, and expectations of all key stakeholders. Third, careful attention to organization change management must be paid. At the initial introduction of IT project management, Cisco had some challenges with business units formulating their own interpretations of the project portfolio. A focused effort to create a common taxonomy and standardized processes provided an important foundation prior to the selection of an IT portfolio management software product. The important take-away here is that business logic should drive the selection of the software solution, not vice versa. Fourth, neither the process nor the analysis should be too rigorous. Operate off the Pareto Principle. Do the 20% of work and analysis that will provide the 80% of the value.

In-Q-Tel

"Bond, James Bond!" "Shaken, not stirred . . ." These ever famous quotes conjure up images of a multitude of simultaneously clandestine and intriguing actors playing the famous role of Ian Fleming's Agent 007—James Bond. Those familiar with James Bond movies will also be familiar with the role most frequently played by Desmond Llewelyn—the role of "Q." "Q" was the famous gadget man who managed to create the unimaginable out of seemingly ordinary items. "Q" was also the inspiration for the name of In-Q-Tel, a relatively new organization that acts as the technology venture capital arm of the Central Intelligence Agency (CIA).

Prior to the 1980s, much of the technology innovation came from the U.S. government and leached into private industry. As the information age exploded, the private sector began to innovate technologically at a more rapid clip. At the same time, venture capital firms became increasing attractive as sources of funding for promising technology startups because of the ease of which much needed capital could be attained. Relative to the procurement process of the U.S. Federal Government, venture capital firms appeared to provide relatively easy money unencumbered with typical Government intellectual property requirements. Innovative technology startups strayed from the U.S. Federal Government; large contractors focused more on Government Off the Shelf (GOTS) or custom solutions, increasing their foothold as the technology service providers of choice for the U.S. Federal Government.

These dynamics were recognized by the CIA as having the significant implications for its technology base. As part of those efforts, In-Q-Tel was formed in 1999 to help identify emerging technology to solve the CIA's toughest technology problems. In-Q-Tel was designed to provide the CIA with access to commercially-based startups that focused on technologies addressing the CIA's problem set. Through In-Q-Tel investments, the CIA would not only have early access to these technologies, but would also have a voice in their development and design. In essence, In-Q-Tel provided some pieces of the IT discovery portfolio for the CIA. In addition, this approach provided the CIA with immediate insight, contacts, and knowledge of the commercial marketplace. If structured properly, equity investments in startups could provide leverage on limited taxpayer dollars by leveraging concurrent private sector investment or through appreciation of the value of In-Q-Tel portfolio companies.

In-Q-Tel, formally incorporated as a nonprofit organization and devised an organizational structure modeled after the corporate strategic venture organizations and the venture capital firms of Silicon Valley. In-Q-Tel also hired leaders from the private sector and compensated them competitively. An annual contract was provided to In-Q-Tel, by the CIA to invest in technology ventures that would meet a broad problem set identified by the CIA. At the same time, the In-Q-Tel Interface Center (QIC) was created within the CIA to act as an intermediary organization between In-Q-Tel and the end user community within the CIA.

Much in the way a more traditional IT portfolio management approach is performed, proposals come into a queue for a first vetting. In this instance, however, the proposals usually come in the form of business plans. Baseline criteria have been set for initial screening. These criteria include:

- Fit and alignment with the client's models and needs. In-Q-Tel works closely with both the CIA and the National Geospatial-Intelligence Agency to understand their needs and align them with commercial technology developments

- Commercial viability of the venture

- Viability and innovativeness of the technology proposed by the vendor

- Ability to take an equity position in the company or establish another strategic business relationship

Generally, between 1,000 to 1,500 proposals are received annually. An initial screening pares the portfolio candidates into about 300 opportunities, which are given to a team of experts in business, technology, and the customer's problem set. At In-Q-Tel, these teams are referred to as the Venture Team, the Technology team, and the In-Q-Tel Interface Center (QIC), respectively. The teams collectively scrutinize the 300 or so proposals, honing in on commercial viability, technical merit, and fit with customer needs. Special attention is paid to focusing on needs of the client—not requirements. This distinction is important as they are after technology breakthroughs and do not want to be limited by system-level requirements. In-Q-Tel is willing to take calculated risks and make early stage investments in companies that have outstanding technology ideas but have yet to bear the fruits of commercializing these solutions. This approach is consistent with the some of the activities found in the discovery phase of the IT life cycle.

After this second filter, each remaining opportunity is documented in a standardized format, much the way a standardized initiative request form would be used for funding approval in a run of the mill corporate IT project portfolio. This document is usually 5 to 10 pages in length. All of the candidate investments are then submitted to a review board as a portfolio. Attention is placed on the specific customers needs being fulfilled by the prospective investment. Often, In-Q-Tel will invest in more than one company to fill a stated need in order to ensure that the best possible technology solutions are available to the end user. This is similar to a real options approach often used in the discovery phase of the IT life cycle. At the review board, each proposal is discussed with the eventual goal of driving to a "go–no go" decision on each proposal in the portfolio.

Even approved investments, however, continued to be monitored as a portfolio. Several end games are in mind. First and foremost is In-Q-Tel's measure of "Return on Technology" which is determined by the delivery of innovative solutions to the United States intelligence community. In order to ensure an optimal Return on Technology, additional funding may be required. In-Q-Tel fundamentally uses a Stage-Gate® approach to determine whether additional funding is warranted. And, while the primary focus is on Return on Technology, In-Q-Tel also pays close attention to the commercial success of its portfolio.

Unlike the famous "Q" of the James Bond movies, In-Q-Tel provides commercially-based solutions—not just nifty technology inventions. This commercial focus provides direct benefit to the Government in terms of support and ongoing improvements to the products. Because most of these solutions were also designed for commercial viability, the costs of support and ongoing development are spread across a wide range of customers and not borne entirely by the customer. Finally, In-Q-Tel works with its portfolio to help them identify and pursue an appropriate exit strategy. While a traditional venture capital firm would focus on maximizing the dollar value of an exit event, In-Q-Tel instead focuses on ensuring that the portfolio company will be stable and in a position to continue to provide value to its government customers. For example, in the case of an acquisition, In-Q-Tel will work with the acquiring company to ensure that the products will continue to be supported under new ownership. Again, this demonstrates the notion of exercising real options on their investments.

Just like other customers of IT, In-Q-Tel's customers want solutions, not education on cool technology. In-Q-Tel learned that a transition team was required to convert the seemingly ephemeral companies and their products in the In-Q-Tel portfolio into the solution delivery life cycle of In-Q-Tel's customers. As part of that transition, In-Q-Tel ensures that each investment has sufficient funding to deal with various contingencies. For example, In-Q-Tel may include a full year or more of operations and maintenance in its initial investment to ensure that appropriate maintenance is available until the customer is able to include those funds in its own budget life cycle. Adapting to these contingencies is a key part of the In-Q-Tel model. Things happen. Needs change. Investments require additional funding. Maintaining contingency consciously has been one of the keys to In-Q-Tel's success.

As with most IT portfolio management initiatives, organizational change management is also crucial. This is why In-Q-Tel learned early on the importance of ensuring that customers understand what's required of them. In that vein, executive sponsorship was critical to the success of In-Q-Tel. This paradigm shift of bringing private sector ideas into the public sector required extreme sponsorship and leadership by senior leaders in the intelligence community and government. In this instance, their need for change was critical. Lives were at stake. In-Q-Tel has been an incredible success, strengthening the IT discovery, IT project, and IT asset subportfolios within the CIA.

Xcel Energy*

Ray Gogel starts his mornings with a close look at his dashboard. Not the one in his car, the one on his office desktop. The Chief Information Officer of Xcel Energy is setting his daily agenda by reviewing the status of his company's IT projects. He speeds through the projects marked with green lights, slows down to scrutinize those marked yellow, and stops to focus on those in red. The portfolio management system instituted by Gogel and his team has already winnowed out low-value or redundant projects, so everything on Gogel's dashboard is critical to Xcel's business. The stark clarity of his dashboard display focuses his attention on projects that aren't currently making their metrics—projects that are falling behind schedule or deviating from budget, in addition to recognizing the improvement of projects that have moved back to a green healthy status. Gogel sees an important part of his CIO's job as getting those yellow and red projects back to green, as they not only are an indicator of his group's delivery levels but are also key value drivers for the organization. As the majority of his portfolio generates a positive return on investment, any delay or problem in delivering the project also means a reduced return to the company and its shareholders.

OLD INDUSTRY, NEW APPROACH

A decade ago, it might have been uncommon to see this kind of innovative information technology in the utility industry. Gas and electric utilities in the United States were almost all regulated by government, commonly guaranteeing the utilities a specified rate of return after covering approved costs. This regulatory

*The authors would like to thank Xcel Energy and Mercury for their contributions to this case study.

structure did not generally encourage cutting-edge approaches to cost reduction or service delivery, since the perceived risk usually exceeded the likely reward.

> "My goal when I arrived at Xcel Energy was to apply commercial rigor and accountability to IT to gain credibility with the corporate and business unit leadership. This in turn provides a solid foundation for evolving IT into a transformational agent and value driver for the business."
>
> *Ray Gogel, CIO, Xcel Energy*

But the wave of deregulation that swept the industry in the late 1990s changed that picture forever. Utilities sought ways to improve efficiency as they were freed to reap the benefits of those efficiencies. Scale became more important, spawning a wave of mergers and acquisitions. The 21st century seemed to promise a much different utility.

As it turned out, this rapid deregulation spawned some excesses and exploitation, such as the Enron experience. Yet beyond the headlines, mainline utilities were making big strides towards innovation and agility—changes for the better, changes that would endure.

Xcel Energy provides an excellent example of a "transformed utility." Formed in 1999 by the merger of New Century Energies of Denver and Northern States Power of Minneapolis, it is the fourth-largest combination electricity and natural gas company in the United States, with 5 million customers in 11 states, 11,000 employees, and annual revenue of $9.5 billion.

When the merger closed, Xcel found itself with two, sometimes three, of every system and application a utility would need. Beyond the disparate systems stood different ways of managing and approaching IT. At first, this wasn't necessarily seen as a problem, since the trend toward deregulation led management to believe they would end up with a group of autonomous business units anyway, each with its own systems. But as the deregulation trend waned, IT strategy shifted toward consolidating these disparate IT systems and functions. Why? Xcel Energy's leadership found that distributed IT made it essentially impossible to get a consolidated picture of overall IT demand, to control aggregate IT spend, or to create technology synergy across the company. Beyond that, the multiple IT organizations were contributing to a technology footprint that was already out of control and getting worse. To cap it all, delayed and over-budget projects had become too common.

ORGANIZING FOR CHANGE

The business and IT leadership of Xcel Energy had a good handle on their business goals. They already had a set of key performance indicators (KPIs) to evaluate business performance. They also believed with a single system and consolidated, reliable, real-time data, they could deliver far more IT value to the business.

But they were keenly aware that the existing business units were accustomed to running their own chunks of IT relatively autonomously. A centralized IT would need authority and standing in the corporate structure to succeed. So a new business unit was established to house IT—Business Systems—with 950 employees including business analysts. The new CIO, Ray Gogel, who arrived in April 2002, would report directly to the chief operating officer. This replaced the old structure, where corporate IT was part of the Shared Services organization reporting to the Chief Financial Office (CFO).

Xcel Energy delivers IT services in close partnership with IBM Global Services. Xcel characterizes this as a "third generation" relationship because of its maturity. IBM is a full partner, sharing the same scorecard for success. The same indicators drive the behaviors of both partners. In the past the relationship was traditional vendor–client with discernible walls between the two. Now, work is seamlessly performed in an integrated team; it's hard to tell who gets a paycheck from which company.

Working with IBM, Xcel Energy's Business Systems unit set out to govern and run IT as a business, with clear processes, accountability, and commercial rigor. The goal: deliver higher value to the business at lower cost. The primary focus: shift the balance of IT spending away from routine "keep-the-lights-on" activities and toward more strategic IT projects that improve business performance and competitiveness. The means: effective governance to provide IT services more efficiently and deliver strategic projects to market more efficiently by improving the decision-making and delivery processes. This focus on project delivery is also a key component in Gogel's efforts to drive business transformation, with his stated mission to "Drive business transformation that results in an extraordinary difference at Xcel Energy."

INVOLVING THE BUSINESS IN IT

Gogel knew he couldn't reach his goal without full participation by the company's business units. As the company recentralized IT, he felt it was essential that the business unit leaders develop trust in the new structure. He worked closely with them to translate their strategic and operating requirements into an enterprise-wide technology strategy.

> "When we designed our IT governance structure, the first thing we did was reach out to the business units to understand their strategic and operating requirements. We then translated these into an enterprise-wide

technology strategy, and put in place a structure that kept the business side involved by giving them real-time visibility and control over the IT initiatives and operations important to them. Our partnership with the business side is so much stronger as a result, because they can see the value we deliver every day."

Ray Gogel, CIO, Xcel Energy

The strategy calls for keeping the business side involved in IT programs and projects to maintain alignment with evolving business goals and priorities. "We want to demonstrate value and resolve problems," said Mike Carlson, Xcel Energy's vice-president of business transformation and customer value. "We are trying to eliminate the black hole between users and IT." This required finding a comprehensive way to capture, analyze, and prioritize IT demand while providing business units clear, easy-to-access views of IT processes and activities.

In other words, Gogel and Carlson wanted to make IT transparent to the business. The participation of business leaders would be both welcomed and facilitated at every stage of projects being created to help their units.

TWO MAJOR INITIATIVES TO TRANSFORM IT: MANAGED PORTFOLIO AND MANAGED DEMAND

Gogel, Carlson, and their team envisioned two major initiatives to transform IT. These two initiatives, implemented in sequence but closely interrelated, were designed to drive down the cost of routine, "keep-the-lights-on" IT activities to free more funding for strategic projects, while more effectively governing both kinds of activities with improved visibility and control.

The first major initiative encompassed a program management office (PMO) to manage delivery of projects and a formal portfolio management system for evaluating and prioritizing strategic IT projects. The PMO was initially set up to manage $100 million of mostly discretionary spending, including all mandatory regulatory and compliance initiatives, via a set of standard and consistent metrics.

The second major initiative was to implement an automated demand management system to capture all routine requests on IT, insert business governance, and manage fulfillment of the demand. Requests captured by the new system include a wide range of typical IT activities for which no consistent corporate-wide processes existed, and which were largely handled manually at significant expense. Purchases of hardware and software; employee additions, subtractions, and moves; password resets; and similar activities contributed to a $135 million annual O&M budget for this "keep-the-lights-on" portion of IT. The demand management initiative would be implemented as a second phase, following successful implementation of the portfolio management system. These two initiatives, combined with consolidating all company-wide IT functions into one business unit, enabled Xcel Energy to manage the complete portfolio of IT investment and begin to drive transformational change into the organization.

Because they wanted these initiatives to be integrated with each other and with overall IT operations, Xcel Energy selected Mercury IT Governance Center software for portfolio management, program management, and demand management. A particular appeal of these products, Carlson said, was their use of customizable desktop dashboards to provide real-time status on requests and projects, with the ability to roll up the data in ways that generated metrics meaningful to Xcel Energy's operation. These dashboards could be personalized on both the IT and business sides, advancing the goal of making IT initiatives and operations transparent to business stakeholders. Due to the strategic nature of these initiatives and the success Xcel Energy has had, Mercury has also become one of Xcel Energy's "third generation" partners and a member of its Strategic Advisory Board along with IBM and three other companies.

METHODOLOGY AND PEOPLE FIRST

Following Ernest Hemingway's famous dictate, "Never confuse motion for action," Xcel Energy's Business Systems group resisted the temptation to dive into its new PMO, determining instead to first establish a solid governance methodology and build an effective team.

They started by identifying essential ingredients for a successful PMO. These included:

- Clear and consistent governance policies, standards, and processes
- Automated core processes
- Support from and mentoring of project managers for the PMO's new "end-to-end" processes
- Achieving and maintaining close alignment with business units on PMO goals and processes
- Special emphasis on the financial management of projects
- Creating an understanding of commercial rigor and accountability
- Driving recognizable business transformation through existing IT investment
- Leading with a "practice what we preach" example by running the PMO initiative itself as a project.

Team members were selected based on specific skill sets determined to be necessary for success. The PMO director position required not only organizational management skills, but also business process reengineering and transformation experience. The manager for policy, process, and standards had to have extensive project management skills and process engineering experience. The manager overseeing PMO finance came from the financial organization and helped build the foundations. The PMO project manager had to be not only an experienced project manager (PM), but an experienced process engineer with extensive subject matter expertise. Business unit liaisons had to be able to promote and facilitate the use of the end-to-end process inside their organizations. All of these people had to have what Carlson calls "a bias for results" in addition to a passion for process.

Of these ingredients, the financial portion of the process soon emerged as especially important. Company leadership wanted a standard measure of value delivered against which the performance of all IT projects could be judged. The measure chosen, economic value add (EVA), is very similar to return on investment (ROI), with a weighted average cost of capital. Exhibit C shows a snapshot of how EVA is measured at Xcel Energy. The bars represent dollars currently committed to IT projects, by business unit. The line graph represents current percentage of return on each business unit's investment. For example, the Energy Markets business unit was receiving a 409% return on its portfolio projects, while the CFO was experiencing a negative return. Negative returns are experienced either when the bulk of projects in the unit's portfolio are mandated by regulation or required for compliance like Sarbanes-Oxley. Throughout the portfolio management process EVA is recalculated, and serves as a key criterion for project approval. EVA serves as a barometer of health. For example when EVA is strong, potentially lower return infrastructure projects can be taken on to increase the return of expected future projects. Beyond the measurement of value, Xcel Energy leadership believed that how the purse strings were controlled could play the decisive role in how successful the PMO would be. It was decided that Business Systems (the IT organization) would control funding for IT projects, even those requested by business units. The business units themselves would have to put some "skin in the game" up front to demonstrate their support of proposed projects and risk charge-backs for "unapproved" projects.

NEW END-TO-END PROCESS

The biggest driver of the PMO was the recognition that the existing method of approving and funding IT projects was seriously flawed. Business units would express a need; IT would respond with a proposal and solution outline. Approval

EXHIBIT C   SNAPSHOT OF ECONOMIC VALUE ADDED (EVA)
FOR IT PROJECTS AT XCEL ENERGY

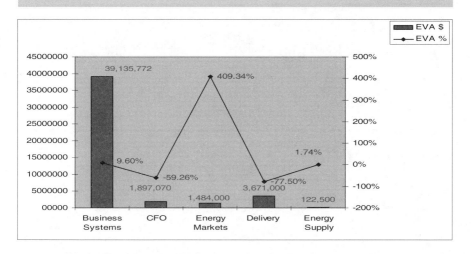

Source: Copyright © Xcel Energy, Inc.

of the proposal by the business unit was coupled to full project funding. However, at this early stage, many projects were "half baked." The business side might not have thought through its needs carefully; IT might not have asked the right questions needed to elicit sufficient detail. The usual result was a continuing stream of project change requests (PCRs) as work progressed and the actual requirements came to light. These PCRs often led to added costs and project delays, which in turn eroded business unit trust in IT's estimation capabilities in particular, and its project management skills in general. As an illustration, prior to the new process PCRs consumed over 69% of Xcel Energy's IT capital budget. The Xcel Energy Business Systems leadership, working closely with the core business units, remapped the prior project process to a stage gate view. This provides a consistent, easy to understand set of requirements to carry an initiative from the idea stage through adoption into the portfolio, then execution through the PMO and post-implementation benefits realization. See Exhibit D.

GOVERNING THE PROCESS

The PMO used powerful incentives to ensure the business units would collaborate closely with IT in selecting only the highest value proposals for implementation. Xcel Energy employs a zero-based yearly budgeting process that places

Then & Now: End-to-End Process at Xcel Energy

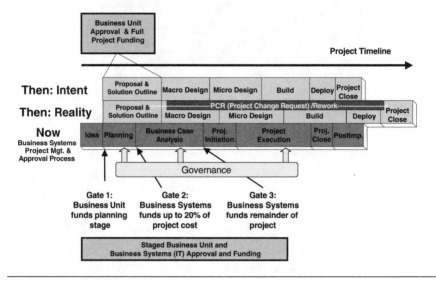

Source: Copyright © Xcel Energy, Inc.

IT project budgets under the purview of Business Systems. These are allocated to mandated legal and regulatory projects first, then to other ideas/projects under consideration for the next year based on their expected EVA. Proposed ideas/projects stand on their merits, with budget going to those expected to deliver the highest value.

Even after an idea/project is budgeted for the coming year, business units must still prove its value through the PMO process. If they cannot, the budget is made available to other opportunities. Business units expense all costs associated with idea development in stage 1 and stage 2 from their operating budgets. When a business unit approves an idea at the end of the planning stage (Exhibit D, Gate 2.) to prepare a business case, up to 20% of the total estimated project budget may be approved to fund the business case stage and prepare the business case. This funding is administered by Business Systems from its central capital budget, and is drawn against the business unit's earmarked funds. If the item under consideration does not have an earmarked budget, dollars can be obtained from the general pool or from canceling, delaying, or otherwise changing other in-process projects or earmarked projects. It is the expectation that all ideas approved for business case stage funding will ultimately be approved for delivery, because if the business case is not approved (the project rejected), the business unit may be required to cover the costs with its operating budget. In addition, that entire earmarked project budget is then removed and made available for reallocation to *any* approved project from *any* business unit.

As an illustration of Xcel Energy's strong governance processes, the business case stage is managed as a project with a funded budget and regular status reporting. At its conclusion, candidate projects face the third gate in the process to receive full funding. When a business case project is approved for full funding, the EVA benefits are communicated to finance and will be subtracted from the sponsoring business unit's next year operating budget. Project approvals are tiered, depending on budget. The business unit project sponsor will present the business case to the PMO director, lead architect, finance director, and the business unit's business technology executive (BU CIO or equivalent). The intent is that the business case is strong enough to fund the remaining 80% of the project's estimated cost. This team can give final approval of all projects with a total budget of up to $250,000. Projects above this level go through a series of sequential reviews depending on size, all the way up to corporate board of directors' approval if the project is budgeted at $10 million or more. It's also important to note that estimated costs are always targeted to be +/− 10% of what will be incurred in the next stage of the process.

This method of governing budgeting and funding may seem punitive on the business units, but it gives them a compelling incentive to choose among candidate ideas carefully, and participate seriously in the evaluation of them. Failing to do so may impact their bottom line. The evaluation activity throughout the governance process is made easier for the business units through detailed real-time metrics of all proposals and projects in various stages, which are available to both IT and business unit participants through the dashboards used in the Xcel Energy PMO.

IDEA AND PLANNING STAGES

The process begins simply with ideas. Anyone in the company may submit an idea within their business unit by providing sufficient information to permit objective evaluation of it. Each idea is reviewed to decide if it merits further attention and approval to continue to the next stage (planning). Each business technology executive (the senior liaison between the business unit and IT) has regularly scheduled meetings where submitted ideas are discussed with each idea's sponsor in the business unit. These leaders decide which ideas are eligible to advance to the next level, the planning stage. Gate 1 in the process occurs here with business units deciding whether they will fund the planning stage, a short feasibility study, to identify potential fatal flaws and further refine the idea. Costs of the planning stage are expensed within the sponsoring business unit. This initial hurdle is a high one. Of the 309 ideas currently in the system only 12% have progressed past the idea gate and into further stages, as shown in Exhibit E.

Each idea submitted for consideration by a business unit is evaluated using consistent metrics. These include nine criteria for scoring business value and seven criteria for scoring technology innovation. These are plotted on axes in bubble charts generated by Xcel Energy's portfolio management system, using the data entered and managed by the project teams as shown in Exhibit F. The data is focused on quantifying the business value (the Y axis) and the technology innovation introduced by the project (the X axis). The estimated cost of the project is used to determine the size of the "dot" plotted on the graph.

Xcel Energy uses nine business value criteria including:

- EVA—Economic Value Add, taking into account hard benefits and all costs

- Does the idea align tightly with corporate priorities? If not, how much is it off?

EXHIBIT E   DISPOSITION OF THE FIRST 309 IDEAS
ENTERED INTO THE PORTFOLIO MANAGEMENT
SYSTEM

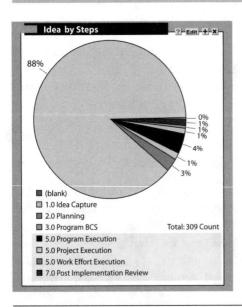

Source: Copyright © Xcel Energy, Inc.

- Would the idea have a corporate-wide customer?
- Would this idea impact Xcel Energy and its customers globally, geographically, or just a specific product line?
- Would it potentially affect Xcel Energy's brand reputation positively or negatively?
- Will it increase or decrease service delivery reliability?
- How positively will it impact daily processes, enhance customer service, and improve capabilities?

Xcel Energy uses seven technology innovation criteria including:

- Does this align with the corporate architecture footprint? If not, how different is it?
- Does this simplify the existing architecture/process, or complicate it?
- How innovative is this initiative in the energy industry? Does it use an ascendant technology or one that is declining? Is it addressing a new industry issue or one that's lagging?
- Will this initiative improve the company's technological flexibility, enabling it to add more value faster in the future?
- Is this a catch-up, status quo, or leapfrog activity in terms of competition?
- Who will Xcel Energy rely on to deliver this initiative: in-house resources, a single vendor, or multiple vendors who can work in a partnering model?

Beyond these business value and technology innovation criteria, other business drivers are captured and analyzed in this process including regulatory impacts, the degree to which the project is discretionary, the strategic nature of the project, and detailed EVA and benefit information.

As demonstrated in Exhibit F, a large number of projects appear on the screen during the initial evaluation round in the idea stage. Those that appear toward the upper right corner of the graphic are those that earned the highest combined score. These are generally the top candidates to move forward, although specific needs and opportunities may dictate projects with somewhat lower scores, such as those required by government and/or industry regulation.

In the next stage, the project planning stage, more research is done on the idea and the business value and technology innovation criteria reevaluated. This refinement process winnows out a majority of candidate projects, determining that they would deliver too little value, are poorly aligned with business priorities, or overlap significantly with other projects. Projects in this stage that don't appear to be above the bar are a challenge to the sponsor to increase the value

EXHIBIT F   BUBBLE CHARTS EVALUATING CANDIDATE
PROJECTS IN IDEAS AND STAGES*

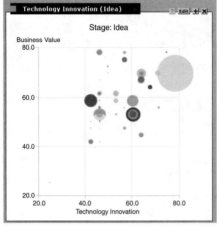
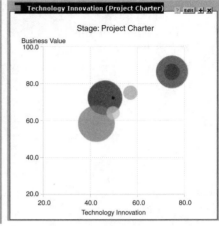

*Note the significant reduction in projects in the right-hand chart, the effect of winnowing out low-value candidates.
Source: Copyright © Xcel Energy, Inc.

of the project or risk losing it. Stopping low-value or redundant projects from being funded in these first two stages is saving Xcel Energy millions of dollars per year.

At the conclusion of the second or planning stage, the business unit sponsor presents the idea (depending on size of the project) to the business unit's business technology executive, finance director, and director of the PMO using an established presentation template. The template ensures all potential projects are comparable and understandable in a short time frame, and that a good decision can be made on whether the idea should be approved to move on to the next stage, creation of a detailed business case funded by the PMO (not the business unit).

BUSINESS CASE STAGE

This stage fully explores the business value, cost, and impact of the potential project on Xcel Energy's business. The first step of the business case stage is where all participants attend business case training. The training is a 40 slide presentation that details what the process is, what lessons have been learned by other projects during this stage and what is expected of the participants. All participants must clearly understand the objective is on-time, on-budget delivery of the business case and the resulting value proposition for the company. Scope creep is allowed only if it adds more value to the business case, and is approved through the formal change request process.

The deliverables of this stage include everything required to execute the project if it were to be approved. Project plans, contracts, required resources, risks, processes, architectural blueprints, integration requirements, integration approaches, and highly detailed cost/benefit or EVA analysis. Similar to the planning stage, the goal of the business case stage is to have financial estimates within plus or minus 10% of what the next phase will cost—in this case the final project cost if execution is approved. Due to the detailed financial analysis performed during this stage, the resulting economic impact of moving the project forward (or holding it back) is very clear. Also in this stage, a detailed architectural viability assessment is performed, determining the alignment to the technology architecture blueprint and extensively evaluating technology risks.

A detailed risk management plan is also prepared in the business case stage. Risks are evaluated in two dimensions: probability (high/medium/low); and impact (high/medium/low). Any risk in either dimension that is medium or high must have a risk mitigation plan created for it. Medium and high risks have an entry created as part of the project plan to ensure it is managed and not overlooked. Each risk is also created in a separate "log" entry within the PMO software to provide visibility to Business Systems and the BU management to the degree of risk outstanding on the project.

Projects are ultimately judged on a combination of EVA, risks, and other factors. Just as important as the number crunching that results in project rankings is clear communication of expectations between top executives. For example, often times when a project is approved, the CIO and business unit president sit down together, discuss, and agree on a set of expectations for project results. This top-level human communication reduces the chance of misunderstandings and finger-pointing later.

CALCULATING CANDIDATE PROJECT SCORES

Xcel Energy calculates detailed return on investment or EVA (Economic Value Add) metrics for every idea as part of the idea, project planning, and business case stages with sharper knives coming out in each subsequent stage. In the business case stage, all prospective costs of the project are analyzed and estimated, including, labor, outside services, hardware, software, and other costs. On the benefit side of the ledger, both "hard" and "soft" benefits are scrutinized. SIXFOLD RETURN: Between June 2003 and July 2004 Xcel Energy approved $100 million in PMO projects that are expected to return $600 million in value to the company over a seven-year life. Hard benefits include increased revenues resulting from the project as well as both capital and labor savings. Particular attention is paid to whether a project would reduce future full-time-equivalent (FTE) employees or contractors. As an example, if solid metrics prove growth in application usage has caused the addition of two FTE database administrators (DBAs) in each of the last several years, then a project to implement an application that eliminates this growth in DBAs can count these future projected labor savings as a hard benefit.

Soft benefits are, as the name suggests, somewhat intangible and difficult to measure, yet nonetheless very important. Project planning and business case stages analyze whether a particular project would improve service quality or improve responsiveness to customers, contributing to an enhanced reputation and a stronger brand. Where these benefits can be objectively quantified, they can be counted as hard benefits and included in the project's EVA. Where such benefits do not flow directly to the bottom line, they are counted toward the project as more of an intangible.

As candidate projects move through these first three stages, the scores earned by each project typically decrease. As ideas are fleshed out and put under the increasingly harsh light of the planning and business case stages, the business value tends to descend from the clouds and the innovation score usually drops as well. This is not viewed as a bad thing, since most ideas of any kind tend to overestimate benefits and underestimate costs and risk. The Xcel Energy PMO puts the emphasis on the *relative* value of projects being considered. The flip side of declining value scores is the increasing confidence in the accuracy of the scores as more analysis is completed.

Xcel does not treat benefits lightly. Business units are held accountable for realized expected benefits when a business case is approved. To ensure this point isn't lost, the last stage of the project process—post-implementation—serves to validate that benefits are being realized and costs were as expected. This stage will be discussed later.

PROJECT VALUATION SCORECARD

As the business case stage nears completion, Xcel Energy Business Systems (IT) performs an independent evaluation before a decision on full funding is made. Each case is evaluated in three areas: project risk, business risk, and financial return. A "perfect" project would score 100, but in practice this is unattainable (example, Exhibit G). The score achieved represents a comparative assessment against the ideal. This is used to demonstrate that risks and return have been carefully evaluated, and is intended to provide a general "yardstick" on the project's chances of success at this point. It's important to remember that all approved projects at Xcel Energy are critical and intended to be successful, so this scorecard is more a metric of how much oversight will be required to ensure the project is successful.

EXHIBIT G   BCS DASHBOARD*

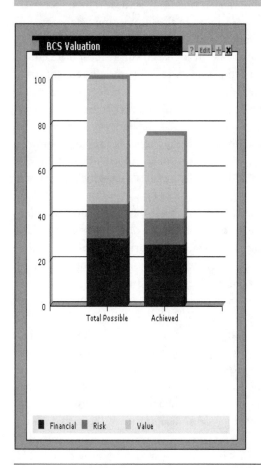

*Note: displays estimated business case value against total possible for the candidate project shown in Exhibit H.

Source: Copyright © Xcel Energy, Inc.

PMO PROJECT EXECUTION STAGE

Once a business case is approved for full project funding, it moves forward rapidly into the execution stages. However, on some occasions other projects may need to be delayed or cancelled to fund very high ROI opportunities that Business Systems and the BU sponsors feel should be accelerated.

Project start-up is expected to take no more than five days, as the preparation has really been done in the business case stage. During start-up, contracts are signed, people are brought on board, the scope is rechecked, kick-off meetings are held and the project plan is baselined. This can all be done quickly because the business case stage included development of all required pricing information and estimates, preparation of required contracts, and legal review. These items are incorporated into the business case stage to ensure that cost estimates are as accurate as possible for decision-making purposes. Therefore, for approved projects, all that should be required in the initiation stage are signatures and kick-off meetings.

Throughout this process, all project actions are consistently monitored, enforced, and reported to stakeholders through Mercury dashboards. Project status can be viewed in any number of ways, depending on the requirements and interests of each executive team member. Major projects with multiple independent components are typically termed "programs," with individual components managed as projects within the program. Each project in a program is managed independently, but tied to the overall program schedule, with all data in the projects automatically rolled up into a single program view.

A typical project dashboard format (see Exhibit H) would include summary information such as business sponsor, project manager, start and end dates, and budget, as well as completion status and detailed performance-to-date against schedule and budget. These dashboards offer drill-down access to more detailed information in each category by clicking on the item of interest.

Xcel Energy uses a measure called "project health" to give a snapshot view of each project's status (Exhibits I and J). Seven key indicators of project health have been identified that are measured against the plan baseline including budget expended to date, budget expected at completion, milestones achieved to date, tasks completed to date, labor hours expended to date, labor hours expected at completion, and project issues. Using this data, project status is distilled into traffic signal (red–yellow–green) displays to instantly alert executives to the relative health of each project. A 10% variance (over or under) on any of the metrics automatically turns the project yellow; a 15% variance turns it red. Similarly, missing a deadline to submit project status reports immediately turns the project red. The use of agreed-upon metrics to measure project health has replaced a variety of subjective measures used by individual project managers, which made truly objective comparisons impossible.

EXHIBIT H   PORTION OF A DASHBOARD FOR A TYPICAL
PROJECT IN XCEL ENERGY PORTFOLIO

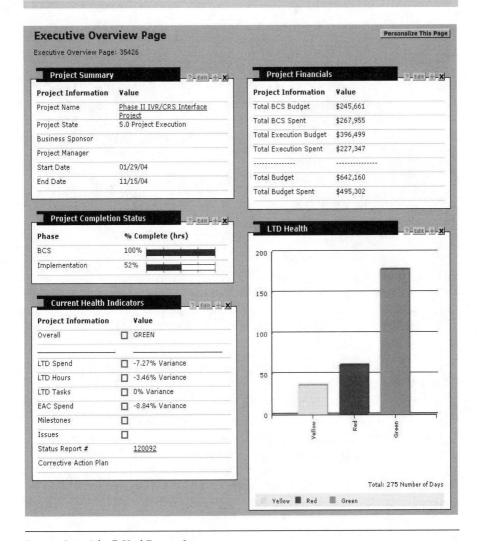

Source: Copyright © Xcel Energy, Inc.

Again, drill-down capabilities in the software allow executives on both the business and IT side to determine causes of project problems. For example, the cause of a project's red indicator might be as simple as the oversight of an executive who forgot to sign off on a required project approval in a timely manner, or more complex, such as the unexpected departure of an alliance partner's key project person or the simultaneous slight delay of multiple unrelated tasks.

EXHIBIT I   GRAPH OF PROJECT HEALTH FOR ACTIVE
PROJECTS WITHIN A BUSINESS UNIT AND
COMPANY-WIDE PROJECT HEALTH ACROSS
BUSINESS UNITS

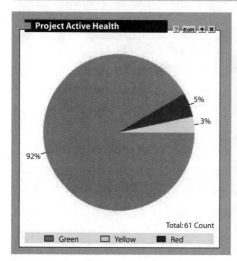

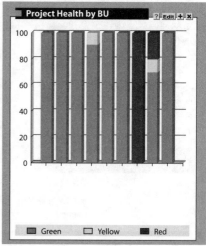

Source: Copyright © Xcel Energy, Inc.

Every time a project goes yellow or red, a root cause analysis is performed, assisted by the drill-down capabilities of the software. An action plan is quickly created and implemented, with results monitored and published for stakeholders to see. The real-time communication of these key status indicators to all levels of the organization, including the individual business unit presidents, drives the collaboration necessary for successful project delivery.

POST-IMPLEMENTATION REVIEW

Every completed project that was approved based on value delivered to the bottom-line is required to undergo a post-implementation review stage driven by the corporate CFO and the sponsoring business unit. Here lessons learned are collected, the real cost of the project reviewed, and actual benefits are validated against the expected value committed to when the project was approved. For example, one project promised an EVA of 20% to be achieved by redeploying people and increasing revenue. The value measurement criteria that were defined during the business case are now validated to determine whether the expected value is being

EXHIBIT J   PROJECT ISSUES, DEPENDENCIES, PCRS, AND
RISKS BY STATUS, WHICH ALSO AFFECT PROJECT
HEALTH

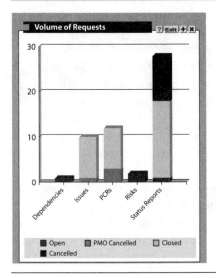

Source: Copyright © Xcel Energy, Inc.

delivered. In addition, costs are reviewed to ensure all relevant costs have been included.

Business Systems participates and helps perform a root cause analysis if promised benefits are not fully realized. Where possible, corrective action is then taken to achieve the full expected value, because the CFO may deduct some or all of the shortfall in projected benefits from the business unit's operating budget. The enforcement of this phase serves as a powerful incentive to all participants to make the business case estimates as realistic as possible. In addition, the sponsor is sent a survey to capture lessons learned which are then used to improve the overall process.

SINGLE SYSTEM OF RECORD

What makes these scorecards, and all the PMO data, reliable and actionable is the acceptance by all project participants at Xcel Energy—from the CEO, CFO, and CIO, to business unit leaders, and all project team members, whether in-house, outsourced, or vendor-related—of a single system for managing the portfolio and projects. Projects cannot proceed except by use of the system, so the practice, still common in some companies, of "renegade" projects operating without sanction has been all but eliminated at Xcel Energy. By performing all project actions through the system—from requesting consideration of an idea, to analyzing costs and benefits, to executing the resulting project—all data is uniformly captured and used to generate consistent metrics. There is no more checking and reconciling versions of project status spreadsheets at update meetings; project data is always available in real time through dashboards, putting everyone on the same page.

This automated data capture also automatically generates a complete audit trail. This is not only beneficial to double-check who performed which actions at what point in time, but it also provides a strong foundation for demonstrating the key processes and policies that IT control assumptions are based on. The single system also plainly displays the resources allocated to each project, making conflicts visible and easier to resolve, as well as greatly facilitating forward planning.

Xcel Energy Business Systems intensively mines the information in the system for continuous improvement analyses. They track and analyze PCR trends, forecasting accuracy, budget accuracy, and many other metrics. The assurance that these metrics are consistent and reliable give them confidence in using them to continually identify opportunities to improve processes and increase value delivered to the business.

MANAGING DEMAND ON IT

While Xcel Energy's leadership believed that effective management of its strategic IT project portfolio was essential to growing and transforming its business, they believed they needed to go farther. The percentage of the overall IT budget spent on routine, "keep-the-lights-on" activities was almost twice as high as the spending on strategic IT projects in 2002—63% to 37%, according to Mike Carlson. At this level, Xcel Energy was actually toward the positive end of the spending-split spectrum. Numerous surveys in recent years show that in most companies the ratio between routine and strategic IT spending is generally between 4 to 1 and 2 to 1.

Even at a 63–37 split, Xcel Energy was spending $135 million annually in routine IT operating and maintenance costs, with limited end-to-end visibility or control. IT services were requested and delivered differently in each Business Unit through disparate, nonintegrated systems, some of which were informal and marginally documented. Xcel Energy's IT leadership saw both an opportunity and a requirement to control these costs: an opportunity to improve service delivery, gain insight into spending trends, and increase the business value provided; and an imperative to drive down these "keep-the-lights-on" costs to free more funding for strategic projects.

At the beginning of 2004, Xcel Energy implemented a unified system to manage demand used by 8,000 employees and contractors. All requests for IT services now had to be submitted through a web browser interface, using a request menu and templates to gather information. Requests move through an automated work flow, gaining review and approval first from the requestor's business unit, then from IT. Requests are routed to authorized approvers, with clear approval criteria built into the work flow and automated reminders and escalations to expedite decision making. The system then automatically routes approved requests through the fulfillment process. See Exhibit K.

Xcel sees multilevel benefits from this demand management system. At the enterprise level, it helps drive the shift toward more strategic spending by reducing routine IT spending, and by making discretionary spending far easier to identify and control. At the Business Systems (IT) level, it enables real-time visibility into all discretionary IT demand, provides the ability to easily adjust approvals based on business priorities, and gives IT leaders the ability to analyze service delivery performance. At the user level, the clear interface and automated processes increase the ease of doing business with IT. The metrics generated by the system and monitored by business unit leaders provide a clear understanding of what it costs, in money and effort, for IT to provide these services and allows them to prioritize their spending to maximize business value and return. The labor-reducing automation increases the value of IT spending on routine activities.

By understanding all the demand on IT, analyzing it, and inserting appropriate controls to manage demand, Xcel Energy's leadership sees the organization transitioning from the common IT model of heavy spending on fixed costs and support activities to a new model focused on strategic investment that grows and transforms the business, and applies innovative technologies to position the company for the future.

Early benefits from the demand management system include significantly improved alignment of IT requests with business priorities and a sharp decrease in discretionary or non–value-added requests. Over time, Xcel Energy expects the combination of demand management and portfolio management discipline to shift that strategic/routine IT spending ratio from the 2002 split of 37% strategic and 63% routine to a ratio of 57% strategic and 43% routine.

REALIZING THE BENEFITS OF PORTFOLIO MANAGEMENT

Xcel Energy is more than satisfied with the initial results of its efforts to manage its IT project portfolio and overall IT demand (see Exhibit L). After one year of portfolio management experience, their KPIs looked like this:

EXHIBIT K   IT DEMAND AT XCEL ENERGY CATEGORIZED BY
REQUESTING UNIT, ONE OF MANY METRICS
AVAILABLE IN REAL TIME

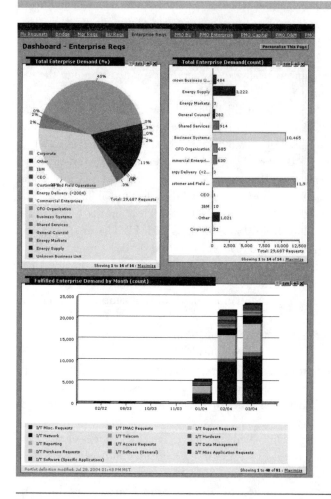

Source: Copyright © Xcel Energy, Inc.

- Identified and stopped $8 million in grandfathered projects determined unlikely to deliver expected business value
- Redeployed $10 million in capital from budgeted projects that couldn't demonstrate value to projects that could
- Reduced operating and maintenance spending by almost $1 million through improved PMO processes

- Reduced project change requests 21% through better front-end analysis and business case development
- Increased the number of healthy (green) projects in Xcel Energy's IT port-folio by more than 70% in the first five months of use—from having only half of the projects meeting schedule and budget criteria to having more than 85% do so
- Reduced the percentage of capital budget consumed by PCR's from over 69% to under 5%
- Between June 2003 and July 2004 approved $100 million in projects that over a seven-year life are expected to return over $600 million in value to Xcel Energy
- 41% turnover in project management resources as result of increasing level of accountability

EXHIBIT L   PORTION OF TYPICAL XCEL ENERGY IT SCORECARD

Business Systems 2004 Scorecard

	Priority	Key Performance Indicator	Champion	Actual 2003	2004 Target	YTD Actual	On/Off Target	KPI Weight
Customer	Improve Customer Satisfaction	Customer Survey Results Governance Council (Gap Closure)	Gogel	1.84	1.66	.90	●	5%
		Customer Survey Results End-Use Customers (Gap Closure)	Marley	2.59	2.33	1.96	◐	5%
	Transform the Business	% Economic Value Added from Capital Projects (% EVA/Capital Invested)	Carlson	7.50%	10.30%	10.24%	◑	15%
	Meet Project Health Objectives	Project Health (% of Projects "Green")	Carlson	77.44%	82.50%	81.9%	◐	10%
	Standardization and Simplification	Reduce Technical Footprint (% Reduction of Architectural Components)	Coady	17,687 Remaining (19%) reduction	15,884 Remaining (10%) reduction	1,090 Components Removed	●	15%
Employee	Enhance Employee Engagement	Employee Engagement Q12 Grand Mean	Newby	3.64	3.84	N/A	●	0%
Investor	Meet Financial Goals	Operating Expenses (O&M Spend $)	McCloskey	$$$	$$$	$$$	●	30%
		Capital Expenses (Capital Spend $)		$$$	$$$	$$$	●	20%

Source: Copyright © 2003, Xcel Energy, Inc.

REFINING PORTFOLIO MANAGEMENT

Xcel Energy's leadership considers portfolio management an iterative process. Early projects in the portfolio skewed toward essential operational activities and strategic initiatives to consolidate and standardize processes and programs that reflected the decentralized era. These projects provided valuable feedback into the portfolio management activity, allowing continuing refinements in processes and success criteria.

As this consolidation effort is completed and the participants in the portfolio management process—the core business units and Business Systems (IT)—reach and maintain a high comfort level with both the methodology and the technology used, Xcel Energy leadership expects to undertake an increasing percentage of transformational projects that materially change the way the company does business. Both the risks and rewards of such projects are higher, but the portfolio management system gives them growing confidence that they can make the right choices and implement them successfully to maximize the return on IT investment.

LESSONS LEARNED

As they gain experience with their new portfolio management and IT governance systems, Xcel Energy team members have taken the opportunity to reflect on lessons learned.

Team members surveyed were unanimous in their views of what went well.

- Complete top-down support proved absolutely critical. The PMO was initially seen by many in the organization as an "unnatural change." Not surprisingly, the underlying reason for the resistance turned out to be fear of a loss of control. Resolute support from the top knocked down this hurdle.

- Continuous, iterative, improvements to build and maintain momentum. Tight, 90 day incremental rollouts supported quick wins, prevented pent-up pushback, and ensured no one got "entrenched."

- Communicating early successes was important in several ways. It reinforced the top-down support, validated the wisdom of giving Business Systems control of overall budgets, and backstopped the team's ability to say "NO" to projects that didn't demonstrate clear EVA.

- The decision to invest the time up front to build the right team, with a strong mix of project management, business process reengineering, and finance experience. That investment of time was more than recaptured in a smoother, faster, rollout process.

What could have been improved? Here, there was no unanimity among team members. The general view was that the strengths of the program far exceeded any weaknesses. However, on reflection, there were a number of "coulda, shoulda, woulda" thoughts from team members.

- A stronger communication strategy, formulated at the front end of the program, would have been helpful. Many of the communications activities were ad hoc.

- More training (one team member asked, "Can there ever be enough?").

- Integrating the PMO to the CFO side of the house at the beginning of the process. Even though the PMO team included a member with experience in the Finance group, some team members thought it would be more effective to "bite the bullet" and integrate with established Finance processes and systems at the start. Doing it later in the program took longer.

- Taking the time to thoroughly understand the capabilities of systems used in the program, rather than just adapting the system to the desired organizational process or the process to the system. In hindsight, team members recognized that the processes implemented early in the program were overly complex. Simpler approaches would have taken less time to implement and might have required less "tuning" later on.

DELIVERING RESULTS

CIO Ray Gogel has told his team that Business Systems mission is to "Drive business transformation that results in an extraordinary difference for Xcel Energy" and "Business Systems credibility begins with the bottom line: ensuring that the right projects move forward on-time and on-budget." Through midyear 2004, the company's IT portfolio was producing an EVA of 10.24% against a 10.30% target. In August 2004, he reported to his team that Business Systems had achieved the best forecast-to-actual performance of any business unit during the preceding period—just 4% variance on forecasted spending—a major improvement largely attributable to the new process and systems. With a passion for continuous improvement and delivering IT solutions that result in an extraordinary transformational difference, Xcel Energy, its PMO, Business Systems, and its partners are off to a great start and still picking up speed.

Sarbanes-Oxley

The Sarbanes-Oxley Act has significantly tightened financial reporting regulations on publicly held companies in the United States. Xcel Energy has built Sarbanes-Oxley requirements into its governance and portfolio management system using a "three-five-nine" approach (three checkpoints, five possible outcomes, nine possible controls).

Three events can trigger financial operations to assess their oversight requirements. The first comes during the planning stage when the project charter is completed and business case funding is being sought. The second occurs during the business case stage when project requirements are completed. The third, when a PCR (project change request) is requested.

When one of the above events occur, any of five outcomes are possible:

- Corporate audit and/or quality assurance oversight required
- Financial oversight required for control change
- Financial oversight required for process change
- Financial oversight required for both process change and control change
- No financial operations oversight required

Depending on which of the five outcomes are selected, nine possible controls exist. One is simply that financial operations participates in requirements definition. Another involves just reviewing requirements to ensure financial reporting, including internal control requirements, is adequately addressed with the appropriate level of involvement/resources. The remaining seven controls include:

- Reviewing business design to ensure that business processes integrate with financial processes

EXHIBIT M   THREE EVENTS TRIGGERING FINANCIAL OPERATIONS AT XCEL ENERGY TO ASSESS OVERSIGHT REQUIREMENTS

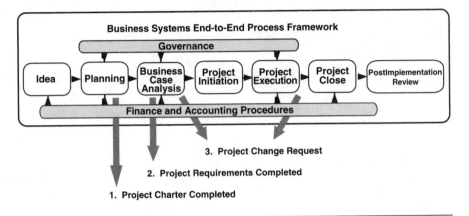

Source: Copyright © Xcel Energy, Inc.

- Validating that financial reporting requirements have been addressed and incorporated into overall technical design requirements
- Reviewing design against GCC (General Computing Controls) requirements
- Reviewing system test results
- Reviewing user acceptance test results
- Validating that financial reporting requirements have been met
- Participating in go/no go decisions

By implementing strong governance, Xcel Energy has designed compliance into its systems and, no matter what, all the data generated in Xcel Energy's portfolio, project, and demand management system is retained in the form of a detailed, documented audit trail that meets Sarbanes-Oxley requirements. See Exhibit M.[1]

NOTES

1. This is not an exhaustive explanation of Xcel Energy's Sarbanes-Oxley compliance initiatives.

Index